A Metaphysics
of Authentic Existentialism

"*One way [of interpreting the word 'existentialism'] is to affirm the primacy of existence, but as implying and preserving essences or natures and as manifesting the supreme victory of the intellect and of intelligibility. This is what I consider to be authentic existentialism.*"

J. Maritain

PRENTICE-HALL INTERNATIONAL, INC., *London*
PRENTICE-HALL OF AUSTRALIA, PTY., LTD., *Sydney*
PRENTICE-HALL OF CANADA, LTD., *Toronto*
PRENTICE-HALL OF INDIA (PRIVATE) LTD., *New Delhi*
PRENTICE-HALL OF JAPAN, INC., *Tokyo*

LEO SWEENEY, S.J.

St. Louis University

A Metaphysics
of Authentic Existentialism

Prentice-Hall, Inc.

Englewood Cliffs, New Jersey

Imprimi
potest
John J. Foley, S.J.
Provincial, Wisconsin Province
23 April 1964

Nihil
obstat
Henri J. Renard, S.J.
Censor Deputatus

Imprimatur ✠ Gerald T. Bergen, D.D
Archbishop of Omaha
7 July 1964

Library of Congress Catalog Card No.: 65-11496

PRINTED IN THE UNITED STATES OF AMERICA/57852-C/

To
Ellen Theresa McDowell
and
John Michael Sweeney

1296294

Preface

A Metaphysics of Authentic Existentialism has resulted from nearly a decade of teaching metaphysics and is intended as a feedback to future classes. It is, then, a textbook of metaphysics.

Because it is a textbook, it endeavors to be as clear and as pedagogically helpful as is possible with difficult subject matter. Pedagogy suggested the use of history (see Chaps. I-III; IV, Sec. 1) as a means of introducing students to philosophical problems and to a philosophic approach in answering them. Yet one should remember that history here is only a means. The historical sections do not always present a full picture of the philosophers studied. Some elements of their position may be emphasized, others downplayed or even passed over in silence (for example, see our remarks on Sartre, Chap. II, n. 19), but references are given to other studies where students may supplement their knowledge.

Pedagogy also advised the length and make-up of the chapter on Aristotle

(Chap. III: "Lessons from Aristotle"). His philosophy of nature (with respect, at least, to substance/accidents and matter/form compositions in material things) still seems true. Hence, rather detailed attention is given it in that chapter and those components are not treated as such in any subsequent chapter.

Good pedagogy also demanded that the book should develop organically. Besides the use of history already mentioned, this organic development is achieved by moving from the known to what is unknown. In Parts Two to Four this movement is implemented by the use of frequent examples and concrete cases. These provide the data, the evidence which stimulates teacher and student alike to think philosophically and which eventually ushers them toward both answers and conclusions—in a word, toward a philosophic position. Concrete examples are absolutely necessary. Without them, a student may parrot terms, memorize definitions, and repeat conclusions, but he will not have thought or philosophized.

As every teacher has experienced, undergraduate students vary greatly in talent, and the time allotted to metaphysics also varies from college to college. Consequently, not all of the sections in this book need be taken in class. Those paragraphs and sections marked with an asterisk may conveniently be assigned to better students as additional reading or for written reports and discussion.

This book also contains a good deal of material on God—for example, Chap. V, Sec. 6: that God exists and the sort of existent He is; Chap. VI, Sec. 2: God and analogy of being; Chap. VI, Sec. 3: God and the transcendents of truth, goodness, and beauty; Chap. VIII, Sec. 3: God as proper cause of existence, with whom creatures co-operate; Chap. IX, Sec. 2b2 and 3b2: God and finality on the cognitive and noncognitive levels; Chap. IX, Sec. 4: God and chance. The result is that it can be used also for a course of natural theology (either separate from or together with general metaphysics).

I am deeply indebted to Fr. Henri J. Renard, S.J., who was my first teacher in philosophy, and to Etienne Gilson, who was my last. I also have profited by my philosophical contacts with Fathers Maurice Holloway, S.J., George P. Klubertanz, S.J., Martin O. Vaske, S.J., and Norbert J. Lemke, S.J. Thanks are due also to Dr. Anton Pegis, Fathers Joseph Owens, C.Ss.R., Armand Maurer, C.S.B., and to other faculty members at the Pontifical Institute of Mediaeval Studies and the University of Toronto; also to Fathers William L. Wade, S.J., John P. Jelinek, S.J., and Francis J. Moriarty, S.J. None of them, though, should be held responsible wherever this book is inaccurate or inadequate. Someone recently has written, "Perhaps only the author can be fully aware of the imperfections of a book." Similarly, only he should be blamed for them.

Finally, I owe a special word of thanks to Rev. Harry W. Linn, S.J., President of Creighton University, Omaha, Nebraska, and to the Jesuit community there for their hospitality. Special gratitude is also due Dennis M. Alvernaz, S.J., who compiled the Index of Names.

LEO SWEENEY, S.J.

Acknowledgments

The author and publishers wish to thank the following for permission to quote or, on occasion, to paraphrase copyrighted material.

George Allen and Unwin, Ltd., for A. H. Armstrong, *Plotinus* (1953), pp. 136-137, 152, 160; for Bertrand Russell, *History of Western Philosophy* (1946), p. 864.

American Association for Advancement of Science and Robert B. MacLeod, George Gaylord Simpson, Ernst Mayr for Robert B. MacLeod, "Teleology and Theory of Human Behavior," *Science*, 125 (March 15, 1957), pp. 477, 478, 479, 480; George Gaylord Simpson, *Science*, 131 (April 1, 1960), p. 973 (this later appeared in *This View of Life* [New York: Harcourt, Brace & World, Inc., 1964], pp. 22, 23, 24); Ernst Mayr, "Cause and Effect in Biology," *Science*, 134 (November 10, 1961), pp. 1503, 1504. Reprinted by permission of AAAS and the authors.

Appleton-Century-Crofts, Inc., for Joseph Owens, *History of Ancient Western Philosophy* (Copyright © 1959 by Appleton-Century-Crofts, Inc.), p. 52; for George P. Klubertanz, S.J., *The Philosophy of Human Nature* (Copyright 1953 by Appleton-Century-Crofts, Inc.) pp. 19-21 (paraphrased), p. 22; *idem., Introduction to the Philosophy of Being*, 2nd ed. (Copyright © 1963 by Meredith Publishing Company), pp. 246-47, 270, 271, 273.

The Atlantic Monthly Press for W. T. Stace, "Man Against Darkness," 182 (September, 1948), pp. 53-55.

A. J. Ayer for *Language, Truth, and Logic*, 2nd ed. (London: Victor Gollancz, Ltd., 1951), p. 45.

Barnes and Oates, Ltd., for Maurice de la Taille, S.J., *The Hypostatic Union* (West Baden Springs: West Baden College, 1952), pp. 19-20.

Basic Books, Inc., for Rollo May and others, *Existence: A New Dimension in Psychiatry and Psychology* (1958), pp. 43, 47-48.

Bollingen Foundation and National Gallery of Art, Washington, D. C., for Etienne Gilson, *Painting and Reality* (New York: Pantheon Books, Inc.,

1957), pp. 5-6, 7, 8, 47; for Jacques Maritain, *Creative Intuition in Art and Poetry* (New York: Pantheon Books, Inc., 1953), p. 10. These works have been copyrighted by the Trustees of the National Gallery of Art, Washington, D. C., and are published by the Bollingen Foundation, New York.

Bruce Publishing Company for Joseph Owens, *An Elementary Christian Metaphysics* (1963), pp. 180, 189; for Henri Renard, S.J., *Philosophy of Being* (1946), pp. 25, 37, 44; for Kevin J. O'Brien, C.Ss.R., *Proximate End of Education* (1958), p. 48.

The Catholic University of America Press for St. Augustine, *Confessions*, VII, Chaps. 10 and 17, from *Fathers of the Church*, Vol. 21, pp. 180, 187.

D. E. Collins for six lines from "A Second Childhood" in *The Collected Poems of G. K. Chesterton*. Reprinted by permission.

Cross Currents for Paul Tillich, "Art and the Ultimate Reality," 10 (1960), p. 13.

The Dial Press for James Baldwin, from "Down at the Cross: Letter from a Region in My Mind," in *The Fire Next Time*, pp. 29-33. Appeared in *The New Yorker*, November 17, 1962. Reprinted by permission of The Dial Press, Inc.

Dodd, Mead & Company, Inc., for six lines from G. K. Chesterton, "A Second Childhood" in *The Collected Poems of G. K. Chesterton*, p. 70. Copyright 1932 by Dodd, Mead & Company, Inc.

Doubleday & Company, Inc., for Etienne Gilson, *Elements of Christian Philosophy* (© 1960 by Doubleday & Company, Inc.), p. 278; for Helen Keller, *Three Days to See*, p. 696. Copyright 1933 by Helen Keller. Reprinted by permission of Doubleday & Company, Inc.

Dover Publications, Inc., for Max Born, *The Restless Universe* (1951, 1957), pp. 154-55.

Farrar, Straus and Company, Inc., for G. K. Chesterton, *Chaucer*, p. 33; for François Mauriac, *The Lamb* (1955), pp. 134-35.

Harcourt, Brace & World, Inc., for Virginia Woolf, *To the Lighthouse* (1927), p. 95; for William Saroyan, "Boys and Girls Together," *Saturday Evening Post*, January 19, 1963, p. 38.

Harper & Row, Publishers, for Aldous Huxley, *Jesting Pilate* (1926), p. 130.

Harvard University Press for Richard von Mises, *Positivism: A Study in Human Understanding* (1951), pp. 62, 271.

B. Herder Book Company for R. Garrigou-Lagrange, O.P., *God: His Existence and His Nature* (1934), Vol. I, pp. 200-203; for Henry Koren, *Introduction to Science of Metaphysics* (1955), p. 223; for John F. Clarkson and others, *The Church Teaches* (1955), nos. 6, 306, 412, 414, 455; for Meister Eckhart, "Renewal in Spirit," quoted in J.F. Anderson, *Bond of Being* (1949), p. 264.

The Heythrop Journal for John L. Russell, S.J., "The Principle of Finality in the Philosophy of Aristotle and Teilhard de Chardin," 3 (October, 1962), pp. 350-51.

The Hogarth Press for Virginia Woolf, *To the Lighthouse* (1927), p. 95.

Holt, Rinehart and Winston, Inc., for Robert J. Kreyche, *First Philosophy* (1959), p. 256.

International Universities Press, Inc., for Charles Brenner, *Elementary Textbook of Psychoanalysis* (1955), p. 2.

Jubilee and Mrs. Molly Ross for Mrs. Molly Ross, "Death of a Man," 6 (September, 1958), pp. 20-23.

Alfred A. Knopf, Inc., for Albert Camus, *The Stranger* (1957), p. 154; for H. L. Mencken, *Minority Report* (1956), pp. 56, 238.

Longmans, Green & Company, Ltd., for P. Coffey, *Ontology or the Theory of Being* (1918), pp. 241, 349, 352, 353, 359-60.

Loyola University Press for John McCormick, S.J., *Scholastic Metaphysics* (1940), pp. 21, 140-41.

The Macmillan Company for Gerard Smith, S.J., and Lottie Kendzierski, *Philosophy of Being* (1961), pp. 278, 360; the Macmillan Company and the Student Christian Movement Press, Ltd., for J. Smart, "The Existence of God," in *New Essays in Philosophical Theology,* ed. A. Flew and A. MacIntrye (1955), p. 46.

David McKay Company, Inc., for Raissa Maritain, *We Have Been Friends Together* (1942), p. 26.

McGraw-Hill Book Company for Allen H. Benton and William E. Werner, *Principles of Field Biology and Ecology* (1958), p. 56; for Martin O. Vaske, S.J., *An Introduction to Metaphysics* (1963), p. 136, n. 4.

The Modern Schoolman for Joseph Owens, "The Causal Proposition— Principle or Conclusion?" 32 (May, 1955), pp. 335, 339.

National Society for Study of Education for Ralph Harper, *Modern Philosophers and Education* (1955), p. 250.

The Nebraska Register for interview of Reverend Alfeo Emaldi, February 22, 1952, p. 1.

New Directions for J. P. Sartre, *Nausea* (Copyright 1949 by New Directions), pp. 15 ff., 54, 130, 171, 173, 210.

The New Yorker for Calvin Tomkins, "A Thing Among Things," March 30, 1963, pp. 49-52. © 1963 by The New Yorker Magazine, Inc.

Robert O'Brien for "Almost Everybody Has Dreams on Every Night," *Life,* May 5, 1958, pp. 121 sq.

Oxford University Press for Gerard Manley Hopkins, *A Hopkins Reader,*

p. 33; for R. G. Collingwood, *An Essay on Metaphysics* (1940), pp. 15-16, 60.

Pantheon Books, Inc., for Josef Pieper, *Guide to Thomas Aquinas*, pp. 135-36. © Copyright 1962 by Pantheon Books, a Division of Random House, Inc. Reprinted by permission.

Philosophical Library, Inc., for J. P. Sartre, *Being and Nothingness* (1956), p. xlvii f.; *idem.*, *Existentialism* (1947), p. 18; for Gabriel Marcel, *Philosophy of Existence* (1949), pp. 43-45.

Pontifical Institute of Mediaeval Studies for Etienne Gilson, *Being and Some Philosophers* (1952), pp. 182-83.

Random House, Inc., for Augustine, *On the Trinity* VIII, 3 in *Basic Writings of St. Augustine*, II, 775-76, edited by Whitney J. Oates, copyright 1948 by Random House, Inc., reprinted by permission; for Jacques Maritain, *Existence and the Existent*, pp. 3, 19, 20, 26, 65, copyright 1948 by Pantheon Books, Inc., reprinted by permission of Random House, Inc.

Henry Regnery Co. for James Collins, *God in Modern Philosophy* (1959), pp. 394, 399.

Review of Metaphysics for John Wild, "Realistic Defense of Causal Efficacy," 2 (June, 1949), pp. 5-6, 8-9, 14.

Charles Scribner's Sons for Etienne Gilson, *Spirit of Mediaeval Philosophy* (1940), p. 37.

Sheed and Ward, Inc., for D. J. B. Hawkins, *Being and Becoming* (Copyright 1954 by Sheed & Ward, Inc.), pp. 71-72; for Jacques Maritain, *A Preface to Metaphysics* (1948), pp. 45-47, 48, 64, 65; for Gerald Vann, O.P., *The Water and the Fire* (Copyright 1954 by Sheed & Ward, Inc.), p. 19.

Student Christian Movement Press, Ltd., and The Macmillan Company, for J. Smart, "The Existence of God," in *New Essays in Philosophical Theology*, ed. A. Flew and A. MacIntrye (1955), p. 46.

United Newspapers Magazine Corporation and United Artists Corporation for "Love Without Measure," *This Week Magazine*, March 23, 1958, p. 2. Copyright 1958 by United Newspapers Magazine Corporation.

Scripta Mathematica, Yeshiva University, for C. J. Keyser, *Mathematics as a Culture Clue and Other Essays* (1947), p. 219.

University of California Press for J. Loewenberg, "The Elasticity of the Idea of Causality," in *Causality*, ed. George P. Adams *et alii* (1932), p. 3.

Joseph F. Wagner, Inc., for F. Van Steenberghen, *Ontology* (1952), pp. 252-53.

John Wiley & Sons, Inc., for George L. Clarke, *Elements of Ecology* (1954), pp. 2-3.

Contents

xiii

PART II: PRIMACY OF EXISTENCE

PART I

Introduction

CHAPTER I

Metaphysics a Valid Science?

In antiquity metaphysics was described by many complimentary terms.[1] It was called a "theology" because it attempted to find and furnish knowledge about God. It was also named an "ontology" inasmuch as the extent of its study was as wide and varied as being itself— indeed, its material object was all beings and its formal object, all beings considered precisely as beings. Moreover, a metaphysician was termed a "philosopher"—literally, one who loved wisdom. In fact, he was "*first* philosopher," and the addition of the adjective implied that the wisdom to which he aspired was most important because it involved God, the First Cause, and was man's greatest achievement in the merely human order. But what is more, it suggested that his wisdom had a genuine pre-eminence over other philosophical disciplines (such as philosophy of na-

---

[1] See Jacques Maritain, *An Introduction to Philosophy* (New York: Sheed & Ward, n.d.), p. 17 sq. and p. 102 sq.; Daniel J. Sullivan, *An Introduction to Philosophy* (Milwaukee: Bruce Publishing Co., 1957), p. 1 sq.

ture, ethics, and others), which received from it some of their basic notions.[2] Actually, too, the term "metaphysics" pointed to the valuable and unique nature of the science. In the phrase, *meta ta physica,* the Greek preposition *meta* means "beyond," and thus "metaphysics" expressed that the science so described was beyond the physical science of cosmology (and, for that matter, all other physical sciences) insofar as it treated of God, of being qua being, and of other topics which transcend the merely physical and material.[3]

In the remote past, then, metaphysics was looked upon with great favor, and any student who endeavored to become a metaphysician was considered to be aiming at a worthwhile goal.

1. Contemporary Opponents of Metaphysics

Currently, though, many hold metaphysics to be of little or no value. True enough, some of these need not be taken seriously, because they themselves are not philosophers and hence probably do not know much about metaphysics. Take as an example H. L. Mencken, the American journalist and satirist, for whom "metaphysics is almost always an attempt to prove the incredible by an appeal to the unintelligible." [4] His judgment can be easily set aside in view of the fact that Mencken himself was no philosopher in any strict sense of the word. So too with the novelist and essayist, Aldous Huxley, according to whom "the Other World—the world of metaphysics and religion—can never possibly be as interesting as this world and for an obvious reason. The Other World is an invention of the human fancy and shows the limitations

---

[2] For example, ethics deals with marriage, the family, the state, each of which basically is the complexus of real relations between the members. Metaphysics properly investigates real relations—what they are, what causes them, whether they are distinct from their causes, and so forth. Hence, metaphysics provides a general theory of relations to the ethician.

[3] See J. Owens, *Doctrine of Being in the Aristotelian Metaphysics* (2nd Ed.) (Toronto: Pontifical Institute of Mediaeval Studies, 1963), pp. 73-74; Anton-Hermann Chroust, "The Origin of 'Metaphysics,'" *Review of Metaphysics,* 14 (June, 1961), 601-16; J. Owens, *An Elementary Christian Metaphysics* (Milwaukee: Bruce Publishing Co., 1963), pp. 1-3.

[4] *Minority Report* (New York: Alfred A. Knopf, Inc., 1956), p. 238. *Ibid.,* p. 56: "The capacity of human beings to bore one another seems to be vastly greater than that of any other animals. Some of their most esteemed inventions have no other apparent purpose, for example, the dinner party of more than two, the epic poem, and the science of metaphysics." Also see *ibid.,* pp. 46, 48, 178, 248.

of its creator." [5] The many undergraduates who know little more after a semester of metaphysics than they knew before also fit into this group.[6]

But metaphysics has other opponents who do deserve serious consideration precisely because they themselves are philosophers. One such is the American author, Rudolph Carnap: "The danger lies in the deceptive character of metaphysics; it gives the illusion of knowledge without actually giving any knowledge." [7] Another is the British writer, A. J. Ayer, for whom every metaphysician inevitably and unwittingly writes sheer nonsense:

> It is in fact very rare for a literary artist to produce sentences which have no literal meaning. And where this does occur, the sentences are carefully chosen for their rhythm and balance. If the author writes nonsense, it is because he considers it most suitable for bringing about the effects for which his writing is designed. The metaphysician, on the other hand, does not intend to write nonsense. He lapses into it through being deceived by grammar, or through committing errors of reasoning.[8]

Why do such opponents so belittle metaphysics? Because for them it is not a genuine, valid science.[9] And why this? Because a genuine science can, they maintain, be based only upon the quantitative, the

---

[5] A. Huxley, *Jesting Pilate* (New York: Harper & Row, Publishers, 1926), p. 130.

[6] Take as an example this verdict passed by an anonymous student and reported by Archie J. Bahm, *Philosophy: An Introduction* (New York: John Wiley & Sons, Inc., 1953), p. 1: "The term 'philosophy' [read: metaphysics] conveys to most people a vagueness and uncertainty. . . . It is a collection of high-flown, meaningless words and phrases on useless subjects." Or this clever comparison: "A metaphysician is like a blind man in a dark room, looking for a black cat—which isn't there" (B. Hagspiel, *Smiles and Chuckles* [Techny, Illinois: Mission Press, 1952], p. 1).

[7] R. Carnap, *Philosophy and Logical Syntax* (London: K. Paul Trench Trubner and Co., Ltd., 1935), p. 20.

[8] A. J. Ayer, *Language, Truth and Logic* (2nd Ed.) (London: V. Gollancz, Ltd., 1951), p. 45.

[9] See R. G. Collingwood, *An Essay on Metaphysics* (Oxford: Clarendon Press, 1940), pp. 15-16: "The science of pure being [= metaphysics] cannot be called a science in the sense in which an ordinary science is so called . . . [because] the 'science of pure being' has a subject matter which is not a something but a nothing. . . . This is only a roundabout way of saying that there can be no such science. There is not even a quasi-science of pure being: not even a thing which in certain ways resembles an ordinary science and in certain ways differs from it. . . . There is not even a pseudo-science of pure being."

measurable. Mathematics, physics, chemistry, experimental psychology, and other empiriological knowledges[10] are rooted in such evidence and, accordingly, are valid bodies of knowledge. But metaphysics as traditionally conceived obviously is not built upon such evidence and, consequently, cannot be listed as a valid science.[11] Hence, any young man or woman who aims at studying metaphysics is simply wasting time and energy.[12]

---

[10] An "empiriological" knowledge is a science (1) which studies material things (hence, the force of the initial syllables in the adjective, "*empirio*logical"), but (2) only as affected by some sort of human activity (hence, the force of the last syllables, "empirio*logical*"). Because of this second factor every empiriological science is constructural.

Contemporary physics is an example of an empiriological science because (1) it is concerned with the structure and activities of material things, (2) but only under laboratory conditions and as mathematically formulated. Although constructural, mathematics or logic is not empiriological science because each lacks the first factor. Although it directly studies actual existents, metaphysics will turn out not to be empiriological because it is not a constructural knowledge.

On constructural knowledge, see Chap. VI, n. 10; Chap. X, pp. 321-22. On empiriological knowledge, see Jacques Maritain, *Degrees of Knowledge*, trans. Gerald B. Phelan (New York: Charles Scribner's Sons, 1959), pp. 202-5; Louis de Raeymaeker, "The One Voice of Science and the Many Voices of Philosophy," *Philosophy Today*, 5 (1961), 83-91; Alden L. Fisher, "The Contemporary Status of Scholastic Psychology," *Proceedings of the American Catholic Philosophical Association*, 31 (1957), 144-56; G. P. Klubertanz, S.J., *Introduction to the Philosophy of Being* (2nd Ed.) (New York: Appleton-Century-Crofts, 1963), pp. 290-93; *idem, Philosophy of Human Nature* (New York: Appleton-Century-Crofts, 1953), pp. 388-96.

[11] For example, see Richard von Mises, *Positivism: A Study in Human Understanding* (Cambridge, Mass.: Harvard University Press, 1951), p. 271: "Contemporary metaphysics often claims to provide an indispensable supplement to the present-day stage of the positive sciences. We reply to this that, wherever science shows gaps and a need for further and deeper elucidation, this elucidation cannot be reached in any other way than that of scientific research, and as soon as it is attained, it will form another part of the positive sciences." Earlier: "Our position seems, in any case, to be in opposition to metaphysics: . . . in our rejection of a 'bifurcation' of the world, in which one part is reserved for the positive sciences, and the other for a purely speculative study" (p. 62). Also see Bertrand Russell, *History of Western Philosophical Thought* (London: George Allen & Unwin, Ltd., 1940), p. 864: "Many questions, formerly obscured by the fog of metaphysics, can be answered with precision, and by objective methods which introduce nothing of the philosopher's temperament except the desire to understand. . . . In the welter of conflicting fanaticisms, one of the few unifying forces is scientific truthfulness, by which I mean the habit of basing our beliefs upon observations and inferences as impersonal . . . as is possible for human beings."

[12] Some of the contemporary authors we have been mentioning do concede a place within the curriculum to metaphysics when understood as "a spirit or

What should be our reaction to such opposition? First of all, let us gladly acknowledge that the various branches of mathematics, chemistry, physics, and other empiriological knowledges are, in their own way and within their own areas, genuine sciences and are extremely valuable for a progressive understanding and mastery of the material universe. Secondly, we should be grateful to our opponents for forcing us at the very outset to take nothing for granted and to face the extremely important and difficult question: can metaphysics be a valid science? At the very outset one thing is also clear: to answer affirmatively we cannot grant their equation of "science" with "empiriological science." We cannot accept their restriction of *science* to knowledge based solely on the quantitative and the measurable. Rather, we must work out a more ample notion. We must attempt to elaborate a description of science which is broad enough to fit metaphysics as well as mathematical and empiriological knowledges.

2. Broader Description of "Science"

How shall we proceed in that elaboration? Let us base it upon the rather evident parallels which such sciences as mathematics, physics, and the like have with sports (for example, basketball), skills (typing) and arts (piano-playing) and, accordingly, let us begin with the latter. From our past experience we know how they are acquired, what they are, and how many an individual person can acquire. First of all, we know that they are acquired by practice, by the repetition of definite physical activity: no one becomes a basketball player or a typist or a pianist except through hours of actually playing basketball, typing, or playing Mozart. We also know what they are—genuine acquired abilities by which we can easily, gracefully, enjoyably perform within given areas of physical activities. Finally, we realize how many an individual person can acquire—everything else being equal (that is,

method of approaching experience, rather than a body of conclusions about experience" (E. S. Brightman) or as a "general theory of criticism" (C. J. Ducasse) or as "an historical science . . . [whose] business is to find out what absolute presuppositions have actually been made by various persons at various times in doing various pieces of scientific thinking" (R. G. Collingwood, *An Essay on Metaphysics*, p. 60). (The quotations of Brightman and Ducasse are from A. J. Bahm, *Philosophy: An Introduction*, p. 2, where I interpret "philosophy" as synonymous with "metaphysics.")

What these critics reject is a metaphysics which claims to achieve knowledge of God, the human soul, the nature of reality, and so forth.

provided he has the requisite natural endowments, talents, time, and so forth), the number of such abilities he can achieve is in proportion to the different sorts of physical activities he engages in. Recreational activity of a prescribed sort on a basketball court will produce proficiency at playing basketball, but not necessarily proficiency at baseball or football and not at all at swimming. Put more generally and abstractly, there are as many distinct sports, skills, and arts as there are different kinds of, diverse areas of physical activities which cause those acquired abilities.

The parallel between such physical abilities and sciences should now be clear. Every body of organized knowledge also is acquired by intellectual activity—by repeated operations of reflecting, reasoning, analyzing, synthesizing, and the like. No one becomes a chemist or a biologist or a physicist except through long hours of actual mental work in a laboratory. Again, such knowledges are acquired mental abilities by which we can with comparative ease and accuracy cope with problems within given areas of intellectual endeavor. Finally, the number of such intellectual abilities an individual person can acquire is in proportion to the different sorts of intellectual activities he engages in (provided, of course, he has the requisite mental endowments and talents). Solving problems concerning plane and solid figures and allied topics will produce proficiency in geometry, but not necessarily proficiency in biology or sociology or economics. Stated in a more general fashion, there are as many distinct sciences as there are different sorts of, diverse areas of intellectual activities from which those sciences result.

The information gained from juxtaposing knowledges with sports and other physical abilities enables us now to focus much more precisely upon the problem we face as a result of the opposition to metaphysics by many contemporary philosophers. A science is an acquired intellectual ability by which one can easily master problems within a given area of mental endeavor and, secondly, there are as many different sciences as there are genuinely different areas of intellectual activity, because these latter cause the former. If, then, metaphysics is to be a science at all, it must arise from an area of intellectual activity which furnishes valid evidence, which has a genuine message for the mind, which delivers insights into what material existents are. If it is to be distinct from other sciences, that area of intellectual activity and evidence must be different from all others, that message and those insights must be truly diverse. According to modern opponents of metaphysics, the only area of intellectual activity which furnishes valid evidence to the human knower is the quantitative and the measurable and, hence, metaphysics as traditionally understood cannot be a genuine science, but is rather a mere collection of high-flown, meaningless, valueless constructs. Hence, our question now has become: do the measurable and the quantitative alone provide evidence for an understanding of material things? Or do not material things also offer evidence of an entirely different sort, which can initiate mental activity issuing into a genuine science of metaphysics? I contend that they do and, accordingly, that a valid science of metaphysics is possible. The present book is an attempt to test and work out that contention.

3. "Evidence of a Different Sort"

Before starting that attempt, let us briefly investigate that "evidence of an entirely different sort" which I have just proposed material existents do offer in order to have an initial and general awareness of what to look for.

As we have previously granted, material things can be legitimately studied within laboratory conditions, and valuable empiriological sciences result. As an instance of such study, consider the experiments conducted on dreams at the University of Chicago.[13] Volunteer subjects went to sleep on plain iron cots in the laboratory. Electrodes were pasted to their scalps, to the bony ledges of their eye sockets, to their backs and chests. A tangle of red, blue, green, and yellow wires sprouted from their heads; these wires were connected to machines in the adjoining instrument room. As the subjects slept, a cardiotachometer clicked away their heartbeats. The swinging pens of the electroencephalograph recorded the infinitesimal brain waves, multiplied a millionfold, that pulsed through the varicolored wires. Through these graphs of some four hundred dreams gathered from more than one thousand hours of sleep, those conducting the experiments finally arrived at several conclusions—that everyone dreams twenty to twenty-five per cent of the time of sleep (except those who are less than six months old and those who are drunk), that we compress and elide time in our dreams, that our eyeballs move greatly during a dream whereas other bodily members move very little, that the direction of

---

[13] For an easily available description of the experiments, see Robert O'Brien, "Almost Everybody Has Dreams on Every Night," *Life*, May 5, 1958, p. 121 sq. Also see Francis L. Harmon, *Principles of Psychology* (Rev. Ed.) (Milwaukee: Bruce Publishing Co., 1951), pp. 348-52.

the eye-movement indicates the direction of events in the dream, that dreams of a schizophrene consist of the image of one object, motionless in mid-air, and so on.

Such a case certainly illustrates that "material things studied within a laboratory" do constitute one area of evidence which can initiate mental activity culminating in valuable conclusions of an empiriological sort (here belonging to physiology and experimental psychology).

But material things also exist outside the laboratory and are not known only through cardiotachometers and electro-encephalographs. Men and women are caught up in the actual events of history. They are immersed in the give-and-take of everyday life in the twentieth century. And what they experience, what they do and suffer can be known through our own direct observation and through their own accounts. As an example, consider an incident which a mother relates concerning her young daughter.

> My daughter F. was about four years old when she first became aware that numbers were not just new words in her vocabulary nor names of digits, but that they can be useful to express quantity. This step, as all parents learn, follows the "so big" stage. One memorable day, F. turned to me to express her love with the help of her new-found knowledge and said, "Mummy, I love you ten times," followed by deep thought and "I love you twenty times." After another short pause, she reached a breathless pinnacle with "I love you six hundred times." A grateful hug and kiss from me produced a tiny frown and more concentrated thought which disappeared in a sigh of relief in her final outburst, "Mummy, I love you outside the line of numbers." [14]

As the last exclamation would seem to indicate, the young girl had achieved the quite significant awareness that some items (here, love) somehow are genuinely immaterial and nonquantitative. She experienced love for her mother, she came to know quantity and number, then by contrast she realized (however momentarily and obscurely) that love under certain circumstances is simply unlike quantity. It cannot be measured by number, it is outside the realm of the strictly material.

How is that incident important to us? It is an indication that human beings are sources for valid knowledge not only when they are within a laboratory but also as they actually live out their daily lives. In the

---

[14] "Love Without Measure," *This Week Magazine*, March 23, 1958, p. 2.

present case an actual event in the life of a child gives an insight into what any human being, by the very fact he is human, actually is and can do. In this incident a child goes through a series of perfective changes and yet remains basically human—and, in fact, the same human being she was since her birth four years earlier: she had grown to her present physical size, she had digested her dinner eaten perhaps two hours earlier, yet she now is actually loving her mother, is thinking of that love and her newly gained awareness of numbers, wishes to express her love, and then comes to the further realization that love is outside the sphere of quantity. Such data (one and the same thing changing and yet remaining basically the same) can initiate reflection terminating in the realization that a human person is a genuine unity, which nevertheless is somehow intimately composed of the permanent and the changing; that some of those changes are material (for example, physical growth, digestion of food), others are not (for instance, love for a parent, intellectual awareness of that love as transcending matter); and, therefore, that a human person who is capable of both material and immaterial activities must himself *be* somehow both material and immaterial.

True enough, such realizations belong properly to the philosophy of human nature and not to metaphysics, but metaphysics is simply a further development along the same line of reflection.[15] Also such conclusions need much more elaboration to be clear and convincing, but enough has been said to see that they have been derived from evidence issuing from a moment in the actual career of a human existent. Accordingly, they testify to the possibility of philosophy as a genuine science and yet distinct from empiriological knowledges and they suggest that material existents as they actually exist and as known by direct perception can and do provide an area of evidence which can stimulate intellectual activity culminating in a philosophy of nature, and eventually in metaphysics.

4. Methodology

Such, then, is an example of evidence belonging to an entirely different order from that which grounds empiriological knowledges and furnishing the foundation of the present book.

How shall we proceed? Our immediate aim must be to understand

---

[15] The difference between philosophy of nature and metaphysics will be explained later. See Chap. X, Secs. 4 and 5.

as thoroughly as possible that material things as they actually exist and as directly perceived are genuinely an area of unique evidence; simultaneously, we shall see precisely what that evidence is. What messages do material existents, precisely as actual, deliver to an attentive human mind? What insights do they furnish?

Undoubtedly there are many ways of achieving that aim, but the one we shall utilize is a brief excursion into the history of Greek philosophy. In the next chapter we shall watch the reactions of various Hellenic thinkers when confronted by the material universe in all its variety, richness, mystery. The advantage of thus beginning with Heraclitus, Plato, and Aristotle is that they formulated intellectual reactions to the universe without any awareness of the revelation God gave the Hebrews and, thus, we can expect that formulation to be the product of human reason alone when working upon data from material things. Moreover, they lived long before the appearance and development of empiriological sciences; hence, material existents as known through direct perception were automatically taken as the starting-point for philosophical reflection. Accordingly, here are thinkers of outstanding intelligence who are without divine revelation and are unprejudiced by modern scientific methodology and yet who face the same material universe as we. What messages do the material existents which fill that universe have for their intellects? How far do they accurately interpret that evidence? Where do they err? Profiting by their successes and their failures, perhaps we can more easily detect the evidence such actual existents really do give and, thus, eventually build up an adequate metaphysics.

5. Summary and Conclusions

(a) According to an articulate group of contemporary philosophers, metaphysics is of no value because it is not a genuine science. Why so? Because the only sort of evidence which can beget a valid science is that which is somehow measured and quantified. Obviously, metaphysics transcends quantity and measurement; accordingly, it cannot be a genuine science, but is a mere collection of high-flown, insignificant, futile statements.

(b) On the other hand, we refuse to restrict science to knowledge based solely on the quantitative, the measurable. We propose that material existents provide evidence for genuine sciences not only as such existents are viewed under laboratory conditions but also as they are directly perceived in their actual day-by-day conditions. Accordingly, a genuine science of metaphysics is possible and the present book is an effort to make good that proposal.

(c) The notion of science, then, has become broad enough to be applicable to any sort of valid, universal knowledge—the empiriological as well as the philosophical.[16] By comparison with such acquired physical abilities as sports, skills, arts, a *science* turns out to be *an acquired intellectual ability by which one can with ease and accuracy solve problems within a given area of mental activity;* secondly, there are as many different sciences as there are genuinely different areas of intellectual activity.[17]

(d) Within this context, then, *metaphysics is that acquired intellectual ability by which one with ease and accuracy knows existents precisely as actually existing through reflection upon material existents in*

---

[16] One must, therefore, go against the current trend of using "science" as a synonym for "empiriological science." Throughout this book, whenever I contrast chemistry, physics, and the like with metaphysics, I shall speak of the former as "empiriological sciences." Whenever "science" is used without the adjective, it means any sort of acquired intellectual ability and can refer to any kind of knowledge—philosophical, empiriological, theological. Its meaning is the same as the Latin term, *scientia.*

[17] We can rather easily translate the present statement into more technical language if we realize that the words, "an acquired intellectual ability by which one can . . . ," are basically equal to "an operative habit," whereas the words, "area of mental activity," are roughly equivalent to "formal object." Put more technically, then, a science is *an intellectual operative habit which has its own formal object;* secondly, there are as many distinct sciences as there are distinct formal objects.

On operative habit, see Henri Renard, S.J., and Martin Vaske, S.J., *Philosophy of Man,* 2nd Ed. (Milwaukee: Bruce Publishing Co., 1956), p. 266 sq.; G. P. Klubertanz, S.J., *Philosophy of Human Nature,* p. 272 sq., especially p. 295; James E. Royce, S.J., *Man and His Nature* (New York: McGraw-Hill Book Company, 1961), p. 238 sq.; Maurice R. Holloway, S.J., *An Introduction to Natural Theology* (New York: Appleton-Century-Crofts, 1959), p. 3 sq.

What is meant by "material" and "formal" objects with reference to a science? The two adjectives are equivalent to "indeterminate" and "determinate." That is, actual existents can be studied both by an empiriological scientist and by a metaphysician and, in this sense, both have the same material object—actual existents considered without the definite, precise aspect under which each properly studies such existents. However, the formal object of each is different: "material existents *precisely as actually existent*" expresses the determinate approach of the metaphysician, "material existents *precisely as within the laboratory*" expresses the determinate approach of the scientists. Accordingly, when we speak of the "material object of a science," the adjective does not refer to matter as such, but is equivalent to "indeterminate," while "formal" is equivalent to "determinate." On this meaning of "material" and "formal," see Chap. III, Sec. 4, *ad finem.*

directly perceived situations.[18] It is distinct from all other sciences because of its unique area of intellectual endeavor: from empiriological
sciences, which deal with material things insofar as they are known
within various laboratory conditions and, frequently, under mathematical formulations; from sacred theology, which deals with (among other
things) material existents inasmuch as they are known through divine
revelation.[19]

Suggested Readings

Ayer, A. J., "The Elimination of Metaphysics," in *Language, Truth and
    Logic* (2nd Ed.), pp. 33-45. London: Victor Gollancz, Ltd., 1951.
Born, Max, "Physics and Metaphysics," *Scientific Monthly*, 82 (1956),
    229-35.
Caldin, E. F., *Science and Christian Apologetic*, Aquinas Papers 17, pp.
    1-12. London: Blackfriars, 1951. On the method of contemporary sci-
    ence.
Chroust, Anton-Hermann, "The Origin of 'Metaphysics,'" *The Review of
    Metaphysics*, 14 (1961), 601-16. On the etymology of "metaphysics."
De Raeymaeker, Louis, "The One Voice of Science and the Many Voices of
    Philosophy," *Philosophy Today*, 5 (1961), 83-91.
Drennen, D. A., *A Modern Introduction to Metaphysics: Readings from
    Classical and Contemporary Sources*, pp. 325-26, 328-30. New York:
    Free Press of Glencoe, 1962. A selected bibliography of writings by
    linguistic analysists and naturalists.
Gilson, Etienne, *The Unity of Philosophical Experience*, pp. 299-320.
    New York: Charles Scribner's Sons, 1940. On the nature of meta-

---

[18] The exact and technical significance of this description will be clarified and
justified later. See Chap. VI, Sec. 1; Chap. X, Secs. 3-5.
[19] Metaphysics has had another group of opponents, the Tertullianists, so named
after one of its early and prominent leaders, Tertullian (ca. A.D. 160-240). According to them, metaphysics (and, in general, any attempt to arrive through
reason at knowledge of God, the human soul, and the nature of reality) is dangerous and harmful because it counteracts or even destroys one's ability to believe
in divine revelation. Faith alone can and does provide all the information needed
on such topics. Hence, metaphysics should be avoided.
   In the twentieth century this position has few defenders, since faith in divine
revelation is not nearly as widespread now as it was in early and medieval Christian eras when this attitude originated and developed. Accordingly, the attempt
of philosophy to know God, the nature of man, and so on is welcomed rather
than rejected by those who in other times might be Tertullianists. Hence, we
shall give no time here to this group. For an excellent study of the Tertullianist
position, see E. Gilson, *Reason and Revelation in the Middle Ages* (New York:
Charles Scribner's Sons, 1939).

physics (after a survey of what happens when nonmetaphysical methods are used to solve metaphysical problems).

———, *Wisdom and Love in Saint Thomas Aquinas,* Aquinas Lecture, 1951. Milwaukee: Marquette University Press, 1951. On the nature of wisdom, metaphysics, philosophy.

Hanson, Norwood Russell, "On the Impossibility of Any Future Metaphysics," *Philosophical Studies,* 40 (1960), 86-96.

Heidegger, Martin, "What Is Metaphysics?" in *Existence and Being,* trans. R. F. C. Hull and Alan Crick, pp. 355-92. Chicago: Henry Regnery Co., 1949.

Hocking, W. E., S. N. Lamprecht, and J. H. Randall, Jr., "Metaphysics: Its Function, Consequences and Criteria," *Journal of Philosophy,* 43 (1946), 365-78, 393-412.

Martin, Oliver, "An Examination of Contemporary Naturalism and Materialism," in *Return to Reason,* ed. John Wild, pp. 68-91. Chicago: Henry Regnery Co., 1953. On the inadequacy of materialism.

Miller, Robert G., "Linguistic Analysis and Metaphysics," in *Proceedings of the American Catholic Philosophical Association,* 34 (1960), 80-109.

Owens, Joseph, *An Elementary Christian Metaphysics,* pp. 1-14. Milwaukee: Bruce Publishing Company, 1963. On "metaphysics": its etymology and meaning.

Sullivan, J. W. N., *The Limitations of Science,* pp. 125-50. New York: The Viking Press, Inc., 1954. A description of how the nineteenth-century mentality of science has been succeeded by an outlook which admits that there are approaches to reality other than those of the empiriological science.

Van Melsen, Andrew Gerard, *Science and Technology,* pp. 9-26. Pittsburgh: Duquesne University Press, 1961. On the difference between philosophy and physical sciences.

CHAPTER II

Lessons from Heraclitus and Plato

By awareness of the position of previous philosophers, our own speculative endeavors are improved and, in fact, can surpass those very predecessors who aided us. "We are," Bernard of Chartres (d. ca. 1125) reminds us, "like dwarfs sitting on the shoulders of giants; we see more things and more far-off ones than they did, not because our sight is better nor because we are taller than they were, but because they raise us up and add to our height by their gigantic loftiness."[1] A similar reminder has recently been sounded by Paul Tillich, prominent contemporary author, who advises that no one should attempt to philosophize without first making the acquaintance of the early Greek thinkers.

Can any philosophy ignore some of the fundamental insights of Parmenides, Plato, and Aristotle? I would say no, and if they do, then they ignore

---

[1] Quotation given by John of Salisbury, *Metalogicon, III,* 4 (PL 199, col. 900).

elements which belong to the very nature of the task of philosophy.
. . . I would say ignoring it [the wisdom achieved by the Greeks],
as some people do who think philosophy starts about 1890, is very
wrong. . . . Therefore, do not let us forget to sit down first and to
learn, both in philosophy and in art.[2]

But even had Bernard and Tillich not spoken out so strongly, we
still would have reason to turn to those Hellenic philosophers by the
very nature of the problem we face. Our task is to realize that material things as they actually exist in directly perceived situations are an
area of unique evidence and, simultaneously, to discover what that evidence is. How better achieve that realization than by observing the
reactions of such intellectual giants as Plato and Aristotle, who were
without divine revelation and were unprejudiced by modern scientific
methodology and yet faced the same material universe as we?

In understanding and profiting by their reactions to that universe,
we must identify ourselves with them as much as possible. In imagination we must turn from our contemporary world with its entertainment
media (TV, movies, radio), its planes and automobiles, its H-bombs
and rockets. We must go back past the Civil War, the American and
French Revolutions, the Renaissance, the centuries of the Holy Roman
Empire, even past the birth of Christ, until the year becomes about
600 B.C. and we find ourselves dressed in cloak and sandals, standing
on Grecian soil.

Setting aside the machines men have made during the past centuries,
we discover that the material universe then is not basically different
from that which confronts us now. Then as now there is the dazzling
beauty of the heavens by night, the golden sunshine and blue skies by
day. There are turbulent storms with blinding lightning, deafening
thunder, driving sheets of hail and rain; the mystery of the earth, rough
with hills and mountains, studded with oceans, lakes, and streams.
There are innumerable plants, big and small, useful and ornamental.
There are animals almost endless in number and kind, in the air or
on the land or in the sea. Finally, there is the greatest mystery of all:
individual men, who walk, sleep, eat, grow, reproduce; who see, hear,
become angry, fight; who think, explain, laugh, write poetry, do as they
please, sin, suffer. Such is the universe which we would try to understand.

And in 600 B.C. no answers are furnished us by modern empiriological sciences or by divine revelation (there is then, for example, no

---

[2] Paul Tillich, "Art and Ultimate Reality," *Cross Currents,* 10 (1960), p. 13.

awareness in Greece of *Genesis, 1, 1:* "In the beginning God created heaven and earth"). We have only the actual universe itself and the innate curiosity and power of our human minds. If these have become dulled under the routine of everyday concerns, we must sharpen and revive them. We must learn to renew the wonder we experienced as children;[3] we must strive for the admiration and astonishment of the artist.[4] We must come to view each situation as if it had never occurred before and might never occur again;[5] we must stare at events transpiring around us.[6] In short, before "the secretive depths and the implacable advance of that infinite host of beings, aspects, events, physical and moral tangles of horror and beauty—of that world, that undecipherable Other—with which Man . . . is faced," we must put on the open attitude and the "feelings of primitive man looking at the all-pervading force of Nature, or of the old Ionian philosophers saying that 'all things are full of gods.'"[7] Then, perhaps, we shall understand

---

[3] Gerald Vann, *The Water and the Fire* (New York: Sheed & Ward, 1954), p. 19: "Wonder is one of the faculties most easy to lose. We have it in childhood, undiscriminating, no doubt, but vivid and deep. We all too easily lose it as we grow older and become immersed in our daily concerns; and so, unless we are very careful, not beauty only but life itself passes us by. For inevitably life loses its meaning when it loses its mystery." We must remember that both Plato and Aristotle link philosophy with the sense of wonderment. Plato, *Theaetetus,* 155D: "This sense of wonder is the mark of the philosopher. Philosophy indeed has no other origin." Aristotle, *Metaphysics,* I, Chap. 2, 882b12: "It is owing to their wonder that men both now begin and at first began to philosophize."

[4] Gerard Manley Hopkins, *A Hopkins Reader* (London: Oxford University Press, 1953), p. 33: "I have particular periods of admiration for particular things in Nature; for a certain time I am astonished at the beauty of a tree, shape, effect, etc.; then when the passion, so to speak, has subsided, it is consigned to my treasury of explored beauty, and acknowledged with admiration and interest ever after, while something new now takes its place in my enthusiasm."

[5] Nan Pendergast, "The Gift of Wonder," *Catholic Digest,* January, 1959, p. 34: "Genius . . . is merely the ability to view each situation as if it had never occurred before."

[6] G. K. Chesterton, "A Second Childhood," *Collected Poems of G. K. Chesterton* (London: Cecil Palmer, 1927), p. 70: "When all my days are ending/And I have no song to sing,/I think I shall not be too old/To stare at everything;/As I stared once at a nursery door/Or a tall tree and a swing." See also Helen Keller, *Three Days to See* (New York: Doubleday & Company, Inc., 1955), p. 696: "I who am blind can give one hint to those who see: Use your eyes as if tomorrow you would be stricken blind. And the same method can be applied to the other senses. . . . Glory in all the facets of pleasure and beauty which the world reveals to you; make the most of every sense."

[7] Jacques Maritain, *Creative Intuition in Art and Poetry* (New York: Pantheon Books, Inc., 1953), p. 10.

and benefit by the reactions of those Ionian philosophers, the first of
whom is Thales (fl. 585 B.C.).[8]

1. An Initial Reaction: Thales

Confronted by the sensible universe, Thales asks, "What are all
those things? What is the common stuff which they all share and
which makes them real?" His answer: water. All things are, basically,
water, and this because of evidence almost too obvious to mention. On
the surface of the earth are countless streams, lakes, oceans. Dig a hole
beneath the surface and one finds water. Pierce the skin of an animal,
cut the bark of a tree, and there comes forth watery liquid. From the
heavens fall constant rain, snow, dew. In a word, all things are water.

Thales's contribution to us is evidently not his answer, because his
doctrine is what can be called a materialistic monism—that is, an identification of all reality with some material component, the reduction of
the whole to one of its physical parts. Every such monism is unsatisfac-
tory because whole areas of the universe are left unexplained—for example, human operations of thinking, of willing, even of sensing are
simply *not* water. He is of great assistance, though, in the sort of question he asks and in the methodology used in answering. The question
he proposes is the basic inquiry of metaphysics: What are actual existents? What makes them be real? What does "to be real" mean? And
his procedure of arriving at a reply is standard for any genuine metaphysician: he turns to actual existents and observes whatever evidence
they may give.

---

[8] In our excursion into Greek philosophy, no one should expect a full treatment of Thales and the other Hellenic thinkers. This can be found in such competent histories of philosophy as J. Owens, *A History of Ancient Western Philosophy* (New York: Appleton-Century-Crofts, 1959) [hereafter referred to as
History]; F. Copleston, S.J., *History of Philosophy, Vol. I: Greece and Rome*
(London: Burns, Oates & Washbourne, Ltd., 1951).

Our concern is not to write a history of philosophy but to philosophize, to
work out our own philosophical position. Hence, we shall emphasize those factors in each philosopher which are conducive to our philosophical endeavor.

On Thales, see J. Owens, *History*, pp. 6-12; F. Copleston, S.J., *op. cit.*, 22-24;
S. Sambursky, *The Physical World of the Greeks*, transl. Merton Dagut (New
York: The Macmillan Company, 1955), pp. 5-6, 12; A. H. Armstrong, *An Intro-
duction to Ancient Philosophy* (London: Methuen and Co. Ltd., 1949), pp. 2-5;
Eduard Zeller, *Outlines of the History of Greek Philosophy* (New York: Meridian
Books, 1955), 42-43.

2. Heraclitus and Radical Existentialism

Heraclitus[9] takes up that basic question and, using the same procedure, comes up with an answer which is as true today as it was in the
sixth century B.C.

What are actual existents? What makes them real? What is reality?
Look at the actual universe, Heraclitus counsels, and there you see a
vast panorama of constant change. Spring replaces winter and in turn
succumbs to summer, which in time gives way to fall. In the heavens,
stars are continually shifting positions, the moon waxes and wanes, the
sun steadily moves from east to west.[10] On the earth springs flow into
creeks, creeks into rivers, rivers into lakes and oceans, whence moisture
is taken up into the atmosphere only to condense into rain, which begins the water-cycle all over again. Falling into the ground, seeds produce plants, which in turn grow, flower, send forth the seeds of new
plants to succeed them. Animals (men included) are born, grow to
maturity, decline, and die, but are replaced by offspring they themselves have begotten. And within the life of any man what do we find
but a constant shift of psychological moods? Now he's up, now he's
down; now he's angry, now he's calm. What is the history of nations
and civilizations but a story of development and decline? The currently
dominant nation has replaced those which previously were supreme,
but it will in time become decadent itself and give way to another,
energetic people now on the rise. "In time," we say—time itself is one
of the greatest mysteries of all, but this much is true: time itself
marches on steadily, inexorably.

The sensible universe is, then, a tremendous complex of unending

---

[9] The proper noun, Heraclitus, as used throughout this book, does *not* refer to
Heraclitus himself (fl. ca. 500 B.C.), but to subsequent philosophers who "were
referred to as Heracliteans or as having Heraclitizing tendencies. . . . They
claimed that there is only flux, with no stability whatsoever, not even such as
would allow the fixed meanings of words necessary for the use of ordinary language. Their teaching was summed up in the formula, 'All things are flowing'
(*panta rei*)" (J. Owens, *History,* p. 52). Heraclitus himself does not seem to
have made that claim. Still for purposes of convenience I shall use his name to
designate those subsequent philosophers who did hold that doctrine.

[10] Of course, the motion of the sun from east to west is only apparent, because
it is the earth which moves, as we know in modern times. But this movement
of the earth, had these Heracliteans known of it, would be but another instance
of the constant change they find in the universe. Current theories that the universe is constantly expanding as galaxies of stars recede from one another at
enormous speeds would be another and impressive instance.

succession, movement, change. Under pressure of that overwhelming evidence Heraclitus concludes that actual things are real precisely because and insofar as they undergo change. The very heart of their reality is change. Their apparent permanence and self-identity are only deceptive masks, covering up the inner currents of fluency which alone make them real. In short, reality *is* change. To be real and to be changing are synonymous.

Such is Heraclitus' conclusion. Although others may hesitate to identify reality with change, reflective men down through the ages have been similarly struck by the ubiquitous and ceaseless flux which the universe involves. One such is the Psalmist, who finds himself crumbling under the attacks of time[11] and for whom all men are

like a dream in the morning, like grass that shoots up—
In the morning it flourishes and is green, in the evening it is mowed down
    and withers. . . .
The sum of our years is seventy and, if we are strong, eighty,
And most of them toil and trouble, for they quickly pass and we vanish.[12]

Another is the author of the *Following of Christ*, who has written a chapter aptly called, "On the Thoughts of Death": "A very little while and all will be over with thee here. . . . Man today is, and tomorrow he is seen no more. . . . When it is morning, think thou wilt not live till evening. And when evening comes, venture not to promise thyself the next morning." [13] Shakespeare is yet another; he has Macbeth, upon hearing of his wife's death, call out:

> Tomorrow and tomorrow and tomorrow
> Creeps in this petty pace from day to day
> To the last syllable of recorded time.
> And all our yesterdays have lighted fools
> The way to dusty death. Out, out, brief candle;

---

[11] Psalm 30, 10 sq.:

Have pity on me, O Lord, for I am in trouble; my eye grows weak with grief, my soul and my body.
For my life is spent in sorrow, my years in groaning.
My strength has failed through affliction, and my bones have wasted away. . . .
I am fully forgotten, as one dead. I am like a broken vessel.

[12] Psalm 89, 5 sq.

[13] Thomas a Kempis, *Following of Christ*, I, Chap. 23.

Life's but a walking shadow, a poor player
That struts and frets his hour upon the stage
And then is heard no more.[14]

The list could be lengthened, but let us move to the contemporary
scene, where one finds such radical existentialists as Jean Paul Sartre
and his followers almost obsessed with the omnipresence of fluency and
change.[15]

What are material things? Each is a series of appearances and nothing more, Sartre tells us in his philosophic *opus magnum, Being and
Nothingness:*

> Modern thought has realized considerable progress by reducing
> the existent to the series of appearances which manifest it. . . . In
> the first place we certainly thus get rid of that dualism which in the
> existent opposes interior to exterior. There is no longer an exterior
> for the existent if one means by that a superficial covering which hides
> from sight the true nature of the object. And this true nature . . .
> no longer exists. The appearances which manifest the existent are
> neither interior nor exterior; they are all equal, they all refer to other
> appearances, and none of them is privileged. . . . The obvious con-
> clusion is that the dualism of being and appearance is no longer en-
> titled to any legal status within philosophy. . . . Appearance be-
> comes full positivity; its essence is an "appearing" which is no longer

---

[14] *Macbeth*, Act V, Scene 4.

[15] Who is a "radical existentialist?" According to J. Maritain, *Existence and
the Existent* (New York: Pantheon Books, Inc., 1949), p. 3, there are two sorts
of existentialism: "There are two fundamentally different ways of interpreting
the word existentialism. One way is to affirm the primacy of existence, but as
implying and preserving essences or natures and as manifesting the supreme victory of the intellect and of intelligibility. This is what I consider to be authentic
existentialism. The other way is to affirm the primacy of existence, but as destroying or abolishing essences or natures and as manifesting the supreme defeat
of the intellect and of intelligibility. This is what I consider to be apocryphal
existentialism, the current kind which 'no longer signifies anything at all.' "
   Those whom Maritain calls "apocryphal existentialists," I call "radical existentialists," but the meaning is the same: those for whom there is only existence
and no essence or, in terms more readily understood at the present stage of this
book, those for whom there is only change and no stability. For them reality is
identified with change.
   There are various groups within radical existentialism (see J. Collins, *The Existentialists: A Critical Study* [Chicago: Henry Regnery Co., 1952]). The best
examples of the particular brand of radical existentialism I have in mind are Jean
Paul Sartre and his followers.

opposed to being but on the contrary is the measure of it. *For the being of an existent is exactly what it appears.*[16]

What Sartre has just explained technically can also be found concretely expressed in this scene from his novel, *Nausea*. First he pictures the fluid state of its hero's mind.

> I think of no one any more. I don't even bother looking for words. It flows in me, more or less quickly. I fix nothing, I let it go. Through the lack of attaching myself to words, my thoughts remain nebulous most of the time. They sketch vague, pleasant shapes and then are swallowed up. I forget them almost immediately.

He goes on to depict a chance meeting of a man and a woman, which can be looked upon as a picture in miniature of the universe itself, the sum-total of such haphazard, contingent, senseless, fluid events.

> You let events flow past; suddenly you see people pop up who speak and who go away, you plunge into stories without beginning or end: you'd make a terrible witness. But in compensation, one misses nothing . . . For example, Saturday, about four in the afternoon, on the end of the timbered sidewalk of the new station yard, a little woman in sky blue was running backwards, laughing, waving a handkerchief. At the same time, a negro in a cream-colored raincoat, yellow shoes and a green hat, turned the corner of the street and whistled. Still going backwards, the woman bumped into him, underneath a lantern which hangs on a paling and which is lit at night. All at once there was the paling smelling strongly of wet wood, this lantern and this little blonde woman in the Negro's arms under a sky the colour of fire. . . . Then everything came asunder. There was nothing left but the lantern, the palisade and the sky; it was still rather beautiful. An hour later the lantern was lit, the wind blew, the sky was black; nothing at all was left.[17]

---

[16] Jean Paul Sartre, *Being and Nothingness: An Essay on Phenomenological Ontology* (New York: Philosophical Library, 1956), p. xlvii f. (Italics mine.) See also Sartre, *Nausea* (New York: New Directions, 1949), p. 130: "I looked anxiously about me: the present, nothing but the present. Furniture light and solid, rooted in its present, a table, a bed, a closet with a mirror—and me. The true nature of the present revealed itself: it was what exists, and all that was not present did not exist. The past did not exist. Not at all. Not in things, not even in my thoughts. . . . Now I knew: things are entirely what they appear to be—and behind them . . . there is nothing."

[17] *Ibid.*, p. 15 sq.

At four o'clock on that Saturday afternoon, then, the lives of two human beings temporarily and accidentally crossed. Two lines of appearances[18] momentarily intersected, and reality then *was* that temporary, unstable, fleeting intersection. A moment later everything came asunder. The woman, let us say, boarded the train, the man continued walking down the street, each heading for other chance events just as temporary and transient as what had occurred in the station yard. And reality at this later moment would be these new temporary intersections. Those streams of appearances, together with the criss-crossings between them, are all there is. The actual universe is itself nothing more than the current aggregation of such fluid appearances.

Quite obviously Sartre is as much preoccupied with the fact of change as was Shakespeare, Thomas à Kempis, or even Heraclitus. Manifestly, too, on this point his is the same philosophy as Heraclitus': reality *is* flux, mobility, fluency.[19] To be real is to be changing, they are identical.

---

[18] Individual existents are, we must remember, nothing but a series of appearances. See *Being and Nothingness,* p. xlviii (just referred to in note 16): "The being of an existent is exactly what it appears." *Nausea,* p. 131: "Things are entirely what they appear to be—and behind them . . . there is nothing."

[19] *Nausea,* p. 171: "And then all of a sudden, there it was, clear as day: existence had suddenly unveiled itself. It had lost the harmless look of an abstract category: it was the very paste of things, this root was kneaded into existence. Or rather the root, the park gates, the bench, the sparse grass, all that had vanished: the diversity of things, their individuality, were only an appearance, a veneer. This veneer had melted, leaving soft, monstrous masses, all in disorder—naked, in a frightful, obscene nakedness." Later: "[This enormous presence] was there, in the garden, toppled down into the trees, all soft, sticky, soiling everything, all thick, a jelly. And I was inside, I with the garden. I was frightened, furious. I thought it was so stupid, so out of place, I hated this ignoble mess. Mounting up, mounting up as high as the sky, spilling over, filling everything with its gelatinous slither. . . ." Also see *ibid.,* p. 180.

See Gabriel Marcel's explanation of Sartre's position: "Thus nausea . . . seems to be bound up in its origin with an experience of fluency . . . insofar as what is fluent slows down and assumes a kind of soft and spurious solidity. The sensation which this suggests is admittedly repellent. . . . 'Gooeyness' is indeed the key word, and it is, for Sartre, gooeyness on an enormous scale: . . . the whole of life is, if not actually gooey, at least tending towards gooeyness. What he has in mind is a certain experience of secretions and of mucus in process of formation" (*Philosophy of Existence* [New York: Philosophical Library, 1949], pp. 34-35).

Sartre's position also gives prominence to the self, the human subject. See J. Collins, *The Existentialists: A Critical Study,* pp. 45-63; H. J. Blackham, *Six Existentialist Thinkers* (London: Routledge & Kegan Paul, Ltd., 1961), pp. 110-48; W. Desan, *Tragic Finale* (Cambridge, Mass.: Harvard University Press, 1954). This aspect of his thought I omit here for pedagogical reasons since it is not directly relevant. See above, note 8, second paragraph.

And Sartre does not hesitate to draw forth the inevitable consequences of his (and Heraclitus') position. If the very heart of reality is
change, then one can acquire no certain knowledge of God, since individual material existents, constantly moving currents of appearances
as they are, provide no stable footing upon which the human mind
can stand in an intellectual search for a First Cause.[20] Moreover, without God and without stable natures which would ground norms of con-
duct, there can be no invariable, universal laws—rather, each man is
a law to himself as he finds himself now in this, now in that actual
situation.[21] Without God, too, there is no divine providence and, hence,
the countless chance events constituting reality are totally meaningless
and unintelligible. The career of each existent begins and ends in random absurdity: "Every existing thing is born without reason, prolongs
itself out of weakness, and dies by chance." [22] What is the resultant
psychological state of man? That of anguish, forlornness, nausea. "The
existentialists say at once that man *is* anguish." [23] "I am bored. From
time to time I yawn so widely that tears roll down my cheeks. It is a
profound boredom, profound, the profound heart of existence, the very
matter I am made of." [24] "As a result man is forlorn, because neither
within him nor without does he find anything to cling to." [25] In the

---

[20] Jean Paul Sartre, *Existentialism* (New York: Philosophical Library, 1947),
p. 60: "Existentialism is nothing else than an attempt to draw all the consequences
of a coherent atheistic position."
For Sartre God is a mere concept—that of a *pour soi* which would simultaneously be an *en soi*, that of a self which would be a thing, of a subject-object, of
emptiness-fullness, of activity-passivity. Manifestly, such a concept is contradictory
and nothing corresponds to it in reality. But the human existent inevitably and
inexorably fabricates it because of the absurd, frustrating unrest built into the
very nature of consciousness and knowledge. See Sartre, *Being and Nothingness*,
especially pp. 617 ff.
[21] *Existentialism*, p. 18: "Atheistic existentialism . . . states that if God does
not exist, there is at least one being in whom existence precedes essence, a being
who exists before he can be defined by any concept, and that this being is man
. . . There is no human nature, since there is no God to conceive it. Not only
is man what he conceives himself to be, but he is also only what he wills himself to be after this thrust towards existence. Man is nothing else but what he
makes of himself. Such is the first principle of existentialism."
[22] *Nausea*, p. 180. Also see *ibid.*, p. 173: "I understood that I had found the
key to Existence, the key to my Nauseas, to my own life. In fact, all that I could
grasp beyond that returns to this fundamental absurdity."
[23] *Existentialism*, p. 21. (Italics mine.)
[24] *Nausea*, p. 210.
[25] *Existentialism*, p. 27. Also see Albert Camus, *The Stranger* (New York:
Alfred A. Knopf, Inc., 1957), p. 154: "It was as if that great rush of anger had
washed me clean, emptied me of hope, and, gazing up at the dark sky spangled
with its signs and stars, for the first time, the first, I laid my heart open to the

face of such a situation, all that an individual human existent can do is to immerse himself totally in the actual moment in which he finds himself. The past is no longer, the future as yet is not, the present alone is. To be sure, the present instant is no sooner here than gone, but there is nothing else to be had.[26]

Those somber consequences caution one to be slow in adopting the Sartrean and Heraclitean identification of reality with change. Actually, abundant evidence exists that things involve not only change but also permanence as well. An individual man does go through a rather constant series of psychological and physical modifications over a period of time, but it is one and the same person who is now angry, now happy, now thinking, now suffering, now speaking. The man himself is the common denominator of the changes, the subject to which they are attributed. Accordingly, no one should say reality is change because existents are also relatively stable.[27]

Nonetheless—and this is one important lesson Heraclitus (and Sartre) teaches—reality does involve change. Real existents do change, and change thus is real, even though reality is not synonymous with change but arises, as we shall see, from an altogether different factor. Accordingly, any metaphysics which claims to be an adequate expression of the actual universe must find room for change as a genuine factor in reality. Secondly, observing the reaction of Heraclitus and company es-

---

benign indifference of the universe. . . . For all to be accomplished, for me to feel less lonely, all that remained to hope was that on the day of my execution there should be a huge crowd of spectators and that they should greet me with howls of execration." Sartre, *Nausea,* p. 180: "[This ignoble mess which is reality] was the World, the naked World suddenly revealing itself, and I choked with rage at this gross, absurd being."

[26] *Nausea,* p. 54: "Something is beginning in order to end: adventure does not let itself be drawn out; it only makes sense when dead. . . . Each instant appears only as part of a sequence. I cling to each instant with all my heart: I know that it is unique, irreplaceable—and yet I would not raise a finger to stop it from being annihilated. This last moment I am spending . . . moment I love passionately, woman I may adore—all is going to end, I know it. Soon I shall leave for another country. I shall never rediscover either this woman or this night. I grasp at each second, trying to suck it dry: nothing happens which I do not seize, which I do not fix forever in myself, nothing, neither the fugitive tenderness of those lovely eyes, nor the noises of the street, nor the false dawn of early morning: and even so the minute passes and I do not hold it back, I like to see it pass."

[27] Moreover, existents not only combine permanence with change but they also are distinct from one another and retain that distinctness and individuality, despite the imaginative picture which Sartre draws (see *supra,* note 19). Your eating nourishes you and not me. My headache afflicts me and not you.

tablishes that the actual universe does provide evidence of a different sort from that encountered within a laboratory—the fact that material existents as they are immersed in the daily give-and-take of actual situations involve various, frequent, deep-seated changes. This is one message which such beings put across to attentive minds and which can be the germ of a genuine science of philosophy of nature and, eventually, of metaphysics.

3. Plato and Radical Essentialism[28]

Another instructive group for our endeavor to build up a valid metaphysics is headed by Plato (428-348 B.C.). He agrees perfectly with the former group that the sensible universe is indeed shot through with change, flux, fluency. But there the agreements ends. He adds: And for that very reason it is unreal and unimportant. Reality is not change, which is rather the very stuff in which unreality centers. To be real is to be stable, to be permanent, to be immutable. The very heart of reality is stability, of which individual material things are totally bereft. Where, then, is it located? Solely in a realm completely separated from the sensible—that of subsistent Forms or Essences.

What evidence leads Plato and his followers to this conclusion? They start with the fact of intellectual knowledge. Human souls discover that they know with certitude and conviction what Man, Dog, Bed, Beauty, Justice, Courage, Circle, and so on are. Such cognition is true and certain because it is stable and immutable. But it could not have come from individual men, dogs, and the like, which are completely unstable and mutable. Hence, the source of my knowledge of man must be, so to speak, the concentrate of manness, with which the human soul comes into contact.[29] That is, that source must be the distil-

---

[28] Who is a radical essentialist? As will become clearer later, he is the counterpart of a radical existentialist (see *supra*, note 15). For him there is only essence and no existence or, in more easily intelligible terms, not change but only stability counts. Stability and reality are interchangeable. The sensible universe is unimportant and unreal. Also see *infra*, note 39.

On Plato's essentialism and theory of forms, see David Ross, *Plato's Theory of Ideas* (Oxford: Clarendon Press, 1951); J. Owens, *History*, pp. 189-229. Both authors give frequent references to relevant passages in Plato's own dialogues.

[29] For Plato this contact was achieved by the human soul when it existed with those Essences before it became linked with a body. To know now is merely to recall those Essences previously known. See J. Owens, *History*, especially pp. 205-6.

For St. Augustine, this contact is achieved by God's illumining the human soul. To know is the result of divine illumination in each intellect. (Incidentally,

lation of what makes man be man and be other from everything non-human, and this is concentrated in a single, eternal, perfectly invariable item, which can be called "the Form of Man" or "the Essence of Man" or "Man-as-Such" or "Absolute Man," or "Humanity-in-Itself" and which alone is genuinely real because it solely is genuinely stable and everlastingly self-identical. And the source of my knowledge of Dog, of Beauty, of Justice, of Courage, and so on would be similar concentrates, similar Forms or Essences. These the sensible universe mirrors, but individual men, dogs, beautiful things and so on, never actually succeed in truly becoming real because of their mutability and materiality.

Accordingly, anyone desiring to acquire true knowledge must first turn away from that universe and from the actual existents which inhabit it. Then let him enter within himself so that he may mentally ascend and find the realm of the Essences. "How shall we find the way [to certain knowledge, to the Forms]? What method can we devise?" asks Plotinus (A.D. 205-270), one of Plato's most intelligent and influential followers. "How can one see the inconceivable Beauty which stays within . . . and does not come out where the profane may see It?" His answer: "Let him who can, follow and come within and leave outside the sight of his eyes and not turn back to the bodily splendors which he saw before. When he sees the beauty in bodies, he must not run after them. We must know that they are images, traces, shadows, and we must rather hurry away to that which they image." [30] In the next chapter Plotinus continues:

> When you know that you have become the perfect work [by turning away from the outside world, by acquiring the requisite virtues], when

the very fact that a man knows any truth is sufficient to prove there is a God, for otherwise he would not know that truth.) See E. Gilson, *History of Christian Philosophy* (New York: Random House, Inc., 1955), pp. 74-77; Vernon Bourke, *Augustine's Quest of Wisdom* (Milwaukee: Bruce Publishing Co., 1945), pp. 116 sq. and 216 sq.; E. Gilson, *Spirit of Mediaeval Philosophy* (New York: Charles Scribner's Sons, 1940), Chap. XII, p. 229 sq.

[30] *Enneads*, I, 6, 8, 1 sq. (A. H. Armstrong translation [*Plotinus* (London: George Allen & Unwin, Ltd., 1953)], pp. 136-37.) The sentences immediately following the quotation just given are also significant: "If a man runs to the image and wants to seize it as if it was the reality (like a beautiful reflection playing on the water, which some story somewhere, I think, said riddlingly a man wanted to catch and sank down into the stream and disappeared), then this man who clings to beautiful bodies and will not let them go, will, like the man in the story, but in the soul, not in body, sink down into the dark depths where intelligence has no delight, and stay blind in Hades, consorting with shadows there and here."

you are self-gathered in the purity of your own being, nothing now remaining that can shatter that inner unity, nothing from without clinging to the authentic man, . . . now call up all your confidence, move upwards yet a step—you need a guide no longer—strain and see [Beauty and the other Essences]." [31]

The Platonist identification of reality with immutability has consequences which are just as inevitable as those flowing from Heraclitus' position, but which are as diametrically opposed as is day to night.

Because reality is coterminous with stability and because the sensible universe is nothing but a complex of change and variation, one must look elsewhere for the realm of what is really real.[32] This is not difficult to find, though, for the very fact that a human soul can and does achieve true and certain knowledge of Man, of Beauty, of Courage and so on proves without a doubt that such a realm does exist and also indicates what it is. Why so? Such knowledge must have an adequate cause. But this, obviously, cannot be individual men, beauties, and so on because of their complete mutability, nor can it be the human soul itself, because this too is variable and inconstant. Hence, there exists a realm of what is really real, which is marked by supreme constancy and perfect permanence and which is the cause of our true

---

[31] *Ibid.*, I, 6, 9, 15 sq. Augustine used the same technique and ended in an awareness of God Himself (*Confessions*, Book VII, Chaps. 9, 10, and 17): "[God having provided for me certain books of the Platonists which were translated from the Greek tongue into Latin] and thus admonished to return unto myself, I entered into my innermost parts under Thy guidance. . . . I entered in and saw with the eye of my soul (whatever its condition) the Immutable Light, above this same eye of my soul and above my mind. . . . Thus, by a gradual process, from bodies to the soul which senses through the body, and thence to its interior power to which bodily sensation takes messages about exterior things. . . . and then further to the reasoning power, to which what is taken by the bodily senses is brought for judgment. And this power, also finding itself mutable in me, lifted itself to its understanding and withdrew the thinking process from the customary level. . . . so that it might discover by what light it was besprinkled when it cried out without any hesitation that the immutable is to be preferred to the mutable; that it might know from this the immutable itself. . . . And, in the flash of a trembling glance, it reached up to That Which Is" (*Fathers of the Church* edition, Vol. 21, pp. 176, 180, and 187).

[32] "Really real" translates Plato's phrase, *to ontōs on*, by which he contrasts the world of Essences with the visible world, which is not genuinely real at all but a mere collection of shadows, images, reflections.

Prescinding from this contrast, we can say that the "really real" is characterized by immutability, permanence, self-identity, intelligibility, truth, and eternity; it will be applied by various authors to whatever has those characteristics—by Plato to the Essences, by Plotinus to the One-Good, by Augustine to the Christian God.

cognition. For Plato himself, as we have seen, this realm consists of the subsistent Forms or Essences—pure concentrates of Man, Beauty, Goodness and the like. For Plotinus it is headed by The One or The Good, Who transcends such essences but from Whom they emanate and Who is absolute immutability and supreme unity.[33] For Augustine the really real is God, Who is the Unchangeable Light, the Eternal Simplicity, Eternal Truth, True Eternity, Subsistent Beauty, and Who contains the ideas of all creatures.[34]

From the very fact that a human soul has intellectual knowledge, then, one also can easily know that the Really Real exists and what it is. Since ultimately the Really Real *is* God,[35] the first consequence of the Platonist position is that one can easily know God—that He is and, to an extent, what He is.

Another consequence of this position is that law is an easily known and ubiquitous factor. Reality as linked with permanence and intelligibility is also coterminous with good order—everything has and should keep its own place and function, the lower subordinated to the higher, the higher ruling the lower. But right order is synonymous with law, which, consequently, is an important and inescapable factor in Plato's view of reality.[36]

Permanence, truth, certitude, easy knowledge of God, law with the

---

[33] For a list of texts from the *Enneads* on The One, see A. H. Armstrong, *Plotinus*, pp. 56-68.

What is the relationship of The One to the Forms? The One transcends the Forms, which are contained within The Intelligence. But the Forms, as well as The Intelligence itself (and, for that matter, all souls), are not really distinct from The One. All such subsequent realities are nothing more than The One deploying Himself on a lower level. See L. Sweeney, S.J., "Basic Principles of Plotinus' Philosophy," *Gregorianum*, 51 (July, 1961), note 13.

[34] See *Confessions,* especially Book VII in its entirety; IX, Chap. 5; X, Chap. 27; XI in its entirety.

[35] True enough, Plato did not consider the Forms to be gods because at his time a god was an "individual living being, similar to those we know from sensible experience," but necessary and immortal (see E. Gilson, *God and Philosophy* [New Haven, Conn.: Yale University Press, 1941], pp. 27-28), whereas the Forms were not individual living beings at all. The Forms are, though, the philosophical first principles of his universe and were supremely real—much more real than if they had been gods. By Plotinus' time the term "god" had lost its pejorative connotations and The One-Good was equated with God (for example, see V, 1, 11 [*Enneads,* Armstrong Ed., pp. 53-54]).

[36] It is significant that Plato wrote dialogues (*Republic, Politicus, Laws*) dedicated to laws—their nature and content, their application to various classes of men and to states. For Plato, actually, Law is as much an Essence as is Man or Courage.

good order and intelligible direction it implants—all such provide for the human soul an atmosphere of well-being, of achievement, of peace, so that the normal psychological state of each person is happiness and joy. And if only he perseveres in stripping himself of the material and the mutable and continues to open himself up more and more to what is higher, his efforts will terminate in perfect union with the Supremely Real. This union is, Plotinus assures us, "a kind of seeing, a being out of oneself, a simplifying, a self-surrender, a pressing towards contact, a rest, a sustained thought directed to perfect conformity. . . . This is the life of gods and of divine and blessed men—deliverance from the things of this world, escape in solitude to the Solitary." [37]

Those consequences of the Platonist *Weltanschauung* are as attractive as those of the Heraclitean view were depressing. Nonetheless, their attractiveness should not prompt us personally to identify reality with immutability because of a grave difficulty that such identification entails. By making reality and stability synonymous, one is forced to conclude that individual material things are basically unreal, insignificant, worthless, because such actual existents are undoubtedly immersed in constant and manifold changes.

This conclusion every Platonist is forced to formulate, implicitly or explicitly. Let us take as an example Plotinus, who in the following passage is outlining to a human soul what happened when it separated itself from God and the world of true reality by descending into matter and becoming an individual man.

> Because something else other than the All [= the sum-total of true reality] added itself to you, you became less by the addition, for the addition did not come from real being (you cannot add anything to that), but from that which is not. You have become a particular person by the addition of non-being.

In order to find God and to become truly real again, it must put off that accretion of individuality and uniqueness.

> When you have become a particular person by the addition of non-being, you are not all till you reject the non-being. You will increase yourself then by rejecting the rest, and by that rejection the All is with you. . . . You must not say even about yourself, "I am just

[37] *Enneads*, VI, 9, 11, 35 sq. (Armstrong Ed., p. 160).

so much." For by rejecting the "so much," you become all, even though you were all before.[38]

That is to say, when a human soul achieves a measure of independence from The One by putting on unique and distinguishing characteristics and by immersing itself in matter to become an individual man, it is to that extent destroying its true reality. Those individual characteristics are a sign of weakness, evil, unreality. Such a soul only becomes truly real and truly itself when it becomes totally identified with The One, Whom it should never have left in the first place. In short, an individual man, precisely in his individuality, uniqueness, and actual existence is unreal, valueless, unimportant.[39]

The only way to see that such an attitude towards the actual universe is false is to look at a concrete case in which actual existents show themselves to be genuinely significant, valuable, and thereby real *in the very actual situations in which they find themselves.* One such is Father Alfeo Emaldi, who thwarted attempts of his Red Chinese captors to learn the identity of his parishioners by a heroic act of courage. He relates his own story:

---

[38] *Ibid.*, VI, 5, 12, 16 sq. (Armstrong Ed., p. 152). For purposes of clarity and emphasis, I have changed the tense and mood of the verbs in the last two sentences, which in the original Greek initiate the excerpt rather than terminate it.

[39] This negative, pejorative attitude towards individual, actual existents is, in fact, so intrinsic a part of radical essentialism that it is a criterion for deciding whether or not an author is an essentialist. Whenever you find someone commenting that actual existence has nothing to do with whether or not a being is real, you are in the presence of a radical essentialist. For example, see Suarez, *Disp. Meta.*, II, Sec. 4: "*Being* as a noun signifies that which has a real essence, prescinding from actual existence." Or J. Kleutgen (a nineteenth-century Suarezian), *La Philosophie scolastique*, Vol. II, p. 89 f: "The *real* is not confused with what is *actual* or *existing*. . . . When we conceive a being as real, . . . *we, leave existence out of consideration*" (quoted by E. Gilson, *Being and Some Philosophers* [2nd Ed.], [Toronto: Pontifical Institute of Mediaeval Studies, 1952], p. 106). [Italics mine.]

So too, it is a sign of radical essentialism when someone makes possible essences more real than actual ones. For instance, see C. Frick (*Ontologia* [Fribourg: Herder, 1934], pp. 74-79), according to whom the philosophy of nature studies actual essences, but only metaphysics, the queen of natural sciences, studies possible essences. The implication is that essences as actual are immersed in change and, thereby, are less real and intelligible, whereas essences as possible are free from change and the debilitating conditions it inflicts upon essences. When so conceived, possible essences do not seem to differ in any important way from Platonic subsistent Essences.

Our missionary activity was reduced to practically nothing by the Communist persecution. Then on November 15, 1951, Father Angelo Lampis and I were arrested in our residence in Tientsin by . . . the Reds. The Communists wanted us to reveal the names of the Chinese Catholics who had remained faithful to us, and tried to force us to sign a list of accusation against them.

I can still remember standing in my small room, thinking of the torture through which other European and Chinese priests had been put. Remembering my lack of courage, I felt myself too weak to resist them. I prayed to God to make me overcome my fear, and suddenly I found myself with a surge of strength, enough to save my Christians. Among my personal belongings I had a safety razor blade. I closed my eyes and with the blade cut off a piece of my tongue. . . . I tried to articulate a word, and found I could still talk. . . . Then I closed my eyes again, and I put out my tongue and cut off more. I tried to articulate words and this time I could make no sound. Then I wrote on the paper the Communists had given me: 'I have become mute for the love of God; and I am ready also to die for Him.' " [40]

This, I would say, is obviously a case in which an individual human existent is significant, valuable, important, and hence *real*, precisely when confronted by an actual, never-to-be-repeated challenge. His courage, his worthwhileness, his value—in a word, his reality—are inseparable from the actual changes he experienced: his remembrance of tortures suffered by other missionaries, his awareness of personal timidity, his prayer for strength, his cooperation with divine grace, his heroic act of bravery. To be real here is located in his very actuality, in his individual acts of fortitude and heroism. Moreover, one's knowledge of what courage is arises from this and other actual acts of courageous men and not from some subsistent idea of courage. Courage is no separate Essence; it is nothing more than a concept within our minds which comes from our directly perceiving individual brave acts and attitudes of actual men and women.

To identify reality with stability, therefore, is erroneous. But a great help can be derived from studying radical essentialism, because this position serves as a warning never to downgrade actual existents. These afford a constant source of data, and without them a philosopher has nothing upon which to build.

[40] *The Nebraska Register*, February 22, 1952, p. 1.

Nonetheless, actual existents involve more than mere change. True enough, they are permeated with frequent and various modifications, but they also are comparatively stable and permanent. He who now is courageous is the same man who previously was afraid. Stability is as great a factor in reality as change (and this is another lesson to be learned from the essentialists) but only as it is embedded in actual things (this the essentialists deny). Any thinker who realizes that individual existents are combinations of both change and stability will transcend all previous insights. Aristotle had such a realization, and we shall study his position in the next chapter.

4. Summary and Conclusions

(a) In this chapter our aim was to understand that material existents are the source of evidence precisely as they are directly observed in the actual conditions of their day-by-day existence. The means used to implement this aim has been to step back into the era of early Greek philosophers and observe their reactions when confronted with the sensible universe.

(b) The initial reaction was that of Thales, who taught us the basic question of philosophy and the general methodology for answering it. The question: what are sensible existents, what is the heart of their reality, and what does "to be real" mean? The methodology: turn to the material universe and carefully observe what goes on there.

(c) Heraclitus, together with radical existentialists of today, put across the important point that reality genuinely does involve change (even though we must add reality is not identical with it because things are relatively stable too). To do justice to the actual world, metaphysics must take change into account.

(d) From Plato and other radical essentialists we learned that stability also must be included as a factor in reality. However, stability is not located in a separate realm of subsistent Essences. Rather it is incorporated into the very fabric of individual material existents, who combine both change and stability into a single, concrete, actual unity. Far from being insignificant and unintelligible, such actual existents are truly valuable and genuinely knowable—in fact, they are the sole sources of whatever natural knowledge we humans have of courage, beauty, justice, value, and the like. They are the starting-point of metaphysics, its constant center of reference, the arbiter of its conclusions.

SUGGESTED READINGS

Armstrong, A. H., *Plotinus*. London: George Allen & Unwin, Ltd., 1953. A translation of significant texts from Plotinus' *Enneads*, with introduction and notes.

St. Augustine, *Basic Writings*, ed. Whitney J. Oates. New York: Random House, Inc., 1948.

Blackman, H. J., *Six Existentialist Thinkers*. New York: The Macmillan Company, 1952.

Charlesworth, Max., "The Meaning of Existentialism," *Thomist*, 16 (1953), 472-96.

Collins, James, *The Existentialists*. Chicago: Henry Regnery Co., 1952. A survey, with critique, of modern existentialists.

Copleston, S.J., F. C., *Existentialism and Modern Man*. Oxford: Blackfriars, 1948.

Drennen, D. A., *A Modern Introduction to Metaphysics: Readings from Class cal and Contemporary Sources*, pp. 218-53, 327. New York: Free Press of Glencoe, 1962. Excerpts from various radical existentialists; a selected bibliography.

Gilson, Etienne, *God and Philosophy*, pp. 1-37. New Haven, Conn.: Yale University Press, 1941. On the answers given by Thales, Heraclitus, and Plato to the question, "What does it mean to be real?"; splendid exemplification of how the history of philosophy helps unravel philosophical problems.

——, *Being and Some Philosophers* (2nd Ed.), pp. 1-40, 74-107, 108-53. Toronto: Pontifical Institute of Mediaeval Studies, 1952. A study of how the following conceive reality: Platonists, medieval and Renaissance essentialists (Avicenna, Suarez, and others), and radical existentialists.

Jowett, B., *The Dialogues of Plato*, 4 Vols. Revised by D. J. Allan and H. E. Dale. Oxford: Clarendon Press, 1953.

Maritain, Jacques, *Existence and the Existent*, trans. L. Galantiere and G. Phelan, pp. 11-19 and 129-53. Garden City, N. Y.: Doubleday & Company, Inc., 1956 (Image Books Edition). On radical and authentic existentialism.

Mounier, Emmanuel, *Existentialist Philosophies*. New York: The Macmillan Company, 1949.

Sweeney, S.J., Leo., "Basic Principles in Plotinus' Philosophy," *Gregorianum*, 42 (July, 1961), 506-16. On essentialistic factors in Plotinus.

——, "Neo-Platonism," *Collier's Encyclopedia* (New York: P. F. Collier and Son, 1961), Vol. 17, pp. 297-98. An aid to intelligent reading of those radical essentialists who are Neo-Platonists.

CHAPTER **III**

Lessons
from Aristotle

The preceding chapter has prepared us to understand and to appreciate Aristotle (384-322 B.C.). From Heraclitus we learned that reality involves change, from Plato that it also entails stability. Obviously, the next step is to combine those two insights. This step Aristotle took by realizing that both change and permanence are factors in reality, and this in such a way that they make up the very warp and woof of individual material things.

In this realization he not only utilizes his predecessors but also corrects them. To Heraclitus he points out that actual existents also remain comparatively stable and identical while changing.[1] To

---

[1] In the final analysis radical existentialists such as Heraclitus or Sartre devaluate individual existents as effectively as do radical essentialists. Even though they concentrate upon them, they reduce them to mere streams of appearances by refusing to see or admit the relative permanence and self-identity they involve. (Sartre, *Nausea*, p. 171: "The diversity of things, their individuality, were only an appearance, a veneer. This veneer had melted, leaving soft, monstrous masses, all in disorder—naked, in a frightful, obscene nakedness.") On the other hand, radical essentialists are guilty of the same refusal and simply ignore individual things by turning away to wherever they locate the really real.

36

Plato he indicates that change too is real because it belongs to the intrinsic constitution of individual things, which are real because genuinely important and valuable. Moreover, stability is not located in any separate realm of Essences, but is within actual things. These are, in fact, combinations of change and stability in such fashion that change and stability are not isolated from one another or from the individual existent itself. Rather, they are the existent, they permeate what he is. An individual man is both a changing stability and a succession of stabilized changes. The task of the philosopher is to observe those units of modification and permanence and then to receive and decipher the evidence they provide.

For Aristotle[2] material things show themselves to involve two different sorts of change and stability. One sort occurs on what he calls the *substantial* level, the other on the *accidental* level. For instance, death affects an existent much more radically than does thinking or becoming angry or growing because it changes the very kind of thing the existent is. Death transforms what is living to what is nonliving, whereas the other states are mere transitions within the life-span of the

---

[2] On Aristotle, see J. Owens, *History*, p. 281 sq. The positions we shall ascribe to Aristotle can just as accurately be attributed to most Aristotelians throughout the centuries. In fact, his description of material things as composites of substance/accidents and of matter/form is, in my opinion, as true today as when he first made it. Hence, in this area he also speaks for me and I shall offer no subsequent chapter on those components.

One should note, though, that my approval of Aristotle's hylomorphism does not automatically extend to his other positions in philosophy of nature, some of which (for example, his theory of natural place) have been shown to be inadequate or even inaccurate by contemporary cosmology and science. Much less does it extend to his scientific views, which are now rather generally obsolete. See Andrew G. Van Melsen, *Philosophy of Nature* (Pittsburgh: Duquesne University Press, 1954), Chap. 2: "A Survey of the History of the Study of Nature," especially Sec. 3: "Aristotle" (pp. 38-52), Sec. 4: "The Explanation of Aristotle's Unchallenged Authority During Twenty Centuries" (pp. 52-70), as well as the final two sections (pp. 70-76 and 76-80). Also see James B. Conant, *Science and Common Sense* (New Haven, Conn.: Yale University Press, 1954), pp. 64-67, 154, 167 f.; Philipp Frank, *Philosophy of Science* (Englewood Cliffs, N. J.: Prentice-Hall, Inc., 1957), pp. 122 f. and *passim*; Werner Heisenberg, *Physics and Philosophy: Revolution in Modern Science*, Vol. 19 of World Perspectives (New York: Harper & Row, Publishers, 1958), pp. 147-66, especially 159-60; Francis J. Collingwood, *Philosophy of Nature* (Englewood Cliffs, N. J.: Prentice-Hall, Inc., 1961), pp. 286-95 and *passim*; Ernest Nagel, *Structure of Science* (New York: Harcourt, Brace & World, Inc., 1961), pp. 42-46; David Hawkins, *Language of Nature: An Essay in the Philosophy of Science* (San Francisco: W. H. Freeman and Company, 1964), pp. 109-14, 178, 252-54.

same thing. Accordingly, the former belongs to the substantial level, the latter to the accidental.[3]

In our attempt to understand Aristotle, then, we shall investigate both sorts. First, however, we must briefly study two rather general propositions which guide Aristotle when observing and interpreting the evidence which material existents afford—namely, that diverse evidences indicate the actual presence within a thing of distinct constitutive parts and, secondly, that an individual material thing is a genuine unity of special stringency and type. Consequently, this chapter has four main sections:

    1. "Diverse evidences indicate. . . ."
    2. Unity.
    3. Change/Stability in the Accidental Order.
    4. Change/Stability in the Substantial Order.

1. "Diverse evidences indicate . . . ."

The affirmation, "Diverse evidences indicate the actual presence within of distinct constitutive parts," will be operative in most of the subsequent processes by which an Aristotelian answers the fundamental questions of philosophy. Nonetheless, its truth can be easily and undubitably grasped through several very simple concrete cases.

Let us imagine that we come to a wood where the trees and underbrush are so thick that one cannot directly see what animals are within. Suppose, however, we notice the fresh footprints of a lion on the wet path leading into the trees. Without having directly perceived the lion, we can conclude from the directly observed footprints that there actually is a lion in the woods. If we see also the footprints of a bear, we can similarly assent that a bear is actually within. What guides us to such conclusions? Our realization that diverse evidences (here, the footprints) indicate the actual presence within of what has caused them (here, the animals). This realization we first acquired early in our intellectual life (however implicitly and ineffably) when we observed some or other agent actually causing an effect. For then

---

[3] The adjectives "substantial" and "accidental" arise from the fact that the former establishes the actual presence of constitutive parts within *substance* (see Sec. 4 of this chapter), whereas the latter points to the actual presence of *accidents* which perfect the substance but are not parts of the substance (see Sec. 3 of this chapter).

we became aware not only that this cause is responsible for this effect, but also that every effect comes about because of a cause, and this because of the very natures of an efficient cause and its effect.[4] Accordingly, diverse effects point to diverse causes and thus arises the affirmation: "Diverse evidences (the effects) indicate the actual presence of diverse efficient causes."

But that affirmation, in view of its elaboration and wording, is concerned with extrinsic and efficient causes, whereas the assertion which gives Aristotle the key for unlocking the secrets of material things has to do with "constitutive parts"—that is, with intrinsic causes. In order to establish this assertion, though, we need only to consider another sort of example. Let us suppose that we enter a room and come upon a cake which we have not seen made. What is in it? What are its ingredients? From the fact that it is moist, we can conclude to some sort of liquid (milk, applesauce, etc.) as an ingredient; from its sweetness, to sugar; from its bulk, to flour; from its tangy taste, to citrus-fruit rinds; and so on. What guides us to such conclusions? Our awareness that diverse evidences (here, the moistness, sweetness, etc.) indicate the actual presence within of what causes them (here, the milk, sugar, etc.), and this awareness we first achieved as a child when we watched, say, our mother make a cake by actually combining sugar, flour, milk, spices, and the like. We then realized not only that that cake (that composite, that combination) was those ingredients-as-mixed-and-baked, but also that every composite (in what it is and appears) *is* its ingredients-as-combined, because such is the nature of ingredients and the resultant composite. In other words, we became aware not merely that those evidences indicated those ingredients, but that external evidences in general indicate internal ingredients, and, even more generally and relevantly, that diverse evidences reveal the actual presence within of diverse constitutive parts.[5]

Such is the proposition which Aristotle will constantly use in han-

---

[4] The case here is similar to our awareness that "Every [nonmathematical] whole is bigger than any of its parts." In the presence of a concrete case (which let us represent thus: [A | B]), we immediately become aware not only that this A is bigger than this B but that every A is bigger than every B, and this because of the very natures of A and B. Such a psychological process we shall later describe as "intellective induction through immediate insight" (see Chap. X, Sec. 3. On the efficient cause proposition, see Chap. VIII, Sec. 4b.

[5] Manifestly, this awareness also is similar to our realization concerning the whole-part relationship (see previous note) and will also be later described as an "intellective induction through insight."

dling the evidences of change/stability, but before outlining those processes we must consider his second general assertion—namely, that an individual material thing is a genuine unity of special stringency and type.

2. Unity

To judge by one of his speeches, Charles de Gaulle, President of France, is keenly aware of the importance of unity as the essential factor in keeping his country strong and independent. "France has regained her national unity and her national cohesion," he said. "Our salvation depends entirely on maintaining our national unity. I say here with special emphasis that outside this unity, there is no salvation for us." [6]

Aristotle too is convinced that unity is important, but his concern is with the role it plays when a philosopher comes to evaluate the internal make-up of individual things. This role will be clear when we present in detail the processes which that evaluation entails, but perhaps a single statement will enable us even now to have an initial appreciation of how significant unity is: "One and the same thing (for example, this man) presents the twofold evidence of change/stability, and, therefore, that thing is made up of two constitutive parts." The parts are not the thing itself, which is truly one, and yet both the thing and its parts are genuinely real because both are actually present. Consequently, although the parts are real, they are not of identically the same nature as the thing itself, because neither part *is* the thing itself but only one of its real constituents. Accordingly, what the parts are is determined by the sort of unity to be found in the whole which they constitute. If the whole is, say, an army or a basketball team, then its parts are themselves individual men. But if the whole is itself an individual man, then his parts are themselves real and yet are not other individual men. As we shall see later, they are that by which the man is human or is mathematical or is angry.

Unity is, then, of supreme importance in our philosophical endeavor; accordingly, we must investigate what it is. When we speak of "one and the same thing," what does *one* mean? If I say that a thing is yellow or round or a cabbage plant, I know what those predicates mean. But when I say, "The thing is *one*," what is signified? Let us answer by looking at some concrete cases.

---

[6] Reported in *St. Louis Globe-Democrat*, Sunday, October 23, 1960, p. 1.

If we contrast a set of bricks, cement, and lumber found in a supply-store with another and equal set which makes up a house, what is the difference between the two sets? Not in the number of bricks or sacks of cement, since the amount in each case is equal, but in the fact that the materials in the second case have been so brought together as to fashion a house. The difference is, then, that the first set is in a state of separation and division, whereas the second is in a state of together-ness, of undividedness, of cohesion. In short, the first is a mere aggre-gation, a pile, a multitude; the second is a unity. The same difference is manifest if we contrast a set of wheels, sparkplugs, upholstery fabric, and other parts found in a store with another set of wheels and spark-plugs which form an automobile, or if we contrast a set of ten students as each eats his evening meal at his own home with another set of ten students actually playing a basketball game in the gymnasium.

According to the present level of consideration, then, unity is a status of togetherness, cohesion, undividedness.

But a more rigorous sort of cohesion exists than that found in a house, machine, or team, as can be readily seen in the constitutive parts of any individual living thing, whether it be a plant or animal or man. If one cuts off a man's arm or a bear's paw or a tree branch, the arm, paw, and branch are no longer alive and can no longer perform their previous functions. In short, they no longer are what they were, and in that sense their very natures have changed. Such a change in-dicates that as parts of the living thing they depend upon the whole in a way totally different from the way in which a soldier depends upon the army or a student upon the football team of which he is a member, for a soldier or a student can leave the army or the team with-out undergoing such a radical change, without ceasing to be human. The former are dependent intrinsically and entitatively: they were orig-inally produced by the living organism as it grew, they are nourished by it, their injuries are repaired by it, they die if removed from it. The whole also shows itself to be intrinsically and entitatively dependent upon its essential parts. Remove a man's liver or a lion's lungs or an oak tree's roots and the entire man, lion, or tree will die. Such internal and ontic (see n. 10, last paragraph) dependence of living parts upon the whole and of a living whole upon its parts points to an inner bond of unity which differs not merely in degree but also in kind from that found in a house or machine or army.

That more stringent unity also is manifested in other ways by living beings. For example, my bodily condition has repercussions upon my psychological state, and vice versa. If I am in good health, I can think clearly; if not, my thought processes are disturbed or perhaps entirely disrupted. If I am struck on the head or take drugs, I become unconscious. On the other hand, if my mental and emotional state is one of shame, I blush; if of anger, I become flushed, my pulse beats faster, adrenalin flows; if of fear, I grow pale and cold, I tremble; if of constant worry, I develop ulcers. This reciprocal influence of matter upon mind and mind upon matter arises from the intrinsic and entitative reliance of each upon the other, and thereby reveals again the strict unity of the whole which they constitute.

Again, the parts of an automobile and of an army work together for a goal which is extrinsic to themselves—that of the driver or of the commander-in-chief. The parts of a living thing, however, work together directly for a goal which is intrinsic to themselves and to the thing, for by their cooperation they produce, nourish, and conserve themselves and the life of the whole. This cooperation can be clearly seen in the coordinating members of a living existent. Not only does a man consist of such distinct organs as senses, glands, brain, lungs, and heart, each with its own function for the benefit of the whole and (ultimately) of itself (for example, the lungs purify the blood, the heart pumps it), but he also has members whose entire function is to coordinate other parts. For example, the circulatory system brings food and oxygen throughout the body and removes waste products. The endocrine and nervous control systems keep all particular functions balanced, in harmony with each other, and adjusted to the requirements of the whole. All such parts can work together because they *are* together in a single living organism which entitatively and internally depends upon them and they upon it.

These evidences, together with much more which could be brought forward,[7] clearly indicate that a man, a giraffe, or a rosebush enjoy (or

---

[7] See G. P. Klubertanz, S.J., *Philosophy of Human Nature* (New York: Appleton-Century-Crofts, 1953), pp. 15-34, where he furnishes evidence for the essential unity of a living thing and interprets facts from modern physical, chemical, and biological sciences which seem to militate against that unity. One such fact (p. 22 sq.) is that the spectrograph of a living thing shows the characteristic spectrum lines of water, carbon, and so forth. In view of that fact a chemist might say that a living thing is (using our terminology) not an intrinsic unity but an accidental unity, a mere collection of chemicals. What can be said in reply? Let us grant the fact, yet recall that water in living human skin does not have all the characteristics of water in a relatively pure liquid state and has some alien characteristics (for example, it shares in the living, sentient, rational state of the whole). To cover this situation, the phrase, "virtual presence," is used (which seems to come from the everyday expression meaning "almost but not quite"—"The fog is so heavy that it's virtually raining," "This wine is virtually

even *are*)[8] a condition of cohesion and togetherness which essentially surpasses that found in a house, an army, or a machine. In short, an individual living thing is a genuine unity of a unique rigor and kind.

In conclusion, then, what have we seen from our examination of concrete cases?

1. *Unity* is a state or condition of cohesion, togetherness, undividedness.

2. There are at least two kinds of unity:

   (a) that which is found in a house, team, or machine and which is traditionally called "accidental" (*per accidens*) or "extrinsic" unity;

   (b) that which is found in a man, lion, or tree and which is called "essential" (*per se*) or, better, "intrinsic" unity.[9]

3. *Accidental unity* is that state of togetherness and cohesion which is comparatively extrinsic and nonentitative[10] because its parts are entitatively independent of the whole.

---

vinegar"). Water is only virtually present in a living human being—that is, it is present *partially* (with only *some* of its own characteristics) and as *subordinated to another* (it is part of another and more complex thing, some of whose characteristics it takes on). Water is formally present in, say, this glass or this river—that is, it is present *fully* (with *all* its own characteristics) and *independently* (it is not an intrinsic part of something else). Thus, because water and other chemicals are only virtually present in a man, he still retains his essential unity.

This notion of virtual presence seems accurately to describe not only how chemicals are present in living things but also how simple elements are present in compounds (for example, how hydrogen and oxygen are present in water) and how the physical counterparts of subatomic particles are present in atoms.

See also James E. Royce, S.J., *Man and His Nature* (New York: McGraw-Hill Book Company, 1961), p. 258 sq.

[8] The state of cohesion and togetherness to be found in an accidental unity is a mere complex of real relations between its members, and this is what "army," "family," and other collective nouns directly express. But the state of cohesion in an intrinsic unity is more than a mere relationship between its parts. It *is* the entire individual, it *is* his very entity. Unity and entity here are coextensive.

[9] Because of the ambiguity of "essence" (see Chap. IV, pp. 90-92 and notes 51-53), we shall generally substitute "intrinsic" for "essential." The other sort of unity, though, can conveniently be designated as either "accidental" or "extrinsic."

There is also a third sort of unity—the state of cohesion and undividedness to be found in something which has no parts. This can be called "unity of simplicity" or "absolute unity" and is found in God, in a substantial form, and in various other constitutive parts.

[10] The significance of "entitative" (and its opposite) should be clear from our previous discussion and examples. It is derived from "entity" and points to the connection which unity has with what a thing is, with its very entity. In some cases the unity is such that if you separate a part from the whole, you introduce

4. *Intrinsic unity* is that state of cohesion and togetherness which is internal and entitative because its parts entitatively depend upon the whole and work together for an intrinsic goal: to produce and conserve the parts themselves and the whole.

The latter sort of unity Aristotle finds within individual material things[11] and, hence, also finds their constitutive parts to be by nature genuinely different from those of a machine or house or army. In the next sections we shall face just what those parts are and how great that difference is.

3. Change/Stability in the Accidental Order

In the example already given (p. 10), the young daughter experiences love for her mother. Then she learns what "one," "two," and

---

little or no intrinsic change into the part itself (nonentitative). But in other instances if you remove a part from the whole, the unity is so stringent that the part no longer remains specifically what it was (entitative). Also see *supra*, note 8.

Incidentally, "ontic" when used in this section (for example, see p. 41) and, for that matter, throughout the entire book, is directly based upon the Greek *on*, *ontos* ("being," "entity") and is intended simply as synonymous with "entitative." It has none of the connotations of the word as used by various contemporary radical existentialists.

[11] So far our discussion of intrinsic unity has been directed to living things, and this for the reason that such offer more easily perceived data. Still there is evidence of intrinsic unity also on the inanimate level. See Phillipus Selvaggi, S.J., *Cosmologia* (Romae: Apud Aedes Pont. Universitatis Gregorianae, 1959), pp. 264-86; Fridericus Saintonge, S.J., *Summa Cosmologiae* (Montreal: Imprimerie du Messager, 1941), pp. 416-39; Petrus Hoenen, S.J., *Cosmologia* (Romae: Apud Aedes Pont. Universitatis Gregorianae, 1956), p. 358 sq.; Jaime Echarri, S.J., *Philosophia Entis Sensibilis* (Romae: Herder, 1959), p. 98 sq.; K. F. Dougherty, *Cosmology* (Peekskill, N. Y.: Graymoor Press, 1952), pp. 125-33; D. Nys, *Cosmology* (Milwaukee: Bruce Publishing Co., 1942), II, 161-264 and 433-40; V. Smith, *Philosophical Physics* (New York: Harper & Row, Publishers, 1950), pp. 189-231.

That inanimates do involve intrinsic unity is not as difficult to see as *where* it is located. Is the water in this glass an intrinsic unit? Or is each molecule of water the unit (and, thus, a glass of water is an accidental unit)? Or is an atom within the molecule the unit? Or are the various subatomic particles (or, more accurately: the physical counterparts to what empiriological scientists call subatomic particles) the units?

At any rate, no matter where one locates the intrinsic unity, the first portion of its definition as worked out for living things seems applicable to nonliving items: "An intrinsic unity is that state of cohesion and togetherness which is internal and entitative because its parts entitatively depend upon the whole."

other numbers mean. Next she tries to express that love in those newly acquired quantitative terms, and then comes the new discovery that love and quantity are incompatible. All those psychological states she goes through while remaining basically human, and, in fact, the same human person who was born some four years earlier, who grew physically, who gradually came to a fuller use of her cognitive powers, who learned to express herself through language, who even earlier that day had spoken and eaten and played. Or take the instance of Father Alfeo Emaldi (see p. 32 f.). (see p. 32 f.) On the single day he describes, the missionary had listened to his Communist captors demand that he reveal the names of his parishioners. He remembered the tortures through which those same Communists had put other priests. He feared what his own timidity before physical and mental torture might cause him to do. He prayed for help. He cooperated with the sudden surge of strength he experienced within. He cut off his tongue so as to be unable to speak the names the Communists wanted. And all the while he remained human, and, in fact, the same human existent who had been born in Italy in 1902, who had labored in China since March 10, 1926, under such hardships as bandits, famine, bombardment, and imprisonment in concentration camps during World War II, who even the day before had fed the hungry and helped the dying.

What would be Aristotle's reaction to such cases? He would first say that they involve accidental changes, since the modifications undergone, frequent and impressive as they are, do not specifically change either person: each remains a living human being. Next, such modifications on the accidental level provide a twofold evidence of change and stability: one and the same thing remains specifically and generically what it is and yet acquires new individual perfections (thinking, loving, praying). Such evidences are clues to the internal make-up of each person, as the following process makes clear.

[Directly perceived fact:] In accidental changes one and the same thing
    (a) remains specifically and generically what it is [stability]
    (b) and yet acquires new individual perfections [change];
But evidence #a is other than evidence #b;
But diverse evidences indicate the actual presence within of diverse constitutive parts;
Therefore, such evidences indicate that the thing is actually made up of diverse constitutive parts:
    (a) that by which the thing specifically and generically remains

what it is and yet receives various individual perfections—"Substance";

(b) that by which the thing, while remaining specifically and
generically what it is, is actually modified through a new individual perfection—"an Accident."

This process[12] indicates both that such parts do actually exist and,
to an extent, what they are. It establishes their actual existence because, as we have previously seen (Chap. III, Sec. 1), the relationship
between an evidence and a constitutive part is that between an effect
and its intrinsic cause. But an effect of an intrinsic cause is present
only because what causes it is also present. But accidental changes involve distinct evidences of modification and stability (effects) and, accordingly, reveal that distinct constitutive parts (causes) actually exist
within the thing changing.

Secondly, it also shows what those parts are, and here the force of
the fact that a material existent is an intrinsic unity (see Chap. III,
Sec. 2) is apparent. An individual man is not a mere accidental unity
such as an army or a hockey team, in which the parts are themselves
individual men and thereby are intrinsically and entitatively independent of the whole which they help constitute. Rather he is an intrinsic
unity, whose parts depend internally and entitatively upon him. Nevertheless, the whole (here, the man) is not any one of its parts, nor is
any part the whole. Still both the whole and its parts are real (because
actually present). Consequently, there is a difference between the reality of the whole and of the parts, between what the whole is and
what each part is. This difference is difficult to put in words, but perhaps the expressions, "that which" and "that by which," will serve.
The whole (the man himself) is *that which* is human, thinking, mathematical, and so forth. Each of its parts is *that by which* he is human,
etc. For example, his substance is that *by which* he is human and remains human while receiving various accidental perfections. His mental
activity (accident) is that *by which* he is thinking. His operative habit[13]
of mathematics (accident) is that *by which* he is a mathematician.

Quite obviously, our knowledge of such parts is more than direct

---

[12] The propositions which make up this process (and subsequent ones) have
been organized into what may look like a syllogism for purposes of clarity and
convenience. No one should think, though, that it is strictly a syllogism or involves deduction. That process is an intellective induction, as we shall see later
(see Chap. X, Sec. 3).

[13] See Chap. I, n. 17.

perception. True enough, we directly perceive that this man is accidentally changing, that he is acquiring some new individual perfection while remaining human. This perception we express in judgments, which furnish the starting point of our process. But our awareness of substance and accidents themselves transcends mere perception. We reflect upon that data offered through perception. We intellectually realize that change and stability are diverse evidences, that diverse evidences indicate the actual presence of distinct constituents, and that accordingly an accidentally changing thing is made up of diverse constitutive parts conveniently called substance and accidents. This last stage is an assent of the intellect to which it is forced by evidence: "There actually *is* substance, there actually *are* various accidents." In short, the process terminates in intellectual judgmental knowledge, by which we become aware that such constituents exist and what they are.

Such constitutive parts, then, are known by reflection upon perceived data, and this reflection is a genuinely intellectual operation. We cannot directly perceive substance or accidents. We cannot imagine or picture them. We know them through genuine intellection.[14]

Manifestly, such constitutive parts are real in an unique sense and differ both from the whole which they make up and from its integral, physical parts (for example, lungs, arms, and heart). Up to this time we have been calling them "constitutive parts," but that general phrase is awkward, and, moreover, is applicable to either an accidental, extrinsic unity (for example, individual soldiers are constitutive parts of an army) or an intrinsic unity. Even when applied to the latter, it fits either integral parts or substance/accidents. Some special term, then, is needed. Sometimes substance and accidents are called "principles" of the thing they constitute, but "principle" can refer also to intramental items, as occurs when one speaks of the premises of a syllogism as

---

[14] The term "substance" is derived from the Latin *substantia,* which in turn translates the Greek *to hypokeimenon* or *hē hypostasis,* which means "that which lies or stands under." If taken literally, the English, Latin, and Greek words all have a spatial connotation, and one must be careful not to conceive substance as lying physically under the accidents as a sort of pincushion or foundation. "Accident" does not so obviously connote the spatial and physical, for it comes from the Latin *accidens,* which translates the Greek *to sumbebēkos,* which is equivalent to "that which befalls or happens"—see Aristotle, *Metaphysics,* V, Chap. 30, 1025a13 sq.

Consequently, one must keep reminding himself that substance and accidents are not spatial items and are not physically separated from one another. Substance permeates the entire entity and is always to be conceived as a "that by which." Various and numerous accidents also permeate the entire entity and each of them is also a "that by which."

its *principles* or of law as a *principle* of morality. Hence, that term wiñi
not do, for care must be taken to stress the fact that substance and accidents (and other such parts still to be considered) are actual, extramental constituents of things.

Is there any other term which might prove suitable? We have decided on "component." True enough, that word is as general as "constitutive part," because it can be applied both to the parts of an accidental unity and to those of an intrinsic unity. But it is a single word,
not a phrase, and seems to have few connotations of the merely intramental. In this book, then, "component" will be arbitrarily restricted
to express only substance and accidents (and similar parts) and can be
defined as follows: *A component is a constitutive part of an intrinsic
unity, is known by intellectual consideration of directly perceived data,
and is a "that by which."* [15]

The process we have been considering also reveals that the relationship between substance and accidents is one of "potency" to "act."
What does this second set of terms mean? Historically, the doctrine of
act/potency arose as a reaction against those who claimed that all
change (even local motion) is impossible, however apparent it may be
in the visible universe.[16] Here is an example of the dialectical way they
argued.

> In a change that which changes acquires something new;
> But that which changes either already is or is not;
> But if it already is, then it cannot change because it would already
>   be what it was to have acquired or else it no longer would be what
>   it had been;
> But if it is not, then it cannot change because there would be nothing
>   to change;
> Therefore, change is impossible.

Aristotle replied by elaborating the theory of act/potency. You must
distinguish the first minor, he advised, for that which will change from

---

[15] One must grant that "that by which" is clumsy, but it seems the best way
to describe the function and nature of a component in contrast to the whole
("that which") of which it is a part. Their counterparts in Latin are *id quo* and
id quod, which are perhaps no less a barbarism.
[16] This group includes Parmenides (fl. ca. 485. B.C.) and Zeno (fl. ca. 465-455
B.C.). See F. Copleston, S.J., *History*, I, p. 47 sq., p. 54 sq., and especially p.
311; J. Owens, *History*, p. 56 sq. and p. 79 sq.

A to *B* is actually *A* but, simultaneously, is potentially *B*.[17] Take a man who is now at *A* but will move to *B*. Now he is actually at *A*, but even while there, he potentially is at *B* insofar as his bone-structure and muscles give him ability to walk. His walking is nothing but the progressive actuation of that potentiality.[18]

The notions of "act" and "potency" simply summarize what Aristotle expressed by the two adverbs, "actually" and "potentially." Thus in the previous example of the walking man, "act" is the perfection of his being at this or that place, whereas "potency" is his capacity of having that perfection. More generally, "act" is any such perfection, "potency" is the capacity of receiving a perfection.[19]

If we return now to substance/accidents, we see that these two components are examples of the potency/act relationship. The substance is that by which a thing receives perfections and an accident is that by which it is perfected. Consequently, substance is as potency to its accidents, which in turn function as acts.[20]

*   One final point, and that is to issue a warning. "Substance" and "accident" are both used in everyday life and in technical contexts to convey various meanings. For example, one commonly hears said of a politician, "The substance of his speech last night was easily grasped," where "substance" is equivalent to "the important points." Or, more technically, a theologian will speak of the "divine substance," in which usage the term is the same as "reality" or "being." [21] Or a logician speaks of an individual thing as "first substance" and of the species or genus to which it belongs as "second substance";[22] he even locates substance on the top of his Porphyrean tree as the supreme genus.[23] Our warning is this: a metaphysician's meaning for "substance" differs from

---

[17] See *Metaphysics,* XII, Chap. 2, 1069b15 sq.: "Since that which 'is' has two senses, we must say that everything changes from that which is potentially to that which is actually." Also, *Physics,* III, Chap. 6, 206a14.

[18] Aristotle's justly famous definition of local motion: "The actuation of what exists potentially insofar as it exists potentially" (*Physics,* III, Chap. 1, 201a10-11). While actually changing, then, a thing is actually-potentially.

[19] Expressed in the more technical language of "that by which," an act is "that by which a thing is actually perfected," whereas a potency is "that by which a thing receives a perfection."

[20] For a further discussion of act/potency, see pp. 95-98.

[21] For example, Thomas Aquinas, *Summa Theologiae,* I, 13, 2 resp.

[22] Aristotle, *Categories,* Chap. 5, 2a11 sq.

[23] Andrew H. Bachhuber, S.J., *Introduction to Logic* (New York: Appleton-Century-Crofts, 1957), p. 245.

all the preceding. He restricts "substance" to a component, to a "that by which." For him substance is "that by which a thing specifically and generically remains what it is and yet receives various individual perfections." Such will be the only meaning which the term has hereafter in this book.

 * Similarly, "accident" commonly signifies a chance event ("An automobile accident just occurred on the turnpike"). Or, technically, a logician classifies "white," "standing," "being an American" as accidents rather than as properties (for example, "capable of speech") because the former express concepts of attributes which belong to the subject only contingently.[24] Again our warning is that the meaning "accident" has for a metaphysician is unlike all of those. For him an accident is a component—"that by which a thing, while remaining specifically and generically what it is, is actually modified through a new individual perfection." The term "accident" will be restricted to that meaning hereafter in this book.[25]

Let us now move on to the evidences offered by substantial changes.

4. Change/Stability in the Substantial Order

In the last section we considered accidental changes—that is, modifications which do not specifically affect the thing. The young daughter experienced love for her mother, learned to count, tried to express her love in those numerical terms, discovered that love transcends quantity. Yet throughout she remained human and actually the same human being she had been.

But material things are subject to other changes which do specifically modify them. For example, the inanimate becomes living when food is assimilated into the human flesh of the man who eats it. The living becomes nonliving when a man dies. Let us consider a concrete case of this latter sort of substantial change—the heroic death of a surgeon,

---

[24] *Ibid.*, p. 243.
[25] The basic difference between "accident" as understood by a logician and by a metaphysician is that for the former an accident is a concept, while for the latter it is a real, extramental component. For a metaphysician the term "accident" embraces what a logician expresses by both "accident" and "property." The addition of "contingent" and "necessary" to our previous definition brings this out—an accident is "that by which a thing . . . is actually modified through a new individual perfection, which is either contingent [logician's "accident"] or necessary [logician's "property"]."

Dr. Andrew Ross, as told by his wife.[26] Her account I reproduce in some detail so as to make clear the difference between the series of accidental changes he went through and the substantial change with which they terminated.

In June of 1951 Dr. Ross was told he had cancer. An operation disclosed that all his abdominal glands were infected and that death was merely a matter of time.

> From then on, there was fear in his eyes. It was a controlled and disciplined fear, probably only visible to those who loved him—but it was there. . . . For all fit and happy people fear death: this terrible step which must be taken alone, and which cuts us off so irrevocably from all those we have known and loved.
>
> However, there were few changes in our life. We both clung to normality. If anything, Andrew worked harder—to accomplish as much as possible in what little time was left to him. He lectured to his students, wrote his medical papers, treated his patients and enjoyed his friends. Toward me and the children, he showed a heightened awareness of the joy of being together and a hunger to lose none of our simple pleasures. The quiet country walks in lanes we knew so well took on an added significance. We looked at beauty with new eyes, because we now knew, as never before, that life was ephemeral. We realized that death gives life its meaning.

Two years and nine months thus passed by until, in the middle of March, new and disquieting symptoms manifested themselves.

> . . . and now the end had begun. Frequently there were depths of weakness so exhausting that it was worse than pain. There was the humiliating loss of speech which made his brilliant brain capable only of an agonized and frustrated gibberish; the useless paralyzed arm, which meant he had to be fed and bathed and dressed; the dragging leg which made movement impossible. . . . These are the times when man's dignity and strength are sublime. His never failed him. Dumb, wasted and worn, he asked for no drugs. . . . He nei-

---

[26] Mrs. Andrew Ross, "Death of a Man," *Jubilee*, 6 (September, 1958), 20-23. Her account was occasioned by Lael Wertenbaker, *Death of a Man* (New York: Random House, Inc., 1957), in which the author describes how her husband committed a carefully planned suicide rather than face a slow, painful death from cancer. This justification of suicide Mrs. Ross found depressing and frightening. To counteract its bad influence she wrote a report on her own husband's death.

ther asked nor took the easy way, but consciously went on paying his debt, with the greatness of his spirit shining through his ravaged body.

On the first of June, his doctor said that he could not possibly live through the night.

Once more I sent for our priest to give him the blessings for his last journey. . . . The blessed candles were lit and flickered on either side of his bed in the warm twilight air. His sons, and I, and his sister-in-law, who had nursed him devotedly, knelt around his bed. Kneeling also in the room and stretching all along a wide corridor, were our friends. Together we prayed for his soul, poised in flight, between this world and the next. . . .
    He did not die that night, and early the following morning, for three precious minutes, he regained consciousness. Once again his dear blue eyes were alight with love and peace and memory, and God granted him three syllables to bid me goodbye. A moment later he closed his eyes, and a cuckoo, on a tree beneath his window, began his heartless calling. The sun was shining into the room—it was warm with the promise of a glorious day. Very soon we folded his pale hands reverently upon his breast. This was the death of a man.

What would be Aristotle's reaction to such a case? First, that the long series of accidental changes (Dr. Ross feared, lectured, wrote, treated patients, conversed with friends, loved his wife and sons, suffered, courageously refused drugs, and so forth) finally terminated in a change which substantially modified him: what was human and living became nonhuman and nonliving—a mass of pure chemicals. Second, that substantial modification provides a twofold evidence of change and stability. Accidental modifications combine change (the loss and acquirement of individual perfections—the Doctor's fear replaced his previous carefree attitude, his illness excluded his former good health) with stability (the substantial continuity—the Doctor feared death and yet remained human). So too a substantial modification combines change (the loss and acquirement of specific perfection—here, the living becomes nonliving) with stability, as illustrated by the "corporeal" continuity which endures through the modification. For death is not an annihilation. What was living remains somehow the same after death, as indicated by the fact that it retains temporarily at least (that is, until subsequent substantial changes or outside interference) the same appearances—the same shape, weight, color.[27] The amount, kind, and location of the pure chemicals which result after death are determined by the amount, kind, and location of virtual chemicals before death.[28] Finally, just as the diverse evidences of change/stability in accidental modifications indicate the actual presence within of substance/accidents, so too the diverse evidences of change/stability in substantial modifications indicate the actual presence within the substance of two additional components. Accordingly, prior to substantial change the very substance is itself composed of two constitutive parts, for otherwise substantial change would be impossible.

The following process establishes and clarifies this composition.

[Directly perceived fact:] A substantial change in a thing involves
   (a) the loss and acquirement of specific perfection [change]
   (b) together with corporeal continuity [stability];
But evidence #a is other than evidence #b;
But diverse evidences indicate the actual presence within of diverse components;
Therefore, such evidences indicate that on the substantial level a material thing is actually made up of two real and diverse components:
   (a) that by which a thing is of such and such a specific nature and, hence, has its own distinctive characteristics—"SUBSTANTIAL FORM";
   (b) that by which a material thing receives a substantial form and yet which is capable, through subsequent substantial change, of receiving other substantial forms—"PRIME MATTER."

---

[27] Our respect for the dead is a witness to this continuity, for if the body of a loved one was not somehow the same before and after death, we might just as well wake and bury the corpse of a stranger. In what sense is the body the same? Not specifically (since death is a substantial change), but generically or virtually (this last adverb arises from the notion of "virtual presence" [see above, note 7], for death can be looked upon as a change in which what was virtually present becomes formally present).

For additional information on substantial change (for example, that it is instantaneous, takes place through accidental changes and material dispositions, and so forth) see G. P. Klubertanz, S.J., *Philosophy of Human Nature* (New York: Appleton-Century-Crofts, 1953), pp. 404-7.

[28] By the substantial change the chemicals which were virtually present in the living thing now become formally present (see *supra*, note 7). I call chemicals which are virtually present "virtual chemicals" and those which are formally present "pure chemicals." A chemist's terminology would be "bound" and "free" chemicals.

That process indicates both that such components do actually exist, and, to a degree, what they are (as the previous process concerning accidental modifications had done for substance/accidents [see Chap. III, Sec. 3], and what we say in the next paragraphs will be an adaptation of what we previously remarked with respect to that former process).

This process establishes their actual presence because the relationship between an evidence and a component is that between an effect and its intrinsic cause. But an effect of an intrinsic cause is present only because what causes it is also present. But substantial modifications involve distinct evidences of change and stability (effects); therefore, they reveal that distinct components (causes) actually exist within the thing changing.

It also shows, to an extent, what those components are, and once again the force of the fact that a material thing is an intrinsic unity is apparent. An individual man is not a mere accidental or extrinsic unity such as is an army or a football team, in which the parts are themselves individual men, and, thereby, are intrinsically and entitatively independent of the whole which they help constitute. Rather he is an intrinsic unity, whose parts depend internally and entitatively upon him. Nevertheless, the whole (here, the man) is not any one of its parts nor is any part the whole. Still both the whole and its parts are real (because actually present). Accordingly, there is a difference between the reality of the whole and of the parts, between what the whole is and what each part is. This difference can again be expressed in terms of "that which" and "that by which." The whole (the man himself) is *that which* is human. His substantial form is *that by which* he is human (and, thus, is specifically like other men and unlike dogs, petunias, hydrogen). His prime matter is *that by which* he has received his substantial form and, ultimately, is this man.[29]

Once again, our knowledge of such components is more than direct perception. True enough, we directly perceive situations in which this or that sort of substantial change occurs. This perception we express in judgments, which furnish the starting point of our process. But our awareness of primary matter and substantial form themselves transcends mere perception. We reflect upon the data offered through perception. We intellectually realize that the loss and acquirement of specific perfection and corporeal continuity are diverse evidences, that diverse evi-

---

[29] On prime matter as the ultimate source of individuation, see Chap. VI, Sec. 5b.

dences indicate the actual presence of the diverse components causing them, and that consequently a thing which is capable of substantial change is made up of the diverse components called prime matter and substantial form. This last stage is an assent of the intellect to which it is forced by the evidence of substantial modifications: "There actually *is* substantial form, there actually *is* primary matter." In brief, the process terminates in intellectual judgmental knowledge, by which we become aware that such components exist and what they are.

Such constitutive parts, then, are known by reflection upon perceived data, and this reflection is a genuinely intellectual operation. We cannot directly perceive prime matter and substantial form. We cannot picture or imagine them. We know matter and form through genuine intellection.

The process we are currently considering also indicates that the relation between prime matter and substantial form is one of potency to act. An act is a perfection and potency is the capacity of receiving a perfection. But prime matter is such a capacity and substantial form is a perfection, for our process ends in our affirming that the former is "that by which a material thing receives a substantial form and yet which is capable, through subsequent substantial change, of receiving other substantial forms," and that the latter is "that by which a thing is of such and such a specific nature and, accordingly, has its own distinctive characteristics and activities." Therefore, prime matter and substantial form are related to one another as potency and act. In fact, prime matter is *pure* potency, because the adjective means "nothing but." Prime matter is *nothing but* a recipient and a capacity. Although it is real because it actually exists within a material existent, still of itself, it has no act whatsoever.[30] Its sole function within the thing of which it is a constitutive part is to receive, to limit, to individuate.

* A final (and important) point is to investigate the force of the phrases "prime matter" and "substantial form." Why call the one component "matter," and, in fact, "prime matter"? What is the force of the

---

[30] Prime matter is thus unlike substance, which is potency with respect to accidents and yet is itself a composite of act/potency—that is, of substantial form/ prime matter. Accordingly, substance is not pure potency but of itself involves an act (substantial form).

One way to establish that prime matter is pure potency is to rely on the fact that there is only one substantial form in each thing, and this because an individual thing is an intrinsic unity. His single substantial form is that by which this man is corporeal, living, sentient, and rational. For prime matter to have an act or form of its own would disrupt the stringent unity each man is.

adjective? Then, too, why call the other "form," and, also, "substantial form"? Again, what is the significance of the adjective?

 * First of all, "material" can be used in opposition to "immaterial." When contrasted with intellection, freedom, courage, value, and the like, such things as these men, these animals, these plants, and these chemicals all have at least one common trait: each has parts outside of parts, each is actually extended, is directly in place. This common characteristic has come to be expressed by the term "material," which therefore means simply "that which has parts outside of parts, is actually extended, is directly in place." Of what can that term be directly predicated? Only of that which itself has parts outside of parts —thus of men, animals, plants, and minerals. Is it directly predicable of components? No, because none of them (whether they be prime matter, substantial form, or various accidents) is a *that which* but rather a *that by which*. None of them is itself actually extended, has parts outside of parts, is immediately in place. Therefore, each one is in itself not material, which is the same as saying that each is, in its own way, immaterial. And this latter adjective then points simply to the fact that of itself each is without parts and is not actually extended.[31] Thus a human soul, a canine soul, and prime matter are not themselves material. What, then, does the noun mean in the phrase "prime matter"? Quite obviously, it does not have reference directly to actual extension, to parts outside of parts, since prime matter and substantial form are themselves, in this frame of reference, both non-material.

 * But what, positively, does the noun signify? In everyday life "material" is also used in another way and here it is in contrast with "formal." For instance, gabardine, silk, wool, and the like are the *ma-*

---

[31] Of course, each of the various components is immaterial in its own way. Some (for example, the human soul) are intrinsically independent of matter and the term "spiritual" is used to describe this status. Others (for example, a canine soul) are intrinsically dependent on matter, and "barely immaterial" or some such expression can be used for their status. Prime matter is still more intimately linked with materiality, for quantity, although a property of the composite, flows more directly from prime matter than from substantial form (see p. 180 f.). Still prime matter of itself is not actually extended, and thus it too is immaterial in its own way (see Chap. V, Sec. 4).

All the components can be classified as "material" only through extrinsic denomination—that is, they are the constitutive parts of a thing which is itself actually extended and to which "material" is directly and properly applied. Of course, this classification too will vary in accordance with the varying function each component has within the thing and with the varying degrees of dependence each has upon matter.

terial from which men's suits are made. Bricks, cement, lumber, and glass are the *materials* going into the construction of a new house. Wood or marble or bronze is the *material* for a statue. Words and rhythm are the *materials* of a poem. But those artifacts do not consist just of the materials from which they are made. Gabardine and the other cloths become a suit only if they are cut according to a definite pattern. Bricks, cement, lumber, and the like become a house only when assembled and set up according to a definite plan and shape. Wood or marble is a statue only when a definite figure is carved or chiseled in it. Words and rhythm become a poem only when organized in a definite structure. If such things as cloth, bricks, marble, and words are the *materials* of the artifacts, then the pattern, plan and shape, figure and structure are their "forms." In such examples "matter" is that which can receive some or other pattern, shape, figure, structure. It is that which is of itself without determination but which is determinable in various ways by the introduction of diverse formal factors—for example, a piece of suitably large cloth can become a suit or a dress or a tent, the difference arising from the pattern used. It is that which can be perfected in this or that manner by submitting to this or that determining element. More generally, then, "matter" is simply *that which receives, that which is perfected, that which is determinable,* whereas "form" is *that which is received, that which perfects, that which determines.*[32]

* Such is the meaning which the noun has in the phrase "prime matter." Within the substance, the component which has substantial form as its counterpart is said to be "matter" not because it is itself extended or has parts outside of parts, but because it receives that form and thereby is perfected and determined. On the other hand, the component within the substance which has prime matter as its partner is called "form" because it is received by prime matter, which it thereby perfects and determines.

---

[32] This general description of matter and form will have to be refined a bit later on. First of all, determination will turn out to be of two sorts—"to limit a perfection" and "to confer a perfection." (See p. 111 on autodetermination.) As used in connection with form, the term signifies the conferment of perfection. Also, form in a strict sense will be seen to be an intrinsic, static, and quidditative perfection in order to contrast it with real relations, operations, and the act of existing; these latter are perfections but are not forms. Finally, matter/form are not synonymous with potency/act but, rather, are potency/act *within the essence.*

These refinements will be made clearer later on, but for the present time and purposes the general description of matter and form is sufficiently accurate and detailed.

＊ But why "*prime* matter" and "*substantial* form"? What is the force of the adjectives? They have traditionally been considered to be at least useful because there are two sets of recipients, as well as two sets of received perfections. This man, say, consists of a component (prime matter) which receives the specific perfection (substantial form) and of a component (substance) which receives individual perfections (accidents). If one were perfectly consistent, the recipients of specific perfections and of individual perfections would be both called "matter" because they are recipients, and then termed "first" or "second" matter to indicate that each receives different perfections: "first" or "prime" matter receives the more basic, ontologically prior, specific perfection; "second" matter receives the less fundamental, ontologically posterior, individual perfections.[33] But language is seldom consistent; hence philosophers commonly designate the recipient of substantial form as "prime matter" while calling the recipient of accidents "substance." We shall abide by this common practice.

＊ The case is somewhat similar with respect to "substantial form." As we have just remarked, there are two sets of received perfections—the specific and the individual. If one were completely consistent, both those perfections would be called "form" because they are both perfections received by potencies. Then, if we were to keep in line with "first" and "second" matter, the specific perfection could be designated as "first form" and an individual perfection as "second form." But the former perfection has come to be called "substantial form" and the latter "accidental form," or simply "accident." We shall again abide by this common practice and use "substantial form" and "accident" to designate the specific perfection and an individual perfection.[34]

＊ The preceding analysis has been rather tedious but it is important in this way. It enables us to realize that the noun in the phrase "prime matter" does not imply that the component to which it is applied is itself actually extended or has parts outside of parts. Rather, it simply indicates that that component is a recipient—the recipient of a specific perfection, which perfects and determines it. This realization is an important factor in gaining an accurate understanding of that component, as well as of the others.

---

[33] In this interpretation, "second matter" is the same as substance. In actual use, though, the phrase has come to be restricted to the realm of artifacts. For example, a block of marble is "second matter" with respect to the statue it can become: it can receive and be perfected by various figures or shapes.

[34] I shall use "accident" rather than "accidental form" because, as will be clear later, not every accident is a form. See pp. 206-7 on relations.

5. Summary and Conclusions

(a) In Chapter III our goal has been to observe and then to profit by Aristotle's reaction to the sensible universe. This Greek philosopher had himself profited by observing his predecessors. From Heraclitus he learned that change is a factor in reality because real things change. From Plato he became aware that reality also involved stability, but maintained that this stability is not located in some separate realm of subsistent Essences but in actual things. Here is a clear token of Aristotle's genius: his realization that actual things are neither total change nor total permanence but rather combine the two. An individual thing is a changing stability and stabilized change, and this on two levels— on the substantial or on the accidental level, depending upon whether or not the modification specifically affects what the existent is.

(b) In exploiting this double evidence of change/stability on the two levels, Aristotle relies on two important insights gained from the actual world in which we live.

1. First of all, *diverse evidences indicate the actual presence within of diverse constitutive parts,* since the latter are the intrinsic cause of the former. Accordingly, change and stability on the two levels point to two sets of distinct, actually present, constitutive parts, for otherwise such evidences would themselves be absent: effects (here, change and stability) are present only because their intrinsic causes (here, diverse constitutive parts) are present.

2. Second, a material existent involves intrinsic (*per se*) unity—*a state of cohesion, togetherness, undividedness which is internal and entitative because its parts entitatively depend upon the whole.*[35] The result of this unity is that the constitutive parts of which we have been speaking are real in a different way from that of the whole which they help make up. This difference let us express by the phrases *that which* and *that by which.* The whole (this man) is *that which* is human or mathematical; his constitutive parts are each *that by which* he is human or mathematical. For purposes of convenience and clarity, let us call such parts "components"; hereafter that term will have the following meaning. *A component is a constitutive part of an intrinsic unity, is*

---

[35] This description would seem to fit both the living and the nonliving. For the living, though, one can also add the clause, "and because the parts work together for an intrinsic goal." On intrinsic (*per se*) unity on the inanimate level, see n. 11 above.

known by intellectual consideration of directly perceived data, and is a "that by which."

(c) So far four such components have been uncovered in material existents. The first set has been named "substance" and "accidents" and is indicated by the accidental modifications which things undergo and which involve the twofold evidence of change (the loss and acquirement of individual perfections) and stability (substantial or specific continuity).

1. This evidence reveals not only that such components actually exist but also, to an extent, what they are. *Substance is that by which a material thing specifically and generically remains what it is and yet receives various individual perfections. An accident is that by which the thing, while remaining specifically and generically what it is, is actually modified through a new individual perfection.* As those descriptions readily indicate, a substance and an accident are each a *that by which*.

2. Although they are known by reflection upon perceived data, this reflection is a genuinely intellectual operation, which terminates in intellectual judgmental knowledge. They themselves cannot be directly perceived or imagined or pictured, but are known by genuine intellection.

3. Finally, substance and accidents are related to one another as potency to act because the role of substance is to receive accidents, which simultaneously perfect it.

(d) The second set of components is named "prime matter" and "substantial form" and is known to exist within an individual thing because of the substantial modifications which such things undergo and which involve the twofold evidence of change (the loss and acquirement of specific perfection) and stability (corporeal continuity).

1. This evidence reveals not only that such components actually exist but also, to a degree, what they are. *Prime matter is that by which a material thing receives a substantial form and yet which is capable, through subsequent substantial change, of receiving other substantial forms. A substantial form is that by which a thing is of such and such a specific nature and, hence, has its own distinctive characteristics and activities.* According to those descriptions, prime matter and substantial form are each a *that by which*.

2. Although the starting-point of the process by which they are known is directly perceived data, those components themselves are known by reflection upon that data and this reflection is a genuinely intellectual operation, terminating in intellectual judgments. They themselves

cannot be directly perceived or imagined or pictured but are known by genuine intellection.

3. Again, prime matter and substantial form are to one another as potency to act inasmuch as the former receives and limits the latter, which simultaneously specifies and thereby perfects it. In fact, prime matter is pure potency, because it is *nothing but* potency. Without any act or form of its own, it itself is nothing but a recipient, a capacity, a limit, although it is real because it actually exists within the substance.

4. Finally, the noun in the phrase "prime matter" does not entail that the component of which it is predicated is itself actually extended, has parts outside of parts, or is directly in place. Like other components, prime matter itself is free of those characteristics, which are applied to it only through extrinsic denomination. Rather, the noun "matter" signifies simply that the component of which it is predicated is a recipient—the recipient of a specific perfection, which perfects and determines it and which for that reason is designated as "substantial form." [36]

(e) Are those four the only components to be found within a material thing? To answer one must ask another question: does a material thing furnish any evidence over and above change and stability on the accidental and the substantial levels? If not, then such are the only components. If it does, then it also contains whatever component is manifesting itself through that additional evidence.

Aristotle's answer to this second question would be negative: a sensible thing offers the double evidence of change/stability on the two levels and nothing more. One must wait some fourteen centuries for a different answer, and then it is given by a Catholic priest and Dominican theologian. The most important clue which a sensible thing gives to its internal make-up, Thomas Aquinas (1224-1273) replies, is not

---

[36] Up to this time the components have been exemplified only with respect to living existents. What of the nonliving? Wherever one finds intrinsic units on the inanimate level, there one also finds substance/accidents and prime matter/substantial form, which can be described as follows. With respect to, say, hydrogen, "substance" would be "that by which this unit is and remains hydrogen and yet receives various individual perfections" (such as weight, transparency, and so forth). "Accident" would be "that by which this unit, while remaining hydrogen, is actually modified by some or other such individual perfection." "Substantial form" would be "that by which this unit is hydrogen (rather than oxygen or any of the other elements)." "Prime matter" would be "that by which this unit has received the substantial form of hydrogen but which is capable, through subsequent substantial change, of receiving other substantial forms (for example, that of water)."

that it changes accidentally and substantially but that *it does actually exist*, that it is an *actual existent*. Since a diverse evidence indicates the actual presence within of a diverse component, a sensible thing involves not only substance/accidents and prime matter/substantial form but also a new and different component—namely, that by which a thing actually exists and which can be called "the act of existing," or simply "existence." This component is the heart of the existent's reality, the ultimate source of all its perfections. To the metaphysician it contributes the formal object of his science, for he studies being as being, which is simply another way of saying that he studies existents precisely *as existent*, existents in the very exercise of their acts of existing.

By making this reply, Aquinas stepped from a philosophy of nature up to the distinct and higher level of metaphysics.[37] But more of this in subsequent chapters.

SUGGESTED READINGS

Aristotle, *Basic Works*, ed. Richard McKeon, pp. 230-36, 253-57, 745-47. New York: Random House, Inc., 1941. On change.

De Raeymaeker, Louis, *The Philosophy of Being*, trans. E. H. Ziegelmeyer, S.J., pp. 170-81. St. Louis: B. Herder Book Co., 1954. On substance and accidents as underlying accidental change.

Gerrity, Brother Benignus, *Nature, Knowledge, and God*, pp. 63-82, 102-44. Milwaukee: Bruce Publishing Co., 1947. On matter and form, substance and accidents.

Gilson, Etienne, *Being and Some Philosophers* (2nd Ed.), pp. 41-73. Toronto: Pontifical Institute of Mediaeval Studies, 1952. A study of how Aristotelians conceive reality.

Hawkins, D. J. B., "Change, Potency, and Act," in *Being and Becoming*, pp. 97-109. New York: Sheed & Ward, 1954.

——, "Substance," *ibid.*, pp. 110-23.

McMullin, Ernan, ed., *The Concept of Matter*. Notre Dame: University

---

[37] Since Aristotle does not seem to have been aware of the act of existing, does that absence mean that he had no metaphysics? No, Aristotle did have a science of being as being, but it was concerned with the First Movers, who alone are being in a strict sense and are fully real, and it dealt with the sensible universe only in reference to them. See J. Owens, *History*, pp. 322 ff.; *idem*, *Doctrine of Being*, pp. 21-26.

On Aristotle's unawareness of the act of existing, see Edward Stevens, S.J., "The Perfection of Being in Aristotle," *Modern Schoolman*, 41 (March, 1964), 227-49.

of Notre Dame Press, 1963. This volume contains valuable articles on "matter" in the Greeks, medievals, moderns, and contemporaries (both philosophers and empiriological scientists). The following are most relevant: Ernan McMullin, "Introduction: The Concept of Matter," pp. 1-41; John J. Fitzgerald, " 'Matter' in Nature and the Knowledge of Nature: Aristotle and the Aristotelian Tradition," pp. 79-98; Joseph Owens, "Matter and Predication in Aristotle," pp. 99-121; Norbert Luyten, O.P., "Matter as Potency," pp. 122-41; Ernan McMullin, "Matter as a Principle," pp. 169-213; Milton Fisk, "Primary Matter and Unqualified Change," pp. 214-41; Harry A. Nielsen, "The Referent of 'Primary Matter,' " pp. 244-54; Ernan McMullin, "Four Senses of 'Potency,' " pp. 295-318.

Stevens, S.J., Edward, "The Perfection of Being in Aristotle," *The Modern Schoolman,* 41 (March, 1964), 227-50.

Van Melsen, Andrew Gerard, *The Philosophy of Nature,* pp. 39-48 and 101-23. Pittsburgh: Duquesne University Press, 1953. On matter and form; on difficulties concerning substantial change.

Van Roo, S.J., William A., "Matter as a Principle of Being," *The Modern Schoolman,* 18 (1940), 1-5.

Veatch, Henry, "Aristotelianism," in *A History of Philosophical Systems,* ed. V. Ferm, pp. 106-17. New York: The Philosophical Library, 1950.

Wild, John, *Introduction to Realistic Philosophy,* pp. 277-95 and 320-30. New York: Harper & Row, Publishers, 1948. On change; on matter and form; on substance and accidents.

PART II

Primacy
of Existence

CHAPTER **IV**

Existence and Essence

There are some who look on the Middle Ages as intellectually barren, on the Catholic Church as a hindrance to original research, on sacred theology as inimical to progress in philosophy. How amazing and even disconcerting it must be for them to discover that the one who transcended Aristotle by making a most significant contribution to philosophy is a thirteenth-century Catholic theologian. For Thomas Aquinas did just that by realizing that actual existents involve a component heretofore overlooked, which is totally different from essence and which he named *esse* or "act of existing." [1]

---

[1] As an evaluation of Aquinas' contribution to metaphysics, see Etienne Gilson, *Elements of Christian Philosophy* (New York: Doubleday & Company, Inc., 1960), p. 278: "The doctrine of Thomas Aquinas has this superiority over the others: that its principles are, in a sense, the same as those of apparently different, and sometimes opposed, philosophies—with this difference only: that in Thomism these principles are taken in the fullness of their meaning. This accounts for the privilege of Thomism to be open to all truth and to provide a place even for truths that its author could not explicitly foresee. All that is true in any other philosophy can be justified by the principles of Thomas Aquinas, and there is no other philosophy that it is possible to profess without having to

1. Position of Thomas Aquinas

When and under what circumstances did Aquinas achieve that realization? This question is important historically, since he originated the
doctrine of *esse* as a component over and above essence, and it would
be interesting and valuable to know how and why he first became aware
of that doctrine. It is also important doctrinally, because understanding
how he achieved that awareness may help us attain it too. But the
question is rather difficult to answer. True enough, even in his early
writings[2] he frequently affirms that *esse* is different from essence[3] and
occasionally states explicitly that the difference is real and not just
conceptual.[4] But in those same treatises we also encounter two difficulties, the first of which is that most frequently he is content to make
those affirmations and statements in strictly theological contexts without offering any proof for that difference. The real distinction is pre-
supposed as already established and is merely used to illustrate some
point of divine revelation. Take as an instance the following text, where
the point at issue is the Scriptural description of God as "He Who Is"
(Exodus, 3, 14). Is that the best possible description for Him? Thomas
answers affirmatively and for this reason.

---

ignore, or to reject, some conclusions that are true in the light of these principles.
Speaking in a more familiar way, one can be a Thomist without losing the
truth of any other philosophy, whereas one cannot subscribe to any other
philosophy without losing some of the truth available to the disciple of Thomas
Aquinas." One must remember that Gilson wrote those glowing words only
after forty years of studying ancient, medieval, modern, and contemporary
philosophers.

[2] His early writings are those written ca. 1254-1260. These include his *Com-
mentary on Lombard's Sentences, On Being and Essence, Disputed Question on
Truth, Exposition of Boethius' Treatise "On the Trinity," Exposition of Boethius'
"De Hebdomadibus,"* and *Quodlibetal Questions VII-XI.* On the chronology of
Thomas' works, see I. T. Eschmann, O.P., "A Catalogue of St. Thomas' Works"
in E. Gilson, *Christian Philosophy of St. Thomas Aquinas* (New York: Random
House, Inc., 1956), pp. 381-437.

[3] This affirmation he makes approximately thirty-five times. For a list of texts,
see L. Sweeney, S.J., "Existence/Essence in Thomas Aquinas' Early Writings,"
Proceedings of the American Catholic Philosophical Association, 37 (1963), 103-5.

[4] See *In de Hebdomadibus,* Lect. 2, #32 (Marietti Ed., II, 398); *De Veritate,*
27, 1 ad 8 (Marietti Ed., p. 513b); *In I Sent.,* 19, 2, 2 sol. (Mandonnet Ed.,
pp. 470-71); *Quodl.,* IX, 4, 1 resp. (Marietti Ed., p. 185b); *In II Sent.,* 16,
1, 2 ad 5 (Mandonnet Ed., p. 419). For a study of these texts, see L. Sweeney,
S.J., *op. cit.,* pp. 128-29.

In every thing which is, there is a quiddity to consider (that by which the thing subsists in a determinate nature) and also an act of existing (that by which it is said to actually be). Now the term "thing" arises from the quiddity, as Avicenna teaches in his *Metaphysics*, whereas the expression "he who is" or "being" arises from the act of existing. *Since in every creature essence is other than existence*, a creature is properly named from its quiddity (for example, "man" from humanity) and not from the act of existing. But God's very existence is His quiddity and, consequently, the expression which properly describes Him and is His own unique name is that taken from existence [namely, "He Who Is"].[5]

Manifestly, Aquinas takes the fact for granted that *esse* is a component actually present within all creatures and other than essence. He makes no attempt to establish that otherness.

* The second difficulty is that the proofs he does provide in those early treatises are not entirely helpful. Two of them are theological rather than philosophical, for they obviously move from God to creatures.[6] A third sort (the genus-argument) aims at establishing the difference between essence and *esse* by pointing to the fact that things agree in belonging to the same genus or species but differ insofar as they have *esse*.[7] It is so complex and awkward as to be ineffectual.[8]

---

[5] *In I Sent.*, 8, 1, 1 sol. (Mandonnet Ed., p. 195).

[6] The first of these can, in fact, be called a "God to creatures" argument (or, more exactly, "God to angels," because the creatures in question are angels); it moves in this fashion: in God alone essence is *esse*; but an angel is not God; therefore, an angelic essence is not *esse*, which however it receives from God. For a study of the five texts in which it occurs, see L. Sweeney, S.J., *op. cit.*, pp. 112-20 and 130.

The second of these theological arguments is based on participation and can be stated as follows: God is subsistent *esse* and thus is Being essentially; but a creature is not God; therefore, a creature is not *esse* and is a being only through participation. For a study of the four relevant texts, see L. Sweeney, S.J., *op. cit.*, pp. 120-26 and 131.

[7] Thomas uses this line of inference in at least six passages. See L. Sweeney, S.J., *op. cit.*, pp. 109-12 and 130.

[8] Here is the structure of that argument drawn from the texts referred to in note 7:

> Genus and species express what things are;
>
> But what things are is that which they have in common;
>
> Therefore, things have in common the fact that they belong to such and such a species and genus: this man and that man agree in the fact that each is a man; this man and that dog agree in the fact that each is an animal;
>
> But the whatness which things entail has *esse* only in individuals;

The final sort centers upon studying the concept of essence rather than upon existence and, besides, needs to be supplemented on two important points in order to be conclusive. Consider the version of it which Aquinas gives in *On Being and Essence*.[9] He is discussing whether separate substances such as angels [note the theological context] and human souls are completely simple. He answers negatively, for the reason that they are composed of potency and act. The key-lines then occur.

> Whatever does not belong to the notion of essence or quiddity comes from without and enters into composition with the essence, for no essence is intelligible without its essential parts. Now, every essence or quiddity can be understood without anything being known of its existing. I can know what a man or a phoenix is and still be ignorant whether it exists in reality. From this it is clear that *esse* is other than the essence or quiddity, unless, perhaps, there is a being whose quiddity is its very *esse*.[10]

*   Why does that argument seem inconclusive if taken by itself? First of all, the mere fact that we can know what a man is and yet be ignorant of whether or not he exists need not establish existence to be other than essence, as this parallel makes clear. I can know what "man" is without an awareness of "this man." Yet *in this man* what "man" signifies is not really different from what "this man" expresses. They

---

But individuals are different, unique;

Therefore, the whatness which things entail also involves difference and uniqueness, and this through *esse*;

Therefore, the whatness which things entail is that in which they both agree and differ, is that which is at once common and unique: *common* insofar as it is generic and specific (that is, ultimately it is the basis for intelligibilities predicable of all), but *unique* insofar as it is individual and has *esse*;

But what accounts for agreement is other than what accounts for difference;

Therefore, the fact that things are individual and have *esse* and yet also belong to a genus and species indicates that in them *esse* is other than whatness.

[9] Besides *On Being and Essence*, the essence-argumentation is to be found in the following: *In I Sent.*, 8, Expositio Primae Partis Textus (p. 209); *ibid.*, 8, 4, 2 sol. (p. 222); *In II Sent.*, 1, 1, 1 sol. (pp. 12-13); *ibid.*, 3, 1, 1 sol. (pp. 87-88); *De Ver.*, 10, 12 resp. (p. 220b). For an exegesis, see L. Sweeney, S.J., *op. cit.*, pp. 105-9 and 129-30.

[10] *De Ente et Essentia*, c. 4 (Roland-Gosselin Latin Ed., p. 34, lines 4-16; Maurer translation, pp. 45-46).

are really identical.[11] They differ only mentally insofar as "man" signifies indeterminately what "this man" expresses determinately. So too
I can know what a man is without an awareness of whether he exists.
But *in this existing man* (and the question concerns whether the act
of existing and the actual individual essence in this existing man are
really distinct), perhaps what "man" signifies is no more really different
from what "this man as existing" expresses than are "man" and "this
man" in our first example. Perhaps they differ merely mentally as the
indeterminate and the determinate. At least, if this man and his
existence are really distinct, that distinction is not established by the
present line of reasoning unless this contrast is added to it: the relationship between an essence as specific and as individual is that of act and
potency, whereas the relationship between essence and *esse* is that of
potency and act.[12] The result of this addition is that essence/*esse* are
not equivalent in this text to essence-as-specific/essence-as-individual
and, thus, are perhaps more than merely mentally distinct.

    * The second reason why Thomas' fourth approach is not convinc-
ing by itself has, I would suggest, been clearly seen by all Suarezians.
Let us grant, they would say, that essence can be understood without
anything being known of its existence. Again, let us grant that essence-
as-known is different than essence-as-existing. But in what does that

---

[11] On this point see J. Owens, *St. Thomas and the Future of Metaphysics*
(Milwaukee: Marquette University Press, 1957), p. 81, note 35: "When ab-
stracted without precision, the essence is predicated of the individual thing and
so is identical with it"; *idem*, "Thomistic Common Nature and Platonic Idea,"
Mediaeval Studies 21 (1959), 222: "According to the metaphysical procedure
followed in the *De Ente et Essentia*, the Thomistic distinction between essence
and being is reached from the way in which predication shows that a sensible
nature is . . . wholly identified in reality with the changeable individual in
which it is found."

[12] Thomas draws this contrast at least by implication. The first relationship
is established by this line of reasoning: what is received and the recipient
(*receptum/recipiens*) are to one another as act and potency (*De Ente*, c. 4
[Roland-Gosselin Ed., p. 35, lines 10-21; Maurer translation, p. 47]); but in
material things specific essence is *received* in signate matter, whence it becomes
individuated (*ibid.*, c. 5, p. 42, line 7 sq.; Maurer translation, p. 54); hence,
essence-as-specific and essence-as-individual are related to one another as act to
potency.

    On the second relationship, see *De Ente*, c. 4 (Maurer translation, p. 47):
"The quiddity itself, then, or the form which is the intelligence must be potential with respect to the existence which it receives from God, and that existence
is received as an act. Potency and act are thus found in the intelligences" (Latin
text in Roland-Gosselin Ed., p. 35, ll. 21-24). See L. Sweeney, S.J., *op. cit.*,
p. 107 and notes 16 and 17, pp. 129-30.

difference consist? In its relationship to God as efficient cause: an essence-as-existing God has actualized by willing it to be. But that actualization is not intrinsic to the essence. It does not arise from a component actually present within the existent. It is merely the effect of God's efficiency; it is the extrinsic state of an essence as efficiently posited by God in the actual universe.[13]

*   Whether the essentialist's interpretation of essence-as-existing is true, is open to question. But the cogency of their attack on Thomas' text seems beyond question, unless it is complemented by the important realization that *esse* is an intrinsic and perfective factor within existents.[14] As such a factor, *esse* is more than essence situated within a framework of efficiency, and thus may be really other than essence.

His endeavors to establish the real distinction are not completely successful in his early writings.[15] He does succeed, though, in subsequent treatises.[16] Setting aside reflection upon the concept of essence as an approach to the real distinction, he turns instead to *actual existents themselves*. There he concentrates upon the fact that they do actually exist and upon what that fact does to those existents: it contributes all their perfections to them. The result is that *esse*, the component to which that fact leads and of which it is the evidence, is clearly seen to be a perfection and act within the existent and really other than what the existent is. In fact, it is the perfection *par excel-*

---

[13] This interpretation of *esse* as nothing more than efficient cause was made long before Suarez by Thomas' own contemporaries. See L. Sweeney, S.J., *op. cit.*, p. 108, n. 19.

[14] On *esse* as an intrinsic factor in existents, see *In II Sent.*, 1, 1, 4 sol.: "Existence is more intrinsic to a thing than that which determines and limits existence" (Latin text in Mandonnet Ed., p. 26). On *esse* as a perfection, see *De Ente*, c. 5 (Maurer translation, p. 51): "Similarly, although God is simply the act of existing, it is not necessary that He lack the other perfections or excellences. On the contrary, He possesses all perfections of all genera of beings; so He is said to be unqualifiedly perfect. . . . But He possesses these perfections in a more excellent way than other things, for in Him they are one, while in other things they are diversified. The reason for this is that all these perfections are His according to His simple act of existing. . . . In the same way, God possesses all perfections in His very act of existing" (Latin text in Roland-Gosselin Ed., p. 38, l. 12 sq.). This can be drawn from that text: God is *esse* and, for that very reason, is all-perfect; therefore, *esse* (in God, as well as in creatures) is itself a perfection. See L. Sweeney, S.J., *op. cit.*, pp. 106-9.

[15] One should remember that the question is not whether he holds that existence really differs from essence (he explicitly asserts that he does—see texts cited above, note 4), but whether he adequately *proves* it.

[16] These would embrace what he wrote both in his Middle (ca. 1260-1267) and Late (ca. 1267 sq.) periods.

lence, the actuation of all other acts, as the following paraphrased texts show.

When is the perfection of being a man or that of being fire actually achieved? When it exists in dry wood [to restrict ourselves to the latter example], or in the hands of the man holding a piece of flint, or in his mind as he thinks about starting a fire? No, fire is *fire* only when it actually exists. This fact shows that the act of existence is the actuality of all actuations and the perfection of all perfections.[17] Again: everything is perfect because of and according to its existence. For example, wisdom would be no perfection for a man unless because of it he actually *is* wise. And the same holds true for all other perfections. Accordingly, the manner in which a thing exists also determines the degree of its perfections.[18] Again, you actually do not have goodness or men unless they actually exist. Hence, existence is the actuality of every form and nature.[19] Again, absolutely nothing has actuality except inasmuch as it exists. Hence, the act of existing is the actuality of all things, even of forms. Accordingly, existence for a horse, a man, or anything whatsoever is its actuation and perfection.[20]

When he came to write the *Summa Contra Gentiles* and other late treatises, then, Aquinas was not only aware that the act of existence is really distinct from essence (this awareness he seems to have had from the first moment he took up his pen),[21] but he also realized that the way in which to establish their real distinction is to turn to the actual universe. Contemplate the myriad existents it contains: the actually

[17] *De Potentia,* q. 7, a. 2 ad 9 (Marietti Ed., p. 192). The Latin reads: "Quaelibet autem forma signata non intelligitur in actu nisi per hoc quod esse ponitur. Nam humanitas vel igneitas potest considerari ut in potentia materiae existens, vel ut in virtute agentis, aut etiam ut in intellectu: sed hoc quod habet *esse,* efficitur existens. Unde patet quod hoc quod dico *esse* est actualitas omnium actuum, et propter hoc est perfectio omnium perfectionum."

[18] *Summa contra Gentiles,* I, c. 28 (Leonine Manual Ed., p. 29d). The Latin: "Omnis enim nobilitas cuiuscumque rei est sibi secundum suum esse: nulla enim nobilitas esset homini ex sua sapientia nisi per eam sapiens esset, et sic de aliis. Sic ergo secundum modum quo res habet esse, est suus modus in nobilitate."

[19] *Summa Theologiae,* I, 3, 4 resp. (Leonine Manual Ed., p. 17b). The Latin: "Esse est actualitas omnis formae vel naturae: non enim bonitas vel humanitas significatur in actu nisi prout significamus eam *esse.*"

[20] *Ibid.,* I, 4, 1 ad 3 (p. 21d). The Latin: "Ipsum esse est perfectissimum omnium: comparatur enim ad omnia ut actus. Nihil enim habet actualitatem nisi inquantum est; unde ipsum esse est actualitas omnium rerum et etiam ipsarum formarum. Unde non comparatur ad alia sicut recipiens ad receptum; sed magis sicut receptum ad recipiens. Cum enim dico esse hominis vel equi vel cuiuscumque alterius, ipsum esse consideratur ut formale et receptum."

[21] See above, n. 4.

existing horses and fires, and men who actually are wise and good and virtuous. There one discovers both what actual existence is and that the fact things actually exist is an evidence different from what they are. The consequence is that the real otherness of the act of existing from essence, as well as its primacy in the existent, opens up before him.[22]

We may add that this interpretation of the genesis of Thomas' position on the real distinction does not deny that Thomas may first have elaborated his notion of the act of existing while engaged in theological meditation upon *Exodus* 3, 14 and other Scriptural texts,[23] but it suggests that he simultaneously had his finger on the pulse of the actual world. This it was which had initially conveyed (and was still conveying) to him the everyday notions of existence, actuality, and the like, now being examined under the light of the Scriptural text. Under that illumination they would be transformed, sublimated, and deepened both with regard to God and to creatures. Nonetheless, it was *they* which would be transformed. They had first to be in his mind in order to undergo that change. Without them there was nothing to work upon.[24]

This interpretation also implies that although a theologian originated the notion of *esse* as the actualizing component within creatures, still that doctrine does not belong of its very nature to theology. It is not a strict mystery, transcending the grasp of human reason. That is to say, the illumination which Thomas experienced while reflecting upon *Exodus* 3, 14 did not superimpose any intelligible content upon the data already gained from material existents through direct experience. Rather, its function was to enable him to see *what actually was already contained within that data* but heretofore overlooked by previous thinkers. And Thomas' role with reference to subsequent students

---

[22] Thomas' concern to ground his metaphysics of *esse* upon direct contact with actual existents is matched by a similar concern in psychology, where important doctrines are established through direct observation of human existents in actual cognitive and appetitive situations. For instance, *S.T.*, I, 76, 1 resp. (p. 358c): man's intellective soul is the form of his body because "intellection is an operation of this man: everyone *experiences* that he it is who intellectually knows (*experitur enim unusquisque seipsum esse qui intelligit*). . . . One and the same man *perceives* that he knows both through intellection and through sensation (*ipse idem homo est qui percipit se et intelligere et senitire*)." Among numberless other instances which could be given, see *ibid.*, I, 84, 7 resp. (p. 414c): ". . . Videmus . . . experiri potest"; *Expositio in Librum de Causis*, Prop. 10 (Saffrey Ed., p. 70, l. 19 sq.): ". . . etiam experimento in nobis percipimus: videmus. . . ."

[23] This is E. Gilson's position. For example, see his *Elements of Christian Philosophy*, pp. 124-33.

[24] See L. Sweeney, S.J., *op. cit.*, pp. 113-14 and note 28.

can be conceived somewhat on a parallel—having discovered the nature and primacy of *esse,* he now can point out to us what to look for within the data delivered by the actual world.[25]

Finally, this interpretation suggests how we should now proceed in our own philosophical endeavors: concentrate upon the material universe and so observe the actual men and women, animals, flowers, and nonliving stuff it contains. From them comes our everyday knowledge of existence, actuality, perfection, limitation, imperfection, deficiency, and the like. Directly perceived, they put across the message that they do actually exist and what they are. And the question now confronting us concerns them in their day-by-day actual situations: does the fact *that* they do actually exist furnish an evidence different from *what* they are? Apparently the only philosophical way of determining whether the answer is yes or no is by looking at them long and hard.[26] This project we shall undertake next.

2. Two Initial Considerations

Our survey of Thomas' endeavors to establish the real distinction has focused attention on how precisely to put the question. What must be asked is: Is the fact that this man *actually exists* genuinely different from the fact that he is *this man*? If so, the first fact reveals a component actually present within, which can be called "act of existing" because of its function and which is other than his quiddity or essence (that by which he is what he is—this man). Why so? Because diverse evidences indicate the actual presence of diverse components (see Chap. III, Sec. 1). Consequently, the act of existing in this human existent is really distinct from his quiddity; thus, their real distinction is a mere corollary of one's affirmative answer to that initial question.

Obviously, one's energy must be expended especially upon that question.

---

[25] His function with reference to philosophy is, then, just that: to indicate evidence we might otherwise miss. But we formulate and assent to conclusions only if we see that evidence and if it warrants them. In general, a Thomistic philosopher is one who finds that the evidence adduced by Thomas for his stand on existence and other matters is still genuine and valid, and who then elaborates the same conclusions. If he should accept that position simply because it is Thomas', he may be a Thomist, but he is no philosopher.

[26] For our earlier recommendations of turning to actual existents and of sharpening our awareness of them, see Chap. II, p. 18 and the texts quoted in notes 3-7.

But first let us briefly discuss two preliminary points: first, what a real distinction precisely entails; second, what "actual existence" signifies when one asserts, for example, "Someone actually is downstairs" or "That kind of fruit tree actually does exist."

(a) WHAT IS A REAL DISTINCTION?

What a distinction, in general, is and what a real distinction is can both be answered by looking at the following statements.

    1. " 'Garment' and 'clothing' are synonymous and, hence, are distinct from one another only in spelling."
    2. "Stan Musial is distinct from cosmonaut Alan Sheppard."
    3. "Musial's substantial form is distinct from his prime matter."

As can easily be gathered from those examples, "to be distinct from" means "to be other than" or "not to be identical with." Distinction, then, is some sort of otherness, some kind of absence of identity. If that condition arises because of my mental activity, it is merely a *mental* distinction.[27] But if it reflects the actual items in question themselves, it is a *real* distinction. Independently of my knowing them, Stan Musial actually is other than Alan Sheppard, his substantial form actually is other than his primary matter.

Notice that Statements 2 and 3 indicate there are at least two sorts of real otherness and nonidentity—that between two individual men and that between components within one and the same man. For clarity and convenience we need two adjectives to differentiate them. Let us arbitrarily call the first "a real *major* distinction" and the second "a real *minor* distinction." [28]

How do we know that the first sort is present? By such obvious signs as physical separation (for example, Mr. Musial is here, Mr. Sheppard is there) and so on. And the second? By diverse evidences

---

[27] As an example consider Statement 1, where "garment" is other than "clothing" only in spelling—when I predicate them both of this coat, they have one and the same meaning.

For more information on various sorts of mental distinction, see Chap. V, n. 29; Chap. VI, notes 39 and 42.

[28] One should guard against thinking that the second adjective in the phrase "real minor distinction" transforms the distinction into a mental one. It does not: one component, which is distinct from another according to a real but minor distinction, is actually not the other. The adjective "minor" states that the distinction is real but is not the same sort as a real major distinction.

within one and the same essential unit. For example, in the accidental order change (loss and acquirement of various individual perfections) is really other than stability (specific continuity), and hence accidents are really distinct from substance. In the substantial order change (loss and acquirement of specific perfection) is really other than stability (corporeal continuity), and therefore substantial form is really distinct from prime matter.

Manifestly, when we ask whether in this man the act of existing is really distinct from his essence, the question concerns a real *minor* distinction because it involves components within the same essential unity. And how will we know whether they are so distinct? Not because they are separated or separable (such is the criterion for a real major distinction), but because there are diverse evidences within one and the same existent—that is, the fact that he *actually exists* is not the same as the fact that he is *this man*. Such is the criterion and, apparently, the sole criterion, and this emphasizes again what we said at the outset of this section—energy must primarily be spent upon determining whether or not the fact *that* actual things exist is genuinely different from *what* they are. And that determination demands, as we also have already said before, that we look long and hard at actual existents, a requirement which leads to the next point on the signification of "actual existence."

(b) WHAT IS "ACTUAL EXISTENCE"?

In his famous discussion of time, St. Augustine remarks: "What is time? If no one asks me, I know; but, if I want to explain it to a questioner, I do not know." [29] What he says concerning time fits also the situation of anyone trying to express what "actual existence" means. Everyone understands immediately and easily what it is—"That type of fruit tree actually does exist," "There actually is a city called Paris," "Someone actually is downstairs now." But putting our meaning into words is another and difficult matter.

Recently, though, a young lady did put it in picturesque words and succeeded rather well. In the following report she is describing what she experienced when confronted with the fact that she had been an illegitimate child.

> I remember walking that day under the elevated tracks in a slum area, feeling the thought, "I am an illegitimate child." I recall the

---

[29] *Confessions*, XI, Chap. 14 (Bourke trans., p. 343).

sweat pouring forth in my anguish in trying to accept that fact. Then I understood what it must feel like to accept, "I am a Negro in the midst of privileged whites," or "I am blind in the midst of people who see." Later on that night I woke up and it came to me this way, "I accept the fact that I am an illegitimate child." *But* "I am not a child anymore." So it is, "I am illegitimate." That is not so either: "I was born illegitimate." Then what is left? What is left is this, "*I Am.*" This *act* of contact and acceptance with "I am," once gotten hold of, gave me (what I think was for me the first time) the experience "Since I Am, I have the right to be."

What is this experience like? It is a primary feeling—it feels like receiving the deed to my house. It is the experience of my own aliveness, not caring whether it turns out to be an ion or just a wave. It is like, when a very young child, I once reached the core of a peach and cracked the pit, not knowing what I would find and then feeling the wonder of finding the inner seed, good to eat in its bitter sweetness . . . It is like a sailboat in the harbor being given an anchor so that, being made out of earthly things, it can by means of its anchor get in touch again with the earth, the ground from which its wood grew; it can lift its anchor to sail, but always at times it can cast its anchor to weather the storm or rest a little. . . . It is my saying to Descartes, "*I Am, therefore* I think, I feel, I do."

It is like an axiom in geometry—never experiencing it would be like going through a geometry course not knowing the first axiom. It is like going into my very own Garden of Eden where I am beyond good and evil and all other human concepts. It is like the experience of the poets of the intuitive world, the mystics, except that instead of the pure feeling of and union with God it is the finding of and the union with my own being. It is like owning Cinderella's shoe and looking all over the world for the foot it will fit and realizing all of a sudden that one's own foot is the only one it will fit. It is a "Matter of Fact" in the etymological sense of the expression. It is like a globe before the mountains and oceans and continents have been drawn on it. It is like a child in grammar finding the *subject* of the verb in a sentence—in this case the subject being one's own life span. It is ceasing to feel like a theory toward one's self. . . .[30]

Obviously, her experience consisted in part of cutting away from existence what is nonessential ("I am an illegitimate child . . . I am illegitimate or, rather, I was born illegitimate . . . I *Am*"). It culminated in a vivid awareness of what actual existence is like—the deed

---

[30] See R. May, *Existence: A New Dimension in Psychiatry and Psychology* (New York: Basic Books, Inc., 1958), p. 43.

to one's house, one's own aliveness, the inner seed of a peach, the anchor of a sailboat, the first axiom in geometry, Cinderella's shoe, the subject of a sentence, and so on. Those figures of speech pointed to what it is: the absolutely basic fact which gives her be-ing and courage in be-ing ("Since I Am, I have the right to be") and which grounds her thinking, feeling, and other activities ("*I Am, therefore* I think, I feel, I do").

To supplement her account, let us attempt a less imaginative explanation by reflecting upon the existential judgment, "Someone actually is downstairs now." As a first step we should reduce that judgment to simply, "Someone actually *is*," thereby eliminating the spatial and the temporal from the notion of actual existence. Actually to exist is not the same as to be in space and time because some items which actually exist (for example, our activities of intellection and free choice, our human souls themselves) transcend the here and now, and also because actual existence reveals itself to be as free of space and time as of illegitimacy or any other nonessential factor. What, then, is the meaning of the statement, "Someone actually *is?*" Negatively, that the person in question is not the result of our imagination or fantasy or daydreams. Positively, that he actually is present rather than absent,[31] he actually is outside nothingness, he possesses the status of be-ing rather than that of not be-ing.

Admittedly, all such descriptions are inadequate, but they will suffice if they are constantly supplemented by our immediate experience of others and especially of ourselves as actually being present outside nothingness and confronted with nonselves.[32]

3. The Crucial Question

Let us now ask: Is the fact that something *actually exists* really different from the fact that it is *something?* Are there any indications that such is the case?

---

[31] Remember, though, that *presence* should not be equated with *presence in space and time*.

[32] Note C. E. Peirce's description: ". . . the being of an individual thing of fact, the being which consists in the object's crowding out a place for itself in the universe, so to speak, and reacting by brute force of fact, against all other things. I call that existence" (*Collected Papers of Charles Sanders Peirce*, ed., Arthur Burks, Charles Hartshorne, and Paul Weiss [Cambridge, Mass.: Harvard University Press, 1931-1958], I. 19).

I would say yes, and this unhesitatingly and certainly. Let us develop and substantiate that affirmative answer in two stages, the first of which (actual existence cannot be mere efficiency) is preparatory for the second (actual existence is other than an existent's quiddity).

(a) ACTUAL EXISTENCE IS NOT EFFICIENCY

First of all, then, what does the adjective "real" mean? It means simply this: "that which has value, worth, perfection." [33] Most philosophers would agree with that answer, but disagreement begins in deciding what factor ultimately causes value, worth, and perfection. Is it the fact that something is material and quantitative, as positivists and other materialists claim? Or is it immutability, as Platonists maintain? Or is it absolute change, as Heraclitus and Sartre answer? [34] No, I would reply, it is actual existence. By the very fact that something actually exists it achieves perfection and value and significance. To realize the difference actual existence makes, one need only reflect on the contrast between what is merely possible and what is actual—the mere thought of a thick steak in contrast to the piping hot, juicy steak actually on the platter set before us; the mere thought of a cold bottle of beer in contrast to the one actually stored in the refrigerator; the mere thought of one hundred dollars in contrast with the one hundred dollars actually in one's pocket; the mere thought of a perfect friend and companion contrasted with the one we actually may have found. That list could be continued indefinitely, but enough has been said to make clear that the difference between the items contrasted is not in *what* they are: a hundred dollars when actual contains not one dollar more than when merely thought of; a bottle of beer, whether in my mind or actually in our icebox, contains the same ingredients. The difference resides in actual existence, in the fact that what was

---

[33] Value, worth, and perfection can be of least three sorts: *arbitrary* (exemplified by paper money: the government arbitrarily declares this piece of green paper to be worth one dollar, this piece ten dollars, and so on); *subjective* (for example, the special value which a watch acquires in my eyes because given to me by my brother); and *objective* (the worth which is embedded in the object itself, which in fact *is* the object). Throughout Section 3 we will speak of value, worth, and perfection in the objective sense.

[34] For Sartre, fluency or change is what is real (see Chap. II, Sec. 2). Paradoxically and perversely, though, it is a reality linked with nonreality, a value equivalent to no-value, being pregnant with nothingness and annihilation. But such is all that existents within his universe are and have, hence the forlornness and nausea caused within them.

once only a thought now actually does exist. And this transition from the merely possible to the actual is simultaneously a transition from the nonperfect to the perfect, from what is without value and worth to what is valuable and worthwhile. Because it does contribute perfection, value and worth to existents, then, actual existence is the factor which makes them real. Despite what radical essentialists may say, it does not nullify, but literally *realifies* them. It does not detract from, but adds to them. It does not lessen, but enhances them.[35]

From the fact that actual existence is what makes an existent be real, it follows that actual existence is necessarily intrinsic to that existent.[36] Why so? Because it helps to constitute him, to set him up,

---

[35] This position is in direct opposition to that of the radical essentialists. For them, to be real is to be immutable. But strict immutability is found solely in the realm of the possibles. Hence, the possibles alone are truly real, and actuality as such is synonymous with unreality. Accordingly, the transition from the state of possibility to that of actuality is a going from the real to the unreal, from the perfect to the imperfect, from being to nonbeing, since by that transition immutable essences are immersed in a world of flux and instability. If one insists, "Surely some positive difference must exist between an essence as possible and as actual," the answer is that the difference is no intrinsic change within the essence for the better (in fact, the essence as actual is less real than when possible), but is merely the addition of the notion of efficient causality. An actual essence is simply an-essence-as-efficiently-produced. In such an interpretation, evidently, actual existence looked at positively *is* the essence and is identified with the essence. Viewed of and in itself, it is nothing, it is unreality and non-being.

On the other hand, if to be real is to be actual, then actual existents alone are truly real, and possibles are on the side of unreality and nonbeing. (They are real only through extrinsic denomination insofar as they are such as to be capable of actualization.) The passage from possibles to actuals is, then, a going from nonbeing to being, from the valueless to the valuable, from the unreal to the real. Consequently, actuality is a positive factor in existents, which is over and above efficiency and which will eventually show itself to be other than what the existent is.

In summary, one can say that one's acceptance or rejection of the real distinction between existence and essence is consequent upon his acceptance or rejection of actuality as the heart of reality.

[36] Something can be intrinsic because it is physically contained by another. For example, the penny within my pocket is intrinsic to the pocket. Or something can be intrinsic because it is identical with or a constituent of another. For instance, lungs are intrinsic to the human body also because they are integral parts of it.

It is especially in the latter sense that actual existence is intrinsic to the existent, because it is a constitutive factor of the existent as the inner source of his reality. In this sense, an efficient cause is extrinsic to the existent it produces because it is really other than its product.

to account for him; as the source of his reality, actual existence is also the source of his perfection, value, and worth. But an existent is nothing more than perfection, value, and worth concretized and realized. He *is* what constitutes him, and his constituents are identical with him. Hence, as a constituent, actual existence is a factor intrinsic to him.

The result is that his state of actuality is not explicable simply through efficient causality, as the essentialists would have it. Actuality is not merely a possible essence in relationship to God or some other agent. True, efficient causes are required, but they always remain other than, and in that sense are extrinsic to their effects. But the fact that this man actually exists is an internal factor which conditions everything about him. It permeates and realifies every fiber of his being. Actuality is, then, an intrinsic condition of each existent and amounts to a good deal more than setting an essence into a context of efficiency. It is the existent himself viewed in the light of what internally perfects, ennobles, constitutes, and realifies him.

(b) ACTUAL EXISTENCE OTHER THAN QUIDDITY

What precedes has prepared us for the next stage. Having shown actual existence to be intrinsic to the existent, how can we now indicate that it is really other than his essence, which obviously is also an intrinsic factor in him? How point out that the fact Paul actually exists is genuinely different from the fact that he is Paul?

The first indication is an immediate sequel of the fact just discussed —that actual existence causes an existent to be real. If the function of actual existence within an existent is to realify, then his quiddity (the other intrinsic factor) is what is realified. If the former perfects, then the latter is perfected.[37]

------

[37] This relationship between actual existence and the quiddity has important consequences. The fact that actuality perfects what an existent *is* does not deny that his whatness may itself entail perfections, but they are perfections subordinated to and dependent upon actual existence. Provided this man actually *is*, then he is *this man* and almost anything can happen. He can become wise and just and skilled. But there is wisdom, there is justice, there is skill only if there are wise, just, and skilled men actually existing.

Expressed somewhat differently: it is important that Shakespeare was Shakespeare, that Toscanini was Toscanini, that Einstein was Einstein, that John F. Kennedy was John F. Kennedy. But in order that Shakespeare should have been

But that which realifies and perfects cannot simultaneously be that which is realified and perfected;

Therefore, *that* things actually exist is genuinely different from *what* they are.

The second indication is a reflection upon another facet of the actual universe. The extremely numerous and varied existents within our universe have one thing in common: the fact that they do actually exist. I can correctly say of this man, this giraffe, this heliotrope, this piece of cobalt, this galaxy of stars that each actually is. But each is unique in *what* it is: this man is not this giraffe or this star—in fact, this man is not that man. They are alike in *that* they are, they differ in *what* they are.[38]

But what is common cannot simultaneously be what is unique;

Therefore, *that* things actually exist is genuinely different from *what* they are.

Other indications of a similar nature could be given, but let us conclude this section by turning to examples of the intuition Maritain describes as "metaphysical" (see Appendix A). For the French author that unique, immediate, sudden awareness is an insight into *being*[39] and terminates especially in an awareness of the act of existing.[40] But the intuitions communicated to me by acquaintances seem rather to

---

Shakespeare, he first had to *be* (and the same, obviously, for Toscanini, Einstein, Kennedy). All the perfections expressed by "Shakespeare" depend upon the fact that Shakespeare actually existed.

[38] This relationship too (between actuality and what an existent is) has significant consequences. The fact that actual existence is a perfection common to all existents indicates that it is independent of any one of them: in order to have actuality one must have some whatness or other, but not *this* one. Otherwise, actuality would be confined to this one existent. Accordingly, although any "thisness" is absolutely dependent on existence, the latter is dependent on the former only relatively and with qualification.

One should remember that the fact something actually exists has already been shown to have two characteristics. It is an intrinsic, constitutive factor of the existent, and thus is not merely a relationship to efficient causes (see Sec. 3a of this chapter). Secondly, it is not the same as being in space or time, or, even more generally, as being material (see Sec. 2b of this chapter). Without those two characteristics somehow established, the current indication that actual existence is other than essence lacks force.

[39] This point he stresses in *Preface to Metaphysics* (New York: Sheed & Ward, 1948). See Appendix A.

[40] This he stresses in *Existence and the Existent* (New York: Pantheon Books, Inc., 1948). See Appendix A.

be a vivid, enduring awareness that they actually exist and that this fact is of prime importance, affecting them profoundly.[41] Thus, this awareness is a stone which kills two birds because it points to the fact that actual existence is a factor of importance and perfection within the existent, and thus also implies its otherness from what the existent is. Here are some samples.

> It has been so long ago, but this is the way it seems to have happened. I was lying in bed waiting for sleep to come when it seemed as though the rest of the created universe had faded into nothingness and that one lone being existed in that void or vacuum and that I was that being. I was intensely conscious of myself, of the fact that I had a body, and of my distinctness from all other things.

Again:

> One evening when I was a senior in high school, I was walking down a long corridor of school at the end of which a window allowed entrance to the rays of the near-setting sun. Between myself and the window, I discerned the silhouettes of my school friends among the long shadows. The difference between the force of my being and theirs, between my knowledge of my own being and theirs at once struck me. I seemed cut off from and yet existing with other things.

Again:

> Two weeks following my first year in college . . . I recall sitting on a hill on a farm where I had spent my memory-filled childhood years and watching a small group of children playing in the yard of a nearby farm down a long, declining slope about a third of a mile away. At some intervals their voices would come through just as clearly as if they were a few feet from me and just as suddenly I could see them playing as before but their happy, carefree, childish voices would not carry to the spot where I was sitting. . . . I clearly recall how I felt at the time. Perhaps this awareness was predominantly unconscious, perhaps not, but I had some vague, yet definite awareness that "I now existed—objectively."

----

[41] Raïssa Maritain's intuition (reported by Jacques Maritain, *Preface*, p. 48) seems to have been of the same sort, since it contains an explicit awareness of existence: "I have often experienced in a sudden intuition . . . the profound first principle which makes me exist outside nonentity." Such too is the experience of the young lady reported (p. 77 f.).

Again:

> There were two windows in my bedroom. My bed was in such a position that I could look out both of them without getting up. I woke up once in the middle of the night and sat up in bed. Somehow the night and the stars shot a message into me. I felt a real surge of joy in just being (although I don't think the word *being* occurred to me at all).

Finally:

> The evening before the priest at a parish mission service had given a sermon on heaven and hell and had stressed their eternity by some such example as the following. Say a man walks for a million years down a road which has no end—he would cover a long distance and yet actually he would be no closer to the end of that road now than at the beginning of the world, for the road has no end. So too a soul after death lives for a million years, yet that soul then is no closer to annihilation than at the beginning, for it is eternal. . . . The next morning during class (sun streaming through windows of the second-floor sophomore classroom) I was suddenly struck by what it meant for me to exist for all eternity and that this unique person would *be* forever. This realization has never left me.[42]

Such, then, are some instances of intuitions which have actually occurred. As we have already mentioned, Maritain interprets such experiences as insights into being as being and into the act of existing itself. I would rather describe them as insights into actual existence as

---

[42] Frequent examples of similar intuitions occur in literature. For instance, see F. Mauriac, *Questions of Precedence* (New York: Farrar, Straus & Co., Inc., 1959), p. 46: "Was I 5 or 10 years old when I used to stand for hours in front of the looking-glass . . . amazed at the thought that I really existed. . . ." Edgar Allan Poe, *The Pit and Pendulum* (New York: Modern Library, Inc., 1938), p. 246 sq.: "Very suddenly there came back to my soul motion and sound—the tumultuous motion of the heart, and, in my ears, the sound of its beating. Then a pause in which all is blank. Then again sound, and motion, and touch—a tingling sensation pervading my frame. Then the mere consciousness of existence, without thought—a condition which lasted long. Then, very suddenly, thought and shuddering horror. . . . In the return to life from the swoon there are two stages: first, that of the sense of mental or spiritual; secondly, that of the sense of physical existence." Fyodor Dostoevsky, *The Idiot* (New York: The Macmillan Company, 1923), p. 224: "Those moments were only an extraordinary quickening of self-consciousness . . . and at the same time of the direct sensation of existence in the most intense degree."

a fact and evidence—the people involved vividly and suddenly become aware that they actually do exist and how supremely important that fact is. Existence as a fact and evidence is, of course, nothing but existence-as-a-component-manifesting-itself and will readily disclose its message when one reflects (for instance) in metaphysics class upon the fact that diverse evidences indicate the actual presence within of components and upon other relevant matters. But some such reflection (however rapid and implicit) seems required, for otherwise the intuition will remain a never-to-be-forgotten psychological experience without formally and explicitly introducing one into metaphysics itself.

Moreover, Maritain makes such intuitions absolutely indispensable for metaphysics—if someone has never had one, he cannot possibly be a metaphysician.[43] I would agree that some sort of personal awareness of the supreme importance of actual existence is absolutely necessary, but I would say intuition is only one way of gaining that awareness. It can also be achieved by making the reflections suggested in the two previous stages (see above, #a and #b).

Summary. Such, then, are considerations designed to show that the fact something actually exists is an evidence really different from the fact that it is something.

First, realize that actual existence is an intrinsic condition of every existent because it is the source of his reality and perfection, and next, that it is other than what he is because the former is what perfects and is common, the latter is what is perfected and is unique.

Second, utilize metaphysical intuitions, which also can underwrite those same two points.

What is the import of this new and different evidence? It reveals the actual presence of a new and different component—that by which an existent actually exists. This revelation will be clear when we formulate the basic process in the next section.

4. The Process

[Directly perceived fact:] An actual material existent
    (a) not only is *what* it is (Paul is this man)
    (b) but also *actually exists* (Paul *is*);
But evidence #a is other than evidence #b (see Sec. 3);

---

[43] See J. Maritain, *Degrees of Knowledge* (London: Geoffrey Bles, 1959), p. 215. Also see Appendix A.

But diverse evidences indicate the actual presence within of diverse
components;

Therefore, such evidences indicate that an existent is actually made
up of two real and distinct components:

    (a) that by which it is *what* it is—"Essence" (that is, the com-
posite of substance [prime matter/substantial form] and accidents);

    (b) that by which it *actually exists*—the "Act of Existing" or
simply "Existence."

This process indicates both that such components actually do exist
and, to a degree, what they are (as the previous processes concerning
accidental modifications had done for substance/accidents [see Chap.
III, Sec. 3] and substantial modifications for matter/form [see Chap.
III, Sec. 4], what we say in the next paragraphs will parallel what we
previously remarked with respect to the former processes).

This process establishes their actual presence because the relationship
between an evidence and a component is that between an effect and
its intrinsic cause. But an effect of an intrinsic cause is present only
because what causes it is also present. But the fact that a material
existent does exist and the fact that it is this existent are genuinely
different evidences (effects), and hence indicate the really distinct
components actually present within (causes).

It also shows, to an extent, what those components are, and once
again the force of the fact that a material thing is an intrinsic unity is
apparent. As we have often remarked before, an individual man is not
a mere accidental unity such as is an army or a soccer team, in which
the parts are themselves individual men and, thereby, are intrinsically
and entitatively independent of the whole which they help constitute.
Rather he is an intrinsic or *per se* unity, whose parts depend internally
and entitatively upon him. Nevertheless, the whole (here, the man)
is not any one of its parts, nor is any part the whole. Still both the
whole and its parts are real (because actually present). Consequently,
there is a difference between the reality of the whole and of the parts,
between what the whole is and what each part is. Let us again express
this difference in terms of "that which" and "that by which." The
whole (the man himself) is *that which* exists. His act of existing is
that by which he actually exists.[44] His essence is *that by which* he
exists as this individual man.

---

[44] The stringent unity to be found in a man (or, for that matter, in any
unum per se) indicates there to be only one act of existing within him. One

Once again, our knowledge of such components is more than direct perception. True, we directly perceive that we ourselves and other material existents do exist, and, within limits, what we and they are. This perception we express in judgments, which furnish the starting point of our process.[45] But our awareness of existence and essence precisely as components transcends mere perception. We reflect upon the data offered through perception. We intellectually realize that the fact this man actually exists offers an evidence really different from the fact that he is this man (see pp. 79-86), that diverse evidences indicate the actual presence of diverse components causing them, and that consequently this human existent, as well as any other material existent, is made up of diverse components called "act of existing" and "essence." This last stage is an assent of the intellect to which it is forced by that twofold evidence: "In this human existent there actually *is* an act of existing, which is really other than his essence." [46] In brief, the process terminates in intellectual judgmental knowledge, by which we become aware that such components exist and what they are.

Existence as a component, then, is known by reflection upon perceived data, and this reflection is a genuinely intellectual operation. We cannot directly perceive it. We cannot picture or imagine it. We know it through genuine intellection.

The process we are currently considering also indicates that the relation between essence and existence is one of potency to act. The function of an act is to confer a perfection, to actuate, whereas that

---

and the same act actualizes the substance and accidents which constitute the individual essence. No accident, then, has its own act of existing; each is existentialized by the single act existentializing the whole. In short, there is no *esse accidentale*. In itself, the act of existing is neither accidental nor substantial. These adjectives can be applied to it only through extrinsic denomination—one and the same existence can be called "substantial" insofar as it is actualizing the substance and "accidental" insofar as it is actualizing the accidents (of course, through the substance in which they inhere).

See James A. Albertson, S.J., *"Esse* of Accidents according to St. Thomas," *Modern Schoolman*, 30 (1953), 265-78.

[45] On existential judgments, see E. Gilson, *Being and Some Philosophers* (Toronto: Pontifical Institute of Mediaeval Studies, 1952), especially Chap. 6, pp. 190-215; Robert J. Henle, S.J., *Method in Metaphysics* (Milwaukee: Marquette University Press, 1951); *idem,* "Existentialism and the Judgment," *Proceedings of American Catholic Philosophical Association*, 21 (1946), 40-53.

[46] This distinction between existence and essence is, of course, a real *minor* one. See pp. 76-77.

of a potency is to limit a perfection, to be actuated, to be perfected. But existence as a component confers the perfection of actuality—it is that by which an existent transcends nothingness and nonbeing, and thus *is* and is real, and, thereafter, is in a position to achieve further perfections through subsequent activity. On the other hand, essence is that within an existent which is actualized and perfected by existence, which it simultaneously limits by confining it to *this* existent (for example, for one to be this man means automatically that he cannot be that man). Accordingly, existence and essence are related to one another as act to potency.

*   In fact, existence is *pure* act in the sense that insofar as it is itself concerned, it is *nothing but* act.[47] Its sole function is to actuate by actualizing, and, literally, realifying. Of itself it involves no potency. It is in no way perfected by essence. "But," someone may object, "the essence of, say, this human existent involves, besides prime matter, a human soul, intellect, will, other operative powers, and various other accidents. Surely, therefore, his essence involves perfections of its own, which it confers upon existence." No, I would answer, for the reason that his essence has those very perfections only because it *is* and is real, and thus only because and inasmuch as it is actuated by the act of existing.[48] The sole *rapport* which existence has to essence is that of what perfects to what is perfected, of what actuates to what is actuated.

*   "But," comes the rejoinder, "compare this man today on his twenty-fifth birthday with what he was twenty years ago. Today he is much more perfect physically, intellectually, and morally than he was

---

[47] The adjective, "pure," can also mean "subsistent." Only God is pure act in this sense, because He alone *is* existence and actuality. His very essence is existence. Existence in all other existents is received and limited by an essence which is a distinct component. Thus, existence in such existents is not subsistent, although it is a pure act inasmuch as of itself it is *nothing but* actuation.

[48] But is it not also true that in material existents one never finds an act of existence except with an essence? Accordingly, essence would seem equally important as existence. No, I would answer, and for this reason. Consider this individual human being. Existence is absolutely necessary for this individual human essence: it could not be this essence unless it *is*. But this individual human essence is not absolutely necessary for existence—otherwise, one could have the act of existing only when actualizing this human existent, with the result he would be the sole actual existent. But one finds many existents, each with an act of existing. Therefore, existence is absolutely necessary for this essence, but this essence is not absolutely necessary for existence.

as a five-year-old child. Surely, his act of existing twenty years ago
was in potency to what he is today; it was perfected by his development. If so, it does involve potency and cannot be pure act." Again,
no: his essence is that by which he then was in potency to those future perfections. His essence it is which was directly perfected by that
gradual growth in physical and other areas. No internal change took
place in his act of existence, which now at his twenty-fifth birthday
simply is actualizing what it would have actualized at his fifth birthday *had his essence then been such as it is now.*[49] In short, perfective
changes occur immediately only within the essence, which goes from
less to more perfect, whereas the function of existence, at no matter
what stage of development the existent finds himself, is simply to actuate by actualizing. It is, then, pure act.[50]

*   Next let us briefly examine the names given those two components. First, concerning "essence": what is the force of that noun? Why
use it to designate the component by which an existent is what it is?
What does it signify?

*   To begin with, whenever the human mind comes upon some
unknown thing (whether it be an object just appearing on the horizon or an abstract painting or a spaceship seen for the first time), it
automatically asks, "What is it?" Then an answer comes (sooner or
later, depending upon our previous experiences and knowledge), which
might run like this if the item in question is a spaceship: "It is some-

---

[49] Perhaps an example will help clarify the relation which the act of existing
has to the essence it is actualizing. Suppose that we compress a metal spring
and put it in a pasteboard box of such a sort that the cover of the box extends
down over the sides and thus can be raised gradually. Let us raise the cover
one inch. That raising of the cover allows the spring to expand now to where
it would have been at the very beginning if the cover then had been where it
is now. The change directly occurs in the position of the box-cover, but any
change there determines the extent of expansion of the spring.

The act of existing is like the compressed spring, the essence it actualizes is
like the box. Essence confines and limits existence to whatever size it is at any
stage in its development. As an essence gradually "grows," as it is perfected by
accidental changes, it allows existence gradually to expand to where it would
previously have been if the essence itself had then been that perfect. Existence
gradually actualizes what it would have actualized earlier had the essence then
been what it is now. Of course, if existence is in no way confined by an essence
distinct from itself, it is unlimited, and thus is infinitely perfect. God is such an
existent. He is existence; He is a spring uncontained in any box whatsoever;
He is pure actuality because He is subsistent existence. (See note 47.)

[50] For additional information on act/potency, see Sec. 6 of this chapter.

thing [here the answer arises from the intrinsic entity of the object] which is dazzlingly bright and moves fast [here the answer is from external appearances], which is made of such-and-such metals [here the answer is in terms of the material from which it is made], which is used for military purposes and for scientific research [here the answer is in terms of its final causes], and so on." The answer which the human mind elaborates expresses *what* the object is. Our intellect now knows what it is, now is aware of its whatness. And the term used to signify that awareness is "quiddity" ("whatness") or "essence."[51]

* Two points should emerge clearly from this analysis. First, there are many different ways of answering what a thing is, depending upon our approach, our level of knowledge, and the intricacy of the thing itself. Consequently, the awareness which "quiddity" or "essence" expresses, and thus the meanings it assumes, can themselves be multiple and varied. Second, one can ask, "What is it?" of any sort of item—of *per se* (intrinsic) unities (for example, "What is a man? a whooping crane? a mammal?"), of accidental unities ("What is an IBM machine? a lunar-ship? a family"), of integral parts of a *per se* unity ("What are the lungs? the liver? the heart?"), of components ("What is prime matter? an accident? the act of existing?"), of intramental items ("What is an irrational number? a surd? a logical species and genus?"). Since "essence" signifies simply the awareness we have of what such items are, it can be applied to all of them. In this sense, then, each of them has an essence. Each has something which initiates that awareness and is signified by that term.

* Let us restrict ourselves to what essence means with respect to a *per se* unit, such as this man. If we inquire what he is, we can give (a) a spontaneous, nonphilosophical reply or (b) a technical, philosophical reply. In the first way of answering we look upon him as a whole, in his entirety; in the second way we consider the components which constitute him. In the first way our knowledge becomes more and more determinate. For example, if I enter a room and unexpectedly come upon something under a sheet of canvas (let us say it will turn out to be a man who is bleeding), my first cognitive reaction is, "There's something or other underneath the sheet." Then as I con-

---

[51] For reasons of clarity and convenience, I am using quiddity and essence as synonymous. Other authors distinguish between them. For example, G. P. Klubertanz, S.J., *Philosophy of Being*, p. 112, n. 23: " 'Essence' implies that we are considering what a thing is as a principle of its being. 'Quiddity' implies rather an absolute consideration of what it is, as a pure intelligibility."

tinue to observe: ". . . which is alive . . . sentient . . . rational."
Such is essence when used in its nontechnical, everyday sense. The
essence of a man is to be something which is living, sentient, and rational. In this usage it signifies the man as a whole and is in no way
contrasted with the act of existing.[52]

* When taken in the other way (b), though, "essence" is a component, although here it can have at least two meanings. For a philosopher of nature, "essence" is the same as "substance." Thus, the essence
of this man consists of his substantial form and prime matter. His accidents are outside his essence.[53] But for a metaphysician, "essence"
includes both substance and accidents: it is everything in an existent
except his act of existing. Unless otherwise stated, such is the meaning
"essence" has in this book.[54]

* Next, what about "act of existing?" What is the force of that

---

[52] The meaning a logician and an epistemologist give to "essence" is similar
to (and arises from) that which it has in the spontaneous, nonphilosophical
approach. For example, according to logic and epistemology, "rational animal"
(specific essence) can be predicated of the whole (for example, "John is a rational
animal"), and thus must signify the whole. Again, "animal" (generic essence)
and "rational animal" differ from one another only as the less determinate differs
from the more determinate.

The upshot of this similarity is that essence for them is not a constitutive part
or component of a thing, but rather is *the thing itself*. Whenever one discusses
whether existence is really distinct from essence, one should remember that the
latter word is not taken in its logical and epistemological sense.

[53] Thus when we describe substance and accident on the level of philosophy
of nature, "essential" and "nonessential" are roughly equivalent to "specific-
generic" and "individual." Hence, to say substance is "that by which a thing
essentially remains what it is and yet receives various nonessential perfections"
is the same as saying substance is "that by which a thing specifically and
generically remains what it is and yet receives various individual perfections."
(A similar substitution can be made in the description of "accident"—see p. 60.)

[54] The different meaning "essence" has for a philosopher of nature and for a
metaphysician arises from the different aim each has. The former is primarily
interested in *natures* and in individuals only insofar as they share in, and thus
manifest, this or that kind of nature. But the latter is primarily concerned with
all actuals precisely as actual. Now that which is actual is each individual
existent, and his status of actuality embraces whatever is actually existing in him
—accidents as well as substance. Hence, "essence" for a metaphysician signifies
substance and accidents, whereas the same term for a philosopher of nature
bypasses accidents.

The following technical definitions attempt to emphasize this difference in
meaning. Essence for a philosopher of nature is "that by which this existent is
what he is as a member of such-and-such a species." Essence for a metaphysician
is "that by which this existent is what he is precisely as an existent."

phrase? Plainly, it describes the function of this component, which actuates a thing by causing it actually to exist. A substantial form actuates by specifying, an accident by conferring individual perfections, but the component we call "act of existing" actuates by actualizing and existentializing. It is the actuation which makes a thing be actually present outside nothingness and be a *being,* a term which means simply "that which actually exists." [55]

5. Summary and Conclusions

(a) From Chapter IV it is clear that discussion of the real distinction between existence and essence should begin with this crucial inquiry: Is the fact that something *actually exists* a really different evidence from the fact that it is *something?* If so, then the first fact points to an actually present component which is really other than essence, and, obviously, their real distinction follows as an immediate corollary.

(b) Is the fact, then, that this man *actually exists* a really different evidence from the fact that he is *this man?* Yes, for a reason which involves two stages of reflection.

1. *Actual existence is not explicable merely by an appeal to efficient causality,* as the following consideration makes clear:

> That which makes an existent real is that which contributes objective worth, value, perfection to it;
> But actual existence makes that contribution;
> Therefore, actual existence literally *realifies* the existent and all its parts;
> But whatever thus realifies an existent and all his parts is intrinsic to him;
> Therefore, actual existence is intrinsic to the existent: it permeates him as that which actualizes and realifies him;
> But efficient causality is other than its effect (the existent), and in this sense remains extrinsic to the existent;
> Therefore, actual existence cannot be identical with efficient causality: it is not merely the existent-as-efficiently-caused, it is more than an essence set within a context of efficiency.

---

[55] For more information on "being," see Chap. VI, Secs. 1 and 2; also see Appendix B.

2. *Actual existence is really different from the other intrinsic factor in the existent—namely, from what he is,* as these two arguments show:

> Actual existence realifies and perfects, his quiddity is realified and perfected;
> But that which realifies and perfects cannot simultaneously be that which is realified and perfected;
> Therefore, *that* things actually exist is genuinely different from *what* they are.

> Actual existence is a factor common to all existents; what each is, is unique;
> But what is common cannot simultaneously be what is unique;
> Therefore, *that* things actually exist is genuinely different from *what* they are.

(c) Accordingly, the fact that an existent *actually exists* is an intrinsic factor in him and is a really different evidence from the fact that he is *this existent.* Hence, it points to a hitherto overlooked component, which can be called "act of existing" in view of its function.

(d) In virtue of the process used in arriving at this component, we know both that it is actually present within an existent and also what it is.

The *"act of existing"* is *"that by which an existent actually exists."* It is the actuation by which a thing is actually present outside nothingness and nonbeing and is no longer imaginary, fictional, or merely possible. *"Essence"* is the counterpart of the act of existing, from which it is distinct by a real minor distinction. As understood by a metaphysician, it encompasses everything in an existent except the act of existing. It is *"that by which an existent is what it is."*

Although what the process has as its starting-point and constant center of reference is actually perceived data (especially important are existential judgments), still those components themselves are known by reflection upon that data, and this reflection is a genuinely intellectual operation, terminating in intellectual judgments. Those components cannot be directly perceived or imagined or pictured but are known by genuine intellection.

The relation between existence and essence is that of act to potency inasmuch as the function of the former is to actuate by actualizing and realifying the latter, which simultaneously receives and limits the former. In fact, existence is *pure* act insofar as in itself it is *nothing but*

act, nothing but actuation. Of itself it involves no potency; it is in no
way perfected by essence. Its sole task is to actuate by actualizing.

* 6. Act and Potency

The last point provides an occasion of clarifying our position on
act/potency. According to some prominent philosophers, this doctrine
comes at the very beginning of metaphysics and then is used to establish subsequent doctrines. For example, Henri J. Renard, S.J., first
works out the "general aspects of this theory [of act and potency]" [56]
in a chapter which culminates in three sets of important conclusions.

> [First:] All beings subject to change must be composed . . . of act
> and potency. . . . A pure act is not subject to change, for it has
> no potency, but is all perfection. . . . Act and potency adequately
> encompass being, for whatever exists is either pure act or a composi-
> tion of act and potency.[57]
> [Second:] Every finite, limited perfection requires an intrinsic po-
> tential principle, which limits it and to which the act is proportioned.
> Consequently, by way of immediate deduction, an act existing with-
> out a limiting potency must be infinite in its own order, and neces-
> sarily unique in that order. Wherever beings are found to be many
> and limited, they must be composed of two principles: one we call
> the actual, the other the potential and limiting principle.[58]
> [Third:] Adequately distinct concepts of realities indicate always a
> real distinction between these realities, even though they be united
> to form an essence, or a being that is strictly one [and, hence, act
> and potency are really distinct].[59]

Renard next applies those general propositions to the three "orders of
existence, of essence, and of activity" [60] and thereby proves that a material existent consists of three sets of constitutive parts—existence/
essence, substantial form/primary matter, and accidents/substance.[61]
Despite the attractive clarity of this approach, we have preferred to

---

[56] Henri J. Renard, S.J., *Philosophy of Being*, 2nd Ed. (Milwaukee: The
Bruce Publishing Co., 1946), p. 17.
[57] *Ibid.*, p. 25.
[58] *Ibid.*, p. 37.
[59] *Ibid.*, p. 44.
[60] *Ibid.*, p. 15.
[61] *Ibid.*, pp. 46-77.

proceed differently. First we established that such components actually do exist within an actual thing and what their natures and functions are[62]—accidents confer individual perfections upon the substance, which simultaneously receives and limits them; substantial form specifies prime matter, which at the same time limits it as the ultimate principle of its individuation; existence actualizes and realifies the essence, which simultaneously confines and limits it. Quite obviously, accidents, substantial form, and existence have a similar function—they confer perfections. Their counterparts (substance, prime matter, and essence) also have a similar function—they limit those perfections. How can we describe those common functions more conveniently and accurately than by utilizing Aristotle's notions of act/potency?[63] Accidents, substantial form, and existence are acts; substance, prime matter, and essence are potencies. This description was made after the process establishing each set of components had been completed.

Hence, our approach is almost the reverse of such metaphysicians as Renard. For them the doctrine of act/potency comes at the very beginning of metaphysics and is an instrument for proving that an existent is made up of various components. For us it comes only after the components have themselves been uncovered and merely summarizes their roles in relation to one another. For them the doctrine is a principle and starting-point, for us it is a corollary and sequel.

In our approach, general propositions concerning act and potency can also be formulated, but this occurs only at the very end of the process, after we know that various components are actually present within the existent and after we realize that their reciprocal functions of conferring and limiting a perfection are aptly expressed by the notions of act and potency. Then we can inspect the various components now depicted as acts and potencies and draw up whatever summary statements they suggest. As an example, consider the following.

(a) All the various acts and potencies are real, since various evidences have indicated them to be actually present within an existent.

(b) They are also really (and minorly) distinct from one another, as is clear from the fact that the evidences which manifest them are genuinely different.

(c) They are components. This important fact entails several con-

---

[62] This we did by relying upon the diverse evidences an individual material existent provides—change/stability on the accidental level, change/stability on the substantial level, the fact that something actually exists/the fact that it is something.

[63] On Aristotle's doctrine, see pp. 48-49.

sequences. First, because they are components, acts and potencies are dependent upon one another and are ordered to one another.[64] Second, an act or a potency cannot exist without its countercomponent, although there are exceptions to this statement—after death the human soul exists without prime matter; some operative powers can be without actually acting.[65] The third consequence concerns the role acts and potencies have towards one another in one and the same order and with reference to one and the same perfection. The function of act is to confer that perfection, that of potency to receive and limit it. Within such a context, then, act of itself says only perfection, whereas potency of itself says only capacity and limitation.[66] Finally, because they are

---

[64] Although acts and potencies are *mutually* dependent, they are not *equally* so. An accident is more dependent upon substance than substance is upon the accident. Prime matter depends more upon substantial form than substantial form does upon prime matter. This essence is more dependent upon the act of existing than the act of existing is upon this essence. For a clarification of this point, see n. 48 above and also Chap. V, Sec. 3.

[65] For instance, when we close our eyes, we no longer see and yet retain our power to see.

[66] The phrases, "in one and the same order and with reference to one and the same perfection" and "within such a context," are important for an accurate understanding of this consequence, as the following point reveals. Although accidents, substantial form, and existence are all acts, still only existence is pure act, because it alone is *nothing but* act and perfection. The perfections which the other two confer are not absolute ones. From one point of view, they are themselves limited. For example, a dog's substantial form is *of itself* without the perfection of a man's substantial form. The limitation which prime matter works upon it is that it be *this* canine soul and not that it be canine rather than human. This latter restriction issues immediately from itself. Hence, a substantial form is an act which says only perfection, but merely in a certain order, merely with reference to the limitation issuing from prime matter: the form does not immediately individuate itself. Hence it involves only perfection, but merely within a curtailed context.

In summary: although an act of itself says only perfection, still not every act is *pure* act (*nothing but* act or perfection), because some acts, while unlimited in one order, are limited of themselves in another order. Only the act of existing is pure act, because actual existence transcends all limitation; it is perfection and nothing but perfection in every order; it is in no way restricted of itself to individuals within the same species or even to any species whatsoever; it is a perfection common to absolutely all existents—to creatures and to their Creator.

Incidentally, by a parallel reflection one can easily see that not every potency but only prime matter is pure potency. Although other potencies (substance, essence) *are* potencies with reference to the acts they receive and limit, from another point of view they are more than mere recipients, more than absolute limitations. Intrinsically they also involve acts of their own (substance = prime matter/*substantial form*; essence = substance/*accidents*).

One should remember, also, that although within a certain context an act of

components, acts and potencies are simultaneously known within the existent because they are indicated by evidences within one and the same thing. But this is also true: an existent is known through its acts —I can know what sort of thing this or that existent is only through its operations, and, even more radically, only if it actually exists. Moreover, within an existent a potency is known and described through its act—for example, substance is "that by which a material thing . . . *receives various individual perfections,*" or prime matter is "that by which a material thing *receives a substantial form* and yet which is capable . . . of *receiving other substantial forms.*" [67] In fact, all potencies can be classified as operative or entitative precisely because of the acts to which they are ordered. They are operative if the acts are either operations or the direct results of operations (that is, operative dispositions and habits). They are entitative if the acts directly pertain to the thing's entity. [68]

Here, then, is the procedure followed with respect to act/potency. First, we realized that accidents/substance, substantial form/prime matter, and existence/essence actually make up an individual existent and that the function of accidents, substantial form, and existence is to confer perfections, whereas that of substance, prime matter, and essence is to limit them. In the light of those functions we next described these components as related to one another as act and potency. Only then did we formulate general propositions concerning acts and potencies, and these are based on reflection upon actual components previously verified.

But let us return to our consideration of the act of existing and now especially in the primacy it has both in reality and in metaphysics.

---

itself says only perfection, still some acts (namely, existence and substantial form) mediately limit themselves. So too, although a potency itself says only limitation, still substance mediately perfects itself. See Chap. V, Sec. 3.

[67] See Chap. III, "Summary and Conclusions," #c1 and #d1.

[68] In line with this classification, operative potencies are all faculties (for example, intellect, will, external and internal senses) and operative powers (the vegetative powers of nutrition, growth, and reproduction). All other potencies (prime matter, substance, essence) are entitative.

The classification of potencies into natural and supernatural (or, more traditionally, obediential) is made on a similar policy. A potency is natural if the act to which it is ordered is on the natural plane (for example, substance with reference to various accidents, the human soul with respect to intellect and will). It is supernatural if the act to which it is ordered is supernatural (for example, the human soul with reference to sanctifying grace, the intellect with reference to faith, the will with respect to charity). See Chap. IX, n. 53.

SUGGESTED READINGS

Anderson, James F., *Metaphysics of St. Thomas Aquinas.* Chicago: Henry Regnery Co., 1953. A selection of quotations on metaphysics from the writings of St. Thomas.

Aquinas, Thomas, *On Being and Essence,* trans. Armand A. Maurer. Toronto: Pontifical Institute of Mediaeval Studies, 1949.

Bourke, Vernon J., *The Pocket Aquinas.* New York: Washington Square Press Pocket Books, Inc., 1960. Excerpts from thirty-two of Aquinas' writings.

Clarke, S.J., W. Norris, "The Limitation of Act by Potency: Aristotelianism or Neo-Platonism?" *The New Scholasticism,* 26 (April, 1952), pp. 167-94. A controversial interpretation of act and potency in Aquinas.

———, "What Is Really Real?" in *Progress in Philosophy,* ed. James A. McWilliams, S.J., pp. 61-90. Milwaukee: Bruce Publishing Co., 1955. On various meanings of "real" and "being"; on the "possibles."

De Raeymaeker, Louis, *The Philosophy of Being,* trans. E. H. Ziegelmeyer, S.J., pp. 115-55. St. Louis: B. Herder Book Co., 1954. A history of the real distinction between the act of existence and essence.

Eslick, Leonard J., "The Real Distinction," *The Modern Schoolman,* 38 (1961), 149-60.

Gallagher, Donald A., "Contemporary Thomism," in *A History of Philosophical Systems,* ed. V. Ferm, pp. 454-70. New York: The Philosophical Library, 1950.

Maurer, Armand A., "Form and Essence in the Philosophy of St. Thomas," *Mediaeval Studies,* 13 (1951), 174-76.

———, "Revived Aristotelianism and Thomistic Philosophy," in *A History of Philosophical Systems,* ed. V. Ferm, pp. 197-211. New York: The Philosophical Library, 1950.

Owens, Joseph, "Unity and Essence in St. Thomas Aquinas," *Mediaeval Studies,* 23 (1961), 240-59.

Phelan, Gerald B., "The Existentialism of St. Thomas," *Proceedings of American Catholic Philosophical Association,* 21 (1946), 25-40.

Pieper, Josef, *Guide to Thomas Aquinas,* trans. Richard and Clara Winston. New York: Pantheon Books, Inc., 1962. Aimed at helping a student to read Aquinas intelligently.

Sweeney, S.J., Leo, "Existence/Essence in Thomas Aquinas' Early Writings," *Proceedings of the American Catholic Philosophical Association,* 37 (1963), 97-131.

———, "Scholasticism," *Collier's Encyclopedia* (New York: P. F. Collier and Son, 1961), Vol. 20, pp. 487-89. An aid to intelligent reading of Aquinas and other scholastics.

Van Roo, S.J., William, "Act and Potency," *The Modern Schoolman,* 18 (November, 1940), 1-5.

Walton, W. M., "Being, Essence, and Existence for St. Thomas Aquinas," *Review of Metaphysics,* 3 (1950), 339-65.

CHAPTER V

Primacy of Existence in Existents

The importance of actual existence has been frequently emphasized by G. K. Chesterton, but nowhere better, perhaps, than in this paragraph.

There is at the back of all our lives an abyss of light, more blinding and unfathomable than any abyss of darkness; and it is the abyss of actuality, of existence, of the fact that things truly are, and that we ourselves are incredibly and sometimes almost incredulously real. It is the fundamental fact of being, as against not being; it is unthinkable, yet we cannot unthink it though we may sometimes be unthinking about it; unthinking and especially unthanking. For he who has realized this reality knows that it does outweigh, literally to infinity, all lesser regrets or arguments for negation, and that under all our grumblings there is a subconscious substance of gratitude.[1]

---

[1] G. K. Chesterton, *Chaucer* (New York: Pellegrini and Cudahy, n.d.), p. 33.

Actual existence is, then, that which perfects an existent and is the factor he has in common with all, whereas his quiddity is that which is perfected and is unique. As we have previously seen (Chap. IV, Sec. 3b), that which perfects and is common cannot be identified with that which is perfected and is unique. Therefore, actual existence is an evidence genuinely different from what an existent is, and thus points to a new component, conveniently called "act of existing" in view of its function and really distinct from the essence it actualizes.

The previous chapter has aimed at establishing the real distinction between existence and essence. In the present chapter we shall endeavor to explicitate what was already implied in the real distinction— the act of existing has primacy over essence. After first outlining what such a primacy entails, we shall next indicate the reasons why the act of existing enjoys such a status: (a) it is the source of all other perfections, (b) it is autodetermining, and (c) it is amaterial.

1. "Existence Precedes Essence"

If we ascribe primacy to the act of existing what does this primacy entail? If we consult a dictionary, primacy is defined as, "State of being prime, or first, as in time, place, rank, etc." [2] Let us omit the reference to time and place, for actual existence is not temporally or spatially prior to essence. This definition is then adequate as a starting-point, since primacy for actual existence does point to the first-rank position it occupies in importance because of its nature and function. As we have already seen, an essence is potency in the order of being, and even in its own order is always a combination of potency/act,[3] whereas actual existence is pure act in any existent whatsoever.[4] Of itself it says *nothing but* actuation and perfection. It receives no perfection from any essence. Its sole function is to perfect, to actualize, to realify. Moreover, any essence whatsoever absolutely depends upon the act of existing actualizing it, since this latter is absolutely necessary for that essence. Yet no one essence is absolutely necessary in order to have an act of existing. For example, consider this individual human person.

---

[2] *Webster's New Collegiate Dictionary* (Springfield, Mass.: G. & C. Merriam Company, 1953), p. 670.

[3] That essence does itself combine potency with act should be clear from the fact that it involves not only prime matter but also substantial form and accidents. See pp. 88-90, 96-98.

[4] See Chap. IV, notes 47-49.

Existence is absolutely necessary for this individual human essence: it could not be this essence unless it *is*. Even in its very "thisness" it depends upon actual existence. But this individual human essence is not absolutely necessary for existence—otherwise, one could have the act of existing only when actualizing this human existent, with the result he would be the sole actual existent. But one finds many existents, each with an act of existing. Therefore, existence is absolutely necessary for this essence, but this essence is not absolutely necessary for existence.

Primacy for the act of existing, then, emphasizes the pre-eminent place it occupies because of its nature and function. This pre-eminence can be well expressed by a statement used by radical existentialists, provided it is correctly interpreted—"Existence precedes essence." What does such an existentialist as Sartre intend by it?

In him it can have at least two meanings, which are quite different but closely related. First of all, existence precedes essence by abolishing and destroying it. This destruction arises from the fact that every existent is nothing more than a mere stream or series of appearances. This identification of existence and reality with total fluency automatically entails that no existent can have any stable nature or essence.[5] Nor does he have one even in the mind of God, and this for an obvious reason: "There is no human nature, since there is no God to conceive it." [6]

In its second signification, the statement is entirely restricted to men.

> If God does not exist, there is at least one being in whom existence proceeds essence, a being who exists before he can be defined by any concept, and . . . this being is man, or, as Heidegger says, human reality. What is meant here by saying that existence precedes essence? It means that, first of all, man exists, turns up, appears on the scene, and, only afterwards, defines himself. If man, as the existentialist conceives him, is indefinable, it is because at first he is nothing. Only afterward will he be something, and he himself will have made what he will be. Thus, there is no human nature, since there is no God to conceive it. Not only is man what he conceives himself to be, but he is also only what he wills himself to be after this thrust toward existence.[7]

What is Sartre saying? An individual man first appears on the scene, turns up, begins to exist and only then defines himself, changes from

---

[5] See Chap. II, Sec. 2.
[6] *Existentialism* (New York: Philosophical Library, 1947), p. 18.
[7] *Ibid.*

nothing to something, chooses what he wants himself to be,[8] hurls himself toward a future,[9] plans himself,[10] fashions his image of man as he thinks he (and all others) ought to be.[11] His prior existence (appearance on the scene, turning up, actual presence in the absurd universe) allows him to determine, fashion, plan himself, his image, his future—in a word, his "essence." At first sight existence precedes essence here by causing and preserving it rather than by destroying it. But the essence which a man attempts to build up for himself must be deceptive and illusory if Sartre's view here is to be consistent with his identification of reality with fluency and appearances.

> By reducing the existent to the series of appearances which mani-
> fest it. . . . we certainly thus get rid of that dualism which in the
> existent opposes interior to exterior. There is no longer an exterior
> for the existent if one means by that a superficial covering which
> hides from sight the true nature of the object. And this true nature
> . . . no longer exists. . . . For the being of an existent is exactly
> what it appears.[12]
> Things are entirely what they appear to be—and behind them . . .
> there is nothing.[13]
> The diversity of things, their individuality, were only an appear-
> ance, a veneer. This veneer had melted, leaving soft, monstrous
> masses, all in disorder.[14]

If indeed reality *is* absolute flux and mere appearances, then man can no more have achieved any sort of permanency (and, hence, genuine nature) for himself at the end of his career than he had at its beginning. The result: here again existence precedes essence or nature by destroying it.

But however one interprets Sartre,[15] the precedence of existence over essence is quite clear in the authentically existentialist approach we have been making. It entails both that existents have genuine es-

---

[8] *Ibid.*, p. 20.
[9] *Ibid.*, p. 19.
[10] *Ibid.*
[11] *Ibid.*, pp. 20-22.
[12] *Being and Nothingness* (New York: Philosophical Library, 1956), p. xlvii.
[13] *Nausea*, p. 131.
[14] *Ibid.*, p. 171.
[15] For interpretations of Sartre, see James Collins, *The Existentialists: A Critical Study* (Chicago: Henry Regnery Co., 1952), p. 60 sq.; J. Maritain, *Existence and the Existent* (New York: Pantheon Books, Inc., 1949), p. 3 sq.

sences or natures and that these are subordinated to the acts of existing actualizing them.

First of all, then, each material existent has an essence—that by which it is this man or this dog or this maple tree. True, each has an essence ultimately because there is a God:[16] God sees Himself imitable in endlessly varied ways, and each creature is one of those ways, actualized and literally realized under God's free creative choice. But one need not assent to the existence of God in order to know that material existents have essences. Let him only observe himself and other existents. There he sees that an individual man is not absolute change or a mere series of appearances, but rather intimately combines change with stability. I who write these lines am basically the same person who some weeks ago wrote Chapter I and who many years ago learned to write in a Nebraskan schoolroom. You who are reading these lines are fundamentally the same person who read Chapter I at an earlier time and who learned to read some years previously under circumstances proper to you. Father Emaldi who related his experience under the Chinese Communists is the same man who previously performed his heroic act of courage in the face of their demands in 1951 and who had come to China in 1926. Each existent, then, combines accidental changes with specific stability, and this unique combination *is* his essence. Within each essence substance is the principle of specific continuity, as we have seen, and accidents account for the existent's development along physical, emotional, intellectual, cultural, and religious lines.

Each material existent, then, has a genuine essence because he is not pure flux but rather unites fluency to permanency within the confines of a single subject. His essence is not discovered in any separate realm of Essences (as Plato would have it), but as concretized in an actual existent. His essence is not static but dynamic and progressive,

---

[16] One can ground each existent in God even more precisely, but this grounding differs from philosopher to philosopher. According to Descartes (who had been anticipated in this by Abelard, Scotus, and Ockham), essences are what they are ultimately because God wills them to be such and such. A man is a rational animal and is thereby other than a canine animal or any other animal because of the divine will; $2 + 2 = 4$ because God so wills it. According to Leibniz and his brand of essentialists, essences are what they are entirely because of themselves and, thus, are ultimately independent of God.

A far better answer is that essences are what they are because God is what He is. In a universe where reality is actuality, God is subsistent actuality. He sees Himself imitable in infinitely varied ways, and each of those ways is a creature, which will actually exist if God freely creates it. In this interpretation divine will and intellect are themselves rooted in divine being.

because within itself it involves accidental changes. Yet those changes do not destroy it (as Sartre would have it) because it also involves substantial stability.[17] Such is the sort of essence each material thing has—a concretized, intimate fusion of change and stability, of accidents and substance.

But in any material existent its essence is also actualized by an act of existing which is other than itself (see Chap. IV, Secs. 3 and 4) and to which it is subordinated. Why the subordination? Because, as we have seen at the beginning of this section, it completely depends upon the act of existing existentializing it, since it has absolute need of it. Yet it is not absolutely necessary in order to have an act of existing. For instance, consider this dog. Existence is absolutely necessary for this particular canine essence: it could not be this essence unless it *is*. Even in its very individuality and particularity it depends upon actual existence. But this individual canine essence is not absolutely necessary for existence—otherwise, one could have the act of existing only when actualizing this canine existent, with the result that this dog would be the sole actual existent. But one finds many existents, each with an act of existing. Therefore, existence is absolutely necessary for this essence, but this essence is not absolutely necessary in order to have an act of existing. Thus, any essence is subordinated to the act of existing actualizing it.

Such, then, is force of "Existence precedes essence" when interpreted within an authentically existentialist context. The nouns in the statement refer to components within one and the same existent—*existence* to the act by which this man actually exists, *essence* to the concretized, unique combination of change/stability by which he actually exists as this man. Each component has its own function—the act of existing actualizes and realifies the essence, which simultaneously limits it by specifying-individuating-individualizing it (see n. 18). Of these two components actual existence is the more important, for in any existent the essence absolutely depends in its very uniqueness and "thisness" upon the act of existing: it could neither be this essence nor perform its proper function unless it *is*. But no one essence is absolutely neces-

---

[17] Even a substantial change does not annihilate the essence, because death entails not only change (the loss and acquirement of specific perfections) but also a corporeal continuity. This latter is indicated by the fact that what was living and is now nonliving retains temporarily the same shape, weight, and other appearances, and by the fact that the amount, kind, and location of the pure chemicals resulting after death are determined by the amount, kind, and location of virtual chemicals before death. The component underlying and causing such continuity is prime matter. See Chap. III, Sec. 4.

sary for the act of existing—it is discovered actualizing this human essence, that human essence, this canine essence, and so on. In brief, it is a perfection common to all existents and in this lies its precedence. Yet this precedence does not destroy but rather establishes and preserves the essence. As actualized and realified by the act of existing, an essence not only *is* but also is *itself*, and thus can and does perform its own task of specifying-individuating-individualizing the existent.[18] Although (and because) subordinated to actual existence, an actualized essence is genuinely real and makes a unique contribution to the existent of which it is a part.

Authentic existentialism, then, affirms "the primacy of existence, but as implying and preserving essences or natures and as manifesting the supreme victory of the intellect and of intelligibility." [19] It finds place for both actual existence and essence; the former is prior in nature and function to the latter, but in such a way that its priority safeguards and enhances the latter.

Let us now investigate in more detail at least three reasons why the act of existing enjoys such pre-eminent rank—it is the source of all other perfections, it is autodetermining, and it is amaterial.

2. Actual Existence and Other Perfections

In discovering whether all other perfections in an existent are ultimately grounded in its act of existing, one must first uncover what a perfection is. We commonly speak of a day or a flower or a picnic or a gentleman or a house as *perfect*, but what is meant? Let us concentrate upon a house which is actually being built. When can we describe it as "perfect"? When it is completely finished—when the last nail has

---

[18] As we shall see in Section 3, "Autodetermination," the act of existing limits itself, but this it can do only mediately, only through the essence it actualizes. Anyone who would reduce essence to a mere limit or negation so as to stress the primacy of the act of existing would thereby seem also to eliminate one of the prerequisites of that very primacy.

Incidentally, in the phrase, "specifying-individuating-individualizing," used to describe how essence limits existence, "specifying" refers to the function of substantial form within essence, "individuating" refers to that of prime matter, "individualizing" refers to that of accidents.

[19] J. Maritain, *Existence and the Existent*, p. 3. This interpretation of authentic existentialism is not accepted by everyone—for example, see John Wild, "Christian Rationalism (Aquinas, Gilson, Maritain)," in *Christianity and Existentialism* (Chicago: Northwestern University Press, 1963), pp. 40-65.

been hammered, the final coat of paint and varnish applied, and so on.[20] Then *it has everything which it should have in order to be a house.*

If we now turn from the adjective "perfect" and ask what the noun "perfection" signifies, the answer should be clear. A perfection is *that which an item ought to possess in view of what it is.* It is *a possession due to an existent.*

Perfections show themselves to belong to at least two classes. Some possessions are due to a material existent precisely *as material*—for example, this man's weight and size, his vegetative and sentient powers, all of which are intrinsically dependent upon his material status. But his intellect and will, together with the operations they elicit and the operative habits which reside in them, are intrinsically independent of matter. Thus, intellection, freedom, wisdom, and the like are possessions due to the spiritual side of his nature,[21] and hence are perfections of a different sort. To this second group belong also those possessions which are due to a material existent precisely *as existent*—existence itself, as well as unity, truth, and goodness, which are consequent upon being.

Accordingly, perfections are of two kinds:

(a) those whose very perfection contains some potentiality or limitation, and hence imperfection—these let us call "mixed";

(b) those which of themselves contain no limitation and imperfection—these let us call "pure." [22]

✳   One final point needs clarification before we investigate the act of existing and its relationship to other perfections. It can be stated in this manner: is perfection synonymous with act? Obviously not, because all the components of a material existent (both acts and potencies) are perfections; they are what it ought to have in order to be either material or an existent. This holds true even with respect to prime matter, which, say, this dog must have if he is to be dog and this dog.[23] Hence, perfection is not identical with act. Rather, some

---

[20] The English adjective "perfect" is derived from *perfectum,* the perfect passive participle of the Latin verb, *perficio* (to make, to complete) and means literally "that which has been completed, finished."

[21] On the meaning of "spiritual," see Chap. V, Sec. 4.

[22] What we here call "pure" perfections, M. R. Holloway calls "perfections proper to a being as being" (*Introduction to Natural Theology* [New York: Appleton-Century-Crofts, 1959], pp. 122, 132). See his entire discussion, pp. 119-24, 132.

[23] These statements can be made with reference to prime matter: (1) It is pure potency because of itself it is *nothing but* a recipient; it has no act of itself. (2) Yet it is a perfection because it is a possession which a material existent ought

perfections are potencies (that is, possessions [substance, prime matter, essence] by which an existent receives other perfections). Some are acts (that is, possessions [accidents, substantial form, act of existing] which an existent receives in and by his potencies).[24]

Having discussed what a perfection is and what the various kinds of perfections are, we are now prepared to ask explicitly what sort of perfection the act of existing is and how all other perfections are rooted in it.

These questions are easy to answer in the light of what has gone before. First of all, the act of existence *is* a perfection, since it is what any and every existent must have if he is to exist. It is a pure perfection, since of itself it contains no limitation and imperfection—it is limited only by the essence it actualizes; it is intrinsically independent of matter.[25] Moreover, it is the only component which even *as a component* is a pure perfection and a pure act. Of itself it is completely free from potency and says nothing but actuation, whereas all other components in an existent are in potency to it (see pp. 88-90).

But why is it the source of all other perfections? Because it is the ultimate reason why an individual thing has those other perfections, as the following argumentation shows.

> A perfection is a possession due to an individual man;
> But he has nothing unless he exists;
> But that by which he exists is his act of existing;
> Therefore, his act of existing is fundamentally that by which he has whatever he does have;
> Therefore, his act of existing is the ultimate source of all other possessions or perfections.

*   Let us apply this to the other components, one by one.

> The function of prime matter in an existent is to limit by individuating;

---

to have. (3) But it is a "mixed" perfection because even though it is a perfection, its very nature is to be a potency and a limitation.

[24] Manifestly, the classification here of perfections as potencies and acts is not identical with the previous one of perfections as mixed and pure. Some potencies entail pure perfections (for example, the operative powers of intellect and will), whereas some acts are mixed perfections (for example, such accidents as quantity and various qualities, substantial forms). The two classifications are made from different points of view.

[25] See Chap. V, Sec. 4.

But this function it can perform only if it actually *is;*
But that by which it actually *is* is the act of existing;
Therefore, that by which prime matter is enabled to individuate is, ultimately, the act of existing;
Therefore, this latter is the ultimate source of prime matter in itself and in its functioning.

The task which a substantial form performs in an existent is to specify—for example, a human soul makes the composite be human rather than canine or equine or geraniaceous or aqueous;
But this task the substantial form can perform only if it actually *is;*
But that by which it actually *is* is the act of existing;
Therefore, that by which a substantial form is enabled to specify is, in the last analysis, the act of existing;
Therefore, this latter is the ultimate source of substantial form in itself and in its functioning.

The function which accidents carry out is to confer individual perfections—for instance, a man's operative habits are that by which he is wise, prudent, temperate, modest, courageous, generous, mathematical, musical, philosophical, and the like; his operations are that by which he is actually thinking, analyzing, reasoning, remembering, loving, freely choosing, and so on;
But this function accidents can carry out only if they actually *are;*
But that by which accidents actually *are* is the act of existing;
Therefore, that by which accidents are enabled to confer individual perfections is the act of existing;
Therefore, this latter is the ultimate source of accidents in themselves and as carrying out their functions.

This entire section on existence and other perfections comes down to this: no component can be itself or exercise its own intrinsic sort of causality unless it *is.* Therefore, by causing every other component to *be,* the act of existing is the ultimate source of all the other components and of the perfections which they are.

Why, then, is that act the source of all perfections? Because it is the ultimate source of all actuality and, thereby, of all reality, for to be real is to be actual. And the fact that it is the source of all perfections reveals the primacy it enjoys within an existent.

3. Actual Existence and Autodetermination

Another revelation of that primacy comes from the additional fact that the act of existence is autodetermining. What does this self-determination involve?

The term is currently used in the daily newspapers with reference to the African and Asian colonies of various European nations. Those colonies which are about to be released from the status of colony find themselves in the process of what is called self-determination. That is to say, various avenues are open to them. They can remain within the economic and cultural orbit of the mother country (as happens, for example, when a British colony becomes a member of the British Commonwealth), they can gradually achieve complete autonomy, they can immediately sever all relations with the mother country, and so on. Of those different alternatives they freely decide upon one. In this free choice lies their self-determination—they themselves determine what sort of nation they will be.

In metaphysics, the term does not have reference to the free decision of a nation or even of an individual man.[26] Rather, it refers to the components within an individual material existent, and, more precisely, to the relationships which they have to one another as intrinsic causes of that existent.

In understanding this point, one must first realize that the verb "determine" can have at least two distinct but complementary meanings even in everyday situations. It can signify "to confer a perfection," as when we say, "Using milk rather than Scotch determines the kind of drink we make." It can also signify "to limit a perfection," as when we say, "The size of the glass determines the amount we drink."

If we apply this information to components, it is evident that the

---

[26] E. Gilson seems first to have used "autodetermination" in our sense. See *Le Thomisme: Introduction à la philosophie de saint Thomas d'Aquinas*, 5th Ed. (Paris: J. Vrin, 1948), p. 54: "Chaque essence est posée par un acte d'exister qu'elle n'est pas et qui l'inclut comme son *autodétermination*." Also see *idem*, *Christian Philosophy of St. Thomas Aquinas* (New York: Random House, Inc., 1956), p. 36.

Aquinas himself occasionally uses *determinare* in the twofold sense of conferring and limiting a perfection. On *determinatio* as conferment of perfection, see *In I Sent.*, d. 24, q. 1, a. 1 ad 3 (Mandonnet Ed., p. 577); *S.T.*, I, 44, 2 resp.; *ibid.*, I, 119, 2 resp. On *determinatio* as limit of a perfection, see *ibid.*, I, 80, 1 resp.; *ibid.*, 84, 2 resp.; *S.C.G.*, III, c. 66.

various acts within an existent determine by conferring perfections (let us refer to this meaning of "determine" as #1). For example, a man's accidents of mathematics and music determine him to be mathematical and musical, his substantial form determines him to be human rather than canine, his act of existing determines him to be existent rather than nonexistent. But his potencies determine by limiting perfections (let us refer to this meaning of "determine" as #2). For example, his intellectual ability and acumen determine how much mathematics he can achieve, prime matter determines him to be *this* man by ultimately individuating his substantial form, his essence determines him to be *this* existent by specifying-individuating-individualizing the act of existing actualizing him.

But what would *self*-determination mean? That an act would not only confer a perfection (and thus, as we would expect, determine the existent in sense #1 of the term), but would also limit itself through its partner-component (and thus determine itself in sense #2 of the term). Likewise, a potency would not only limit a perfection (and thereby, as one would expect, determine that perfection in sense #2 of the term), but would also perfect itself through that act (and thus determine itself in sense #1 of the term).

What decides whether a component, be it an act or a potency, actually is autodetermining? *The fact that the intrinsic causality it exercises upon its partner-component within the existent* (conferring or limiting a perfection) *is of such a nature that the latter relies absolutely upon the former in order to exercise its own intrinsic causality* (limiting or conferring a perfection).[27] If such is the case, if the former necessarily helps the latter in carrying out its own causality, if the former in the function it uniquely performs is absolutely necessary for the latter's function, then the former determines itself through the latter. If the former is an act, it limits itself through the potency it actuates ("determine" in sense #2). If a potency, it perfects itself through the act it receives ("determine" in sense #1).

---

[27] A somewhat similar relationship exists between the principal and instrumental efficient causes. Take the case of a teacher using a piece of red chalk to write a meaningful word on the blackboard. The proper effect of the chalk is that word *as red*. This it can cause, however, only insofar as it is moved by the writer. Hence, the chalk depends upon the principal cause in order to exercise its own proper causality. Because of this dependence, then, the writer also has produced the redness in the effect, although only through the instrument. On intrinsic causality, see pp. 223-24.

(a) WHICH COMPONENTS ARE AUTODETERMINING?

Which components are self-determining? This we can answer rather easily if we examine the intrinsic causality which various acts and potencies reciprocally exercise. Let us begin with prime matter and substantial form.

* Is, then, prime matter self-determining? Does the prime matter of (say) this man specify itself through his human soul? Does it even mediately humanize itself? It does if each proposition of the following line of argumentation turns out to be true.

> Substantial form determines [sense #1] prime matter by specifying it;
>
> But substantial form is specifically such and such only because it is individuated, because it is in this individual, because it is this individual substantial form—for example, a human soul is human only because it is *this* human soul;
>
> But prime matter is ultimately that by which the substantial form is individuated, that by which it becomes *this* form;
>
> Therefore, prime matter is mediately self-specifying through the substantial form, and thus is autodetermining [sense #1].

Is, then, prime matter mediately self-determining? Obviously not, for the second proposition of the argument is false. No substantial form is specifically such-and-such because of the individuation it receives from prime matter, for if this were the case, the substantial form could be found only in this individual. The species would be confined to him alone. Rather, the substantial form is what it is specifically *from itself,* from its own nature. A human soul is human rather than canine proximately because its very nature is to be human. Accordingly, the individuation which prime matter exercises upon a human soul does not make that soul be human or contribute directly to the humanization which the latter carries out in the existent. The result is that prime matter is not self-specifying, even through the substantial form it receives and limits.

* But is substantial form autodetermining? Does it mediately individuate itself? Once again, it does if each proposition of the following argument is true.

> Prime matter determines [sense #2] substantial form by receiving and individuating it;

But prime matter can receive and individuate the substantial form
  only if it is in an existent which is specifically such-and-such;
But that by which an existent is specifically such-and-such is the
  substantial form;
Therefore, the substantial form is mediately self-individuating through
  prime matter, and thus is self-determining [sense #2].

Is, then, substantial form mediately self-determining? Yes, since the
crucial second proposition of the argument is true. That is to say,
prime matter is the basic cause of individuation, because quantity, although a property of the composite and not of either form or matter
taken alone, flows more directly in the composite from prime matter
than from substantial form because it is a generic rather than a specific property of material things.[28] But prime matter cannot *by itself*
be the more immediate source of quantity because of itself it is only
pure potency. Quantity can issue from it only when it is informed,
only inasmuch as it is a component within an existent which is material, which is of such a nature as to be extended, as to have physical
parts outside of parts. But an existent has such a nature only insofar
as it is also aqueous or geraniaceous or canine or human, for we
never find any existent which is *only* material, which is without some
or other specific perfection. In brief, what makes a nature to be specifically such-and-such also helps make it to be material, because the
specific perfection is built upon the generic and carries it along.[29] But

---

[28] On individuation, see Chap. VI, Sec. 5b. Why is quantity not a specific
property? Because nothing exists simply as body, but always as such-and-such a
body—as aqueous body, living body, canine body, human body, and so forth.
Therefore quantity is not a specific property, and hence its more direct source
within the composite is not the substantial form, from which specific properties
more immediately flow. That source is, then, the other component within the
substance—namely, prime matter.

[29] In an actual thing, the specific perfection is not really distinct from the
generic. For example, a man's rationality is fundamentally identical with his
animality. In fact, his rationality permeates his entire sentient, living, chemical,
and material constitution. That is to say, his nature as rational is not really other
than his nature as sentient, as living, and as material. True enough, the properties which flow from that single nature as rational (intellect, will) are really
distinct from those issuing from that nature as sentient (internal and external
sense faculties), as living (vegetative operative powers), and as material (quantity). Also, his substance is made up of two really distinct components (prime
matter, substantial form), which provide an objective basis for the mental distinction between rationality and animality and the other essential perfections. But
the fact remains that those essential perfections are only mentally distinct (de-

that by which an existent is specifically such-and-such is the substantial form. Hence the substantial form, in carrying out its own function of specifying the existent, also enables prime matter to carry out its function of individuation. Accordingly, through prime matter the substantial form individuates itself, and thus is self-determining (sense #2).[30]

* Let us now turn to substance and accidents. First of all, is substance self-determining? Is it self-accidentalizing? Does it through accidents confer individual perfections upon itself? It does if all the propositions of the following process are true.

> Accidents determine [sense #1] by bestowing individual perfections upon substance—for example, a man's intellect is that by which he is capable of intellection, his will is that by which he is capable of free choice, his external senses are each that by which he is able to see or hear or taste and so on; his operative habit of mathematics is that by which he is capable of coping easily with problems concerning discrete and continuous quantity; his act of reasoning is that by which he actually goes from premises to a conclusion;

scribed by some as: *distinctio mentalis ratiocinati maior seu cum fundamento perfecto in re*). Why so? Because an individual man *is* an *unum per se*, as indicated by the fact that all those various operative powers cooperate together for the intrinsic good of themselves and of the whole. And, secondly, because "rational" and other terms expressing those essential perfections simply describe one and the same whole in a more or less determinate way.

[30] If the substantial form, indeed, is self-individuating, this fact may throw some light on the centuries-old problem of how prime matter can individuate a human soul (or, for that matter, any substantial form). How can individuality (with its connotations of uniqueness, autonomy, and perfection) be rooted in the component which is of itself only pure potency?

Various answers have been offered. Some distinguish individuality from individuation as the positive from the negative: "Individuality is the sum total of positive perfections pertaining to this individual as *this* individual. Individuation is the quasi-negative, limiting principle; individuality is the correlative, positive perfection (George P. Klubertanz, *Introduction to Philosophy of Being*, 2nd Ed. [New York: Appleton-Century-Crofts, 1963], p. 106, n. 15). For others, "the original and individual differences of each concrete being . . . are *made possible* by its matter [but] they *proceed from* its form, which alone gives actuality" (Etienne Gilson, *Spirit of Mediaeval Philosophy* [New York: Charles Scribner's Sons, 1940], p. 466, n. 7).

The answer which autodetermination offers need not detract from the above solutions; instead, it complements them. Prime matter does individuate the human soul insofar as it is the more direct source of quantity (and of materiality). But it can be this source only through the influence of the soul, which thereby individuates itself through prime matter. Hence, individuation and individuality arise indirectly from the soul itself.

> But accidents can bestow individual perfections only if they inhere in a substance and only because they are caused somehow by the substance;
>
> But, as we have just intimated, substance is that in which accidents inhere and that by which they are caused;
>
> Therefore, a substance confers individual perfections upon itself through its accidents, and thus is mediately self-determining [sense #1].

Is, then, substance indirectly autodetermining? The answer is affirmative because the crucial second proposition is true. The accidents mentioned in the first proposition (operative powers, operative habits, operations), as well as all other accidents, can confer individual perfections only by inhering in the substance which they perfect and through which they are existentialized—the substance is the channel through which the act of existing actualizing the substance also reaches the accidents.[31] Moreover, the substance causes its own accidents. It is what might be called the "emanative" cause of all its properties (for example, quantity, faculties, operative powers, and so on), which automatically and naturally flow (emanate) from it once it has itself been efficiently caused.[32] It efficiently causes others through its operative powers. For example, through its will it is the efficient cause of its free choices. Through its intellect it efficiently causes operations of reflecting and reasoning, which in turn produce various operative habits. Accordingly, by receiving and causing the very accidents which are individually perfecting it, the substance simultaneously is accidentally perfecting itself, and thus is mediately self-determining (sense #1) through those accidents.

＊ What about the accidents themselves? Are they autodetermining? First of all, some distinctions must be made before we formulate the argument. As we have seen in the previous paragraph, substance not only receives accidents but also causes them. Its efficient and emanative causal relationship to accidents will not be taken into consideration when we discuss whether accidents are self-determining, because autodetermination involves intrinsic causality. Also, by receiving acci-

---

[31] See Chap. IV, n. 44.

[32] On this causality see Michael Montague, S.J., "Active Causality," in *Proceedings of the Twenty-Third Annual Convention of the Jesuit Philosophical Association* (Woodstock, Maryland: Woodstock College Press, 1961), pp. 37-65. Also see Henri J. Renard, S.J., *Philosophy of Man*, 2nd Ed. (Milwaukee: Bruce Publishing Co., 1956), pp. 84-87.

dents, substance determines them in sense #2 of the verb: it limits them. Hence, in inquiring whether accidents determine themselves, we are taking the verb in the same sense: do they receive and ground themselves through the substance, and thus mediately limit and determine themselves?

* Second, the substance directly receives accidents which are properties, but only indirectly receives those which are not properties, since these it receives through the former. (For instance, operative powers [properties] inhere in the substance itself, whereas the operations and resultant operative habits which the substance produces through those powers reside directly in the latter and in the substance only through them.) Accordingly, the question of self-determination with respect to accidents can be twofold, depending upon whether we are considering those which are properties or those which are not.

* Because there are two kinds of accidents and because the relationship which substance has to each is somewhat different, we should not discuss the question of autodetermination with reference to accidents in general, but rather with reference to each of the two kinds. In order to simplify matters, though, let us restrict ourselves to properties.[33] Our question now is: are those accidents which are properties self-determining? Are they mediately responsible for their own reception and limitation?

* Once again, they are if the propositions of the following argument are true.

> Substance determines [sense #2] accidents[34] by receiving them;
> But substance can receive accidents only because it has the individual perfections which accidents confer and are;
> But accidents are each that by which a substance is individually perfected;
> Therefore, accidents receive and limit themselves through the substance, and hence are mediately autodetermining [sense #1].

In the light of that process, are accidents mediately self-determining? The answer is negative, because the second proposition is incorrect. The reason why substance can and does receive accidents is located in

---

[33] Besides, it is sufficient to inquire concerning properties, for if they do not receive and thereby ground themselves, *a fortiori* those accidents which are not properties will not either.

[34] Throughout this process and the rest of the paragraph, "accident" stands for "those accidents which are properties."

the very nature of the substance itself—in itself it is a potency to such accidental perfections and needs to be complemented by them.[35] Consequently, the individual perfections which accidents confer upon the substance are not the source of its receptivity and potentiality. Therefore, they are not even mediately responsible for their own reception and limitation. They are not self-determining.

Let us now turn to essence and existence, beginning with essence. Is the essence of this man self-determining? Does it actualize itself through the act of existing it is limiting? Once again, it does if the following propositions are true.

> The act of existing determines [sense #1] this essence by actualizing, realifying, existentializing it, and this task it performs because it is what it is—namely, actual existence;
> But the act of existing is what it is (that is, is actual, real, and existence) only because it is received and limited by this essence, only because it is *this* act of existing;
> But this essence is that by which the act of existing is *this* act of existing;
> Therefore, this essence actualizes itself through the act of existing, and thus is mediately autodetermining.

Is, then, this essence self-determining? Evidently not, because the second proposition is inaccurate, as will be clear if we refer to what we said some paragraphs back concerning substantial form/prime matter. A substantial form is not specifically such-and-such because of the individuation it receives from prime matter, for if this were the case, the substantial form could be found only in this individual. The species would be confined to him alone. Rather, the substantial form is what it specifically is *from itself,* from its own nature. A human soul is human rather than canine proximately because its very nature is to be human. Likewise, the act of existing is not what it is (the actualizing, realifying, existentializing principle) because it is actualizing this essence—otherwise, it could be found only in this one existent, who alone would be actual and existing. Rather, the act of existing is what it is *from itself,* from its own nature. Accordingly, the limitation which this essence carries out within the existent does not actualize and ex-

---

[35] The very nature of the substance also accounts for its causality with respect to accidents. For instance, intellect and will emanate from the human soul because by nature it is human. Sense faculties flow from the sentient composite because its very nature is to be sentient.

istentialize the act of existing. Hence, this essence is not self-actualizing, even through the act of existence it specifies-individuates-individualizes.[36] In a word, it is not mediately self-determining.

Finally, what of the act of existing? In this existent is it autodetermining? Does it mediately cause its own limitation? Does it indirectly specify-individuate-individualize itself through this essence? Once again, it does if each proposition in the following line of argumentation is true.

> This essence determines [sense #2] the act of existing by receiving it, by specifying-individuating-individualizing it, by limiting it;
>
> But this essence can receive, specify-individuate-individualize, limit only if it actually exists;
>
> But the act of existing is that by which this essence actually exists;
>
> Therefore, the act of existing specifies-individuates-individualizes and limits itself through this essence and, thus, is mediately self-determining [sense #2].

In the light of this argument, is actual existence autodetermining? Clearly yes, because the crucial second proposition is true. The essence in, say, this man can carry out its own unique causality of specifying-individuating-individualizing him only if it actually exists. The act of existing which it is receiving and limiting is absolutely necessary for it: it could neither be this essence nor perform its own causal function unless it *is*. Consequently, the act of existing specifies-individuates-individualizes and limits itself through whatever essence it actualizes, and hence is mediately autodetermining (sense #2).[37]

(b) CONCLUSIONS

If we look back on those previous paragraphs, these points should be clear—when autodetermination occurs, what it is, which components do determine themselves, why the autodetermination of other compo-

---

[36] One must remember that the essence of any material existent is always this essence or that essence and never essence simply. If this latter were the case, such an essence might conceivably be autodetermining as self-actualizing. But, actually, one never comes upon essence simply (which is an abstraction) but only this human essence, that human essence, this canine essence, and so on.

[37] For another approach to autodetermination, see Maurice R. Holloway, S.J., "Towards the Fullness of Being," *Proceedings of the Twenty-Fourth Annual Convention of the Jesuit Philosophical Association* (Woodstock, Maryland: Woodstock College Press, 1962), pp. 6-37.

nents is rooted in the act of existing, and, lastly, why the fact that the act of existing is mediately determining reveals the primacy it enjoys in an existent.

1. Autodetermination occurs whenever *the causal function of a component is absolutely necessary for that of its partner-component.* If so, this latter can carry out its own intrinsic causality within an existent only insofar as it is genuinely influenced by the former. By the necessary influence it exerts, then, the former determines itself through the latter.

2. Accordingly, *autodetermination* is *the self-limiting or self-perfecting property of a component whose causal influence necessarily permeates also that of its partner-component.* If an act, that component limits itself through the potency it actuates. If a potency, that component actuates itself through the act it receives and limits.

3. The components which are autodetermining are three—*substance, substantial form,* and *the act of existing.* The first is a potency, the last two are acts. Substance is self-determining (sense #1) inasmuch as it individually perfects itself through the accidents which it receives and causes (either emanatively or efficiently). A substantial form is self-determining (sense #2) insofar as it individuates itself through prime matter, which it informs and thereby allows to be the more direct cause of quantity. The act of existing is self-determining (sense #2) because it specifies-individuates-individualizes itself through whatever essence it actualizes.

4. The self-determination which characterizes the first two components is rooted in the act of existing, because a substance can receive and cause accidents (and thereby be the means by which accidents come to be existentialized) only if it actually exists. Likewise, a substantial form can inform and specify prime matter only if both these substantial components actually exist. Accordingly, the self-perfection and the self-individuation which, respectively, a substance and a substantial form achieve, rest on the act of existing.

5. Finally, the self-essentialization which the act of existing mediately achieves in each existent reveals the primacy this component enjoys. For actual existence in this man specifies-individuates-individualizes itself through this human essence by actualizing it. This actualization is absolutely necessary for this essence, for it can be this essence and can carry out its own causal function of specification-individuation-individualization only if it *is.* Even in its uniqueness and particularity it absolutely depends upon the act of existing, which, however, is relatively independent of it: in order to have an act of existing, there must be

some essence or other, but it need not be *this* essence. Consequently, in any existent the essence is subordinated to the act of existing which is actualizing it and which is thereby shown to have primacy in the existent. Because of its nature and function, it is pre-eminent in rank and importance.

4. Actual Existence and Amateriality

Another indication that the act of existence has primacy is its unique independence of matter even in a material existent.

In order to understand how extraordinary this independence is, let us contrast it with the immateriality to be found in other components. But this contrast requires that we first discuss what materiality is, since immateriality is its negation, and anything negative can be understood only in light of what is negated.

(a) MATERIALITY

What, then, is meant when we say that something is material? We mean that it is of such a nature as to have parts outside of parts, as to be actually extended, as to be directly in place, and so on. This meaning becomes clear when men, animals, plants, and chemicals are juxtaposed to such items as intellection, freedom, courage, unselfishness, love, value, and the like. The former all have at least this one common trait: each is of such a nature as to have parts outside of parts, as to be actually extended and directly in place. That common characteristic has come to be expressed by the term "material," which therefore means simply "that which is of such a nature as to have parts outside of parts, as to be actually extended and directly in place, and the like." [38]

* Of what can that term be predicated? Obviously, of all men, animals, plants, and chemicals, each of which receives the predication as *that which* is material.

* But each material existent is made of two components:

(a) *essence*—that by which that-which-is-material is precisely what it is (namely, material);

(b) and *act of existing*—that by which that-which-is-material actually exists.

---

[38] See p. 56.

Manifestly, the essence itself within a material existent also is strictly material, but only in the sense that it is *that by which* such an existent is material.[39]

*. But such an essence is itself constituted of prime matter, substantial form, and accidents. Can such components also be described as "material"? Since no essential component *in and of itself* has parts outside of parts or is actually extended or in place, each of them, when considered in itself, may be termed "immaterial" (thereby meaning simply "that which does *not* have parts outside of parts, and so on"). But since they actually go together to fashion a strictly material essence, each can also be called material through extrinsic denomination, meaning simply that it is a component of a material existent (to which the term is intrinsically applied) and, even more precisely, that it is a component of the essence within that existent. As a constitutive part of a material essence, it is within that by which a material existent is, precisely, material.[40]

*   But a material existent is not only made up of essence but also of an act of existing. Can this latter also be classified as "material"? Yes, and again through extrinsic denomination insofar as it too is a component of a material existent. But because it is other than the existent's essence (which is that by which the existent is material), the act of existence is not a component of the material existent as material, but only *as existent*. Consequently, one describes actual existence as material through extrinsic denomination in a different and weaker sense than when the term is applied through extrinsic denomination to the essential components.[41]

---

[39] Should "material" also be strictly predicated of quantity? Possibly, although differently than when predicated even of essence. The essence is material as "that by which that-which-is-of-such-a-nature as to have extended parts outside of parts does have such a nature." Quantity is material as "that by which that-which-is-of-such-a-nature as to have extended parts outside of parts does have such parts." It is the component within the essence which accounts for extension.

But one should remember that neither quantity nor essence is material as *that which* has parts outside of parts. Only the thing, the existent is thus material.

[40] Although prime matter, substantial form, and various accidents are all material through extrinsic denomination, yet they are not all equally so because of the varying degrees of dependency they have upon matter, as will be clear in the following section, "Immateriality."

[41] One might designate this difference thus: essential components are material through extrinsic denomination as "within the essence," *esse* as "within the existent."

(b) IMMATERIALITY

But all the components can be described as immaterial when viewed in and of themselves, inasmuch as none of them has of itself such a nature as to be actually extended and directly in place or to have parts outside of parts. Yet that blanket description is not very helpful, for components are immaterial in varying degrees in view of the different connection they have with matter.

The human soul, together with its faculties of intellect and will and the operations and operative habits it produces through them, is only, so to speak, *extrinsically* dependent on matter.[42] True, it is the substantial form of the body; it can be created only within matter, and the source of its natural intellectual knowledge is data it receives from the senses. Nonetheless, it also is an intellectual principle; it does have intellection and free choice as its typically human operations; it continues to exist after the human composite itself is dissolved at death. Accordingly, it is intrinsically independent of matter. This kind of freedom from matter is traditionally described by the term *"spiritual,"* meaning *"a component which is within a material essence and yet which is immaterial* [it does not have parts outside of parts] *in such a way as to be intrinsically independent of matter."*

All other essential components except the human soul and the accidents immediately consequent upon it (the faculties of intellect and will, their operations and operative habits) are intrinsically dependent on matter insofar as they totally rely upon the material status of the essence of which they are constitutive parts. And this total reliance extends not only to prime matter, quantity, and the physical qualities of, for example, this dog, but also to his soul, together with the sense faculties and other operative powers consequent upon it. This soul depends on matter from beginning to end in its very being and operations —it is educed from matter; it ceases to exist when the canine composite is dissolved through substantial change; all its operations occur necessarily within physical organs. Still none of those components, when considered in and by itself, has parts outside of parts or is actually extended and directly in place. Hence, each of them is in itself immaterial. But their immateriality cannot be described as "spiritual," because

---

[42] We presuppose what is said here of the human soul and its faculties and operations to be discussed and established elsewhere (for example, in the philosophy of human nature or sacred theology). We make use of it so as to understand *esse* and its immateriality better.

here the term expresses *"a component which is within a material essence and yet which is immaterial in such a way as to be intrinsically dependent on matter."* Let us say such a component is *"barely immaterial,"* the adverb differentiating its immaterial status both from that of the human soul and from that of the act of existing, to which we now turn.

This last component, too, is immaterial, because it obviously does not of itself have parts outside of parts and it is not actually extended or directly in place. Nevertheless, its immateriality is unique. True enough, in this man or this dog or this oak tree it is a constitutive part of a material existent, but it is there not because the existent is material but because he is an *existent*. In this it differs even from a human soul, which is a component of a material existent precisely *as material* (because it is part of his essence) and can begin to exist only through creation in matter as the substantial form of the body, and thus is at least extrinsically dependent upon matter. But the act of existing has no such dependency upon matter in any material existent whatsoever; hence it can hardly be described as "spiritual." Still less is it intrinsically dependent upon matter as is a canine soul or various other essential components. Hence it is not fittingly termed "barely material."

Such, then, is the extraordinary immateriality of the act of existing —*a component which is within a material existent and yet which is immaterial to such a degree as to be both extrinsically and intrinsically independent of matter* because it is other than his essence, whence arises his materiality. What is the best word for it? Manifestly, neither "spiritual" nor "barely immaterial" will do. Let us use *amaterial* and reserve it solely for the act of existing, thereby expressing that *of itself* it simply has no connection with matter whatsoever.[43]

Here, then, is a component whose unique status of immateriality arises from its unique nature and function. All other components are within a material existent because he is material, whereas the act of existing is present in him because he is an *existent*.

Little wonder, then, in view of its uniqueness, that the act of existing has primacy over essence in an existent.

---

[43] Traditionally, God and angels are also termed "spiritual" to express that the divine essence and an angelic essence are, each in its own way, entirely independent of matter. This is a legitimate and easily recognized extension of the term. They also can just as easily be described as "amaterial" through a similar extension of the latter term.

5. Summary and Conclusions

(a) In Chapter IV we aimed at showing that the act of existing is a component within an existent, really distinct from the essence it actualizes. In this chapter we have discussed the primacy which that act has within the existent.

(b) In what does that primacy consist? In the fact that the act of existing in any existent is such in nature and in function as to outrank the essence it actuates. It realifies and perfects; the essence is realified and perfected.[44] It is pure act, whereas an essence is solely potency in the order of being and even in its own order is always a combination of potency/act. Existence is absolutely necessary for any essence whatsoever, since no essence can be what it is unless it actually exists. But no one essence is absolutely necessary in order to have an act of existing; otherwise, existence would be confined to this one existent. It is a factor common to all existents; the quiddity is unique in each.

In short: existence precedes essence. In opposition to Sartre, we argue that material existents have genuine essences (concretized, intimate combinations of change and stability, of accidents and substance), but that they are subordinated to the acts of existing which actualize them and which relatively are more important.

(c) Can the reasons why *esse* is of greater importance and enjoys such precedence be stated more precisely and developed more thoroughly? First of all, the act of existing takes precedence because it is the perfection *par excellence* and because it is the source of all other perfections.

1. It is the perfection *par excellence* because it is what any and every existent must have if he is to exist. It is a pure perfection since of itself it contains no limitation and imperfection—it is limited only by the essence it actualizes; it is intrinsically independent of matter. Moreover, it is the only component which even *as a component* is a pure perfection and a pure act.

2. It is the source of all other perfections because of the fact that it is the ultimate reason why an individual thing has those other perfections, as this consideration shows.

---

[44] Obviously, these remarks refer directly to cases in which essence is other than *esse*. But even in God *esse* is paramount as the heart of His reality and root of all His perfections (see Sec. 6 of this chapter).

A perfection is a possession due to an individual man;

But he has nothing unless he exists;

But that by which he exists is his act of existing;

Therefore, his act of existing is fundamentally that by which he has whatever he does have;

Therefore, his act of existing is the ultimate source of all other possessions or perfections.

(d) The second reason for the primacy of the act of being is that it is autodetermining: it limits itself through the essence it actualizes. Why so? An essence limits the act of existing by specifying-individuating-individualizing it; but no essence can specify-individuate-individualize *unless it actually exists;* therefore the act of existing limits itself through the essence it actualizes by enabling it to be this or that essence and to carry out its causal function of specification-individuation-individualization. Even in its uniqueness and particularity, the essence of this man absolutely depends upon the act of existing, which, however, is relatively independent: in order to have an act of existing, there must be some essence or other, but it need not be this essence. Consequently, in any existent the essence is subordinated to the act of existing which is actualizing it, which thereby limits itself through the essence actualized and which is thus shown to have primacy in the existent.

(e) A final reason why the act of existing has primacy is its unique independence of matter even in a material existent: it has no direct connection with matter whatsoever, it is simply *amaterial.* Every component without exception is immaterial of and in itself in the sense that it itself has no extended parts outside of parts. But actual existence is extraordinary in that essential components are present in a material existent because the existent is material, whereas existence is present only because the existent is an existent. To express this diversity among components, let us say that

1. with the exception of the human soul (together with its intellect and will and their operations and operative habits), essential components are "barely immaterial" because *they are within a material essence and yet are immaterial in such a way as to be intrinsically dependent on matter;*

2. the human soul (as well as its intellect and will and their operations and operative habits) is "spiritual" because *it is a component within a material essence and yet which is immaterial to such a degree that it is intrinsically independent of matter;*

3. but *esse* is "amaterial" because *it is a component which is within a material existent but outside the material essence, and hence is immaterial in such a way as to be both extrinsically and intrinsically independent of matter.* Accordingly, the act of existing has no direct connection with matter at all, and thus is a component with a unique status of immateriality and with a consequent primacy over all essential components.

6. Actual Existence and God

This primacy makes the act of existing an excellent basis for easily proving the existence of God, because it reveals material existents to be signposts pointing to an Existent Who is totally greater and significantly other than themselves. Why so? Because actual existence, which is perfection *par excellence* and which is autodetermining and amaterial, is other than the essence of a material existent; hence it does not belong to the nature of any such existent: none exists of its very nature. Nevertheless, they do exist, they do have that supreme and unique perfection. Therefore, there must be an Existent Whose very essence is to exist, Who of His very nature is actuality and thus needs no cause, and yet Who can and does cause all else to exist.[45]

---

[45] But why must the cause be an existent in whom actual existence and essence are identical? Why could not other material existents suffice? Because also in such existents existence is really other than essence, and hence, instead of a solution we merely have another question: Who causes *them* to exist? We have only managed to transfer the problem back one step. No solution is possible as long as the cause posited is merely a creature: an existent (whether material or immaterial) whose existence is really distinct from his essence. No creature can properly cause the existence of another because one properly causes only what he causes in acting according to his nature, and it is not the nature of any creature to exist.

But might not an infinite series of such existents be an adequate cause? No, because even if creatures are endlessly added to other creatures, they still remain creatures, just as the endless addition of zeros to other zeros never amounts to anything other than zero, and creatures are zeros when it comes to properly causing existence. In a word, an infinite series is no more powerful than any one of its members, each of which is a creature and, accordingly, incapable of properly causing another creature to exist, as we have just seen.

On the impossibility of an infinite series, see Henri J. Renard, S.J., *The Philosophy of God* (Milwaukee: Bruce Publishing Co., 1951), pp. 22-25; Maurice R. Holloway, S.J., *Introduction to Natural Theology*, pp. 83-84; Arnold Benedetto, S.J., *Fundamentals in the Philosophy of God* (New York: The Macmillan

The situation here is like that which occurs when one sees a young, indigent, and (let us suppose) entirely honest child playing with a diamond necklace. We know that the youngster does not have those precious jewels of and from himself, and yet he now does actually possess them; therefore, someone must have given them to him. In a word, wherever there is a gift, there must also be a giver. The gift with regard to the very existential status of material things is their actual existence, and the donor is an Existent Who *is* actuality.

Rather obviously, this line of reflection not only establishes that God actually exists but also enables us to know to some extent the sort of existent He is.[46] In order to be the cause of existents in whom actual existence is really other than what they are, He must Himself not be that sort of existent. He is necessarily a noncreature. As we have already stated, He *is* actual existence, His very nature is to exist, and in Him existence is identical with what He is. The consequences of this identity are multiple and important. Actuality is being, its lack is nonbeing. Because God *is* actuality, He is Being, the subsistent and perfect fullness of reality. Moreover, since unity, truth, goodness, and beauty are all inevitable consequences of being (by the very fact and to the extent that something actually *is*, it is also one, true, good, and beautiful),[47] He is also subsistent unity, truth, goodness, and beauty. Furthermore, He is endowed with intellection, volition, love, and freedom, because these pure perfections[48] are ultimately rooted in and flow from actual existence. In order to know, choose, or love we must first actually *be*, but there are actual existents without knowledge, freedom, or love. Again, intellection is intellection only because there actually *are* beings which know; love is love and freedom is freedom only inasmuch as there actually *are* existents who love and freely choose. In brief, then, actual existence is more common, more universally present than

---

Company, 1963), pp. 44-49; G. Smith, *Philosophy of Being* (New York: The Macmillan Company, 1961), pp. 369-71.

For a nontechnical version of this line of reflection based upon the existentiality of things, see Jacques Maritain, *Approaches to God* (New York: Harper & Row, Publishers, 1954), pp. 1-15. It is what he calls, "The Primordial Way of Approach: Natural or Prephilosophic Knowledge of God."

[46] This knowledge will be largely negative and indirect because derived through creatures. On the difficulties encountered in knowing God, see Leo Sweeney, S.J., "Metaphysics and God: Plotinus and Aquinas," *Die Metaphysik im Mittelalter*, Vol. 2 of *Miscellanea Mediaevalia* (Berlin: Walter de Gruyter, 1963), pp. 232-39.

[47] On the transcendents, see Chap. VI, Sec. 3 sq.

[48] On pure perfections, see p. 108.

any other pure perfection, and it is the ultimate source for them all. Consequently, He Who *is* actuality is thereby also intelligent, loving, and free.

Admittedly, this sketch of God needs much development in order to be satisfactory,[49] but enough has been said, we hope, to indicate that the act of existing in its primacy and real otherness from essence allows us to answer affirmatively to the question, "Is there a God?" Yes, God does exist, because how else could these material existents possess actual existence, that pearl of great price? It is other than what they are; it neither has been nor is now nor ever will be part of their natures. And yet they do exist. Hence, there must be an Existent Who by nature *is* actual existence and Who is giving them that gift.[50] This Existent we call God, Who by the very fact He is *actuality* is also all-perfect (He possesses all pure perfections) and by the fact that He is *subsistent* actuality is infinitely perfect (He possesses each perfection in an unlimited degree).

Recently a British linguistic analyst openly admitted the awe he experiences from reflecting upon actual existence.

> The only rational thing to say if someone asks "Why does this table exist?" is some such thing as that such-and-such a carpenter made it. We can go back and back in such a series, but we must not entertain the absurd idea of getting back to something logically necessary. However, now let us ask, "Why should anything exist at all?" Logic seems to tell us that the only answer which is not absurd is

[49] Such development can conveniently be found in the basic treatises on natural theology cited in n. 45.

[50] Interestingly and significantly, James Collins recently reviewed the positions taken by modern and contemporary philosophers on God and then concluded that one can legitimately attain a philosophical knowledge of God only by moving from the structure of material existents precisely as existents. See *God in Modern Philosophy* (Chicago: Henry Regnery Co., 1959), pp. 394 and 399: "[The proposition that God exists] rests upon an inference, the force of which comes from the given, actual existents of our experience. The proposition which gives meaning and validity to our philosophical conception of God ultimately gets its causal foundation and inferential warrant from our analysis of composite, sensible beings. There is no more radically determinate and relevant a basis for assent than this one, since the inference is made and the assent given to God as a consequence of inspecting some given sensible things in their composing principles of being. . . . A humanly developed philosophy of God must examine the structure of the existing sensible thing of our experience, discover its intrinsic composition and causal dependence in being for its concrete act of existing, and in this way infer the truth of the proposition that there exists a first, purely actual cause of this being." See *ibid.*, p. 387.

to say, "Why shouldn't it?" Nevertheless, though I know how any answer on the lines of the cosmological argument can be pulled to pieces by a correct logic, I still feel I want to go on asking the question. Indeed, though logic has taught me to look at such a question with the gravest suspicion, my mind often seems to reel under the immense significance it seems to have for me. That anything should exist at all does seem to me a matter for the deepest awe. But whether other people feel this sort of awe, and whether they or I ought to is another question. I think we ought to. If so, the question arises: If "Why should anything exist at all?" cannot be interpreted after the manner of the cosmological argument, that is, as an absurd request for the nonsensical postulation of a logically necessary being, what sort of question is it? What sort of question is this question "Why should anything exist at all?" All I can say is, that I do not yet know.[51]

The awe he feels before existence is, as he has rightly concluded, no request for a logically necessary being.[52] Yet it is the initial and valid step towards an Existent Who is necessarily known to exist and to exist of His very nature, because material things do exist and yet in such a way that existence is always other than what they are. And this Existent we call God.

SUGGESTED READINGS

Aquinas, *Basic Writings,* ed. A. Pegis, Vol. I, pp. 18-24. New York: Random House, Inc., 1945. On the existence of God: the "Five Ways."

Gerrity, Brother Benignus, *Nature, Knowledge, and God,* pp. 188-210. Milwaukee: Bruce Publishing Co., 1947. On the meaning of "spiritual."

Gilson, Etienne, *Being and Some Philosophers,* 2nd Ed., pp. 152-215. Toronto: Pontifical Institute of Mediaeval Studies, 1952. On Aquinas' authentic existentialism: primacy given to the act of existence in existents and in metaphysics.

————, *Christian Philosophy of St. Thomas Aquinas,* pp. 29-45, 84-95. New York: Random House, Inc., 1956. On the act of existence: its primacy and autodetermination, its distinction from essence.

————, *Elements of Christian Philosophy,* pp. 43-87. Garden City, N. Y.: Doubleday & Company, Inc., 1960. On the "Five Ways" of Aquinas.

---

[51] J. Smart, "The Existence of God," in *New Essays in Philosophical Theology,* ed. A. Flew and A. MacIntyre (London: SCM Press, 1955), p. 46.

[52] See W. Norris Clarke, S.J., "Linguistic Analysis and Natural Theology," in *Proceedings of American Catholic Philosophical Association,* 34 (1960), 110-26.

————, *God and Philosophy*, pp. 38-73. New Haven, Conn.: Yale University Press, 1941. On the primacy given to the act of existence by Aquinas.

————, *The Spirit of Mediaeval Philosophy*, trans. A. H. C. Downes, pp. 42-63. New York: Charles Scribner's Sons, 1940. On God: His existence and nature.

Gornall, S.J., Thomas, *A Philosophy of God: The Elements of Thomist Natural Theology*. New York: Sheed & Ward, 1962.

Hawkins, D. J. B., *The Essentials of Theism*. New York: Sheed & Ward, 1949.

Holloway, S.J., Maurice R., "Towards the Fullness of Being," *Proceedings of the Twenty-Fourth Annual Convention of the Jesuit Philosophical Association*, ed. Leo Sweeney, S.J., pp. 15-37 and 57-82. Woodstock, Maryland: Woodstock College Press, 1962. An interpretation of autodetermination.

Maritain, Jacques, *Approaches to God*, trans. Peter O'Reilly. New York: Harper & Row, Publishers, 1954.

Owens, Joseph, *An Elementary Christian Metaphysics*, pp. 311-34, 335-64. Milwaukee: Bruce Publishing Co., 1963. On the meaning of "spiritual"; on God: His existence and nature.

Phelan, Gerald B., "The Being of Creatures," *Proceedings of the American Catholic Philosophical Association*, 31 (1957), pp. 124 ff. On essence as an intrinsic limiting mode in subordination to the act of existence.

Sweeney, S.J., Leo, "Metaphysics and God: Plotinus and Aquinas," in *Die Metaphysik im Mittelalter*, Vol. 2 of *Miscellanea Mediaevalia*, pp. 232-39. Berlin: Walter de Gruyter, 1963.

Wild, John, *Introduction to Realistic Philosophy*, pp. 356-91. New York: Harper & Row, Publishers, 1948. On God as First Cause.

CHAPTER VI

Primacy of Existence in Metaphysical Knowledge

In the previous chapter we have aimed at unveiling the primacy that the act of existing has within existents. After indicating what such primacy entails (Chap. V, Sec. 1: existence has preeminence because of its nature and function), we developed reasons why existence precedes essence: the former is the source of all other perfections (Sec. 2), it is autodetermining (Sec. 3), it is amaterial (Sec. 4). We concluded by mentioning that the act of existing in its otherness from essence and its primacy provides a valid basis for knowing that God exists and what sort of Existent He is (Sec. 6). In this chapter we shall emphasize its primacy in metaphysical knowledge.

The foundation upon which this preeminence rests is completely solid, as this consideration shows. Existence has primacy within existents; but metaphysical knowledge is the intelligible representation of those existents; hence, existence has primacy also in our metaphysical knowledge, as well as in the definitions, descriptions, and other expressions of that knowledge. In other words, the act of existing should somehow (either explicitly or implicitly) enter into all discussions inaugurated by a metaphysician and into all definitions elaborated by him.

* This entrance can be easily illustrated by listing the descriptions of various components we previously formulated in terms of change/stability (see Chap. III, Secs. 3-5) and translating them into metaphysical language.

> *Previously:* "Substance is that by which a material thing is and remains what it is specifically and generically and yet receives various individual perfections."
>
> *Now:* "Substance is that by which an existent so exercises its act of existing[1] that it is and remains what it is specifically and generically while receiving various individual perfections."
>
> *Previously:* "An accident is that by which the thing, while remaining what it is specifically and generically, is actually modified through an individual perfection, which is either contingent or necessary."[2]
>
> *Now:* "An accident is that by which an existent so exercises its act of existing that, while remaining what it is specifically and generically, it is actually modified by some or other individual perfection (either contingently or necessarily)."[3]

---

[1] The English phrase "exercises its act of existing," here and in the subsequent definitions, is an attempt to put across the dynamic relationship between an existent and its existence. Other expressions might be: an existent "carries out," "fulfills," or, passively, "is actuated by." Josepf Pieper's word is "does": "This factor [of existence] is not co-ordinal with the others; it is something fundamentally different. It has something of the quality of doing. The tree, determined by all those contentual peculiarities, also 'does' something: it grows, turns green, bears fruit. And in addition it 'does' something else before all these other individual acts: it exists. This act of existing is not only something 'of the nature of doing'; it is 'doing' in a distinctive and wholly unique sense. The ancients called it 'doing' without restriction or further specifications; they simply termed it *actus*" (*Guide to Thomas Aquinas* [New York: Pantheon Books, Inc., 1962], pp. 135-36).

No expression so far discovered is completely successful, but at least this should be clear: to exist is not merely something static, not simply to be outside nothingness. Rather it is a dynamic, vibrant actualization and realification of the entire being; substance and the other components within essence function merely in reference to it.

[2] On the force of "contingent . . . necessary," see p. 50, n. 25.

[3] One should recall that a single act of existing actualizes both substance and accidents within an existent. There is no so-called "accidental act of existing." See p. 87, n. 44.

Existents show themselves to be perfected by at least four sorts of accidents: quantity, various qualities, operations, and relations. See Chap. VII, Sec. 4.

Previously: "Prime matter is that by which a material thing receives a substantial form and yet which is capable, through subsequent substantial change, of receiving other substantial forms."

Now: "Prime matter is that by which an existent so exercises its act of existing that it receives a substantial form and yet which is capable, through subsequent substantial change, of receiving other such forms."

Previously: "Substantial form is that by which a thing is of such-and-such a specific nature."

Now: "Substantial form is that by which an existent exercises its act of existing in such a way as to be specifically such-and-such."

Previously: "Essence is that by which a thing is what it is as a member of some or other species."

Now: "Essence is that by which an existent precisely as an existent is what it is," [4] or "Essence is that within an existent by which the act of existing is received and limited."

These definitions are not the only ones a metaphysician could work out for substance and the other components, but they are simple enough and have the added advantage of showing how differently a philosopher of nature and a metaphysician view such components. The former conceives them solely in terms of the change and stability encircling a material thing. The latter sees them only in relationship to the act of existence. They function solely under its influence. They immediately account for the fact that each material existent exists uniquely—specifically similar to some existents but individually different from all.

1. Actual Existence and "Being"

Nowhere must the primacy of the act of existing be clearer or more important than with respect to our metaphysical awareness of "being." Existence must occupy the prominent place within "being" because it holds that spot in beings. That which makes any being be *being* is the fact that it actually is, and provided it does actually exist, it is being and is real, no matter how significant or insignificant it may be in *what* it is. God, this man, this insect, the soul within this dog, his prime matter, his accidental perfection of quantity—all differ greatly

---

[4] On essence, see p. 92, n. 54.

in what they are, which determines their way of existing. But all are alike in that they all actually are, and thus each is real and being.[5] The term "being," then, must express a meaning sufficiently supple and rich to fit any and all of them. Let us settle on "being" as meaning "an actually existing item." In that phrase the noun points to what is existing (for example, God, this man or any other such existent, prime matter or any other component, this machine or any other accidental unity); the other words point to actual existence, that whence such items derive their perfection, reality, and being. In understanding and interpreting that definition, one must remember that these words ("actually existing") are to be given emphasis and prominence. They point to the very heart of reality in each being.

* If "being" has that meaning, one must conclude that the term cannot be properly and directly predicated of the intentional universe. One may not apply it to the content of any concept except through extrinsic denomination.[6] This conclusion is diametrically opposed to the radical essentialists, for whom the possibles alone are fully real and are true beings. Because of this opposition let us spend some time on this point.

* First of all, how can there even be a question of predicating "being" of concepts if it means "an actually existing item"? One describes oxydized iron as "rusty" and various household furnishings as "plastic," but no one says meaningfully that his knowledge is rusty or plastic. On the other hand, we sometimes depict the conclusions to which we assent as "probable" but we do not say this wire fence or this barking dog is "probable." The intramental and the extramental universes are so disparate that adjectives apt for one cannot be applied

---

[5] This status of diversity and similarity is the basis of analogy. See Sec. 2: "Analogy of Being."

[6] With regard to human knowledge, one must carefully distinguish between its concepts and operations (a) as actually existing and (b) as to their content. Because they actually exist within the knower, they are real, and "being" is predicated of them through intrinsic denomination, as it is of such operations as freely choosing, loving, becoming angry, and of any other accident. But knowledge has this peculiar and wonderful characteristic: through the operations and concepts which comprise it and which actually are within the knower, the thing known exists intentionally within the knower, who thereby becomes the known. Knowledge, then, has a *content*: what-is-known as it is intentionally within the knower. Of this content (for example, Caroline Kennedy-as-known, Pope Paul VI-as-known, prime matter-as-known, mathematical infinity) "being" is predicated only through extrinsic denomination.

to the other. Why, then, predicate "being" of the intentional world at all?

* Throughout the history of thought such predication has often been made because philosophers conceived "being" differently. For instance, being to Plato was coterminous with immutability, and thus he called separate essences "beings" and linked actuals as such with nonbeing and unreality.[7] He turned from the sensible to the intelligible universe, and those he influenced automatically applied "being" to the latter and questioned whether the term could fittingly be extended to sensible existents at all. Thereafter the inquiry of whether and how "being" is predicated of the intelligible realm became a commonplace.

* But even one who views "being" as signifying "an actually existing item" can reasonably and usefully apply the term to the intramental universe, provided proper safeguards are observed, in order to express the fact that it is similar and is related causally to the one outside. The similarity lies in the fact that each universe has, so to speak, its own inhabitants. One is full of actual existents, caught in skeins of relationships (cause-effect) to one another. The other is full of *cognita*, and these too are interrelated: for example, the cause-effect relationships between the fictional characters in *Hamlet*, in William Faulkner's *As I Lay Dying*, in Graham Greene's *Heart of the Matter*;[8] the various functional relations between elements within modern mathematical systems; and so forth. The inhabitants of each world also involve an actuation: in the one it is that of actual existence, in the other it is that of being-known.[9]

* The relatedness between the two universes consists in the fact that knowledge is both the cause and the effect of actual existents. Knowledge within an artist causes artifacts (for example, the vision of beauty a painter wishes to communicate helps produce the painting), whereas speculative knowledge is caused by existents (for instance, metaphysics arises from the reflection which beings as being initiate).

* In the light of the similarity and especially of the causal relatedness between the intelligible and actual universes, then, "being"

---

[7] See Chap. II, Sec. 3: "Plato and Radical Essentialism," especially n. 39; also p. 81, n. 35.

[8] Perhaps in this interrelatedness of fictional characters whom we become through reading lies the reason why literature offers an escape from the humdrum, broadens one's perspectives, and enriches one's experiences and eventually one's personality.

[9] With respect to the latter, Berkeley is right: here *esse* is indeed *percipi, cognosci*.

can be transferred to the former, but this only through extrinsic denomination: items within it can be called "beings" insofar as they are
such as to be either the causes or the effects of actual existents, to
which alone the term pertains properly and directly. Thus a possible
can be described as "being" or "real" inasmuch as it is the blueprint
of what can actually exist, or the memory of a past existent is "being"
inasmuch as it is an awareness of what once was actual. And this
predication through extrinsic denomination admits of various degrees,
which depend upon how closely linked various intelligibilities are to
actual existents. The first degree is that of nonconstructural knowledge—that is, awareness based proximately on actual existents and
exemplified by actual-existents-as-known (these can be past, present,
or future existents, which are known either spontaneously or philosophically). The other and lower degrees are occupied by various kinds of
constructural knowledge, since these are awarenesses only remotely
based on actual existents.[10] This entire intramental universe is that
of "intentional being."

    ✻ Let the following table clarify and summarize the previous para-
graphs.

    "BEING" or "REAL" = "an actually existing item"

      is
      predicated

   A: *strictly and through intrinsic denomination*

        of all actual existents (*e.g.*, this man, that lion)
        of all the components within each (prime matter, accidents)
        of all accidental unities (a family, an artifact)

----

   [10] What is constructural knowledge? From reflection upon various sorts of constructs found in logic, mathematics, physics, and other empiriological sciences, as
well as in our spontaneous knowledge of physical and moral evils, constructural
knowledge seems to consist in these two factors: (a) The mental activity involved helps constitute (and thus affects) the very content of the intelligibilities
in question, within which it shows up as an integral part. (b) Consequently, the
basis of those intelligibilities is not directly any actually existing item, but rather
that mental activity.
   By contrast, in nonconstructural knowledge (a) the mental activity involved
is merely the means the knower uses to receive the intelligible message which
actual existents themselves deliver; (b) accordingly, the basis of such intelligibilities
is directly those actual existents.

B: *with qualification and through extrinsic denomination*: of the
content of all concepts

1° actual-existents-as-known
    past
    present
    future (possibles)
	nonconstructural
	knowledge
		I N T E B

2° conceptions of logic,
    mathematics, empiriological
    sciences, etc.
 	
3° Contradictory notions
    (square circle)
	constructural
	knowledge
		N E T I I N O G N A L

*   "Being," then, is predicated in two widely different ways, depending upon whether the subject of the predication is an actually existing
item or is the content of an intelligibility. The primacy of actual existence with respect to our knowledge and predication of "being" dictates
that the term be properly and intrinsically applied to nothing except
whatever actually is.

*   Two subsidiary points remain to be made. It already is obvious
that we differ greatly from a radical essentialist with respect to the
possibles. In his position they are supremely real, and, in the last
analysis, constitute the subject of metaphysics, because being-as-being
is being in its immutability, its intelligibility, its possibility.[11] As we
have often said, for us they are in themselves nonbeing;[12] they achieve
reality only in relation to what is actual and at best are on the fringe
of metaphysics.[13] But there is another way in which we differ from

---

[11] To a radical essentialist the treatise on the possibles is at the heart of his
metaphysics. For example, Carolus Frick, S.J., devotes approximately one-fourth
of his metaphysics book to them (*Ontologia* [Friburgi Brisgoviae: Herder and
Co., 1934], pp. 67-101).

[12] See pp. 80-81 and n. 35. Aquinas speaks similarly—see S.T., I, 14, 9:
"Whether God has knowledge of nonbeings" (*Utrum Deus habeat scientiam non
entium*). As the body of the text makes clear, the nonbeings referred to are possibles. Also see Norris Clarke, "What is the Really Real?" in *Progress in Philosophy*, ed. James McWilliams, S.J. (Milwaukee: Bruce Publishing Co., 1955),
pp. 61-90.

[13] They play an important role only in that section of metaphysics which is
natural theology, where they enter into discussions of divine knowledge, freedom,
and causality. See Henri J. Renard, S.J., *Philosophy of God* (Milwaukee:
Bruce Publishing Co., 1951), *passim* and especially pp. 119-37, 152-61;
Maurice R. Holloway, S.J., *Introduction to Natural Theology* (New York: Appleton-Century-Crofts, 1959), pp. 290-306, 319-32.

an essentialist on the possibles, and this has to do with their very inner constitution. For him they are blocks of permanency and intelligibility, not yet actualized and hence still isolated from fluency and unreality. They are essences in an intelligible status, each of which exhausts the entire reality of the thing capable of existing, each of which *is* the thing. To our way of thinking, a possible is not just an essence. It is rather a composite of [essence/act of existing] which currently is not, but which can be. Each is an [essence/act of being]-known-as-capable-of-existing. Each is an *existent*-which-is-possible, each is an *existent* which can be and perhaps will be.

*   The reason why the act of existing as-known enters into the internal constitution of a possible seems indestructible. It is a constituent (in fact, the most important constituent) of an actual existent. But a possible existent is a future actual existent, or, stated from the other side, an actual existent is what was once a possible existent but now actualized. Therefore, the internal make-up of an existent as possible should match that of an actual, with the sole (but important) difference that the components of the former are there only as-known, whereas those of the latter are actual. Accordingly, a possible existent is an [essence/existence]-known-as-capable-of-existing.[14]

*   The importance of this conclusion is apparent. Within authentic existentialism the very structure of a possible is radically modified.[15] No longer is it just an essence; it is now an essence/*esse* in the intelligible order. No longer is it real in and of itself, but only by relation-

---

[14] The only reason why the act of existing (as-known) could be omitted from the make-up of a possible existent is if it were not a component of existents. As long as it is a constitutive part of them, no existent, whether actual or possible, can be accurately understood without it. See E. Gilson, *Being and Some Philosophers* (Toronto: Pontifical Institute of Mediaeval Studies, 1952), pp. 182-83: "Ideas represent possible beings, including both their actual existence and their becoming. In other words, if *esse* (to be) is the supreme act of creatures, their idea must needs include it as the active energy through which the corresponding essence shall progressively receive all its determinations. . . . The second error [in wrongly conceiving 'possibles'] is to forget that the essence of a possible being necessarily includes the possible existence through which alone it can achieve its essential determination. To repeat, essential possibility is no sufficient reason for existential possibility, and, since its essence is what a being is going to become, if it exists, existence itself necessarily enters the calculation of its essential possibility."

[15] This modification parallels a similar one in the very structure of *essence* itself, already referred to (see Chap. II, Sec. 3: "Plato and Radical Essentialism," and Chap. V, Sec. 1, "Existence Precedes Essence"). An essence does not consist merely in stability, as a radical essentialist would have it, but is an intimate fusion of stabliity with change, of substance with accidents.

ship to the status of actuality it can and perhaps will attain. And the presence of *esse*-as-known within even its intentional make-up is a sign and a reminder of that radical modification. Within a possible existent *esse*-as-known assumes a primacy over the essence-as-known which is analogous to that assumed by *esse* over essence in an actual existent.

＊ The second subsidiary point involves the problem of how "being" is to be predicated of artifacts. Take literature or music. In what sense can *Hamlet* or the *Ode on a Grecian Urn* or any other poem be said to be actually existing and thus be describable as real and being? "In the beginning, everything is simple: a poem exists while somebody reads it or hears it being read. . . . But while it is not being actually read, or heard, in what sense can it still be said to exist?" [16] In what sense can a musical piece be said to actually exist? "A sonata, a symphony, or an opera endures as long as the time of its performance. As soon as an orchestral mass and the choirs it supports have sounded the last chord of Beethoven's Ninth Symphony, the whole structure vanishes into nothingness. Nothing of it is left except grateful memories and the hope to hear the same masterpiece again, or, rather, another rendering of it." [17] Moreover, "a musical piece has no simultaneous existence. . . . What do we actually hear of a sonata? Not the sonata as a whole. Not even one of its movements, its themes, or its bars; all that we actually hear of it at a time is one of its chords. While this one is actually sounding, the next one has not yet come and the preceding one has already ceased to be." [18]

＊ If "being" signifies "an actually existing item," it is applicable to literature, music, and other artifacts only because each of them is something which actually is, and this in its own way. The problem is to ascertain what each is and how each does actually exist.

＊ The artifacts listed are accidental unities; hence, let us begin by studying such commonplace unities as a family or an automobile. What is the unique reality of a family but the sum of the real relations binding together mother, father, and children and expressed by the collective noun "family?" Why, then, is "being" predicable of a family? Because that complex of relationships is an actually existing item, to which the term is applied properly and through intrinsic denomina-

---

[16] Etienne Gilson, *Painting and Reality* (New York: Pantheon Books, Inc., 1957), pp. 5-6.

[17] *Ibid.*, p. 7.

[18] *Ibid.*, p. 8.

tion.[19] What is the unique reality of an Oldsmobile? It is the ordering and arrangement of suitable parts in such a way as to form an attractive and sturdy vehicle capable of self-propulsion. Why is "being" applicable to it? Because that good order is an actually existing item, of which the term is said properly and intrinsically.

* Moving over to the area of fine arts, let us ask what the unique reality of a mosaic is. The answer: a decorative arrangement of small pieces of colored glass or stone inlaid into cement or plaster. Why can "being" be said of it? Because that arrangement is an actually existing item, aptly expressed by "being" through intrinsic and proper predication. What is a painting? It is the right ordering of various pigments upon a canvas or some other background material. Once again, "being" is predicable through intrinsic denomination because that good order is an actually existing factor.

* To summarize: "Being" is predicated of all such accidental unities (and this through intrinsic denomination) because all their parts are actual existents in their own right and yet coalesce to fashion a new actually existing item, designed for utility or for beauty. Now we should be ready to consider those same questions concerning literature and music.

* What is the unique reality of *Hamlet?* It is twofold: first, the definite order of letters, syllables, and words upon a printed page; second and especially, the actual production of the play—those words uttered by actors and heard by an audience. Why can "being" be predicated intrinsically and properly of it? Because in those two states it is an item which exists actually and in its own fashion. What is the unique reality of music? Again, it is twofold: first, the definite order and sequence of notes as they are written on a score; second, and more important, an actual performance of the piece: those notes as played by an orchestra and heard by the audience. Why can a musical piece be properly described as "being"? Because however tenuous and fluent it may be ("Music [is] the very type of that which, because it never is but ceaselessly becomes, is much less a being than an existent striving to be without ever quite doing it"),[20] still it *is* an actually existing item, and thus deserves the name "being."

* "Being," then, is any actually existing item, and this fact has

---

[19] Of course, "being" is also applied through intrinsic denomination to the members of the family (who are the subjects of the relationships expressed by "family") as individual existents and intrinsic unities.

[20] Gilson, *op. cit.,* p. 8.

two important consequences. First, it is properly and directly predicable of any such item, whether it be this man, his components, his family, his automobile, his portrait, the literature he writes, the music he plays. Second, it is thus predicable only of such items. The possibles and the contents of all other intelligibilities are real, at best, through extrinsic denomination.

2. The Analogy of Being

We shall next discuss the primacy which actual existence enjoys in our metaphysical knowledge of truth, goodness, and beauty, which together with being are the transcendent traits characterizing all actual existents and triggering corresponding awarenesses in the human knower (see pp. 151-64). Before that step, though, let us briefly consider analogy. This is a consideration which is needed for a more adequate understanding of being (and, for that matter, of the other transcendents too); it has in fact been prepared for by Section 1 of this chapter as well as by Chapters IV and V.

From what has gone before, it is clear that actually existing items are many in number and extremely different in kind. Some we directly perceive: ourselves, other men and women, animals, plants, inanimate things,[21] as well as the machines we use, the buildings we dwell and work in, the masterpieces of painting and music we enjoy.[22] Others we know only intellectually (although working within data furnished by perception) either through reflection (the components: the act of existing, substantial form, prime matter, various accidents—see Chaps. III and IV) or through reasoning (for example, God—see Chap. V, Sec. 6). The diversity between these existents is too manifest to need comment—for example, that between God and any other actual item, no matter what it is; that between an intrinsic and extrinsic unity (this man and this typewriter); that between two such intrinsic unities as this man and this mosquito, or even between this man and that man, who are numerically distinct and individually unique; that between such extrinsic unities as this typewriter, that garage, Leonardo da Vinci's *Mona Lisa*, Beethoven's *Violin Concerto*; that between this man and his substantial form or other components, or even that between one component and another, each of which has its own causal function to

---

[21] All these we have technically said to be or to involve "intrinsic" or *per se* unities. See Chap. III, Sec. 2.

[22] These we call "extrinsic" or accidental unities.

perform, each its own nature.[23] And yet, however diverse they are in what they are, they are similar in that they all do actually exist.

The extramental world is, then, everywhere shot through with similarity and diversity. But it is the content-determining cause of our metaphysical knowledge of "being," which, as "an actually existing item," is deliberately designed to be predicable of all existents (be they God, an intrinsic unity, an extrinsic unity, or a component)[24] and, equally important, to signify everything within each ("item" refers to *whatever* each is, "actually existing" to the fact *that* each is).[25] Accordingly also, our awareness of "being" is marked by a parallel similarity and diversity.

But to predicate "being" is simply to reverse the initial movement from actuals to the knower: by affirming "God is real" or "This man is real," we simply apply back to actuals the knowledge gained from them. Hence, our predication of "being" involves similarity/diversity. When directed to God or to this man, his act of existing, and his portrait, "real" or "being" has a meaning which is neither completely identical nor totally different, but which weds diversity to similarity.

In brief, actual beings, our knowledge of them as beings, and our affirmation of being concerning them are all characterized by similarity/ diversity. How can this characterization common to those three distinct areas be conveniently described? By the single term "analogy." Actual existents are analogous to one another; our metaphysical knowledge of

---

[23] Besides Chaps. III and IV, see also Chap. V, Sec. 3: "Actual Existence and Autodetermination."

[24] On the deliberate elaboration of the meaning given to "being," see Appendix B.

One should note that in subsequent pages the noun "existents" is restricted to men, animals, and other intrinsic unities, whereas "actuals" is applied also to components and to extrinsic unities—in brief, to any actually existing item, whatever it be.

[25] This dog is actually similar and diverse to all other dogs and is the content-determining cause of our awareness of him as "dog." Still that awareness is not analogous, but univocal, because it grasps this dog only in his similarity to other dogs: in a word, it does not signify everything in each dog. But our awareness of this dog as "being" catches him not only in his similarity to all other beings (the fact that he actually exists) but also in his diversity from them (the fact of what he is: this dog [although not precisely as this dog but as actual]): rightly interpreted, it signifies everything in him. (Incidentally, our *perception* of him as "this dog" would seem to be describable in its own way as analogous, for we are aware of him in his similarity to other dogs ["dog"] and in his diversity from them ["this"].)

For a fuller explanation of this important point, see below, pp. 149-50 and p. 145, n. 29, 2nd par.

them is analogous; our predication concerning them is analogous. In each case the adjective simply points to that situation of similarity/diversity. Analogy is nothing more than the condition of similarity/diversity in actuals, in knowledge, and in predication.[26]

One can even speak legitimately and usefully of various *kinds* of analogy in view of the various kinds of similarity/diversity which are to be found among actuals (as well as in the ensuing knowledge they cause and in the predications they receive). Why so? Similarity/diversity is a relational situation, and relational situations vary from one another insofar as their ingredients vary, one set of which is the *relata*—the existents which are referred to one another. That is to say, the sort of similarity/diversity obtaining between God and a creature is not identical with that between two creatures, with that between a creature and his components, or with that between the components themselves. Consequently, the analogy between God and creatures is somewhat unlike that between two creatures or between the other two sets of actuals. There are, then, various sorts of analogy, some of which we shall now try briefly to elaborate by reflecting upon the various kinds of similarity/diversity that actually existing items manifest.

First of all, God and a creature differ with respect to being inasmuch as actuality is of the former's very nature, whereas it is really other than the latter's. God *is* perfectly and subsistently, whereas the creature *is* only through an act of existing limited by what he is. Despite this grave difference, though, they are alike in that each *is,* each does actually exist. Here, then, is truly a situation of similarity/diversity, but one in which diversity is almost maximal, similarity minimal. It is a similarity/diversity which might be termed "eminence" if we describe it from the side of God, Who is being pre-eminently.[27] But analogy is nothing more than similarity/diversity. Accordingly, the analogy between God and a creature can be called one of *eminence:* namely *the similarity/diversity in being* (as well as in consequent

---

[26] Traditionally, analogy seems restricted to knowledge and predication; thus it is contrasted with the univocal and equivocal: a *notion* is analogous if its *meaning* is similar/diverse, whereas a *notion* is univocal if its *meaning* is similar but equivocal if its *meaning* is diverse. In view of the facts, though, it is better to say that analogy is any sort of similarity and diversity, whether found within existents, knowledge, or predications.

[27] It might just as easily be called one of "participation" or of "dependence" if viewed from the side of the creature. The lesson to be learned is that descriptions of the kinds of analogy are somewhat arbitrary. Our criterion should be the one which best fits the situation of similarity/diversity in question.

metaphysical knowledge and predication) *between the Existent Whose very essence is to exist and an existent whose existence is really distinct from his essence.*[28]

Another sort of similarity/diversity is that between two creatures. For example, take these two men.[29] They differ with respect to being inasmuch as each is numerically distinct and individually unique: although each is human, still each is so differently, singularly, in a manner never to be exactly reduplicated. Still they are also alike in being—each actually exists, and this in the same fashion: in each the act of existing really differs from essence. Here, then, is another situation of similarity/diversity, but one in which neither diversity nor similarity is extreme. It is a similarity/diversity which has traditionally been described as "proportionality"—somewhat as with mathematical proportionality (for example, 2 : 4 : : 5 : 10), whence the name seemingly was derived, there exists within each creature a similar proportion between existence and essence: that of real distinction and composition (John : existence : : Paul : existence). Since similarity/diversity is equivalent to analogy, the analogy in being (as well as in the metaphysical knowledge and predication paralleling being) between one creature and another can be termed that of *proportionality: the similarity/diversity between existents in each of which actuality is really other than what they are.*[30]

---

[28] If we interpret it more generally, the analogy of eminence might be depicted as the similarity/diversity between the more and less perfect, between the entitatively higher and lower. If so, it can for obvious reasons be applied to substance/accidents, matter/form or to existence/essence; in its strict interpretation, however, it is reserved for God/creature.

[29] What is true of individuals within the same species will a fortiori be true of other creatures. They will differ not only individually but also specifically (for example, this man and this dog), generically (this man and this tree) or even more drastically (this man and an angel).

Even though two individuals of the same species are specifically alike, still they are individually different, and this is more than sufficient to cause them to differ also in being. Being encompasses their very individuality; for them to be actual is precisely to exist each in his own way. Being is not formulated simply as "actually existing," but as "an actually existing item." It embraces both existence and essence, and this latter in its actual and hence individual and singular status. To refuse to ascribe an analogy of proportionality to individuals of the same species is a serious mistake. For further discussion see L. Sweeney, S.J., "Analogy and Being," *The Modern Schoolman*, 39 (March, 1962), 259.

[30] Frequently, it is called "*proper* proportionality," the point of the adjective being to distinguish it from the proportionality involved in metaphor. In the latter (for instance, "John is an ox") what is signified by the predicate is not found intrinsically in the subject. With regard to being, though, what is signi-

* Still another sort of analogy is that between a creature's components. Consider within this man the act of existing by which he actually exists, prime matter by which ultimately he actually exists as individuated, substantial form by which he exists as man, various accidents by which he exists in an individual fashion. They differ in being insofar as each is really distinct from the others, each has its own causal function to perform, each is what it is and nothing more. But they also are similar, for each actually exists and does so within one and the same human existent: they are intrinsic causes of the same effect (this man), upon which they in turn depend and within which they actually are. Because they all are and are what they are *only with reference to the single existent they constitute,* this similarity/diversity (and hence analogy) can aptly be described as one of "reference." Accordingly, the analogy of *reference* is the *similarity/diversity between the components of one and the same existent.*[31]

* A final type of similarity/diversity with respect to being[32] is that found between the extramental and the intramental universes. These two are similar because each has, so to speak, inhabitants. As we have already remarked (Chap. VI, Sec. 1), one is full of actual existents caught in webs of relationships (for example, cause-effect) to one another; the other is full of *cognita,* and these too are interrelated: for

---

fied by the predicate is intrinsic to the subjects ("John is a being and Paul is a being"). (For a different interpretation of metaphor, see Robert Boyle, S.J., "The Nature of Metaphor," *Modern Schoolman,* 31 [May, 1954], 267-80.)

Can the analogy of proportionality also be applied to God/creature? Yes, provided one realizes that this analogy is itself analogous and one broadens its definition a bit: "the similarity/diversity between existents in each of which actuality is somehow *other* (whether really or conceptually) than what they are." On this controverted point, see L. Sweeney, S.J., "Analogy and Being," pp. 257-58; John J. O'Brien, S.J., "Analogy and the Fourth Way," *Wisdom in Depth: Essays in Honor of Henri J. Renard, S.J.* (Milwaukee: Bruce Publishing Co., 1966).

[31] We have lumped all components together in reference to the existent they constitute, but additional comparisons are possible (and hence additional kinds of analogy) because the components are variously interrelated to one another—for example, substance to accidents, existence to essence, existence to prime matter (as pure act to pure potency), and so on. But not enough profit would be gained from working out these other comparisons and analogies to warrant the labor and tedium.

[32] Actuals involve still other types of similarity/diversity—for example, that between this man and any one of his components, that between this man and any of the components of another man, that between two extrinsic unities, and so on. But as was the case with regard to the components (see previous note), so here too: too little profit would be gained for the amount of energy expended. Besides, it should be clear now how such types of similarity/diversity and of analogy can be worked out if there is need.

example, the cause-effect relationships between the fictional characters in (say) *Macbeth*, in J. D. Salinger's *Catcher in the Rye*, in Graham Greene's *End of the Affair* or between the various functional relations between elements within modern mathematical systems. The extramental and intramental universes are also alike because of their dependence on one another, which arises because knowledge is both the cause and effect of actual existents. Knowledge within an artist, whether human or divine, helps cause his artifacts (for example, the vision of beauty a painter wishes to communicate helps produce the painting), whereas speculative knowledge is caused by existents (for instance, metaphysics arises from the reflection which beings-as-being initiate).

＊ Yet these two universes also differ inasmuch as the "inhabitants" of the former (that is, actual existents) are genuinely real: they actually exist and their actuation is actual existence. But the "inhabitants" of the latter (that is, intelligibilities as to their content—see p. 135, n. 6) are unreal: precisely as what-is-known they do not actually exist and their actuation is nothing more than being-known (*cognosci*).

＊ Thus there is another situation of similarity/diversity with respect to being, but one which joins minimal similarity to extreme diversity. Because of the similarity "being" is predicated through intrinsic denomination only of actuals and of *cognita* merely through extrinsic denomination: these latter are, strictly speaking, nonbeing and unreal.[33] How can we best describe this similarity/diversity? Since it issues into such disparate predications that actuals are named (denominated) "beings" intrinsically but *cognita* are so named only extrinsically, let us call it one of "denomination." Consequently, the analogy of *denomination* is *the similarity/diversity between the extramental and intentional universes,* and "being" is predicated of the former through intrinsic denomination but of the latter through extrinsic denomination.

Such, then, are several kinds of analogy. Although elaborating them is a somewhat intricate task, still its fundamental methodolgy should be clear: one works out the kinds of analogy by investigating various

---

[33] From one point of view the diversity here is greater than that found between God and creatures, since despite their great dissimilarity "being" is predicated intrinsically of both. But not so of the *cognita*, which are so far removed from entity as themselves to be nonbeings and to be termed "beings" only through extrinsic denomination.

We might note that the predication of "being" here is counteracted by that of "true," which is predicated through intrinsic denomination of knowledge and of actuals only through extrinsic denomination. See Sec. 3 of this chapter.

kinds of similarity/diversity. And despite its grave importance,[34] analogy itself is easy to understand in its basic meaning: it is simply the status of similarity/diversity found in actuals, as well as in the knowledge they cause and the predication they receive, with respect to being. In fact, it is a mere corollary, an automatic consequence of the rest of one's metaphysics. That is to say, one's acceptance or rejection of it is already determined by the stand he takes on the nature of existents and the meaning of "being." If one holds, as do monists, that existents are all identical with one another or with some basic stuff of which they are mere manifestations, then diversity is lacking and analogy is impossible. Or if one maintains, as do Ockham and other nominalists, that existents are totally diverse from one another (here, to be real is to be entirely other and different), then similarity is lacking and so too is analogy. But if one views existents as really distinct and yet also similar, he has the requisite combination of diversity and similarity and a doctrine of analogy is possible, although this possibility is still dependent upon the second point—the meaning one gives to "being."

If one restricts "being" to one level of existents (for example, Neo-Platonists define "being" as "one-many" and thus God is above being because of His utter unity and absolute simplicity;[35] whereas others

---

[34] For example, Karl Barth declares analogy to be the crucial difference between Catholicism and Protestantism. See Niels C. Nielsen, "Protestant Faith and Catholic Unity," *America*, August 14, 1954, p. 479: "Barth made one central idea the essential point of difference between the Protestant and Roman Catholic positions. He announced that he regarded the rejection of the analogy of being, central in Thomistic analysis, as the only valid reason for refusing to accept the claims of Roman Catholic authority." Walter Lowrie, *Kierkegaard* (London: Oxford University Press, 1938), p. 9: ". . . The Catholic doctrine of the *analogia entis* . . . Barth accounts the dividing line between Protestantism and Catholicism." On Barth's views of analogy, see Sebastian A. Matczak, *Karl Barth on God: The Knowledge of the Divine Existence* (Staten Island, New York: Alba House, 1962), Chap. V: "Abyss Between God and Man (Analogy)," pp. 173-221.

[35] For a Catholic version of this Neo-Platonic position, see Meister Eckhart, "Sermon on Renewal in the Spirit," quoted in J. F. Anderson, *The Bond of Being* (St. Louis: B. Herder, 1949), p. 264: "If I say God is good, it is not true: I am good, God is not good. I say more: I am better than God is, for what is good can be better, and what is better can be best. But God is not good, therefore He cannot be better, therefore He cannot be best. These three: good, better, best, are remote from God Who is above all. And if, again, I say that God is wise, it is not true: I am wiser than He. Or if I say, God is a being, it is not true: He is a transcendental essence, a superessential nothing."

reserve it for God with the result that creatures are unreal, no-good),[36] then it is not analogous. Or if its content consists of a single factor— if it means simply "something" rather than "something actually existing"—then it still need not be analogous, even though it is not confined to any one area of existents. It could be equivocal if "something" is taken as including all the individual differences of each thing, or it could be univocal if understood as prescinding from individual and even specific and generic differences. Thus "being" in its content is the most indeterminate, most indigent concept possible. Pushed to the ultimate of abstraction and of indefiniteness, it is predicable of everything (whether infinite or finite, whether spiritual or material, whether human or nonhuman) because it in no way expresses those differences. It points simply to the fact that each subject of which it is predicated is "something" rather than "nothing."

But if the content of "being" consists of two factors, if it means "an actually existing item," then it is analogous. "Item" has to do with the diversity of existents since it points to what each is (and in this "each" differs from all else). "Actually existing" deals with their similarity since it indicates that each is (and in this they are all alike, no matter how disparate they may otherwise be).

Still there is more. This last factor has to do with existents also in their diversity. Nothing actually exists except in a determinate, concrete, unique, individual fashion, thereby, making it different from all else. Hence, its status of actual existence is one also of diversity. In expressing existents as "actually existing," then, "being" also expresses their diversity.[37] Accordingly, "being" is truly analogous,

---

[36] The position of those Lutherans who hold that original sin has cast men into a condition of total ruin and intrinsic worthlessness would seem to fit here. Perhaps Barth's declaration (see n. 34) becomes intelligible in the light of this position.

The doctrine of Christian Scientists also appears to be a case in point. See Rosemary Lauer, "The Philosophy of Christian Science," *The Thomist*, 20 (1957), pp. 194 and 201: "From the original principles of Christian Science, if one interprets them in a univocal sense, certain metaphysical conclusions follow as surely as night follows day: *If God is, then whatever is not God is not;* if all reality is God, then all reality is intelligent, or Mind; if God is all reality and good, then evil is nothing; if God is immaterial, then matter is nonexistent. . . . In the realm of pedagogy [Christian Science] serves the teacher of metaphysics as a superb example of the consequences to be expected from taking univocally such terms as 'being,' 'real,' 'truth,' and 'good.' "

[37] Manifestly, the autodetermination of existence (see Chap. V, Sec. 3) is at the basis of analogy. Because existence is independent of any one particular essence,

and its analogy rests mainly[38] on the second factor of its content.

Also because of that second factor, because it signifies all actuals precisely as actual, "being" has this prerogative: it is as rich in content as is possible for a concept having maximal extension, for it is designed not only to be predicable of all but also to signify everything in each. As we have seen, what an actual *is* is always determinate, concrete, unique, individual. Hence by signifying an actual in what it actually is, "being" catches it in its very determinateness, concreteness, uniqueness, individuality, for nothing exists except in a determinate, concrete, singular, individual way. But if it signifies everything in each, how can it still be predicated of all? Because it does not signify an actual in what it is precisely as determinate, as concrete, as unique, as *this*— if it did, it would only be predicable of this one existent. Rather, it signifies an actual in what it is (which actually is determinate, concrete, and so forth) precisely *as actual,* and thus is predicable of all actuals, because all agree in being actual (even though, we must add, their status of actuality is simultaneously one also of diversity).

Consequently, because "being" expresses actuals as actuals, it is predicable of all, since all actuals are being inasmuch as they are actual. And yet it also signifies everything in each because the actual status of each encompasses each in its very individuality, uniqueness, and determinateness. Therefore "being" is a concept which is maximal in extension and in comprehension.

In its signification of what is actual precisely as actual is also rooted its analogy, as we have already mentioned. In its status of actuality

---

it essentializes itself through whatever essence it does actualize. But essence is the direct source of diversity in an existent. Therefore, the act of existence also causes its own diversity. But existents, together with the knowledge they cause and the predication they receive, are analogous as combining diversity with similarity. But actual existence is the mediate source of their diversity, as well as the immediate source of their similarity: all are diverse in that each exists in its own way, all are alike in that they do exist. Therefore, analogy of existents, knowledge, and predication is based on actual existence in its autodetermination and its primacy within the existent.

Underlying the analogy of being in whatever sphere is the fact that to be actual is, in the last analysis, to be both similar and diverse.

[38] Mainly, I say, but not entirely, because "item" too is necessary as indicating what is actualized. Essence functions as the immediate source of diversity, and this function actual existence could itself usurp only at the price of no longer being actual existence. (Similarly, actual existence is relatively independent of essence, but it can be autodetermining only if there is some essence or "other." The act of existing can itself usurp the limiting function of essence only if it is no longer actual existence.)

an actual is similar to and yet also diverse from all else: all actuals are alike in that they do exist, all are diverse in that each exists in its own way. Therefore, by expressing actuals precisely as actuals, "being" signifies actuals in their similarity and diversity, and hence is analogous.

Such is the analogy of being. Let us now move on to the other transcendents.

3. Actual Existence and Other Transcendents

Manifestly, the analogy of being reaffirms the primacy of actual existence. Existents, together with ensuing metaphysical knowledge and predications, are analogous by reason of the similarity/diversity they entail. Actual existence is not only the immediate source of their similarity (all are alike in that they exist) but also is the mediate source of their diversity (each exists in its own way) because of its autodetermination: the act of existing essentializes itself through whatever essence it actualizes, and thus also diversifies itself and the existent. Therefore, actual existence is at the heart of analogy, and is thereby again shown to have primacy.

Let us next consider the primacy of existence in the transcendents other than being.

*   (a) TRANSCENDENTS AS KNOWN SPONTANEOUSLY

Whenever we are unexpectedly confronted with what is unknown (for example, suppose we return to our room to find an object concealed under a sheet on the floor), our spontaneous knowledge gradually moves from a condition of relative indetermination to one of determination, from the more to the less general, as the object in question gives off more and more evidence of itself. Let us say that the object under the sheet is an injured, bleeding man, which we observe without removing the sheet. Our first awareness would be, "something or other actually there," followed by "which is living . . . sentient . . . human," as it slowly moves about under the sheet, stains the sheet with blood, then groans and speaks.

There is, then, in our human knowledge a movement with respect to content from the less to the more definite; there is a cognitional growth. Subsequent awarenesses are added to prior ones, and these additions are immediately based upon the thing manifesting itself to the knower. They are useful, even necessary, in our coming to know things and in our communicating with one another about them. The terms we use to express them are not synonyms, since each subsequent one has a fuller and hence somewhat different meaning.[39] As our knowledge grows, subsequent awarenesses contain more than prior ones (for instance, "something actually present which is living" says more than merely "something actually present"). But they are predicable of fewer things (the former awareness can be applied only to what is living, the latter to the nonliving as well). As a logician would state it, their increase in comprehension is matched by a decrease in extension. In view of this situation, let us call such subsequent awarenesses and the words signifying them *"restrictive"*—they are *restricted* to definite classes of things.

But we also experience another sort of spontaneous knowledge, as reflection upon our reactions to that previous scene disclose. On coming upon that object hidden under the sheet, our first awareness is that of "something or other actually present," which then develops into the additional restrictive awarenesses already listed as we come to know the kind of thing it actually is. But that initial awareness also issues into that of "real," of "one," of "other than." These we find ourselves to spontaneously have if anyone questions us later about the scene and we reply that no, it was not just something we imagined, but was *real:* something actually *was* there; no, there were not several, but only *one;* no, it was not merely the sheet: there was something there *other than* the cloth.

Here, then, is a second type of cognitional growth, a movement from what is implicit to the explicit.[40] The subsequent awarenesses of "one"

---

[39] What sort of distinction or difference is there between such awarenesses? As we have previously seen (p. 114, n. 29), it is a mental one in view of the fact that what "rational" signifies is not really other in this man than what "sentient" and other such intelligibilities signify. A man's rationality permeates his entire sentient, living, chemical, and material constitution. His nature as rational is not really different from his nature as sentient, as living, and as material. The terms are descriptions of that single nature from a more or less determinate point of view.

For a contrast with transcendent awarenesses, see p. 153, n. 42.

[40] This movement is also one from a condition of relative indetermination to one of determination, as is that in restrictive knowledge. But the awarenesses in which it terminates are to some extent different from those encountered in the latter (for instance, an increase in comprehension does not lessen extension). To emphasize the difference, we shall arbitrarily reserve the phrase "from the indeterminate to the determinate" for restrictive awarenesses and "from the implicit to the explicit" for transcendents. Besides, the latter words are especially apt, since subsequent transcendents merely explicitate what "being" implicitly contains. In designating all actuals *as actual,* "being" also embraces them as undivided, as "other than," and so on.

and "other than" are added to what is prior,[41] and these additions are directly based upon the thing exhibiting itself to the mind. They are useful and necessary in our knowing things, as well as in our communicating with one another about them. The terms we use to signify them are not synonyms, because each subsequent awareness has a fuller, more explicit and, therefore, somewhat different meaning.[42] As our knowledge grows, the subsequent awarenesses contain more than the prior one—for instance, "something actually present and other than all else" explicitly says more than merely "something actually present." But even so—and this is their extraordinary characteristic—they remain predicable of an equal number of things—for example, "something actually present and other than all else" is applicable as extensively as is "something actually present," since every actual thing automatically is also distinct from everything else by the very fact that it is an actual thing. Here, increase of comprehension does not lessen extension. These awarenesses and terms, accordingly, are not

---

[41] "One" and "other than" (as well as the other subsequent transcendents still to be investigated) are added to "something actually present," but not so "real," which is not subsequent to but rather concomitant and on a par with it. "Something actually present" is what "real" or "being" means. Hence, "real" or "being" is prior to the other transcendents and is that to which they add.

At least as far back as Avicenna (born A.D. 980) philosophers were saying that "being" is what a human knower first knows. In light of the fact that our initial spontaneous awareness is "something or other actually present," which the terms "real" or "being" designate, one can understand why they so spoke. Yet the content of that knowledge is not "being" so much as "something actually present." The former is the term, the latter the awareness.

[42] What sort of distinction is between such awarenesses? As with restrictive intelligibilities (see p. 152, n. 39), it is a mental one, since what "being" designates is not really other in this actual thing than what "one" and "other than" designate: his entity, unity, and otherness all revolve around his actuality; each merely highlights now one, now another aspect of it.

They differ, though, from restrictive awarenesses (see p. 152, n. 40), and hence the mental distinction between them is divergent from that between the latter. Some express this divergence by calling the first a "minor," the other a "major" mental distinction. Others express it by depicting the first as a "mental distinction only imperfectly grounded in reality," whereas the second is a "mental distinction perfectly grounded." This description is drawn from the fact that the second rests upon really distinct components within the existent (that is, substantial form and prime matter, from which issue the specific and the generic perfections, respectively), whereas the first has no such basis. Rather, it results from the fact that an actual is so complex and rich in its very actuality that it cannot be grasped by a human knower in a single concept but only in a series of them.

Either description is satisfactory. What is important is to remember that the transcendent awarenesses only conceptually differ from one another, and differ in a way unlike that of restrictive ones.

confined to any certain classes of things, but rather *transcend* them. Let us call them, then, "*transcendents.*" [43]

Besides "real," "one," and "other than," our automatic knowledge of things also entails several other awarenesses of an identical nature, although these are more easily illustrated and substantiated by stepping outside the previous example and by simply showing that they too transcend any one type of thing. Consider "good." We meaningfully ascribe it to such divergent things as food and drink, houses, apple-trees and other plants, dogs and almost any other animal, men and women. When listening to Jascha Heifetz play a cadenza or watching an expert skater do a Triple Sal Chow, we instinctively exclaim, "A good job!" We speak also of a good choice, of good attitudes, of a good scholar. To be applicable to such various classes of things, then, "good" also must be a transcendent. [44]

So too is "beauty," since a sunset, a landscape, trees and flowers, race horses and other graceful animals, men and women are all de-scribed as beautiful. Likewise with "truth." Although it is primarily a mark of knowledge ("The District Attorney knows the truth about the incident"), still we also say things are "true" or "false" (for example, a father after investigating his teen-age son's handiwork in the base-ment reports to his wife, "Yes, it's a true bomb, all right!"). And the things so described are many in kind, as evidenced by such phrases as "a true Rembrandt," "a true likeness," "true, not fool's gold," "a

---

[43] Other authors call them "transcendentals." For example, see Martin O. Vaske, S.J., *An Introduction to Metaphysics* (New York: McGraw-Hill Book Company, 1963), Chap. VII, pp. 178-208; Robert J. Kreyche, *First Philosophy*, Chaps. 8 and 9, pp. 167-204; Henry J. Koren, *An Introduction to the Science of Meta-physics* (St. Louis: B. Herder Book Co., 1955), Chap. 2, pp. 48-103; Herman Reith, *Metaphysics of St. Thomas Aquinas* (Milwaukee: Bruce Publishing Co., 1958), Chap. 6, pp. 109-40. Because of Kant's use of it (as well as for other reasons), though, this term can be misleading. I prefer to call them "transcend-ents" (which, incidentally, is Aquinas' term—see, for example, *Disputed Ques-tions on Truth*, 21, 3 resp.). They simply *transcend* any one class of things and for that reason are in contrast with restrictive ones.

[44] Upon additional reflection such divergent examples fall into three categories: (a) those in which "good" means "that which is perfect because it is the effect of love"—for instance, the cadenza, the figure-skating; (b) those in which "good" means "that which causes love because it is perfect"—for instance, the food, drink, buildings, and so forth; (c) those in which "good" is predicated only through extrinsic denomination—for instance, a free choice, which is called good because a man freely chooses a good object (#b). See p. 160, sq. and n. 54. On the meaning of "perfect," see pp. 107-9.

true rocket," "a true or a false friend," "a true Republican," "false teeth," "false storefront," "a true Socialist," and so on.[45]

"Good," "beautiful," and "true," then, are also transcendents and share in all the above-mentioned characteristics of "real," "one," and "other than." [46]

All six transcendents testify to two complementary factors as their causes: the complexity of things and the nature of human knowledge. Things actually are undivided within themselves, and thus each is somehow one; are distinct from one another; are perfect to some extent and thus worthy of appreciation and love; are intelligible and thus can cause true knowledge; are well proportioned and thus trigger admiration and joy. They are, in brief, so rich and complex in themselves and in their multiple interrelations that they cannot be adequately caught except in multiple intelligibilities, and these are the various transcendents. Secondly, if the human mind were so powerful as to exhaust in a single intuitive grasp all the intelligible wealth of things, there obviously would be only one transcendent awareness. Although it is a tribute to man's cognitive ability that he can spontaneously achieve such transcendent awarenesses at all, still his knowledge is comparatively imperfect and weak: it is gradual, progressive, and piecemeal. The multiplicity of the transcendents testify to that aspect of human cognition.

(b) TRANSCENDENTS AS KNOWN METAPHYSICALLY

Such, then, are the transcendents on the spontaneous level—awarenesses which all persons automatically achieve and the meaning of

---

[45] If truth is a property of knowledge, it can be applied to things only through extrinsic denomination. This application occurs in a twofold manner. Something can be called "true" insofar as it is the result of truth (for example, the bomb with respect to the teen-ager, who must know truly what a bomb is and how to make it in order for there to be a bomb) or insofar as it causes truth (the bomb with regard to those witnessing an explosion for the first time). In reference to this second application, some things are of such a nature as easily to deceive, to convey an erroneous impression, to cause a false judgment, as their very names imply—false teeth, fool's gold, false storefronts, a mirage, counterfeit money, a wig, a forged signature, and so on. See p. 158 sq.; also n. 51 and n. 53.

[46] This list of transcendents is not intended to be complete. Most likely "cause" is another, since it is predicable of everything—of agents, goals, components (see Chap. VIII). So too, perhaps, is "love" or "tendency"—on this, see William Rossner, S.J., "Love and Being," *Wisdom in Depth: Essays in Honor of Henri J. Renard, S.J.*

which transcends any one of the various classes of things. By making the implicit be explicit they add to prior knowledge, and thus are not synonyms. In them the content of our knowledge grows, but its extension remains constant: all of them are predicable wherever any of them is predicated. Because of the fact that these awarenesses are the direct reactions of the human knower to the actual universe itself, we can accurately say that in the last analysis the transcendents are nothing more than actual things re-presenting themselves within our minds in all the rich complexity of their interrelations. In the light of this, transcendents will necessarily be found wherever the actual universe confronts attentive minds.

They will be found, then, on the metaphysical level too, for metaphysics is the result of such a confrontation. It is the science of existents precisely as existent, immediately caused by actuals registering themselves in their very status of actuality upon our intellect. The effect is awarenesses which in a special manner transcend any definite kind of thing, which explicitate what previously was only implicit, which add to prior knowledge, which mark a growth in comprehension with no decrease in extension. In a word, they are transcendents.

Let us briefly look at some of these. The initial awareness which actually existing items set up within the metaphysician has as its content "an actually existing item" and is expressed by "real" or "being." On the spontaneous level those terms mean "something or other actually present": "something" points to something material (be it an intrinsic unity such as a man or an extrinsic unity such as a wristwatch) because known only through direct perception; "actually present" points to its actual existence merely as a fact. No longer, though. Now they signify "an actually existing item": "item" indicates any sort of actual whatever, whether material or immaterial, whether a man, a clock, a component, or God; "actually existing" now highlights actual existence as the heart of the item's reality, whether this be identified with that actuality (as in God) or really other than it (as in other actuals).[47] Manifestly, such an awareness is predicable of absolutely every sort of actual because it has been consciously derived from them and signifies each in its very actuality, whence all are similar.[48] It is, in short, a transcendent.

Every actual *is* also in an undivided and cohesive way, whether this

---

[47] See Appendix B: "How the Meaning of 'Being' is Worked Out."

[48] Since "being" also designates them in their diversity, such predication is analogous, of course, and this according to the kinds of analogy previously outlined. See Sec. 2 of this chapter.

indivision, cohesiveness, togetherness be that of an extrinsic unity (this telescope, this mosaic), an intrinsic unity (this man), or of simplicity (as in God or in a substantial form or any other component).[49] Addressing themselves in that condition to a metaphysician, actuals add to the previous notion, and the result is the awareness of "an actually existing item as undivided," expressed by the word "one." "Item" still points to any sort of actual whatsoever and "actually existing" to actual existence as the center of its reality, but "as un-divided" indicates what is both a condition and a consequence of actuality, for whatever is actual could be divided only at the risk of not being what it is and, above all, of not be-ing at all. This awareness continues to be predicable of all actuals because it too has been deliber-ately derived from them so as to be reapplied to them in their varying states of unity. It is, then, a second metaphysical transcendent.

Inasmuch as it actually exists and does so in a unique fashion, every actual also is other than all others. This fact is clear from even a mere inventory of them. Various intrinsic unities such as this man and that man, as well as various extrinsic unities such as this pipe organ and that electric fan, are all known to be distinct through direct per-ception: we see them physically separable. The act of existing and other components within this man we know to be distinct through intellection: we reflect upon the diverse evidences he gives of change/stability, of actual existence.[50] By reasoning, we know God to be totally other than all else because He alone exists of His very nature. In their otherness, then, actuals cause within an alert metaphysician the aware-ness of "an actually existing item as other than all else." "Item" and "actually existing" retain their previous meanings, but the addition, "as other than all else," points to a second condition and consequence

---

[49] Manifestly, such actuals are not all equally one, but are analogous in their unity. They are similar in that all are to some degree undivided and cohesive. They differ in that each is so in its own way—for example, the members of a family are themselves individual persons, held together by relations arising from common origin, love, and other factors; the integral parts of an individual man depend entitatively upon a single human nature, which is itself specifically one because informed by a single substantial form, itself actualized by a single act of existence simultaneously existentializing all the other components and all inte-gral parts; God is totally free of divisive parts and thus is subsistent unity.

For portrayal of a philosophy in which unity holds primacy, see L. Sweeney, S.J., "Basic Principles in Plotinus's Philosophy," *Gregorianum*, 42 (July, 1961), 505-16.

[50] Components differ really from one another by what can be described as a "real but minor distinction"; intrinsic, as well as extrinsic unities, differ really among themselves by a "real major distinction." See Chap. IV, Sec. 2a.

of actuality: every actual is distinct from all else by the very fact it actually *is* and is what it is. Because it can be predicated of all actuals (and this for the same reasons which held good for "being" and "one"), this awareness is also a metaphysical transcendent.

With respect to their status of actuality, actuals entail relationships also to knowledge. As we previously saw when analyzing situations on the spontaneous level, truth when strictly interpreted is a characteristic only of knowledge—the conformity of the mind to what actually is ("The prosecutor knows the truth about the racial incident"). But what actually is (a bomb made by a disgruntled teen-ager) is the result of true knowledge in the mind of its maker (unless the youth had true knowledge of what a bomb is and how to make it, there would be no bomb, and this fact is recognized in the father's statement, "Yes, it's a true bomb, all right"). What actually is also is the cause of true knowledge in other minds (as indicated by the mother's remark after the bomb exploded: "Now, I truly know what a bomb is"). Because of its relationship to truth, then, what actually *is* can be termed "true" through extrinsic denomination.[51]

Once we ascend to the philosophical level and discover that all actual existents whose essence is really other than existence have been made by an Existent Whose very nature is Actuality and thereby is also Knowledge (see Chap. V, Sec. 6), then we realize that all such existents can be called "true." They actually *are* and are what they are because in knowing Himself perfectly God knows them truly as finite

---

[51] No one should imagine that this mode of predication is arbitrary or meaningless or without objective foundation. When we apply health to medicine through extrinsic denomination (for example, "Declomycin capsules are health-giving for anyone having the flu"), that application is grounded in and points to the very chemical constitution of the medicine. Change the chemical formula and the application is no longer possible. Likewise, the application of truth to an actual is grounded in and points to its very entity, which *is* and is exactly what it is because it conforms to its maker's true knowledge, and which in turn causes our minds to be conformed to itself because of the fact that it *is* and is what it is. To say an existent is true is to limelight the connection which *being* has to knowledge and truth.

Some define truth as any type of conformity. In such an approach, it can be predicated through intrinsic denomination not only of knowledge (conformity of the mind to things), but also of things (conformity of things to the mind). But this approach does violence to the primary connection truth seems to have to knowledge. We depict the conclusions to which we intellectually assent as "probable," "certain," and "doubtful" but no one describes a barbed-wire fence or a barking dog as probable or certain or dubious through intrinsic denomination because these are clearly properties of knowledge. So too is truth, which should accordingly be reserved, in its intrinsic predication, for knowledge.

re-presentations of His infinite actuality, and He produces them in accordance with that knowledge.[52] They are, then, the effect of truth in the mind of Him Who makes them. As the content-determining source of human cognition, they also are the cause of truth in the minds of us who observe them. They are situated midway between divine and human truth.

When this situation in which all creatures are located gets through to a metaphysician, the result is the awareness of "an actually existing item in its relationship to truth." "Item" continues to indicate any kind of actual and "actually existing" indicates actuality as the heart of its reality, whereas "in its relationship to truth" stresses that in their existential status actuals are linked with true knowledge—either as its effect or as its cause. Nothing *is* or is what it is unless its maker knows truly; no one else knows truly unless things actually *are* and are what they are. Since this awareness has arisen from the universal condition of all actuals, it is predicable of all, and thus is another transcendent on the metaphysical plane.[53]

---

[52] For a substantiation and development of God's knowledge and its link with His causality, see the treatises in natural theology referred to in n. 45, p. 127.

Why bring God into a consideration of truth (as well as goodness and beauty, soon to be considered)? Because His existence has already been proved, and the sort of Existent He is has also been sketched, at least in a general fashion (see Chap. V, Sec. 6). His knowledge, love, and joy in contemplation add a necessary dimension to the transcendents.

They can, nonetheless, be validly (although incompletely) viewed without God—that is, in relation to the truth, love, and joy through contemplation which they cause in us. Existents themselves actually are intelligible, and as the content-determining causes of our intelligibilities they bring our knowledge into conformity with themselves. Existents themselves actually are perfect and thereby capable of exciting in us love and desire. Existents themselves actually are splendent (for the force of that word, see n. 56) and call forth joy and admiration when we behold them. Consequently, transcendent descriptions of things in their relations to human knowledge, love, and delight as true, good, and beautiful are not only possible but also accurate, valid, worthwhile, philosophically necessary. Seeing them against the background of divine truth, love, and delight simply completes and balances the picture.

[53] The subject of this predication through extrinsic denomination (see p. 155, n. 45 and p. 158, n. 51) is not only this man but also his components, each of which is known truly by God and can cause us to know them truly.

Can we also say God is true? Creatures are said to be true because they are the effect of God's true knowledge and the cause of ours. They are conformed to divine truth and bring our knowledge into conformity with themselves. Can we apply this twofold situation in any way to God? Clearly, God is true with reference to us inasmuch as through creatures He causes us to know Him truly. What of the first sort? Yes, if properly understood. Within God there can be no question

Actuals also are immersed in a context of love. Let us momentarily return to the spontaneous plane. Whatever actually *is* (for example, the cadenza bowed by Heifetz, the Triple Sal Chow executed by a champion figure skater, the pirouette of an expert ballerina) is the result of love in its maker (one does not endure the long hours of practice unless he loves music, skating, or dancing, and the perfect cadenza, Triple Sal Chow, or pirouette does not occur except from painstaking practice). Whatever actually *is* also is the cause of love in us witnessing it (because perfectly executed, a cadenza, Triple Sal Chow, pirouette can trigger in us a desire to do likewise: "How wonderful! I would love to do that too."

Upon moving to the metaphysical plane, we realize that the context of love encompasses absolutely every creature. As existents whose existence differs really from what they are, they point to God, Who by His very essence is Actuality, and thus is Love and Freedom also. They actually exist and are what they are because in loving Himself God also loves them as limited reproductions of His limitless perfections, and He effects them according to that love. In brief, they are the result of His love. Because their perfections initiate love in us, they also are the cause of our love. They occupy a halfway house between divine and human love.

When existents bring home to the metaphysician the place they thus occupy, there ensues an awareness of "an actually existing item as perfect and thus in relationship to love," designated by the term "good." "Item" and "actually existing" preserve their former significations, but the addition, "as perfect and thus in relationship to love," emphasizes the connection all actuals in their very actuality have to love: they are perfect because they are the effects of love or they cause love because they are perfect. Nothing is perfect unless its maker loves; no one else loves except because existents are perfect. Issuing from that common situation in which all existents find themselves, this awareness can be predicated of all and is, clearly, still another metaphysical transcendent.[54]

---

of cause/effect between knower/known. Moreover, conformity is replaced with absolute identity: what is known and the knower are identical because each *is* God, subsistent Actuality. God knows Himself by actually being Himself (whereas we know only by intentionally being the known). Hence, God could no more not know Himself than He could not be Himself. Here, truth is predicated of God's very being no longer through extrinsic denomination, because knowledge here is identified with actuality. God *is* Truth.

[54] Manifestly, good is predicated of all actuals without exception (men and all other material existents, their components, God) through intrinsic denomination,

Finally, existents prove also to be inserted into a third milieu—that of joy and contemplation. As is clear with regard to a human artist, what he actually makes (a painting, a poem, a sonata) results from his compelling inspiration, from his vision of beauty and the thrill and delight it instills. In turn, what he actually makes communicates delight and joy to us beholding it. Simply stated, what actually *is* is at once the effect of the artist's joy through contemplation and the cause of the spectator's joy from contemplation. For both reasons it can be named "beautiful." [55]

To a metaphysician, that environment of joy and contemplation is the habitat of every created existent. By their very existential status as creatures, such existents establish the existence of an Existent Who by nature is Actuality, and thereby is subsistent Perfection, Order, Harmony, Clarity—in a word, Beauty—, issuing into joy through self-contemplation. They actually *are* and are what they are because God,

---

and this analogously, since all are perfect, each in its own way. This analogous predication would be according to the same kinds of analogy as that of "being" —namely, eminence, proportionality, and reference.

Is good predicated of any thing through extrinsic denomination? Apparently it is predicated of our free choices, which can be depicted as good or bad with reference to whether the objects chosen are good or evil. If so, a moral good is something objectively, entitatively good in relation to freedom.

[55] The beautiful has traditionally been described as "that which pleases upon being seen" (*id quod visum placet*). On the spontaneous level that description concerns aesthetic beauty and consists of three elements: (a) *"That which"* points to the beautiful thing itself, whether in nature (a sunset, a landscape, a person) or an artifact (a painting, a sonata). Beauty in those objects resides in their having at least these three properties: integrity or abundance of perfections; proportion, order, or harmony; clarity and refulgence. (b) *"Upon being seen"* indicates any sort of artistic perception (seeing, hearing and the like). (c) *"Pleases"* points to the effects of #a and #b: joy, delight.

When transferred to the metaphysical level, the same three elements should be present, but in a different manner: (a) *"That which"* indicates any actual whatsoever in the very force of its actuality (which for God *is* His very nature and for creatures is the act existentializing all other components, through which it in turn essentializes itself). Thence reside the actual's perfections, unity, right order and harmony, luster. (b) *"Upon being seen"* points no more to mere artistic perception but to the austere, heightened intellection by which a metaphysician understands all actuals in their very actuality (see #a). (c) *"Pleases"* signifies the resultant delight and joy.

On beauty, see Jacques Maritain, *Art and Scholasticism* (New York: Charles Scribner's Sons, 1937); idem, *Creative Intuition in Art and Poetry* (New York: Pantheon Books, Inc., 1953); E. Gilson, *Painting and Reality;* G. Smith and Lottie Kendzierski, *The Philosophy of Being* (New York: The Macmillan Company, 1961), pp. 359-63; M. Vaske, *An Introduction to Metaphysics,* pp. 197-205.

in beholding and rejoicing in Himself, also rejoices in them as partial mirrorings of His beauty, and He produces them in accordance with His joy and delight. They are the results of His joy in beholding the splendor of His beauty. Because their order, right proportions, clarity, and integrity stimulate joy in us beholding them, they are the source of our joy. They reside between divine and human joy.

When actuals address themselves in this condition to a metaphysician, they set up the awareness of "an actually existing item as splendent and, hence, in relation to joy and contemplation," signified by "beautiful." [56] "Item" and "actually existing" again express what we would expect; the other words highlight the liaison which actuality has with joy and contemplation: all actuals as actual are splendent because they result from joy through contemplation or because they effect joy from contemplation due to their splendor. Whatever actually is flashes forth in splendor only because of its maker's delight in contemplation; we take delight in contemplating whatever actually is only because it does so flash forth. Since this awareness has issued from a characteristic common to all actuals, it is predicable of all, and thus is another (and final) transcendent. [57]

(c) IN RETROSPECT

Here, then, are the metaphysical transcendents:

being	an actually existing item as actual
one	an actually existing item as undivided
individual [58]	an actually existing item as other than all else

---

[56] This definition is only an attempt to explicitate the traditional one just discussed (see previous note). "Splendent" (as well as the noun, "splendor") is used in the original force of the Latin word: *"splendere: to shine, to be bright."* The integrity, perfections, right proportion, and good order inherent in their actuality enable all actuals to be bright, to shine forth upon human knowers sufficiently prepared to behold them, with resultant joy and admiration. See G. Smith and L. Kendzierski, *op. cit.*, p. 360: "Only some knowledge acts are delightful. The question is, why is this so? The explanation seems to lie here. Some knowns are integral wholes, with properly proportioned parts and bathed, so to say, in their own light. The knowledge of such knowns, causes an intense knowledge delight."

[57] See n. 46 as to the number of transcendents. The present list is not exhaustive.

[58] A single word is needed to express "other than," and "individual" is the adjective we have chosen as sufficiently appropriate to be applied to God in His otherness from all else, to material things, even to components. Each actual is *individual;* in saying this we mean simply that each is *other than* all others. On "individuated," see n. 87.

true	an actually existing item in relation to truth
good	an actually existing item as perfect, and thus in relation to love
beautiful	an actually existing item as splendent, and thus in relation to joy and contemplation

Together with their counterparts in one's spontaneous knowledge, they have the following characteristics. They are awarenesses whose meanings are not restricted to any of the various classes of things. They explicitate what previously was only implicit. They add to prior knowledge, and hence are not synonymous. In them knowledge grows in comprehension, but its extension stays constant: all of them are predicable wherever any of them is predicated.[59] They are the immediate re-actions of the human knower to the actual universe itself—things actually are undivided, are distinct from one another, are perfect and intelligible and well proportioned. In fact, they *are* actual things reproducing themselves intentionally within us in all their complex richness. This reproduction, though, is no longer through mere direct perception, as that which occurs when the transcendents are spontaneously known and which results in matter showing up in their content. Rather it is through intellection (initiated, however, and nourished by data gained perceptually, and thus inductively). Through analysis, reflection, and reasoning the human knower becomes (to paraphrase Maritain) sufficiently purified, sufficiently empty, sufficiently attentive to listen to actual existents speaking directly in terms of their very actuality, and the science of metaphysics is begotten within him.[60]

That status of actuality is the core of reality in all actuals, and therefore all their other transcendent marks are its sequels. This man is one not only because a single substantial form specifies his nature, but also and especially because the single act of existence actualizing that substantial form also actualizes all of his other components. Why is he really distinct from other members of the human species?

---

[59] Because "one" and the other transcendents subsequent to "being" merely explicitate what "being" already implies, they also share in the properties of "being." But "being" is as rich as is possible for a concept with maximal extension: it signifies everything in each actual of which it is predicated, and it is predicable of all. Therefore, the other transcendents too are as rich in content as is "being": although predicable of all, they too signify everything in each, even though they do so each from its own point of view.

[60] Jacques Maritain, *Preface to Metaphysics* (New York: Sheed & Ward, 1948), p. 48.

Proximately because his quantified matter physically sets him apart from them, although quantified matter exercises its intrinsic causal function of individuation only if it actually *is*.[61] The fact that he is a *man* enables others to know truly what human means, but humanity and its ability to communicate itself intentionally are anchored in the fact that men do exist. Why is he virtuous, witty, wise, and perfect in various other ways? Because granted that he actually *is*, then virtue, keen wit, wisdom *are* and are virtue, wit, and wisdom. Whence his ontological splendor? From the right proportion, good order, ontic integrity to be found (among other places) in the harmonious sub-ordination of all other components to actual existence (they are, are what they are, and are causally functioning because existentialized), which in turn autodetermines itself through them. In brief, the act of existing is the fundamental source not only of reality but of unity, of otherness, of intelligibility, of perfection, and of beauty as well. Its primacy in existents is reaffirmed.

But metaphysical transcendents are nothing more than actually existing items immediately re-presenting themselves within the human knower in their very actuality. Hence, actuality should have primacy in those awarenesses too. If it would not be too complicated, the phrase "as actual" should show up not only in the definition of being but in that of one, individual, and all the rest: "an actually existing item *as actual* and thus undivided . . . *as actual* and thus other than everything else . . . *as actual* and thus with relations to truth," and so on. At least henceforward their definitions should be so read and interpreted that prominence be given that phrase, whether expressed or not.

4. Actual Existence and Evil

If actual existence indeed is the source of reality, and thereby of perfection and of splendor, the inevitable result should be that the universe is full of goodness and beauty by the very fact that it is

---

[61] As we have already seen, substantial form individuates itself through prime matter (see pp. 114-15 and n. 30). But since this cannot specify unless it actually exists, its self-individuation rests upon the act of existing, which is thereby shown to embrace individuation within its own autodetermination.

The role of actual existence in regard to otherness is even more clearly seen when one considers a man's otherness as a person. See Section 5 of this chapter.

actual.[62] But to realize that such is not the case we need only scan our daily newspapers, even in times of what we now call "peace." A relentless hurricane lashes the East Coast with incalculable damage to buildings, property, and crops. On the West Coast savage fires race through tinder-dry forests, leaving only blackened hillsides in their wake. In a Far East city a *coup d'état* replaces one corrupt regime with another possibly just as corrupt, while its streets run red with blood and its stores are invaded by looters. And in an American city, several Negro children attending church are killed by a bomb planted by segregationists. A gang of juvenile delinquents knife two helpless youths in an alley. A nationwide network of hoodlums is uncovered. Within the walls of a major hospital a mother of three children is dying from cancer; a newly married couple are injured when the drunken driver of an oncoming car careens into theirs; a middle-aged man attempts suicide because of unemployment, loneliness, or anxiety.

Despite the many perfections it does contain, then, our universe is not totally perfect. Its inhabitants are, for one reason or another, deprived of many goods they should have. In a word, it is marred by evils, and the question now arises of *what* evil is.[63] We ask the same question concerning a substantial form, a cabbage or a man, or running or thinking or courage. Now the inquiry has to do with the blindness, sickness, death, destruction, injustice, dishonesty, and the like which

---

[62] This optimistic mood is well expressed by Augustine, *On the Trinity*, VIII, Chap. 3 (from *Basic Writings of St. Augustine*, ed. W. J. Oates [New York: Random House, Inc., 1948] II, 775-76): "Since good is the earth, with the loftiness of its mountains, and the due measure of its hills, and the level surface of its plains; and good is an estate that is pleasant and fertile; and good is a house that is arranged in due proportions, and is spacious and bright; and good are animal and animate bodies; and good is air that is temperate and salubrious; and good is food that is agreeable and fit for health; and good is health, without pains or lassitude; . . . and good is the mind of a friend, with the sweetness of agreement, and with the confidence of love; and good is a righteous man; and good are riches . . . ; and good is the heaven, with its sun and moon and stars; and good are the angels, by their holy obedience. . . ."

[63] Evil initiates other questions too. For example, from what causes does evil flow? Does it have an efficient or final cause? (See p. 293, n. 78.) How can we reconcile the presence of evils in the world with God's power and love? For answers to this last, see the natural theology treatises listed on p. 127, n. 45.

No solution to the problem of evil can be satisfactory without bringing in truths from divine revelation (especially the doctrines of original sin and Christ's redemption of mankind through suffering and death), as well as points from the philosophy of man and ethics on the nature and conditions of human freedom and moral activity.

scar our world. What is meant by tagging each of them as "evil"? How can it find a place within a universe which, theoretically at least, should be a plentitude of goodness and perfection? In view of its apparent omnipresence and its far-reaching effects, some have granted evil a positive reality and made it a co-principle with good.[64] Others, perhaps no less aware of its extent and force, have thought the only way to cope with evil is simply to ignore it, to deny its existence, to reckon it as an illusion which can be overcome by positive thinking.[65] What is the answer? Can one find a middle position between those two extremes?

Some items are known and described in themselves—for instance, a cabbage, a vertebrate, a man, his visual power, his actual seeing, his operative habit of mathematics, and the like. Others are known only through reference to something else with which they are contrasted. For example, darkness is the absence of *light*, a hole is the absence of *earth* or *cloth* or *dough*, nonbeing is the absence of *being*. In order to understand this sort of item, one must be acquainted with whatever positive factor is missing (light, earth, cloth), realize that such are absent, and then affirm that these items *are* that very absence. Evil fits here, for it is the absence of a *good* which an existent ought to have.[66] Consequently, as the first step to understanding evil, let us consider again what good consists in.

As previously defined, "good" is "an actually existing item as perfect, hence in relation to love," and is predicable through intrinsic denomination of all actuals—a man, his components, God (see Sec. 3 of this chapter). For greater maneuverability, let us rephrase this definition as follows: *a good is a perfection which an existent ought to have.* Suppose we now concentrate momentarily upon this man. He is composed of various components (actual existence, substantial form, prime matter, multiple and various accidents), each of which is a perfection, and hence a good. When compared to one another, some are recipients of other perfections (that is, essence, prime matter, substance), others are the perfections received (that is, act of existing, substantial form,

---

[64] This is the position of the Manicheans. Perhaps Sartre also fits here, although he pushes the position to its extreme: nothing is good, all reality is evil, and the result is the boredom, forlornness, nausea overwhelming us. See p. 80, n. 34.

[65] This stand is that apparently taken by Christian Scientists and by other religious groups who spurn medicine and doctors.

[66] For instance, blindness is the absence of seeing; deafness, that of hearing; a fever is the absence of the degree of temperature suitable to the human organism; blasphemy is a blatant absence of reverence and adoration towards God.

accidents).[67] Through his own efficient causality and that of agents external to him, he can gradually increase in accidental perfections—for example, he can grow in virtue and become more open to God, he can gain intellectual operative habits in speculative or practical matters, he can contemplate what is beautiful (whether in nature or in artifacts) and thus avoid sinking to a merely impersonal, superficial, inhuman way of living.

What is important for our present purpose is to garner two facts from the preceding. Such an increase is also an increase in goodness, since a good is nothing more than a perfection which one should have. Second and more significantly, to grow in goodness is also to grow in reality and being. Goodness involves the *presence* of due perfections, which *actually exist* within whatever is perfected; but presence and actual existence are coterminous with being and reality; therefore, goodness too is coterminous with being or reality, and an increase in the former is simultaneously also an increase in the latter. Because a newly acquired accident is received by the human existent, and because both what is received and the recipient are good, an increase in goodness is equivalent to a perfection-in-perfection, a good-in-good, a being-in-being.

In contrast, an evil is the *absence* of a good which an existent should have: some or other perfection does not actually exist within a subject. But absence and nonexistence are coterminous with nonbeing and unreality; therefore, evil is also coterminous with nonbeing or unreality. Accordingly, to become more evil is simultaneously a decrease in being and reality, as well as in perfection. Although evil itself is this absence, nonexistence, nonbeing, still it involves the subject or recipient which is deprived of the perfection and yet which itself is comprised of other perfections and thus is good.[68] Consequently, evil is equivalent to imperfection-in-perfection, nongood-in-good, absence-in-presence, nonbeing-in-being.[69]

---

[67] See p. 108 f.

[68] For example, the subject of blindness is the man, and, more immediately, his visual sense, which for some reason or other cannot see. The more immediate subject of poor vision, though, is his actual activity of seeing as without the degree of vision that could and should be there. The immediate subject is always that which directly lacks the perfection in question, that which would itself receive the perfection were it there. On the human level this frequently is a faculty or its operations.

[69] This method of describing evil reveals how heinous evil is when freely chosen. By preferring what is entitatively not good for us (see p. 160, n. 54), we deliberately insert imperfection into perfection, absence into goods already pres-

Perhaps it is now somewhat clear what evil is. It entails three factors.

(a) *In itself* it is the very absence, nonexistence, privation, lack of a due perfection.[70]

(b) It has a *subject*—the existent which is deprived of its due perfection and thus is affected by and suffers from the privation. But the subject in itself is good, and hence is something positive and real.[71]

(c) It is known through a *concept or intelligibility*, the content of which is "the absence of a due perfection" but which is itself an actually existing awareness within our minds, and, accordingly, is also something positive and real.[72]

---

ent, nonbeing into being. Knowingly and freely we begin to destroy and (literally) to annihilate ourselves, to downgrade our degree of reality. These privations are unlike those which come from alien or inescapable sources: they could have been prevented, they are our own doing.

To stress this difference, as well as their seriousness, freely chosen privations are given the special name of *moral* evils and thereby distinguished from *physical* evils. A moral evil is the absence of due perfection in a free choice, as well as in any operation which comes under its direct influence. All other absences of due perfections (whether in men or in subhuman existents) are physical evils.

[70] In the phrases above (imperfection-in-perfection and so on), the first word designates evil *in itself*.

One should take care not to invest evil itself with anything positive. This investiture is not liable to occur with reference to, say, total blindness, which is the absence of all vision, but it can occur when we think of poor vision. Evil there is not the actual vision itself: this the man does have and is a good to the extent it is there—in fact, it is the subject of the privation. Rather it is the amount of vision which is lacking, which he should have but does not. Similarly, the evil connected with such a disease as fever is not the high temperature itself but rather the absence of well-being brought on by that temperature in this type of animal, the lack of suitability and proportion between that temperature and this man.

[71] In the phrases referred to in the preceding note, the last word indicates the subject of the evil (imperfection-in-*perfection*). On the subject, see n. 68.

[72] Obviously, we can easily (although unwittingly) project this concept out upon the actual subject affected and begin to imagine evil itself as something positive and real.

This concept is itself a construct (see p. 137, n. 10). In order to understand this, let us contrast our awareness of "seeing" with that of "blindness." The direct basis of the first is an actually existing item—the operation of seeing which this man is now performing. That of the second is no such actually existing item (in fact, blindness is its very absence) but is the mental activity by which we produce the concept—namely, our knowledge of what seeing is; our affirmation that seeing is absent here, that this man does not see; our concomitant awareness that blindness is "not-seeing," "the absence of seeing." Obviously, the mental activity involved helps constitute the very content of the intelligibility in question,

Here, then, is the intermediate position sought. With the Christian Scientists one can agree that in itself evil is nothing—an absence, a lack. To the Manicheans, though, we concede that evil has a positive side—the subject it afflicts and (frequently, at least) the awareness it produces in those observing that subject. Without a real subject, there could be no evils. Without the positive, there could be no negative. And even though evil itself is a mere absence and a nothing, still it does affect its subject, it does generate a tension, a seeking or reaching out for what is not there but should be. And there lies part of the mystery of evil. If the actual universe were not permeated with reality, perfection, and goodness, evils would be impossible. But it is so permeated, and evils not only can be, but, alas, actually are found in it—privations of perfections in existents which make those very privations possible.[73]

---

within which it shows up as an integral part ("seeing-*denied*," "*not*-seeing," "the *absence* of seeing").

On this point see Aquinas, *S.T.*, I, 48, 2 ad 2: "In another sense, *being* is said to be that which signifies the truth of a proposition which consists in composition, revealed by the verb *is*. In this sense, being is what answers to the question, *Does it exist?* It is in this sense that we speak of blindness as being in the eye; or of any other privation. In this way even evil can be called a being." The only "is" that blindness itself has is the "is" in the intellect's affirmation that, for example, "Helen Keller *is* blind," whereas seeing has a double "is": that of the intellect affirming, "Anne Sullivan is seeing" and that of the visual operation within her.

[73] The picture is not entirely black, however. Evils offer us the challenge needed to become better human beings. "[The fundamental purpose of education is] to introduce a human being to the secrets of his own power to create and thereby to win, through freedom and through suffering, if necessary, the will which is inseparable from all greatness: the will to suffer in creation. Unless we have that will to suffer in creation, we are unworthy to take our part in the travail of humanity" (William E. Hocking in an interview to R. L. Hartzell, Jr., quoted in the *St. Louis Post-Dispatch*, March 20, 1960).

Frequently evils are a great obstacle to assenting to the existence of God. For example, see Raïssa Maritain, *We Have Been Friends Together* (New York: David McKay Co., Inc., 1942), p. 26: "Toward the age of fourteen I started asking myself questions about God. Now that I knew how unhappy or wicked men could be, I wondered if God really existed. I recall very clearly that I reasoned thus: If God exists, He is also infinitely good and all-powerful. But if He is good, how can He permit suffering? And if He is all-powerful, how can He tolerate the wicked? Therefore He is not all-powerful nor infinitely good; therefore He does not exist."

Nonetheless, others prove there must be a God from those very evils. See Nicholas Berdyaev, *Dostoievsky*, trans. Donald Attwater (New York: Sheed & Ward, 1934), p. 87: "The argument everlastingly used against God is the existence of evil in the world, and the whole of Dostoievsky's work is an answer to that argument. I would sum it up, in a paradoxical form, thus: *The existence*

5. Actual Existence and the Individual

Of the six transcendents, the one which deserves special attention and needs more detailed discussion is "other than" or "individual." It undubitably is a transcendent, for it is a trait common to all extramental items, and, we may add, even to intramental ones. For example, in their content our awareness of "animal" is conceptually somewhat *other than* that of "rational"; similarly, our awareness of "being" is *other than* that of "good" or of the other transcendents; our awarenesses of "rational animal" and "man" or of "being" and "real," although identical in content, still are at least expressed by terms which are *other than* one another.[74] But otherness is especially operative in the extramental world. The heart of this man is somehow really *other than* his liver, feet, and other integral parts. His substantial form is really *other than* his prime matter, actual existence, and other components. He himself is really *other than* his twin brother, mother, father, and all other men.[75]

✳ (a) DATA FROM REVELATION

This last otherness it is which demands special discussion, since it actually is twofold. As we learn from divine revelation, this man is really other than that one as an individual member of the human species and, secondly, as an individual human supposit or person. Those

---

of evil is a proof of the existence of God. If the world consisted wholly and uniquely of goodness and righteousness there would be no need for God, for the world itself would be god. God is, because evil is. And that means that God is because freedom is.

"Thus does Dostoievsky arrive at the existence of God through a consideration of the freedom of the human spirit: those of his characters who deny this freedom deny God, and inversely."

[74] The otherness in the first set of awarenesses is that of a "major mental distinction" (see n. 29 and n. 42); that in the second set is a "minor mental distinction" (see n. 42); that in the third might be called a "purely arbitrary" or a "merely semantic mental distinction"—that between synonymous terms (see p. 76, n. 27).

[75] The otherness between integral parts can be described as an "inadequate real distinction" or a "potentially real distinction." Such parts are actually united in and to the whole they constitute; still they are extended, and thus are spatially other than one another. Hence, they *can* become really other than the whole when severed from it. The otherness between components is that of a "minor real distinction"; that between two things, a "major real distinction" (see Chap. IV, Sec. 2a).

two othernesses are really different: nature and supposit are not identical, as revelation in its elaboration and statement by the Catholic Church makes clear. Although we shall discuss this nonidentity only with regard to Christ for reasons of convenience and for obviously direct relevance to our inductive approach in philosophy, still it is to be found also in the Trinity, and this in a magnificent way. Let us quote a few of the Church's statements on the Trinity before turning to Christ. "This is what the Catholic faith teaches," we read in the Athanasian Creed. "We worship one God in the Trinity and the Trinity in unity; we distinguish among the *persons,* but we do not divide the *substance.* For the Father is a distinct *person;* the Son is a distinct *person;* and the Holy Spirit is a distinct *person.* Still, the Father and the Son and the Holy Spirit have *one divinity,* equal glory, and coeternal majesty." [76] Some centuries later the Fourth Lateran Council stated: "We firmly believe and profess without qualification that there is only one true God . . . the Father, the Son, and the Holy Spirit: *three persons* but *one essence* and a *substance* or *nature* that is wholly simple." [77]

But, as we said, we are confining our discussion to Christ. Briefly, how does the Church speak of Him? After its declarations on the Trinity, the Lateran Council turns to the Incarnate Word: "The only-begotten Son of God, Jesus Christ, made incarnate by a common action of the Holy Trinity, and conceived by Mary ever Virgin with the cooperation of the Holy Spirit, became a *true man* composed of a rational soul and human flesh, *one person* in *two natures.*" [78] The Church takes pains to emphasize that His human nature is complete in every way: it consists of soul and body and all the properties any man has.

> [In Christ] the proper character of each *nature* [both divine and human] was kept inviolate, and together they were united in *one person.* Thus was lowliness assumed by majesty, weakness by power, mortality by eternity; and a *nature* that could not be defiled was united to one that could suffer in order to repay the debt attaching to our state. . . . In the full and perfect *nature of true man,* there-

---

[76] John F. Clarkson, S.J., *et al.* (translators), *The Church Teaches: Documents of the Church in English Translation* (St. Louis: B. Herder Book Co., 1955), #6. [Italics added here and in the next three quotations.] The Athanasian Creed was probably written in the fifth or sixth century. In this and subsequent documents "supposit" and "person" are equivalent. "Nature," "substance," and "essence" are also equivalent.

[77] *Ibid.,* #306. The Fourth Lateran Council was held in 1215.

[78] *Ibid.,* #455.

fore, the *true* God was born—perfect in every characteristic proper to us as well as in every one proper to himself.[79]

However little inclined philosophers may be to attend to divine revelation, nevertheless here is a fact revealed by God that casts an important light on existents, and hence cannot be ignored: a Man once actually existed Who had a complete human nature and essence but Who was not a human supposit. Because of that human nature He was really other than every other member of the human race. By reason of His quantified matter He was physically separate from them. By reason of His soul, together with His intellect, will, and other faculties, He had his own operations—His own knowledge, His own free choices, His own prayers, His own feelings, His own sufferings. But He was not really other than them as a human supposit for the simple reason that, as revelation informs us, He was not a human supposit. The question is, then: what makes a nature be a supposit? What is added? How, precisely, do supposit and nature differ?

Revelation itself does not explicitly answer that question, and theologians have given various answers. According to Scotus and others, supposit adds to nature solely the negative characteristic of incommunicability, of noncommunication—my human nature is a supposit because I do not share it with someone else; it has not been assumed by another, whereas Christ's human nature was taken up by God and thus is no supposit.[80] For both Suarez and Cajetan, as well as their

---

[79] *Ibid.*, #412. The quotation is from St. Leo's Letter to Flavius in 449, accepted by the Council of Chalcedon as an accurate expression of the Church's teaching on Christ. Also see the Athanasian Creed: "Our Lord Jesus Christ . . . is a perfect man, with a rational soul and human flesh" (*The Church Teaches,* #7). Council of Chalcedon in 451: "We declare that He is perfect both in His divinity and in His humanity, truly God and truly Man composed of body and rational soul; that He is consubstantial with the Father in His divinity, consubstantial with us in His humanity. . . . We declare that the one selfsame Christ, only-begotten Son and Lord, must be acknowledged in *two natures* without any commingling or change or division or separation; that the *distinction between the natures* is in no way removed by their union, but rather the specific character of each *nature* is preserved and they are united in *one person* and *one hypostasis.* We declare that He is not split or divided into two persons, but that there is one selfsame only-begotten Son, God the Word, the Lord Jesus Christ" (*ibid.,* #414).

Such declarations are against those who would make Christ be one existent by eliminating part either of His divine nature or of His human nature.

[80] For a clear account of Scotus' position, see M. de la Taille, S.J., *The Hypostatic Union* (West Baden Springs, Ind.: West Baden College, 1952), pp. 15-16. On Scotus (as well as other positions), see L. de Raeymaeker, *Philosophy of Being,* pp. 240-47; H. J. Renard, S.J., *Philosophy of Being,* pp. 222-34.

modern followers, supposit adds a really distinct mode to nature—according to the former it is a sequel to existence; according to the latter it is preparatory for existence: it enables essence to exist independently.[81] For theologians whose philosophical approach is an inductive one and to whom material existents have shown themselves to be composed of an act of existing really distinct from what each is, the answer is simple and ready-made. Supposit adds to nature or essence the act of existing; a supposit is a nature actualized by its own act of existing.

> The difference between a human nature that is a person (as in the case of Peter) and a human nature that is not a person (as in Christ's case) is reducible to this: in the one case the nature exists through an existence of its own, in the other through the existence of an uncreated Being. . . . In the first case (the case of Peter) the humanity is possessed of an existence of its own; it exists, not only as a substantial power of action, but as an agent, with its own initiative and its own ends; it exists, in a word, for its own sake, because it exists independently of any one existing, except the Creator as such. Clearly it does not exist of itself, or without cause: that is God's exclusive privilege. But it exists *by* itself, apart from any companionship or partnership in existence; it is *self-enclosed:* which is the definition of a person.[82]

Again:

> What do we call a person, or a subsisting individual, in opposition to a mere nature? We mean one that exists as a complete whole: not as a part of a whole, like my hand; nor as an associate only, like my body; nor as a mere belonging or dependency, like Christ's humanity. We mean one existing separately as well as independently: self-governed no less than self-contained. All that is verified at once when you have, in the created sphere, a complete nature fitted with what is required to make it exist by itself and for itself. What then is required for this? Nothing more than the ordinary connatural existence of a human nature. Have that, I would say to the nature, and at once you are a man, you are somebody: because to exist in such manner is to subsist as a whole, as an independent unit.[83]

---

[81] See M. de la Taille, *The Hypostatic Union,* pp. 16-19. One of Cajetan's most prominent followers is J. Maritain. See his *Existence and the Existent,* pp. 62-68; *Degrees of Knowledge,* Appendix IV, pp. 430-44.

[82] M. de la Taille, *Hypostatic Union,* p. 19.

[83] *Ibid.,* p. 20.

Several philosophically important conclusions can be drawn from the preceding theological excursion. By following the inductive methodology already outlined (see Chaps. III and IV), one can have achieved the realization that a material existent involves more than a mere essence or nature: it also comprises an act of existence, which existentializes that essence and is the heart of reality in that existent. When he comes upon the revealed dogma that nature is not supposit, that they are different, that the latter adds still further independence to the former, he can easily agree. Of course, they are not identical: nature or essence is only part of the existent, which also involves actual existence. A supposit is the entire existent—the essence as actualized by existence. Unlike a philosopher who follows the lead of Scotus or of Cajetan, he need add nothing to his philosophical interpretation of existence when he encounters divine revelation.[84]

---

[84] The matter actually is not that simple, since historically the revealed dogma came first and the philosophical contrast between nature and person was worked out under its influence. This influence produced what Gilson calls *Christian philosophy*. See E. Gilson, *Spirit of Mediaeval Philosophy* (New York: Charles Scribner's Sons, 1940), p. 37: "If [Christian philosophy] is to deserve that name the supernatural must descend as a constitutive element not, of course, into its texture, which would be a contradiction, but into the work of its construction. Thus I call Christian, *every philosophy which, although keeping the two orders formally distinct, nevertheless considers the Christian revelation as an indispensable auxiliary to reason.* . . . It includes in its extension all those philosophical systems which were in fact what they were only because a Christian religion existed and because they were ready to submit to its influence." See *ibid.,* Chaps. I, II, and XX; *idem, Reason and Revelation in the Middle Ages* (New York: Charles Scribner's Sons, 1939), *passim; Christianity and Philosophy* (New York: Sheed & Ward, 1939) in its entirety.

Despite this historical priority, though, a student who works out the authentic existentialist philosophy presented in this book *before* he learns of, or at least meditates upon revelation could experience the re-actions indicated—a ready assent to revelation with no change in his philosophical analysis of existents.

One should remember that prior to revelation philosophers showed no awareness of the otherness issuing from person or supposit. The terms were known, but they had quite a different meaning. *Persona* in Latin and *prosōpon* in Greek mean a mask—literally, "that through which sound comes" and "that which is placed before the face." *Suppositum* is "that which is placed under." Aristotle was aware of the otherness issuing from nature (see, for example, *Metaphysics,* VII, Chap. 8, 1034a5-8; V, Chap. 6, 1016b32; VII, Chap. 9, 1035b30; X, Chap. 3, 1054a33; X, Chap. 9, 1058b5; XII, Chap. 8, 1074a33). But even for him an individual member of the human species was important not so much in himself but as a link in the endless chain of the species. This attitude to individual men is still to be found in Averroës—see Roland J. Teske, S.J., "The End of Man in the Philosophy of Averroës," *New Scholasticism,* 37 (October, 1963), 431-61.

Does he learn nothing new from that encounter, then? Yes, he discovers that not only does nature differ from supposit as part from whole, but also that a nature can, absolutely speaking, actually *be* and yet not be in a supposit, since once at least there actually was a human nature which was not in a human person. Accordingly, emphasis is placed upon the fact that every man (for that matter, every material existent) entails two sorts of otherness, of independence, of autonomy, of individuality: that of his human nature, by which he is really other than the members of any other species, human or otherwise; and that of his human personality, by which he is really other than all other supposits, human or otherwise. However much contemporary thinkers may lump both sorts together[85] and however difficult or even impossible it is for anyone perceptually and experientially to discern their difference, nonetheless different they are. Divine revelation is there to assure us that this is so, and an authentically existentialist philosophy helps explain how this is so.

Finally, actual existence is again disclosed to have primacy because it proves to be the source of the otherness which existents have as supposits. The nature of this human existent is that by which he exists in such a way as to be independent and autonomous as a member of the human species. But his act of existing is that by which he subsists

---

[85] Perhaps one might more correctly say they simply are ignorant that there are two sorts. They are, though, keenly alive to the importance, validity, and value of the individual. Upon that keen awareness is built democracy as a form of government. Karl Marx, *Das Kapital*, First Edition, says on p. 580: "The democratic concept of man is false, because it is Christian. The democratic concept holds that . . . each man is a sovereign being. This is the illusion, dream, and postulate of Christianity." Adolph Hitler said: "To the Christian doctrine of the infinite significance of the individual human soul . . . I oppose with icy clarity the saving doctrine of the nothingness and insignificance of the human being" (quoted by Hermann Rauschning, *The Voice of Destruction* [New York: G. P. Putnam's Sons, 1940], p. 25). See also Moorhouse F. X. Millar, S.J., "The History and Development of the Democratic Theory of Government in Christian Tradition," in *The State and the Church* (New York: The Macmillan Company, 1924), pp. 99-144.

From that awareness flow modern approaches to education. See Ralph Harper, "Significance of Existence and Recognition for Education," *Modern Philosophers and Education* (Chicago: National Society for the Study of Education, 1955), Part I, p. 250: "Both students and teacher are individuals . . . The teacher should recognize the student . . . as an individual. . . . To see another man as an individual is to treat him as if he personally mattered, as if he was irreplaceable, as if he was different from all others. This requires a sensitivity to differences, a humor, and even a certain tenderness that one does not extend to a person in so far as one is thinking of him as one of a type."

—that is, that by which he exists not in someone else, but in, for, and through himself: that by which he exists in such a way as to be independent and autonomous also as a human person. Rightly understood, it is the cause of his human personality.[86]

(b) THE PRINCIPLE OF INDIVIDUATION

Material existents have, then, two kinds of otherness or individuality, the first of which issues from their status as supposits, the other from

[86] Throughout Section 5a we have rather constantly linked supposit with person, and especially with human person. No one should think, though, that supposit and person are synonymous. A person is a certain kind of supposit, one with an intellectual nature; but its having an intellectual nature, its transcendence through knowledge, love, and freedom are not what make it a supposit—this comes from its independence in existence. Analysis solely in terms of such transcendence is inadequate or even irrelevant to its status as supposit. Accordingly, supposit is broader than the human level. It extends to all existents who subsist, whatever their natures—whether divine, angelic, human, or subhuman.

Accordingly, the fact that the presence or absence of knowledge, love, and freedom in an existent flows directly from his nature explains how it was possible for there to have been a human Existent (Christ) Who had such human operations and yet was not a human supposit. But that same fact also emphasizes a point in us who are human supposits: our transcendence through knowledge, freedom, and love, our ability to enter into an "I-Thou" dialogue with other selves, our subjectivity and openness to other subjects issue immediately from the *sort of* existents we are and not from our existential status itself, not from the fact that we subsist, that we exist in, for, and through ourselves because each has its own act of existence. The result is that the consideration of supposits precisely as human, precisely as persons, as subjects *vs.* objects, as selves *vs.* nonselves does not pertain to metaphysics, which studies existents qua existent and not qua this or that kind of existent. Such a consideration can (and should) be made after one has studied metaphysics, philosophy of man, ethics, and philosophy of God. It then serves as an informative and inspiring synthesis of those other philosophical disciplines. But it is itself not metaphysics, and those who locate it at the heart of metaphysics thereby reveal that theirs is not authentically existential. "To be real" is no longer "to be actually existing" but "to be a subject," with the unfortunate result that "real" or "being" can have become univocal (see p. 149) and is predicable only of subjects (and, consistently, perhaps only of *human* subjects). Whatever is not a subject, whatever is subhuman or even nonhuman, is unreal and nonbeing. Such a price is too high to pay even for the most attractive feature which a metaphysics of subjectivity or personalism has to offer: the primacy of being human, "the manwardness, the natural or intrinsic predestination of all physical things to be humanized" (Jerome Diemert, S.J., "Comments," *Proceedings of the Twenty-fifth Annual Convention of the Jesuit Philosophical Association,* ed. John E. Gurr, S.J. [Woodstock, Maryland: Woodstock College Press, 1963], p. 78).

their natures or essences.[87] This latter sort we experience constantly. Because of his concrete nature a man is this material, living, sentient, and rational existent. By reason of his quantified matter he is physically separate from everything else. His vegetative powers nourish and develop him and not others. Through his sensitive powers, together with intellect and will, he has his own knowledge, his own feelings, his own free choices, his own appreciation of beauty, his own sufferings. As this corporeal, living, sentient, rational existent, then, he is other than all other existents, human or otherwise.

Accordingly, the fact of difference seems beyond doubt, and the question is rather: what is its intrinsic cause? If the act of existing is the source of independence and autonomy in an existent as a supposit, what is its source in him as a distinct member of a species? Within a concrete nature what is there to ground otherness and individuality?

First of all, one should note that by one's nature one is specifically different from members of other species. Our inquiry does not concern this difference since, obviously, its source is the substantial form—that by which an existent is human and thus is not canine, feline, and so on. By his nature, though, one also is specifically like members of the same species and yet is unlike them individually. Both John and Paul are similar in that both are men and yet differ because one is this and the other is that man. This difference is the problem.

In its general outline the solution seems foolproof. The natures of John and of Paul are not simple, but are composed of substantial form and prime matter. If his substantial form is that by which John is specifically similar to Paul (and, we may add, specifically unlike a dog or a tree), then prime matter should at least basically be that by which he is individually dissimilar to him. Materiality plays such a function in artifacts.

---

[87] In our interpretation "individuality" is an analogous awareness. All individual items, whether intramental or extramental, are similar in that they are other than one another, and yet are diverse in that they are so each in its own way. This holds true even with respect to nature and supposit. The otherness which marks existents because of their individuated natures is both like and unlike that which marks them as supposits. The first is like the second because both are othernesses; they differ, though, in that the one issues from the sort of being the existent is, the other from his existing independently.

Incidentally, "individuation" and the adjective, "individuated," are restricted solely to the otherness of nature or essence. Although one can talk about both nature and supposit as "individual," one should not speak directly of a supposit as "individuated." Every individuated item is individual, but not every individual is individuated.

Each and every [painting] is a distinct entity, which cannot be duplicated, even by its own author. However carefully he may copy himself, a painter can turn out only another painting. Now, the fundamental cause assigned by philosophers to this character of physical substances lies in the very matter that enters their composition. The classical formula—matter is the principle of individuation —means something quite simple. *It merely expresses the fact that each definite portion of matter, delimited by certain dimensions, exists only once.* A man, or even a machine, can turn out any number of similar chairs made out of the same kind of wood, but the same kind of wood is not the same piece of wood. The number of similar chairs it is possible to make depends only on the available quantity of wood, *but the particular piece of wood that goes into the making of one particular chair cannot enter the structure of another one.* This is what the philosophers give us to understand in saying that, on account of its fundamental incommunicability, matter is the principle of individuation.[88]

What is true of artifacts is a pari or even a fortiori true of intrinsic unities. By the very fact that it is educed from *this* sperm/ovum, a canine substantial form is unique—no other will ever be educed from identically the same sperm/ovum, and hence no other will ever be totally like it. The very fact that a human soul is created within a particular sperm/ovum (with *its* store of genes) eliminates the possibility of another soul being created within the same matter; thus it is unique and differs from all others. Once a substantial form is educed or created within this or that matter, individuation has so thoroughly marked every fiber of its being, as well as that of its faculties and other properties, that the nature it specifies will develop thenceforward in a singular, never-to-be reduplicated fashion.

* But there are difficulties in this theory, as this series of questions reveals.

* *First:* "Is prime matter the sole principle of individuation? If so, how can that which is itself pure potency accomplish such a feat?" *Answer:* Prime matter is only the ultimate principle of individuation. The proximate principle is quantified matter[89]—matter at its lowest de-

---

[88] E. Gilson, *Painting and Reality*, p. 47. (Italics added.)

[89] Traditionally, this principle has been called "matter signed by quantity" (*materia quantitate signata*)—matter made definite by quantity, matter "delimited by certain dimensions" (Gilson, *ibid.*), matter in such a condition that it can be designated and pointed out. This is what we intend by "quantified matter." For a survey of Aquinas' texts, as well as of those of many other authors, see M. D. Roland-Gosselin, O. P., *La 'De Ente et Essentia' de S. Thomas d'Aquin* (Paris: J. Vrin, 1948), pp. 51-134.

gree of essential perfection, matter in such a state that besides whatever other perfections it may have it has extended parts outside of parts. The result is that *this* parcel of matter is other than *that* parcel [90] and, hence, what happens in and develops from this parcel is necessarily other than what happens in and develops from that parcel.

*   *Second:* "But is not matter quantified only when substantial form is present in the composite? If so, is not form the principle of individuation? Or how can substantial form somehow be genuinely necessary and yet matter remain the individuating principle?" *Answer:* Substantial form is necessarily present as conferring the specific perfection which inevitably carries along with it the generic perfection of corporeity—that by which the existent is of such a nature as to have extended parts outside of parts, as to have quantity as a property. In and through its proper function of specifying, then, form is also that by which a composite is of such a nature as to have extended parts outside of parts. The composite as so constituted individuates the additional perfections of life, sensitivity, and rationality by receiving them in a unique way. This it can do because, by reason of the quantity, it is physically separate from and is thus other than any other composite receiving its own set of essential perfections. The intrinsic cause which is directly responsible for individuation, then, is the composite itself in that initial stage of composition—the composite as being of such a nature (whatever specifically it may be) as to have extended parts outside of parts, as to have quantity as its property. And this is what we call "quantified matter."

*   *Third:* "But such an answer only suggests a new difficulty. Either those essential perfections are really distinct from one another (and then one has as many really different substantial forms as there are such perfections; thus man is no longer an intrinsic unity). Or they are solely mentally distinct (and, in that case, they are merely arbitrary disjunctions and theoretical constructs—just different synonyms for one and the same reality); if so, they cannot be real factors in causing individuation within actual existents." *Answer:* There is a third possibility: their mental distinction is not arbitrary but is such as to be objectively grounded in actual existents, as this evidence shows. Although rationality, sensitivity, and the rest are only mentally distinct in this human existent, they are sources of faculties and other properties which

---

[90] Gilson, *Painting and Reality*, p. 47: "[The principle of individuation] merely expresses the fact that each definite portion of matter, delimited by certain dimensions, exists only once. . . . The particular piece of wood that goes into the making of one particular chair cannot enter the structure of another one."

are really distinct—for example, his intellect and will (which flow from rationality) differ really from his sense faculties (which flow from sensitivity), from his vegetative operative powers (which come from life), and so forth.[91] Again, even though such perfections are not really distinct in this man, they show themselves to be genuinely different when those in a man are contrasted with those in a dog, a plant, or a chemical compound. The lower perfections *are actually found to exist without* the higher ones and thus they cannot be totally identical—for instance, a dog has sensitivity but not rationality, a geranium lives but is not sentient, water has various chemical properties but is without life. Moreover, when found within one and the same nature, the higher perfections are never found without the lower (no rationality without sensitivity, no sensitivity without life, no life without an apt chemical constitution in the body), and the higher depends on the lower, which receives, affects, and influences the higher. Accordingly, although various essential perfections are only mentally distinct when considered in any one nature, that distinction is not merely constructural but has a real basis in actual existents.[92] Among these perfections the higher depends upon the lower, and in this sense the lower is to the higher as the prior to the posterior. Because of this atemporal dependence and priority, quantified matter can individuate the further essential perfections which it receives and from which it is genuinely and objectively (although mentally) distinct.

    *   *Fourth:* "But a problem remains. If substantial form is the source of the essential perfection of corporeity (as was indicated in the answer to the second question) and hence is the reason why matter is quantified, then form still seems to be the principle of individuation." *Answer:* This might be true were it not for the fact that prime matter is more directly the cause of corporeity and quantity than is the substantial form. True enough, quantity is a property of the composite and thus comes from both. Nonetheless, it flows more proximately from matter than from form. The latter is the proximate principle of specific perfection and properties; but "quantified body" is not a species—nothing actually exists simply as "quantified body" but always as such-and-such a body—as a hydrogeneous body, a geraniaceous body, a canine body, a human body; consequently, the substantial form is not the proximate principle of body or quantity. This role must be filled

---

[91] See p. 114, n. 29.

[92] It is the mental distinction we previously called "major" or "perfectly grounded"—see n. 42 and n. 74.

by its partner-component in the nature or essence—prime matter.[93] Accordingly, quantity is a property of the composite itself and yet is more directly the result of prime matter than of form because it is a nonspecific and generic perfection. Prime matter is pure potency, yes, but it is not merely a negation. It is an actually existing and hence real component, now revealing itself to be capable of more immediately causing quantity than does substantial form, provided the latter is informing it and specifying the existent. True enough, substantial form, because it is autodetermining, individuates itself through prime matter, since this latter can individuate only if it is in an existent which is specifically such-and-such, which has been formally and essentially perfected. Still, as the more direct cause of quantity prime matter performs a function which the form could itself take over only at the price of no longer being substantial form.

Such, then, is the intricate answer to the question of what causes the otherness and individuality which issues from the natures or essences of material existents. The intricacy of the solution is proportioned to the intricacy of the problem. No principle of individuation is needed at all if with Plato one says there are no individuals but only Natures, or if with Ockham and Sartre one says there are no natures but only individuals. In the first case there is only unity, in the second sheer multiplicity.[94] A principle of individuation is demanded only when unity mingles with multiplicity, when individuals share a common specific nature. Each is truly and equally human, although one is this man, the other that man. All are specifically alike, although individually different. How can these disparate characteristics arise from the single, concrete natures they have? Because that nature is itself composed of two components. Substantial form is that by which this man is human and thus specifically similar to all other men; prime matter, because the more immediate source of quantity, is that by which ultimately he is *this* man and thus is unique and singular. Embedded within the concrete and composite nature itself is the intrinsic

---

[93] See p. 114 f.

[94] Plato equivalently says there are no individuals by viewing them as unreal. To Ockham nature is nothing but a name, a term. Sartre explicitly eliminates natures (*Existentialism*, p. 18: "There is no human nature, since there is no God to conceive it"). Although in his interpretation individuals are alone real, theirs is a reality heading towards unreality, for they are mere series of fluid appearances, streams of chance events. See p. 22 ff. On Plato and Ockham, see L. Sweeney, S.J., "Existence/Essence in Aquinas' Early Writings," *Proceedings of the American Catholic Philosophical Association*, 37 (1963), pp. 110-11.

cause not only of specific perfection, similarity, and unity, but also of individuation, dissimilarity, and multiplicity.

6. Summary and Conclusions

(a) Our intention in Chapter VI has been to reveal the primacy which the act of existing has in metaphysical knowledge. This primacy rests upon unshakable foundations: actual existence has primacy in actual existents (see Chap. V); but metaphysical knowledge is nothing more than the re-action set up in the human knower by existents precisely as existent; therefore, actual existence has primacy also in metaphysical knowledge—it should somehow (either explicitly or implicitly) enter into all discussions inaugurated by a metaphysician and into all definitions elaborated by him, where it should occupy a prominent place. He studies (and subsequently describes) all other components only in relation to the act of existing.

(b) The metaphysical definition of "being" is a clear illustration of this pre-eminence, for in its signification of "an actually existing item" it is designed to express all actuals *in their very actuality*—whether this be really other than (as in creatures) or identified with (as in God) what they are.

(c) Because it signifies all actuals in their very actuality, "being" also expresses them in their similarity and diversity, and thus is analogous. How can this be shown?

> 1. Actuals themselves are similar and diverse to one another: they are similar in that they all do exist, but diverse in that each exists in its own way. They are, in a word, entitatively analogous.
>
> But actuals as actuals are the content-determining cause of our metaphysical knowledge of "being."
>
> Therefore, the metaphysical notion of "being" as "an actually existing item" combines similarity with diversity and thus is analogous: "item" has to do with the diversity of existents since it points to what each is (and in this each differs from all else), whereas "actually existing" deals directly with their similarity because it indicates that each is (and in this they are all alike).
>
> 2. But "actually existing" also has to do with existents in their diversity, as this line of argumentation shows.
>
> Nothing actually exists except in a determinate, concrete, unique, individual fashion, and thereby is different from all else.

Therefore, its status of actual existence is one also of diversity.

Hence, in expressing existents as "actually existing," "being" also expresses their diversity—it catches them in their very determinateness, concreteness, uniqueness, individuality.

Therefore, by designating all actuals in their very actuality, "being" expresses not only their similarity but also their diversity and, thus is analogous.[95]

(d) There are as many different kinds of analogy as there are different kinds of similarity/diversity in actuals, as well as in the ensuing knowledge they cause and in the predications they receive. Some of these are:

1. *Analogy of Eminence*: the similarity/diversity in being (as well as in consequent metaphysical knowledge and prediction) between the Existent Whose very essence is to exist and an existent whose existence is really distinct from his essence.

2. *Analogy of Proportionality*: the similarity/diversity in being, knowledge, and prediction between existents whose actuality is really other than what they are.

3. *Analogy of reference*: the similarity/diversity in being, knowledge, and prediction between the components of one and the same existent.

4. *Analogy of denomination*: the similarity/diversity in being, knowledge, and prediction between the extramental and intentional universes.

(e) Actual existence is the basis of all analogy, and thus again reveals its primacy, as is clear from the following.

> Actuals themselves are analogous because they are both similar (all do actually exist) and yet diverse (each exists in its own unique fashion).   ,

----

[95] Another way of stating the same thing is this:

> The characteristics of determinateness, concreteness, singularity, and individuality (which account for the diversity of existents) directly flow from what each is, and by expressing what each is precisely as actual, "being" expresses each in its diversity.
>
> But the fact that something actually exists accounts also for its similarity with all other actuals.
>
> Accordingly, by expressing actuals in their very actuality, "being" also expresses them in their similarity.
>
> Because it deals with an actual precisely qua actual, then, "being" expresses both the diversity and the similarity within existents, and hence is analogous.

But actual existence is the source of both similarity and diversity—
immediately of similarity inasmuch as it is that by which they
actually exist;
mediately of diversity inasmuch as it essentializes (and, thus,
diversifies) itself through whatever essence it actualizes.
Therefore, actual existence is the chief source of analogy in actuals,
as well as in the metaphysical knowledge they cause and the
predication they receive, and its pre-eminence therein is manifested.

(f) That pre-eminence is also clear in metaphysical transcendents
other than "being," which these merely amplify. They explicitate additional aspects and consequences of actuality. "Being" stresses actual existence as the source of all reality; these emphasize its role as the source
of undividedness, of otherness and independence, of intelligibility, of
goodness, and of beauty.

being	an actually existing item as actual
one	an actually existing item as undivided
individual	an actually existing item as other than all else
true	an actually existing item in relation to truth
good	an actually existing item as perfect, and thus in relation to love
beautiful	an actually existing item as splendent, and thus in relation to joy and contemplation

(g) Whereas "good" is "an actually existing item as perfect, and
thus in relationship to love," an evil is "an actually existing item as
lacking perfection, and hence as out of step with love." If the item
without due perfection is one's free choice (together with operations
it directly influences), the evil is called *moral;* absences of due perfection in any other item are *physical evils.*

1. Every evil entails three factors. (a) *In itself* it is nothing but the
very absence of a due perfection. (b) But it has a *subject*—the existent which is deprived of the perfection but which is composed of other
perfections, and hence is good and is something positive and real. (c)
It is known through a *concept or intelligibility,* the content of which
is "the absence of a due perfection," which is accordingly a construct,
but which is itself an actually existing awareness within our minds,
and consequently is also something positive and real.

2. Since evil itself is nothing (#1a), it would seem to lie outside the
primacy of actual existence. Nonetheless, that escape is only apparent,

because evils require actual existents as the subjects of which they are predicated and without which they would be impossible.[96] Consequently, the primacy of actual existence is maintained, however mysteriously and indirectly, even with regard to evil, the very privation of perfection, goodness, and reality.

(h) That primacy is not merely indirect in the otherness or individuality arising from one's status as a person, or, more generally, as a supposit. Actual existence is the intrinsic cause of that very status. A supposit is the existent in its entirety, the existent as consisting of a complete nature or essence actualized by its own act of existing. The act of existing is that by which this man exists in such a way as to be independent and autonomous as a person. It is that by which he *subsists*—exists not in another, but in and thereby through and for himself.

(i) Because it is autodetermining, actual existence has primacy even in the second sort of otherness and individuality—namely, that springing from nature or essence. Prime matter is the basic principle of that individuation because it more directly causes quantity than does substantial form, which is the cause of specific perfection and properties. However, because matter can perform its own causal function only if it is within a specific nature, prime matter relies upon substantial form, which thus individuates itself through matter. But the intrinsic causality of both form and matter is dependent on that of actual existence: unless they actually exist, matter cannot quantify, form cannot specify. Consequently, by actualizing a complete essence or nature and thereby essentializing itself, the act of existing also individuates itself and also helps ground the otherness and individuality indigenous to essence and nature.

(j) This primacy which the act of existing has in supposits and natures should register in their definitions. However variously these are formulated, actual existence should have a prominent place. For example, *supposit* is "that which subsists," "that which exists in, by, through, and for itself," "an existent which is independent and autonomous in the order not only of essence but also of existence itself." *Nature,* though, is "that by which an existent exists in such a way as to be independent and autonomous solely as a member of some species or other," "that by which an existent exists in an individuated fashion." The *act of existing* is "that by which an existent (immediately) subsists and is a supposit, and (mediately—through prime matter and

[96] They also have actual existents as their extrinsic causes. On the causes of an evil, see p. 293, n. 78.

substantial form) exists also in an individuated way, as an individual member within a species."

SUGGESTED READINGS

Anderson, James F., *The Bond of Being*. St. Louis: B. Herder Book Co., 1949. On the analogy of being.

————, *Metaphysics of St. Thomas Aquinas*, pp. 44-98. Chicago: Henry Regnery Co., 1953. Aquinas on the transcendents.

Bobik, Joseph, "Dimensions in the Individuation of Bodily Substances," *Philosophical Studies* (Maynooth), 4 (1954), 60-79.

————, "Matter and Individuation," in *The Concept of Matter*, ed. Ernan McMullin, pp. 277-94. Notre Dame: University of Notre Dame Press, 1963.

————, "Saint Thomas on the Individuation of Bodily Substances," Doctoral Dissertation, University of Notre Dame, 1953.

————, "St. Thomas on the Individuation of Bodily Substances," in *Readings in the Philosophy of Nature*, ed. Henry J. Koren, pp. 327-40. Westminster, Md.: Newman Press, 1958.

Bourke, Vernon J., *The Pocket Aquinas*, pp. 261-82. New York: Washington Square Press, Pocket Books, Inc., 1960. Aquinas on beauty and art.

Cajetan, *Analogy of Names*, trans. E. Bushinski and H. Koren. Pittsburgh: Duquesne University Press, 1953. A sixteenth-century interpretation of Aquinas' doctrine on analogy.

De la Taille, S.J., Maurice, *The Hypostatic Union*, trans. Cyril Vollert, S.J. West Baden Springs, Ind.: West Baden College Press, 1952. On individual, nature, and supposit.

De Raeymaeker, Louis, *Philosophy of Being*, trans. E. H. Ziegelmeyer, pp. 61-69 and 212-25. St. Louis: B. Herder Book Co., 1954. On unity and distinction; on good and evil.

Diemert, S.J., Jerome, "Thomistic Psychology and the Social Dimension of Man," *Proceedings of the Twenty-First Annual Convention of the Jesuit Philosophical Association*, ed. Reginald F. O'Neill, S.J., pp. 11-64. Woodstock, Md.: Woodstock College Press, 1959. Locates man within a philosophy of subjectivity and personalism.

Gilson, Etienne, *Elements of Christian Philosophy*, pp. 145-63. Garden City, N. Y.: Doubleday & Company, Inc., 1960. On God and the transcendents.

————, *Painting and Reality*. New York: Pantheon Books, Inc., 1957.

————, *The Spirit of Mediaeval Philosophy*, trans. A. H. C. Downes, pp. 108-27, 189-208. New York: Charles Scribner's Sons, 1940. On good and evil; on individuality, supposit, and individuation.

Hart, Charles A., *Thomistic Metaphysics*, pp. 325-404. Englewood Cliffs, N. J.: Prentice-Hall, Inc., 1959. On the transcendents.

Johann, S.J., Robert O., "The Problem of Love," *Review of Metaphysics*, 8 (1954), 225-45. With reference to a philosophy of subjectivity, where "to be real" is equivalent "to be a subject."

———, "Subjectivity," *Review of Metaphysics*, 12 (1958), 200-234.

Journet, Charles, *The Meaning of Evil*, trans. Michael Barry. New York: P. J. Kenedy & Sons, 1963.

Kaelin, Eugene F., *An Existentialist Aesthetic: The Theories of Sartre and Merleau-Ponty*. Madison: University of Wisconsin Press, 1962.

Klubertanz, S.J., George P., *St. Thomas Aquinas on Analogy*, pp. 157-293. Chicago: Loyola University Press, 1960. Useful collection of texts on analogy from Aquinas.

Lyttkens, H., *The Analogy Between God and the World*. Stockholm: Almquist and Wiksells, 1952. One of the first authors to challenge Cajetan's interpretation of analogy in Aquinas' writings.

Marien, S.J., Francis J., "Dualism Revisited," *Proceedings of the Twenty-Third Annual Convention of the Jesuit Philosophical Association*, ed. Leo Sweeney, S.J., pp. 21-36. Woodstock, Md.: Woodstock College Press, 1961. Gives primacy to the human knower and subject.

Maritain, Jacques, *Art and Scholasticism*, trans. F. J. Scanlon. New York: Charles Scribner's Sons, 1937. On beauty and our perception of it; on art and related questions.

———, *Creative Intuition in Art and Poetry*. New York: Pantheon Books, Inc., 1953.

———, *Existence and the Existent*, trans. L. Galantiere and G. Phelan, pp. 70-91. Garden City, N. Y.: Doubleday & Company, Inc., 1956 (Image Books Edition). On subject and supposit (on this latter Maritain follows Cajetan).

———, "On the Notion of Subsistence," in *Progress in Philosophy*, ed. James A. McWilliams, pp. 29-45. Milwaukee: Bruce Publishing Co., 1955. A renewal of Cajetan's theory on supposit.

———, *The Person and The Common Good*, trans. J. Fitzgerald. New York: Charles Scribner's Sons, 1947.

———, *St. Thomas and the Problem of Evil*, Aquinas Lecture, 1952. Milwaukee: Marquette University Press, 1943.

McCall, Robert E., "The Metaphysical Analysis of the Beautiful and the Ugly," *Proceedings of the American Catholic Philosophical Association*, 30 (1956), 137-46.

McInerny, Ralph M., *The Logic of Analogy*. The Hague: M. Nijhoff, 1961. A study made of analogy from a logician's point of view.

O'Neill, Martin S., "Some Remarks on the Analogy of God and Creatures in St. Thomas Aquinas, "*Mediaeval Studies*, 23 (1961), 206-15.

Owens, Joseph, *An Elementary Christian Metaphysics*, pp. 43-67. Milwaukee: Bruce Publishing Co., 1963. On the apprehension and conceptualization of "being" (multiple references are given there to other authors).

————, "Thomistic Common Nature and Platonic Idea," *Mediaeval Studies*, 21 (1959), 211-23. Valuable study with reference to the possibles.

Pegis, A., "The Dilemma of Being and Unity," in *Essays in Thomism*, ed. R. E. Brennan, pp. 151-83. New York: Sheed & Ward, 1942.

Phelan, Gerald B., *St. Thomas and Analogy*. Milwaukee: Marquette University Press, 1941.

————, "Verum Sequitur Esse Rerum." *Mediaeval Studies*, 1 (1939), 11-22.

Reichmann, James B., "St. Thomas, Capreolus, Cajetan, and the Created Person," *The New Scholasticism*, 33 (1959), 1-31, 202-30.

Ryan, John K., "The Problem of Truth," in *Essays in Thomism*, ed. R. E. Brennan, pp. 65-79. New York: Sheed & Ward, 1942.

Salmon, Elizabeth G., *The Good in Existential Metaphysics*, Aquinas Lecture, 1952. Milwaukee: Marquette University Press, 1952.

————, "Metaphysics and Unity," in *Progress in Philosophy*, ed. James A. McWilliams, pp. 47-60. Milwaukee: Bruce Publishing Co., 1955.

Sciacca, M. F., "Individuality and Personality," in *The Human Person and the World of Values*, ed. B. V. Schwarz. New York: Fordham University Press, 1960.

Siwek, Paul, *The Philosophy of Evil*. New York: The Ronald Press Company, 1951.

Smith, Gerard, "Avicenna and the Possibles," *The New Scholasticism*, 17 (1943), 340-57.

Sweeney, S.J., Leo, "Analogy and Being," *The Modern Schoolman*, 39 (March, 1962), 261-69.

————, "Basic Principles in Plotinus' Philosophy," *Gregorianum*, 42 (July, 1961), 506-16. A study of a philosophical position giving primacy to unity.

Symposium: The Principle of Individuation, Aristotelian Society Proceedings, Suppl. Vol. 27 (1953).

Tournier, Paul, *The Meaning of Persons*, trans. Edwin Hudson. New York: Harper & Row, Publishers, 1957. On the difference between persons and things.

Weiss, Paul, *Nine Basic Arts*. Carbondale: Southern Illinois University Press, 1961.

————, *Religion and Art*, Aquinas Lecture, 1963. Milwaukee: Marquette Universtiy Press, 1963.

————, *The World of Art*. Carbondale: Southern Illinois University Press, 1961.

Wilhelmsen, Frederick D., *The Metaphysics of Love*, pp. 13-52, especially 23-24, 46-49. New York: Sheed & Ward, 1962. On supposit, nature, and individuation; against an exaggerated primacy to subject.

CHAPTER **VII**

Existence

and Relations

In the light of Section 5 of the preceding chapter, existents show themselves to be independent and autonomous because of the twofold otherness and individuality they enjoy. Each of us is "an unsurrenderable core which in the end determines everything." [1] Each is himself—unique, self-centered (literally), self-enclosed, self-reliant, resistant to what is alien, inviolable in his innermost depths, mysterious.

Nevertheless, each also is open to the outside. Each is necessarily exposed to what is without. This openness, this vulnerability is not a characteristic just of human beings but of subhumans as well. All inanimate things, plants, and animals are (to give but two examples) affected by their space-time environ-

---

[1] Edwin O'Connor, *Edge of Sadness* (Boston: Little, Brown & Co., 1961), p. 249. See also Virginia Wolfe, *To the Lighthouse* (New York: Harcourt, Brace & World, Inc., 1927), p. 95: *"She could be herself, by herself.* And that was what now she often felt the need of—to think; well, not even to think. To be silent, *to be alone.* All the being and the doing, expansive, glittering, vocal, evaporated; and one shrunk, with a sense of solemnity, to *being oneself, a wedge-shaped core of darkness,* something invisible to others." (Italics added).

ment.[2] All are used by others—absorbed, cooked, eaten, intussuscepted, grafted, trained, harnessed, driven, and so on. But with man it is especially clear, frequent, and profound because of his knowledge and love.[3] Although remaining ourselves, we *become others* through these tremendous powers. Thereby we are affected for better or for worse. We are helped or we are hindered, but no matter what, we are influenced by them, and deeply so. And other human existents too, while continuing to be themselves, *become us* through their cognition and love, and thereby we affect them. Complex webs of interrelationships are spun, and we are caught in their powerful strands.

> Nobody has the power to leave another. . . . So much to answer for! . . . All these personal relationships between men and women, between man and man, for which each one of us will, separately,

---

[2] A science has, in fact, grown up to study just that—*ecology,* described recently as "the study of these interrelations of plants and animals with their environment." And what is the environment? "In referring to the natural environment one tends to think first of the broad aspects of the landscape, such as water, soil, desert, or mountain. These types of environment can be more exactly described in terms of physical influences—differences in moisture, temperature, texture of material, and the like—and of biological influences. [But] other organisms form part of the environment just as much as the soil or the rocks. . . . Modern ecology goes beyond the mere description of the habitat, or the listing of its inhabitants, to an analysis of causal relationships and a coordinated understanding of constructive and destructive processes in the community" (George L. Clarke, *Elements of Ecology* [New York: John Wiley & Sons, Inc., 1954], pp. 2 and 3). Again: "Ecology is a broad field—the study of the relations of organisms with their environment. . . . It has been divided into smaller fields, including plant and animal ecology and marine and fresh-water ecology" (Allen H. Benton and William E. Werner, *Principles of Field Biology and Ecology* [New York: McGraw-Hill Book Company, 1958], p. 56). Both books give abundant examples.

Also see W. K. Brooks, "Heredity and Variation: Logical and Biological" (quoted by Benton and Werner, *ibid.,* p. 56): "Every reflective biologist must know that no living being is self-sufficient, or would be what it is, or would be at all, if it were not part of the natural world. . . . Living things are real things . . . but their reality is in their interrelations with the rest of nature, and not in themselves."

On men, too, as subject to cosmic influences, see Pierre Teilhard de Chardin, *The Divine Milieu* (New York: Harper & Row, Publishers, 1960), pp. 27-29.

[3] E. Gilson, *Spirit of Mediaeval Philosophy,* Chaps. 12-14; Robert O. Johann, S.J., *Meaning of Love* (Westminster, Md.: Newman Press, 1955); Frederick D. Wilhelmsen, *Metaphysics of Love,* (New York: Sheed & Ward, 1962); Joseph de Finance, S.J., *Être et Agir,* 2nd Ed. (Rome: Libraire Ed. de l'Univ. Grég., 1960), pp. 266-72, 295-312, 326-41.

have to answer. The question—"What hast thou done with thy brother" will be asked of us as often as in the course of our existence we have influenced anybody, have exercised power over another's heart or body, have used, and abused, a body.[4]

I underwent, during the summer that I became fourteen, a prolonged religious crisis. . . . What I saw around me that summer in Harlem was what I had always seen; nothing had changed. But now, without any warning, the whores and pimps and racketeers on the Avenue had become a personal menace. It had not before occurred to me that I could become one of them, but now I realized that we had been produced by the same circumstances. . . . My friends were now "downtown," busy, as they put it, "fighting the man." They began to care less about the way they looked, the way they dressed, the things they did; presently one found them in twos and threes and fours, in a hallway, sharing a jug of wine or a bottle of whiskey, talking, cursing, fighting, sometimes weeping: lost, and unable to say what it was that oppressed them, except that they knew it was "the man"—the white man. And there seemed to be no way whatever to remove this cloud that stood between them and the sun, between them and love and life and power, between them and whatever it was that they wanted.[5]

They were four and a family—the man, the woman, the small boy, the small girl, and [as with all families] there was something wrong with the whole thing, only now it was too late. In each of them there seemed to be a secret anguish about the struggle it was, every day, to understand the others. By turns they were enchanted and perplexed, delighted and outraged, entertained and bored; and yet most of the time in the most unaccountable manner *all* of it was fun of one kind or another, or at any rate could become pleasantly memorable, as when after the stupidest fight imaginable the man and woman began to move about in the house in silence, as if in memory of chances lost from long before they had met, and suddenly they looked at one another and each saw a total stranger but loved the stranger because now they were tangled in time and held captive by the two kids, and therefore laughed softly about it all, or hummed or sang or said strange words.[6]

---

[4] Francois Mauriac, *The Lamb* (New York: Farrar, Straus & Co., Inc., 1955), pp. 134-35.

[5] James Baldwin, "Letter From a Region in my Mind," *New Yorker,* November 17, 1962, p. 59; later published as "Down at the Cross" in *The Fire Next Time* (New York: The Dial Press, 1963), pp. 29-33.

[6] William Saroyan, "Boys and Girls Together," *Saturday Evening Post,* January 19, 1963, p. 38.

The stark otherness and distinction we experience in ourselves, then, are matched by an almost total vulnerability and openness to others, which terminate in intricate skeins of countless relationships.[7]

These relations are our next topic of study. Somewhat surprisingly, perhaps, some philosophers deny their existence. They see in friendship or marriage or a family or Harlem nothing more than the mental activity of a human knower when confronted with two or more existents in a definite sort of situation. The question which ultimately awaits us, then, is whether or not a relation is itself genuinely real. Is it a perfection actually existing over and beyond the existent at which it terminates, the subject of which it is predicated, the source within the subject from which it flows? Or is it merely a name given those three factors when an observer grasps them together in a single awareness? [8]

1. The Relational Situation

In order to understand the problem better, let us consider various descriptions given an individual human existent.

1. "Stephen is blind."
2. "Stephen is an oak."
3. "Stephen actually is human."
4. "Stephen actually is quantified,
      healthy,
      angry,
      a mathematician."
5. "He actually is smaller than the hoodlum lurking in the alley
      and larger than his wife."

---

[7] See Cassius Jackson Keyser, *Mathematics as a Culture Clue and Other Essays* (New York: Scripta Mathematica, Yeshiva University, 1947), p. 219: "Most words, perhaps all of them, denote relations either directly or indirectly. Familiar specimens are: father, mother, child, brother, sister, uncle, king, subject, citizen, inhabitant, author, above, below, in, out, greater, less, better, worse, mayor, taller, shorter, area, diameter, derivative, integral, volume, lower, sweeter, savior, president, premier, and so on and on.

"The number of relation-denoting terms is huge; yet, compared with the multitude of relations, it is exceedingly small, for most relations are nameless. . . . C. W. Wood [has said]: 'The web of reality is woven of relations, and the so-called things or individuals which the relations connect are themselves composed of relations, being, so to say, only branch-points or nodes or knots or ganglia formed in the web by the meeting and intersection of relations.'"

[8] See the second paragraph of n. 28 for the serious consequences of this position.

6. "He actually is more intelligent than his brother."
   "He actually is similar to him as a man and as a being."
7. "He actually is a friend of Bernard,
   the husband of Grace,
   the father of Mary,
   the teacher of eighty-nine students in geometry."
   "He actually is a member of the Roman Catholic Church,
   of St. Matthew's Parish,
   of the National Guard,
   of the Greenbriars Country Club."
   "He actually is an inhabitant of St. Louis' Harlem."
   "He actually is a creature of God."

Statement #1, obviously, is negative; #2 is affirmative but figurative; #3 is affirmative, literal, and describes what he is substantially; #4 is affirmative, literal, and describes what he is accidentally. Statements #5 to #7 likewise are affirmative. They are as literally true as #3 and #4—if I affirm the opposite of them, I either am in error or I misrepresent the man in question. Like #4, they are in the accidental order, but unlike #4, they are relational—they have to do with him in reference to various other existents. The relational situations they express arise actually from various reasons—from quantity (#5), from the presence of perfection other than quantity (#6), from efficient causality (#7).[9] These reasons let us call the *foundation* of the relation—that which grounds and causes them, that from which they flow. Their *subject* is that in which they inhere, or at least that of which they are predicated (in this case, Stephen). Their *term* is that to which the subject is referred—the hoodlum, wife, brother, students, and so forth. The relation itself is that which is expressed by "smaller than," "similar to," "friend of," and so on—the order, the being-open-toward, the liaison between subject and term.

---

[9] Actually, causality other than efficient causality is also operative in many situations. For example, there is the influence exercised upon us by the place where we live—an Iron Curtain country affects its inhabitants' attitudes, values, psychological moods, and culture differently than does Italy or France or the United States. And the same holds proportionally true of where one lives within the country—whether in a rural or urban area, in what city, in what district in the city, and so on. There is also the effect brought about in us by the times in which we live. We who live in the Cold War decades are thereby different than those living in the Depression or in the nineteenth century, and so forth. Such causes are not efficient ones, or if they are, are greatly different from those generally encountered (the sculptor, carpenter, and so on).

Let us keep such information at hand as we approach the problem.[10] Manifestly, the question of whether relations are real does not arise in situations in which the S, F, and T (one or all of them) are only mental—for example, friendship between Pogo and Albert in the comic strip is no more real than are Pogo and Albert themselves.[11] But it does arise when those three factors do actually exist—when my acts of knowledge and love (F) make me (S) a friend (R) of another (T), when your entrance into a marriage contract (F) causes you (S) to be the husband (R) of Lenore (T), when your quantity (F) makes you (S) smaller than (R) the bully next door (T), when a young man's environment (F) turns him (S) into rebellion (R) against his fellow men (T). Does "friend of," "husband of," "smaller than," or "rebellion against" express an actually existing perfection which is over and above the S, F, and T? If not, then the R is itself not genuinely real. If so, it is. For example, friendship would be the actual entitative condition of my entire person through knowledge and love towards another. It would be an accident really distinct[12] from its S (me), from its F (operations of intellect and will), and from its T (the other person): it is that by which I so exist as to be orientated to another through cognition and love.

Let us consider those two answers more in detail, beginning with the affirmative one.

2. The Affirmative Reply

Although this position is commonly associated with Thomists, still some contemporary non-Thomists also espouse it.[13] Unless I misread

---

[10] In subsequent pages we shall use these obvious abbreviations: S = subject, F = foundation, T = term, R = relation.

[11] Mental relations are especially important in logic (both Aristotelian and modern) and in mathematics. In the latter, a relation is defined as "the class of couples (x, y) for which some function $\phi (x, y)$ is true." See Louis Kattsoff, *A Philosophy of Mathematics* (Ames, Iowa: Iowa State College Press, 1948), p. 35. A class or set is in turn described as any collection into a whole, M, of definite distinguishable objects m (which will be called "elements" of M) of our intuition or thought.

Recently Robert W. Schmidt, S.J., has suggested that "mental relations" be called *"rationate* relations"—see "The Translation of Terms like *Ens Rationis*," *Modern Schoolman*, 41 (November, 1963), 73-75.

[12] This distinction would, of course, be a real minor one because the relationship is a component, an accident. See p. 76.

[13] For an excellent survey of nonscholastics on relation, see C. Kossel, S.J., "The Problem of Relation in Some Nonscholastic Philosophies," *Modern Schoolman*, 23 (1946), 61-81.

him, one such is John Wild. After listing those who denied the reality of relations in favor of an atomism and essentialism,[14] he explains why noetic relations must be real:

> If we drop our *a priori* prejudices as to what cognition must be, and turn to the examination of any given instance of those recurrent facts which are commonly referred to as cognitive, we shall find that they are all relational in character. Something in the knowing organism, a sensation or a concept, is related in some very intimate way to something distinct from itself. This cognitive relation is normally expressed in our language by the word *of*. All knowledge is *of* something. Take the case of tactual feeling. When I press this table there is something in my finger, the sensation or sense impression. But this is definitely not all there is. The sensation is not an isolated atom. *It is a relation to something quite distinct from itself, and quite distinct from my finger.* The sensation is *of* something external pressing. Now this relation and its term are not merely added on to the impression as external atomic accretions or inferences. They are essential parts of the complex, initial datum which cannot occur without them. I cannot touch without touching *something*. Nor does the relation succeed the impression in time. *They occur all together and simultaneously, as the foundation, the relation, and the term of any relation occur all at once and simultaneously, as distinct but inseparable aspects of one composite structure.*[15]

He ends by urging philosophers to put off their a priori atomism and to acknowledge the real relations which actual existents reveal so strikingly.

> This false assumption [that every part of a whole must ultimately be an atomistic globule, merely juxtaposed with the rest] has been laming and distorting our analysis, and blinding it to the rich relational structure of reality, especially its causal dependence. Why not free our analytic methodology from the shackles that chain it to the prejudices of an a priori atomism trying to disguise itself as an empiricism? Experience fairly flaunts her complex relational structure before our eyes with little or no concealment. We cannot express ourselves intelligibly or scientifically without recognizing this in the

---

[14] John Wild, "A Realistic Defense of Causal Efficacy," *Review of Metaphysics*, 2 (June, 1949), 1-9, especially 4-5. In his list he names Antisthenes, Nicolaus of Autrecourt, Ockham, Descartes, and Hume. Wild is concerned with relations in the following three areas: human knowledge, efficient causation, and logical inference.

[15] *Ibid.*, pp. 5-6. (Italics added.)

very form of our expressions. Why not then sharpen up our tools of analysis, and refine them? Why not a truly empirical and relational mode of analysis? [16]

However infrequent this acknowledgement may be elsewhere, it is rather common among contemporary Thomists. Aquinas himself leads the way and even indicates the methodology to be followed. "Are names implying relations to creatures [for example, 'Creator,' 'Lord'] predicated of God temporally?" he asks early in the *Summa Theologiae*.[17] After answering affirmatively, he states: "In order to see this we must realize that some have held relation is not something real but only mental. This position is plainly seen to be false from the very fact that things themselves have a natural ordering and reference to one another." By opposing that false opinion Thomas shows his own hand, and this in strong Latin. A relation is not a mere thing of the mind (*res rationis tantum*), but is itself a thing of nature (*res naturae*)—an accidental perfection actually existing in things. And the methodology by which to proceed? Simply observe the actual ordering, reference, openness, liaison to be found among existents themselves.[18]

However little some of those who call themselves Thomist may have followed an inductive procedure in other areas, still down through the centuries and up to the present day many conclude with him that friendship, marriage, family, larger than, and the like are accidents really other than the S, F, and T.[19] Let us quote one of the most recent and most prominent:

---

[16] *Ibid.*, p. 14. Also see *idem, Introduction to Realistic Philosophy* (New York: Harper & Row, Publishers, 1948), pp. 347-51. (Since ca. 1958 Wild has moved from realism to phenomenology. Perhaps this move has affected his position on relations, too.)

[17] *Summa Theologiae*, I, 13, 7.

[18] "Ad cuius evidentiam sciendum est quod quidam posuerunt relationem non esse rem naturae sed rationis tantum. Quod quidem apparet esse falsum ex hoc quod ipsae res naturalem ordinem et habitudinem habent ad invicem." Also see *De Potentia*, 7, 9 resp. For a list and exegesis of Thomas' texts, see A. Krempel, *La doctrine de la relation chez saint Thomas: Exposé historique et systématique* (Paris: J. Vrin, 1952); William J. Kane, *Philosophy of Relation in the Metaphysics of St. Thomas* (Washington, D. C.: Catholic University Press, 1958); C. Kossel, S.J., "Principles of St. Thomas' Distinction Between the *Esse* and *Ratio* of Relation," *Modern Schoolman*, 24 (November, 1946 and January, 1947), 19-36 and 93-107; *idem*, "St. Thomas' Theory of the Causes of Relation," *Modern Schoolman*, 25 (March, 1948), 151-72. The latter seems to interpret Aquinas as holding the negative position on relations; if so, his interpretation is mistaken.

[19] For a historical survey of positions within scholasticism on relations, see A. Krempel, *op. cit.*, especially pp. 170-79 and 245-71. On Scotus, see *ibid.*, pp. 249 ff. and 270.

Two sugar cubes, in their real being, are equal to each other regardless of any consideration by the human mind. If they are both white, moreover, they are like each other in color without the human intellect's help. They are therefore related to each other in reality as equal and as similar. Their equality and similarity are accordingly real relations. Real relations, of course, add no absolute reality to their subject, but they do add relative reality. They make the subject really related to something else, as the cubes are really equal to each other and really like each other in color. . . . Because it is a referring, a relation requires a subject, ground, and term. Where it is real, it inheres in its subject, but depends also upon ground and term in both its notion and its being. It is specified by its term. As a real accident, it is really distinct from its own being as well as from its subject, and its being is really distinct from the being of the substance in which it inheres.[20]

How can we establish this affirmative answer? What reasons can be offered to show that it is true?

First of all, how do we know other accidents? How are we sure that an operative habit such as mathematics, acts of free choice, a musical talent, good health, color, and so on actually exist within us? By direct experience of ourselves and others in the concrete circumstances of our day-by-day lives. We are directly aware that now we are working quantitative problems with facility and accuracy, that now we are freely choosing to turn from such problems to study metaphysics, that now we are strumming a calypso tune on a guitar, and so on. In those direct awarenesses we realize that such accidental perfections exist within us and hence are real, we realize what they are (within sufficiently exact limits) and we are aware that they are really other than one another.[21]

The same hold true for relations. In the give-and-take of daily life we experience the actual order, reference, being-directed-towards, de-

---

[20] Joseph Owens, C. Ss. R., *An Elementary Christian Metaphysics* (Milwaukee: Bruce Publishing Co., 1963), pp. 180 and 189. Other recent authors in this group include Henry J. Koren, S.S. Sp., *An Introduction to the Science of Metaphysics* (St. Louis: B. Herder Book Co., 1955), pp. 216-26; Charles A. Hart, *Thomistic Metaphysics* (Englewood Cliffs, N. J.: Prentice-Hall, Inc., 1959), pp. 232-39; P.-B. Grenet, *Ontologie* (Paris: Beauchesne, 1959), pp. 114-23; Maurice Holloway, S.J., *Introduction to Natural Theology*, pp. 350-52 and 360-61; John A. Peters, *Metaphysics* (Pittsburgh: Duquesne University Press, 1963), pp. 382-86.

[21] These realizations are, of course, intellection upon data supplied by the immediate awarenesses. No accident, technically understood, is itself directly perceived. See p. 47. What is said there also applies to relations.

pendence-upon, openness-to between ourselves and others.[22] I am directly aware of the bond (as well as of consequent duties and rights) I have to my parents and you have to yours;[23] of the orientation of my very being to Christ by my status as a religious;[24] of a liaison with my fellow men because of my priesthood and with these students because I am their teacher; of my openness towards and communion with a certain person because of the love of friendship. That bond, orientation, openness are relations; and thus in directly perceiving them we understand that relations do exist within us as accidental perfections (and hence are real) and that they are really other than the subject which they perfect, the activity from which they result, and the terms at which they point.

Some may say, "Granted that we are directly aware of such situations. Still their real constituents are S, F, and T and nothing more. For example, the son-parent complex is equivalent really to the fact that you (S) have been begotten (F) by this man and woman (T). It is adequately explained by those three factors alone." I must disagree. Something more is entailed and experienced in such situations. My sonship is not the mere fact that I have been produced by such parents, but the actual ordering to and dependence upon them which are consequent upon that production. My status as a religious is not merely the fact that I have pronounced vows at such-and-such a date, but the ensuing actual condition of belonging to God, of being-directed-towards and dedicated to Him. Your state of husbandhood is not solely the fact that at a definite point of time you freely exchanged marriage vows with your bride, but the resultant ontic conditioning of yourself, body and soul, by which you belong to her and are orientated towards her. Your being bigger than she is not merely the fact that you both have quantity, but also the actual physical, comparative status we express by "bigger than." Such ordering, dependence, belonging to, dedication, direction, orientation, or openness are entitative: they are

---

[22] This is, after all, Thomas' advice. See n. 18.

[23] Filiation is quite complex. It can be viewed as springing solely from the act of reproduction, or, secondly, from that act plus the knowledge and love between parents and child. When does it cease? In the first interpretation, when the offspring has physically developed to a certain stage, as is especially evident on the subhuman level: at a definite point of time the female of various species rebuffs her offspring and physically separates herself from them. In the second interpretation, filiation ceases when knowledge and (especially) love have broken down. Of course, the R also disappears when the mother or father dies.

[24] Each one must dwell upon and utilize the unique orderings and references which personally affect him.

there whether we think of them or not. The mind does not construct them, but only recognizes them for what they actually are.

* A second way of substantiating this position is the following inference.[25]

> Actually existing items are the content-determining cause of our immediate knowledge and predication.
>
> But one may validly move from effect to cause.
>
> Therefore, we may validly go from our immediate knowledge and statements to actually existing items.
>
> But we have direct, perceptual knowledge issuing
>
> *not only* into these affirmative, literal statements:
>
> [4] "Stephen actually is quantified, healthy, thinking, freely choosing, a mathematician,"
>
> *but also* into these equally affirmative and literal statements:
>
> [5] "Stephen actually is smaller than the hoodlum and larger than his wife"
>
> [6] "He actually is similar to his brother in intelligence and in being"
>
> [7] "He actually is a friend of Bernard, the husband of Grace, the father of Mary, the teacher of certain students, a member of St. Matthew's Parish, and so forth."
>
> Therefore, among actually existing items are to be counted
>
> *not only* quantity, entitative and operative habits, and other qualities, various activities;
>
> *but also* smaller than, greater than, similar to, friend of, husband of, and the other accidental perfections we call "relations."

* Through the direct perception and statements they cause, then, existents show themselves to possess not only such accidents as quantity, various qualities, and operations (all of which are really distinct from one another), but also *relational accidents,* which also are distinct from one another, from other accidents, and from the subject which they perfect and in which they inhere. Such immediate awarenesses

---

[25] This process seems especially helpful with respect to quantitative and other relational situations where the actual ordering and reference are not so vividly experienced. When I meet an enormous stranger in a dark alley and realize that I am smaller than he, my experience of "smaller than" is sufficiently vivid. But in less perilous circumstances my awareness of such orderings based on quantity is more subdued.

In the inference the numbers in brackets refer to the statements as previously listed in Section 1, "The Relational Situation."

and statements are nothing more than those actually existing accidents (relational and otherwise) as intentionally re-presenting themselves within the human knower.

3. The Negative Reply

There is another view on relations, though. Some have denied to them any reality other than that of their S, F, and T. They can be called real only because those three factors do actually exist. The relation itself is, at best, the mental activity stimulated by the S, F, and T situation. When a human knower observes that Stephen (S) loves (F) someone (T), he affirms that Stephen is a friend of the other. But "friend of" expresses no unique ontic condition or status within him. When contrasted with the S, F, and T, friendship is "an abstraction, the work of the intelligence," [26] "a product of our mental comparison of subject with term," [27] a construct imposed by the mind upon the S-F-T complex.[28] The same holds true for all other so-called real relations.[29]

Historically, those upholding this negative position have mainly been essentialists, especially those in the Suarezian tradition.[30] Recently, though, some Thomists have made the same denial. One such is the prominent British author, Denis J. B. Hawkins, who ends his chapter on relations with this paragraph:

---

[26] Fernand Van Steenberghen in the passage cited in n. 32.

[27] P. Coffey in the passage cited in n. 36.

[28] George P. Klubertanz, S.J., *Introduction to Philosophy of Being*, p. 315: "In metaphysics itself, we deal with pure intelligibles; this is especially true in the case of the predicaments. For example, *relation* as a form is a construct." This author is perfectly correct in describing relations as constructs *if* they are not in themselves anything real beyond their S, F, and T. But one must also face the result of this description: whatever is relational (for example, the family, the state, the Mystical Body, morality, analogy) is, *of and in itself*, also constructural. On constructs, see p. 137, n. 10.

[29] Therefore, "spouse of," "son or daughter of," "parents of," "smaller than," "similar to," and so on are likewise abstractions, mental products, constructs. We should recall that "real" here means those relations which are contrasted with the *purely* conceptual or rationate ones—the Pogo-Albert kind, as well as those in logic and mathematics. In all of these S, F, and T are intramental. See n. 11.

[30] On Suarez and his followers, see Krempel, *op. cit.*, pp. 253-54. Albert the Great, together with early Dominicans he influenced, is also a fellow traveler of Suarez (*ibid.*, p. 248 sq.), as well as Ockham and other nominalists (*ibid.*, p. 172 sq. and p. 245), together with John of St. Thomas (*ibid.*, p. 253).

It seems that there are three questions which we can ask about the reality of relations and to which the answers are as follows. Are there real relations? Yes, relatedness is as much a feature of the real world as terms in relation; the world is presented to us as an interconnected whole from which terms and their relations have to be analytically distinguished. Are relations ever the source of new reality? Yes, that is precisely the nature of the originative type of relation, and, wherever we find a relation which gives rise to novelty, we should look for the originative relation or relations involved in it. Are the relations which we discover in the world of experience ever really distinct from the terms which they relate? No, for to say so would be to convert relations into pseudo-absolutes; they are logically distinct aspects of things in their togetherness.[31]

Across the Channel his Belgian counterpart, Fernand Van Steenberghen, is of the same opinion.

> The scholastics asked whether there were *real* predicamental relations, that is, relations which would constitute *real accidents,* distinct from the two related subjects. Such entities, however, are superfluous. The relation as such is an abstraction, the work of the intelligence. It is real when it rests upon real foundations. Thus the relation of filiation between a son and his father is real, because this son was actually begotten by this father. It is based upon a real biological activity, of which the father is the principle and the son is the result.[32]

But many of those taking this negative view have been Suarezian essentialists. Let us take as representative of them P. Coffey, who is the author of a once widely used textbook, *Ontology or the Theory of Being: An Introduction to General Metaphysics* and who acknowledges that his greatest intellectual debt is to two nineteenth-century Suarezians, Urraburu and Kleutgen.[33] His long chapter on relations (pp. 332-56) consists of six sections, two of which are especially pertinent to us. In the first (pp. 341-43) he defines a real relation.

---

[31] D. J. B. Hawkins, *Being and Becoming* (New York: Sheed & Ward, 1954), pp. 71-72.

[32] Fernand Van Steenberghen, *Ontology* (New York. Joseph F. Wagner, Inc., Publishers, 1952), pp. 252-53. Also see L. de Raeymaeker, *Philosophy of Being,* p. 202; G. P. Klubertanz, S.J., *op. cit.,* 269-76.

[33] (London: Longmans, Green & Company, Ltd., 1918); his acknowledgement to Urraburu and Kleutgen, p. viii.

A real relation is *one which is not a mere product of thought, but which obtains between real things independently of our thought.* For a real relation there must be (a) a *real,* individual *subject;* (b) a *real foundation;* and (c) a *real,* individual *term,* really distinct from the subject.[34]

He then proceeds to vindicate its existence against "the specious sophistries of . . . Subjective Idealism" by emphasizing that at least some relations "are not merely logical, are not a mere product of our thought." In the second section (pp. 349-56), he faces this question. Precisely in what sense are those relations real? Do such predicamental relations embody "any mode of real being adequately distinct from those modes which constitute the other categories"?

Considered adequately, the predicamental relation adds to the reality it has in its foundation the *actual reference* of subject to term. In fact, it is in this reference of subject to term, this *"esse ad,"* that the relation *formally* consists. The question therefore may be stated thus: Is this formal relation of subject to term, this *"esse ad,"* a real entity *sui generis,* really distinct from the absolute entities of subject, term, and foundation, and in contradistinction to these and all absolute entities a "relative entity," actually existing in the real universe independently of our thought? Or is it, on the contrary, itself formally a mere product of our thought, a product of the mental act of comparison, an *ens rationis,* an aspect superadded by our minds to the extremes compared, and to the foundation in virtue of which we compare them? [35]

The question could hardly be formulated more clearly, and Coffey's reply is just as lucid. Although "a good many scholastics . . . have espoused the former alternative," still he personally agrees with

the great majority of scholastics [who] espouse the second alternative: that the relation, considered *formally,* *"secundum esse ad,"* is a product of our mental comparison of subject with term. It is not itself a real entity or a real mode, superadded to the reality of extremes and foundation.[36]

---

[34] *Ibid.,* p. 341. Relation is not a *mere* product of thought, as it will turn out, because of the real S, F, and T. The R itself, though, is a product of thought.

[35] *Ibid.,* p. 349. In the phrase "actual reference," the adjective is to be understood as equivalent to "mental," as is clear from the text cited in the next note: the actual reference is "a product of our mental comparison of subject with term. It is not itself a real entity or a real mode, superadded to the reality of extremes and foundation."

[36] *Ibid.,* p. 352.

And his reasons?

> In the first place there is no need to suppose the reality of such a relative entity. *Entia non sunt multiplicanda praeter necessitatem.* It is an abuse of realism to suppose that the *formal* element of a relation, its *"esse ad,"* is a distinct and separate reality. The reality of the predicamental relation is safeguarded without any such postulate. Since the predicamental relation, considered *adequately, i.e,* not merely formally but fundamentally, not merely *secundum esse ad* but *secundum esse in,* involves as its foundation an absolute accident which is real independently of our thought, the predicamental relation is not a *mere ens rationis.* It has a foundation in reality. It is an *ens rationis cum fundamento in re.* This is a sufficient counter-assertion to Idealism, and a sufficient reason for treating relation as a distinct category of real being. . . . In the second place, if a subject can acquire a relation, or lose a relation, *without undergoing any real change,* then the relation considered formally as such, or *secundum "esse ad,"* cannot be a reality.[37]

We have quoted from Coffey rather extensively because he states the negative, essentialist position so lucidly. Moreover, the reasons he lists for maintaining it provide a transition to our next consideration. Why do philosophers hold this view? What arguments do they offer? In his second reason Coffey gives an important clue: ". . . the relation considered formally as such . . . *cannot be* a reality."[38] One of the basic convictions which influences them is that it is *impossible and unintelligible* for a relation to be itself a real perfection distinct from S, F, and T.

> There are thousands of eggs in existence, all of which are like each other. When a new egg is laid, all the other eggs are now similar to it. How many relations of similarity does each egg have? It seems *foolish* to say that there are thousands of perfectly similar accidents in each egg, differing only in their term, and it is *impossible* to say that there is a general relation of similarity, because a general relation is abstract and cannot be found in the real order, but only in a mind. *These absurdities and impossibilities* should be enough to show us that the question has been wrongly understood.[39]

---

[37] *Ibid.,* pp. 352-53.

[38] We shall consider Coffey's first reason in the next section, "The Predicaments." Italics have been added to the quotation taken from the second reason.

[39] G. Klubertanz, S.J., *op. cit.,* p. 271. Interestingly enough, Owens finds no trouble with a similar situation in sugar cubes: see text cited in n. 20.

In what does this impossibility, absurdity, contradiction consist? In at least two points: first, a relation so conceived would have to be a form, and, second, would be almost totally influenced by its term. Let us consider each separately.[40]

If a relation were an actually existing accident really other than its *S, F,* and *T,* then, it would necessarily be a *form.*

> Relation is understood as a kind of form which is between two beings, and joins or unites them like a bridge or a rope.[41]

> If the *"esse ad"* were a separate real entity, a relative entity, really distinct from extremes and foundation, what sort of entity could it be? Being an accident, it should inhere in, or be a mode of its subject.[42]

But its being a form, or, what amounts to the same, an intrinsic mode of a subject, puts a relation in an embarrassing predicament. A form is an inward-looking, self-enclosing modification of a subject, but by a relation a subject goes out and opens up to what is without. As a form, then, either a relation would no longer be relational or it would simultaneously be inward-outward and shut-open.

> [But if a relation were a form,] it would lose its formally relative character by becoming an inherent mode of an absolute character. While to conceive it as an entity astride on both extremes, and bridging or connecting these together, would be to substitute the crude imagery of the imagination for intellectual thought.[43]

In view of such patent contradictions and impossibilities, one must conclude (they say) that a relation is nothing real in itself, but is only

---

[40] Each consideration will proceed as follows: first, the explanation given by those holding this negative view, followed by my own comments and evaluation.

[41] Klubertanz, *op. cit.,* p. 273. Also see G. Smith and L. Kendzierski, *op. cit.,* p. 278: "As referred to George's, John's size 'stretches' towards George's, and this 'stretch' is precisely an *esse ad,* a new category of accident, a relation. A relation is thus a sort of 'in-between' being, in between an accidented subject and its correlative, a sort of metaphysical antenna by which John's size 'feels' George's (this 'feeling' is the *esse ad*), and by which even *before* John's size 'feels' George's it is all set (*esse in*) to do the 'feeling' without the slightest change in John's size, even when it 'feels' differently, that is, even when John's size is differently related to George's."

[42] Coffey, *op. cit.,* pp. 352-53. An inherent, absolute mode is the same as form, as is clear from the context.

[43] *Ibid.*

the mental reaction set up in a human knower by a S, F, and T complex.

What can be said by way of *comment?* All must readily sympathize with Coffey's aversion to substituting "the crude imagery of the imagination for intellectual thought." To conceive of relation as a bridge, rope, antenna, and so on is not to think but to imagine, and no philosophical problem can be decided by the imagination. If it proves to be a real accident, a relation is a *component,* a *that by which,* and accordingly can no more be accurately known through imagination or even through mere direct perception than can any of the other accidents.[44]

But to judge that a relation, if real, must be a form is, we admit, entirely consistent with essentialism. They say that to be real is to be intelligible and thereby also to be form, because intelligibility accrues to a thing from its form. This equivalence between form and reality determines the rest of their metaphysics. If real, prime matter must itself have a form or act, however imperfect, and thus is not pure potency.[45] Actual existence (*esse*) cannot be a real component, because if real it would have to be a form, and what function would it perform when added as another form to a human soul or to any other substantial form? A relation too, if it is to be real for an essentialist, must also be a form, but then the patent absurdities and contradictions already alluded to would arise.

But having granted that consistency, what can we say? The equivalence between reality and form vanishes in an authentic existentialism, where to be real is to be actually existing. Thus relations can be real (they actually exist), can be accidents (they perfect the S in which they inhere), and still need not be accidental *forms.* There are, then,

---

[44] See n. 21. See H. Koren, *An Introduction to the Science of Metaphysics,* p. 223: "How can we represent such things [entities having nothing absolute and merely pointing to something else] in our mind? As a kind of gossamer web linking every creature to all other creatures by innumerous threads, possessing a higher degree of elasticity than the best grade of bubble gum, so that they can stretch and shrink with every move of every correlated being without becoming hopelessly entangled in one another? The answer is that we should beware of using our imagination in metaphysical problems. Just as any effort to imagine what potency and act, essence and 'to be,' substance and accident, look like if taken by themselves can end only in disaster, so also any effort to draw a mental picture of real relations."

[45] See C. Frick, S.J., *Ontologia* (Friburgi Brisgoviae: Herder & Co., 1934), p. 45; T. Pesch, S.J., *Institutiones Philosophiae Naturalis* (Friburgi Brisgoviae: Herder & Co, 1880), pp. 241-43 (Pesch there gives prime matter both an *essential* and an *existential* act of its own).

various components which are real (because actually existing) but which are not forms—for example, the act of existing itself, prime matter, our operations,[46] as well as various relationships. Of course, some components are forms (for example, human soul and other substantial forms; such accidents as color, operative habits, intelligible and sensible species), although they are real not because they are forms but because they actually exist. In our existentialism, what is a *form*? By contrasting the various components just listed as forms with those which are nonforms, we arrive at this description: strictly speaking, a form is that [a] by which a subject or recipient is perfected [b] within the essence [c] in a static [d] and totally intrinsic way.[47]

In view of that definition, friendship, fatherhood, similarity, smaller than, and other relations are not accidental forms: even though each is that by which a subject is perfected within the essence in a static way, still they do not perfect it in a *totally* intrinsic fashion. True, they do inhere in, and thus perfect, the subject (hence, they have an intrinsic side), but their unique nature is to orientate, refer, and open up the subject to what is without. In Aquinas' excellent language: *Forma ponit aliquid sed relatio ponit ad aliquid* ("A form places a 'something' but a relation places a 'to something'").[48] Hence, they are real because they do actually exist. They are accidents because they are individual perfections of the substance in which they inhere. Yet they are not accidental forms, and accordingly, we rather easily escape the absurdity and impossibility their reality might entail in an essentialistic conception.

Let us move on to the second point which the proponents of this negative position see as a cause of unintelligibility and impossibility: a relation, if a real perfection distinct from S, F, and T, would be almost entirely dominated by its term. For example, [1] an S acquires an R solely because of changes in the T.[49]

---

[46] Operations are dynamic actuations of our operative powers, and thus seem to be so different from accidents which are obviously forms (for example, color, intelligible and sensible species, operative habits, and so forth) as to be nonforms.

[47] Because of the words in #a, prime matter is not a form: it is itself a subject or recipient. The words in #b eliminate the act of existing, which is other than and hence outside the essence; #c eliminates operations, which are dynamic actuations (see n. 46); #d excludes relations.

[48] See *In I Sent.*, d. 20, q. 1, a. 1 sol. (Mandonnet Ed., 504); *ibid.*, d. 26, q. 2, a. 1 sol., p. 630; *ibid.*, d. 30, q. 1, a. 1 sol., p. 702; *Quodl*, IX, 2, 3, resp. (Marietti Ed., p. 182); S.T., I, 28, 1 resp.

[49] Numbers in brackets are affixed to sentences in this paragraph for easy reference in my subsequent comments.

A child already born is neither larger nor smaller than its brother that will be born two years hence. But after the birth of the latter child the former can acquire those relations successively *without any real change in itself,* and merely by the growth of the younger child. Again, one white ball *A* is similar in color to another white ball, *B.* Paint the latter black, and *eo ipso* the former loses its relation of resemblance *without any real change in itself.*[50]

One white page of paper is *like* another, but if the other turns brown with age, the white page is *unlike* the brown one. The white page has changed from like to unlike without any cause influencing the white page. How can this be? [51]

[2] Again, an S loses an R when its T disappears: the paternity which a man acquires by an act of reproduction is lost when the offspring dies. [3] Moreover, multiple relations arise from a single F because of a multiplicity of terms: in this man one and the same quantity grounds the triple relations of smaller than, equal to, larger than when he is referred to his father, twin, and wife. [4] This last example discloses even further complications, because by reason of that same quantity he is smaller than, equal to, and greater than *many other men* (to say nothing of trees, various animals, buildings, machines, and so forth). How many relations of smaller than, equality, greater than does he have? If there were as many relations as there are terms, they would be infinitely numerous.[52]

In view of such difficulties, how much simpler and more intelligible to withdraw from relations any reality which would be distinct from their S, F, and T and to affirm that they *are* those factors as grasped together by the mind in a single awareness? Such is, in fact, precisely what the upholders of the negative view do.

Comment: Although offering matter for serious consideration, such examples also provide an opportunity for further clarifying the affirmative side. Let us briefly take them up one by one.

[1] First, when a new R is produced by a change in the T, the S

---

[50] Coffey, *Ontology or the Theory of Being: An Introduction to a General Metaphysics,* p. 353.

[51] Klubertanz, *op. cit.,* p. 271.

[52] A man having several children would offer a similar problem (although not because of the multiple terms so much as because of the multiple foundations: the individual acts of generation which produced the children): does he have several relations of paternity? Similarly, how many relations does a teacher instructing sixty-five students have?

also changes: it acquires a new accidental perfection—that of the R, which comes to inhere in it and which perfects it by ordering it to another. Of course, it does not change absolutely or formally, as the T does by increasing in quantity or by acquiring a different color. Second, such examples reveal that the T genuinely helps cause the R. What sort of cause is it? It appears to fit into none of the Aristotelian classification of causes (efficient, final, exemplary, formal, material), which should, then, be enlarged to cover this new evidence. We might aptly call it a *"presential* cause"—*by its very presence* the T brings the R into existence. The F is an "emanative cause" of the same R, which emanates or flows forth from the quantity or quality in the S.[53]

[2] If a T is truly a cause of an R, there is nothing strange about the latter vanishing when the former disappears. The T, which causes the R by its presence, is no longer present, and hence is no longer causing the R, which the S thus loses.

[3] The fact that many terms produce many relations from one F is not surprising in view of the fact that the T is a *presential* cause of the R and in view of what quantity is. Although a quantitative continuum such as a man is a unity, the very nature of quantity is such as to have extended parts outside of parts and to be potentially multiple.[54] Because of this it *can* do what it shows itself *actually to be doing*: when helped by several terms, it grounds several relations.

[4] Finally, no matter how many terms there may be, an individual existent has only three quantitative relations (smaller than, equal to, greater than), each of which however has multiple "respects" insofar as each "looks towards" (the literal force of *respicere,* from which

---

[53] On emanative cause, see p. 116, n. 32. Also see n. 9 above for a list of causes which overlap or even escape Aristotle's list. Moreover, the physical universe offers several cases of causality which are accepted as facts but which still have no adequate explanation—gravity, extrasensory perception (ESP), magnetic forces, dowsing, and so forth. One attitude toward such instances is to deny that they can be causes because they do not fit traditional categories of causes. Another is to grant the fact that they *are* causes and then enlarge the categories and explanations to include these newly discovered instances of causality.

[54] Not only is quantity potentially multiple, but it is also virtually and (in a literal sense) radically (*in radice*) related before the terms exercise their causality. See Aquinas, *In V Phys.,* lect. 3 (Leonine Ed., no. 8): "If someone through change in himself [T] becomes my size, while I undergo no change [in quantity], this equality was somehow in me beforehand, that is, in its root, from which it has real being" (*ista aequalitas primo erat in me quodammodo sicut in sua radice*). For an exegesis, see Kossel, "St. Thomas' Theory of the Causes of Relation," *Modern Schoolman,* 25 (March, 1948), 158.

respectus is derived) its multiple terms. The multiple "lookings-toward" of each *R* are its "respects." [55] Take the actually existing relation of "smaller than" in this man. In him it is his entitative condition of actually having such "respects" to *A, B, C*, and so on. It is no general, abstract relation,[56] but one which is definite and concrete because it inheres in and perfects a particular *S*. Someone observing it in reference to those terms recognizes those "lookings-toward" and applies them now to this, now to that term by saying, "He actually is smaller than *A*, than *B*, than *C*, than *D*. . . ." Those objective "lookings-toward," now recognized and applied by an observer, are its "respects," which are as many as there are terms. The same can be said of equality and greater than.[57]

Such, then, is at least one basic reason why some philosophers withhold from relation any reality which would be other than that of its *S, F*, and *T*: conferment of such reality is impossible, absurd, unintelligible, contradictory. Why so? Because an *R*, if real in itself, would have to be a form, an inherent and absolute mode of a subject, and, second, would be under the complete domination of its term. Such an approach appears to square best with a radical essentialism, where intelligibility is the criterion of reality and where philosophy keeps itself protected from the actual universe. Whether or not relations are real is not only a question concerning such innocuous things as eggs and balls and pieces of paper. It has also to do with marriage and family and friendship and slums and religion. If a philosopher should say to a lover or a husband or a mother or a Negro, "The relationships

---

[55] "Respects" translates Thomas' *respectus*—for example, see *Quodl.*, I, 2, 1, p. 3: "Propter unam enim quantitatem est in uno corpore una aequalitas tantum, *quamvis sint respectus plures*, secundum quod diversis corporibus dicitur esse aequale. Si autem secundum omnes illos respectus multiplicarentur realiter relationes in uno corpore, sequeretur quod in uno essent accidentia infinita vel indeterminata." Other English equivalents would be "exposures" or "facets."

One should note that at times Thomas identifies *respectus* with the relation itself—see *In I Sent.*, d. 33, q. 1, a. 1 sol., p. 765; *In III Phys.*, lect. 5, no. 618; *S.T.*, I, 28, 1 resp.; *ibid.*, a. 2 resp.; *ibid.*, a. 3 resp.

[56] See Klubertanz, *op cit.*, p. 271: "It is impossible to say that there is a general relation . . . because a general relation is abstract and cannot be found in the real order but only in a mind."

[57] The same explanation answers the problem of a father and his several children or of a teacher and his numerous students (see n. 52)—a single *R* with several or even numerous "respects." See Owens, *An Elementary Christian Metaphysics*, p. 184, n. 19.

One should remember that the sole function of the mind observing a relational situation with many terms is to recognize and apply (not to construct) the multiple "respects" of the single *R* which are actually there.

which give you your name and make you what you are are themselves
only abstractions, mental comparisons, constructs," he might well have
Hamlet's words addressed to him: "There are more things in heaven
and earth/Than are dreamt of in your philosophy."

In his approach the authentic existentialist tries to listen to those
things of heaven and earth and then simply records what he hears.[58]

4. The Predicaments

Before formulating the conclusions which the previous sections warrant, we must briefly turn to the predicaments. This necessity arises
from the powerful role some authors offer them when deciding the fate
of relations. According to Coffey, relation "is a product of our mental
comparison of subject with term," and "is not itself a real entity"
because "there is no need to suppose the reality of such a relative entity."
Why not? Precisely because "the reality of the predicamental relation
is safeguarded without any such postulate." [59] And what is predicamental relation? It is a concept, an intelligibility: although "it is not
a *mere ens rationis*," nonetheless "it is an *ens rationis cum fundamento
in re*." [60] As long, then, as the predicament, the concept, the genus of
relation is saved, nothing else really matters. In such a perspective,
relation has little chance of gaining a hearing for itself as an actual
perfection.

Or consider Klubertanz, who apparently proposes moving from the
predicaments to existents as the proper methodology for evaluating the
nature of relations. First comes a general remark:

> [1] When we consider substance and accident as principles *by* which
> something has *esse* in itself and *by* which something is modified, we
> are trying to understand them according to the manner in which
> things exist. Such an understanding is difficult and roundabout—a
> fact which is manifested by the awkward circumlocutions necessary

---

[58] Proponents of the negative view also offer another reason why it should be
accepted: it does adequate justice to actual relational situations. We have already
seen this reason as an objection to the affirmative view—see p. 199.

[59] *Op. cit.*, p. 352. What he says immediately thereafter shows that he is primarily interested in the *category* of R (p. 212): "[R as an *ens rationis cum fundamento in re*] is a sufficient reason for treating relation as a *distinct category* of
real being." And "real being" for him? It is " 'being' considered *substantivally* as
essential (whether possible or actual)."

[60] *Ibid.* Also see pp. 207, 212, and 349.

to express it. On the other hand, it is very easy to understand and deal with these principles when they are *conceived as things;* in other words, it is easy to deal with the principles of things *by means of intelligibilities.* When we classify *these intelligibilities* according to what they represent, we have the predicaments. The predicaments, therefore, are *conceived in the manner proper to the human understanding.*[61]

After several pages he begins to study relations.

> [2] Our particular problem then is: What is "relation" considered in itself? It is, of course, a predicate, and so something understood, an *intelligibility* (a *ratio*). But our question means more than this; it means, Is a real relation *as such* and *according to its mode of intelligibility* to be found in the order of being?[62]

After depicting the havoc which newly laid eggs create upon the metaphysical scene, he continues:

> [3] These absurdities and impossibilities should be enough to show us that the question has been wrongly understood. Let us go back briefly to accidents. The *intelligibility,* "accident," which is *mentally understood after the manner of a form,* is variously and differently realized in existent material beings. In saying that accident is *conceived after the manner of a form,* we mean that it is *thought of* as a form or quasi-form determining and modifying a substance, in a way somewhat like that in which substantial form determines and specifies matter. . . . The way in which these three principles of relations [S, F, and T] are *understood* is unlike the way in which they are in the real order. *Relations* is *understood as* a kind of form which is between two beings, and joins or unites them like a bridge or a rope. What is there in the real order which corresponds to the *intelligibility conceived after the manner of a form?*[63]

---

[61] *Op. cit.,* pp. 246-47 (Italics added). Dealing with accidents "when they are conceived as things" is equivalent to treating them as substances: "By means of formal abstraction, we can consider these modifications (accidents) in themselves apart from any substance. Indeed, we can consider them *as if* they were substances (*per modum substantiae*); and it is precisely as considered in this way that they are placed in the predicaments" (*ibid.*).

Numbers in brackets are affixed to this and the two later quotations for easy reference in my subsequent comments.

[62] *Ibid.,* p. 270.

[63] *Ibid.,* p. 271 and p. 273. See also *ibid.,* p. 315: "In metaphysics itself, we deal with pure intelligibilities; this is especially true in the case of the predicaments. For example, *relation* as a form is a construct."

In the light of those quotations, there seems little doubt but that such is the procedure this author proposes: go from intelligibilities to actual accidents, and, more relevantly, from relation as an intelligibility and predicament to actual relational situations.[64] But this procedure already predetermines one's position, and it is negative. If a relation in itself is "a predicate, and so something understood, an *intelligibility* (a *ratio*)" (see #2), of course it is not an accidental perfection other than its S, F, and T—it is what it is defined to be from the very start: a predicate, an intelligibility, a *ratio*. Nor can a relation be that sort of accidental perfection if a relation in itself is "understood as a kind of form" (#3), for, as we have already noted, such a situation would be contradictory: either the relation would not be relational or it would be inward-outward at one and the same time.

However easy this methodology may be and however difficult and roundabout understanding relations and other accidents may be according to the manner in which they exist (see #1), still the very aim of a metaphysician is knowing them precisely as they do exist, understanding them precisely qua actual. The difficulties and hardships of attaining that knowledge he must bear if he is to achieve his goal. There is no shortcut.

But what is a predicament? Where do they fit into an authentically existentialist metaphysics? Have they any function to perform? Those are the questions we shall now answer briefly.

What are the predicaments? In my interpretation, they are intelligibilities, *rationes,* awarenesses which emerge when one reflects upon various grammatical predications made about material existents. For example, take these statements:[65]

    (a) "Terence actually is the father of Helen."
    (b) "He actually is also the sculptor of this statue."
    (c) "He actually is an inhabitant of St. Louis County."
    (d) "He actually is a beatnik."
    (e) "Yet he actually is a dandy, too."

---

[64] This is also equivalent to going from relations conceived as a substance (see n. 61) to them as actual accidents.

[65] We shall concentrate upon the last six predicaments in traditional Aristotelian lists—relation, action/passion, time, place, posture, and state. "Posture" (*situs*) is not explicitly treated, but what is said of place is true of it, *mutatis mutandis.*

A good treatment is to be found in Owens, *op. cit.,* pp. 191-209. Also see his article, "Aristotle on Categories," *Review of Metaphysics,* 14 (1960), 73-90.

All those statements are grammatically intended to express the actual relationships he has to various terms.[66] But those same relational situations can also be stated in such a way as only to imply the relations and explicitly to express their foundations or terms. For instance:

(a) "Terence did actually beget Helen."
(b) "He actually is carving this wood (which also is simultaneously being carved)."
(c) "He actually lives here in St. Louis."
(d) "He actually is twentieth-century in his attitudes and outlook."
(e) "He actually wears such-and-such clothes."

The difference between these two series of predications, then, is merely one of grammatical expression. They both involve relations, but the first explicates the relation (and implies the F and sometimes the T), whereas the second explicates the F and/or T (and implies the R). By reflection upon the first series there emerges the awareness or predicament of "relation," whereas by reflection upon the second there emerges the awareness or predicament of "action" (#a and first clause of #b), of "passion" (second clause of #b), of "place" (#c), of "time" (#d), and of "state" (#e).[67] In view of their origin from statements which differ only grammatically, these six predicaments also differ only grammatically and mentally: they all have to do with relational situations and merely designate them from different points of view.[68]

---

[66] Even #c, #d and #e involve relations, since each expresses a cause-effect complex. On #c and #d, see n. 9. With respect to #e, the clothing one wears may cause him to be warm, to be protected, confident, vain, and so on. The adage "Clothes make the man" is relevant here.

[67] "State" is Owens' word (*op. cit.*, p. 208) for *habitus*.

[68] The mental distinction operative here is somewhat like the "minor" one between the transcendents (see p. 153, n. 42): they all have to do with relational situations, but "relation" is primarily concerned with the actual relations themselves, whereas "action" and the others are concerned with the F and/or T. But the distinction is also like the "major" one between restrictive awarenesses (see p. 152, n. 39): the distinction, although only mental or rationate, ultimately entails really distinct items—the R itself, the F, and the T, all of which are really other than one another.

One should carefully note that the distinction in question here is not between an actual R, S, F, and T (which of course is real), but between "relation," "action," and the rest precisely as intelligibilities or predicaments. In their content all of them deal with a relational situation, but some explicitate the R and others the F or T. Thus they somehow differ. They are not identically the same predicament.

Despite this mental distinction, though, they are not constructural intelligibilities because there is an actually existing item which directly corresponds to them—namely, the real relation explicated or implied in each situation.[69]

Can they meaningfully be called "accidents"? Yes, if one remembers he is viewing "accident" against a grammatical, predicational background. A predicate which is essentially constitutive of its subject is "substantial" (for example, "Terence is a man"),[70] and consideration of this sort of statement produces the predicament of "substance." Predicates which are not essentially constitutive of their subjects "happen to" them, and thus are "accidental" (for instance, "Terence actually is quantified, actually is a mathematician," as well as the above two series of statements). Consideration of this sort of proposition gives rise to the predicaments of various "accidents"—"quantity," "quality," "relation," and so on. They are not directly, however, accidents in a metaphysical or (perhaps) even a philosophical sense.[71] They are not components, but are mere awarenesses, intelligibilities, predicaments.

Can they be termed "forms"? Again, yes, if one recalls he is using

---

[69] Of course, that direct correspondent also is the S, F, and T, which too are actually existing items.

"But are not the predicaments which are accidents all constructural by the fact that they are abstract rather than concrete? For example, everyone agrees that 'humanity' is constructural because in contrast to 'man' it is abstract. So too, 'quantity,' and not 'quantified,' is the predicament, or 'fatherhood,' and not 'father.'" Although the accidental predicaments are abstract rather than concrete, they are still not constructs. The difference between them and such an intelligibility as "humanity" is that what immediately corresponds to the latter is one's mental activity, whereas what immediately corresponds to the former is actual accidents. An actual man is subsistent, is a composite and a whole, and the concrete awareness of "man" intentionally re-presents him directly in those characteristics. But "humanity" results from one's concentrating solely on what makes this man be *man* and by *prescinding* from his individuality and all else. "Humanity" then, stands for what is merely a part (the *forma totius*) and not for the whole of man. But any actual accident is itself inherent, simple, and a part. To match those properties directly, an intelligibility must be abstract rather than concrete. Hence, the very abstraction of an accidental predicament proves rather than disproves it to be nonconstructural.

On "humanity," see Aquinas, *De Ente et Essentia*, c. 2 (Roland-Gosselin Ed., pp. 21-23); on the accidental predicaments, see *ibid.*, c. 6 (Roland-Gosselin Ed., pp. 46-47).

[70] If spelled out, one would say: "A predicate which signifies that which is essentially constitutive of what is signified by the subject of a proposition. . . ." But the shorter version used here (and in the subsequent sentence) is sufficiently clear.

[71] A logician, though, would accept them as his nine categories of accidents.

"form" and "matter" solely in a predicational, grammatical signification. Outside a proposition a subject is of itself indeterminate—for example, "Cassius" says nothing about whether it designates a parrot or a man, white or black, metaphysician or pugilist. But it is determinable, and this occurs through predicates, the very function of which is to determine the subject of a proposition—"Cassius is a *man,* is *colored,* is a *prizefighter,* and so on." But the determinant is to the determinable as form is to matter. Therefore, the predicate is to the subject as form is to matter. Accordingly, predicaments which emerge from meditation upon the function of predicates within propositions can be called "forms." Remember, however, that here we meet "form" and "matter" solely in a grammatical context. They are not the components encountered in the philosophy of nature and in metaphysics.

What function do these predicaments perform in metaphysics? Absolutely none, as far as I can see. They certainly play a role in logic, and, possibly, in a philosophy of nature. But they are totally missing from the cast of metaphysics.[72]

---

[72] But what about the use made above (p. 200 sq.) of statements in arriving at a knowledge of relations? Does it not insert the predicaments into metaphysics? Direct statements can be utilized in two different ways. (a) When considered in a strictly grammatical fashion, they can lead to the elaboration of intelligibilities, formalizations, predicational classes called "predicaments." These in turn can be used as guidelines for returning to the actual existent and for deciding whether or not he has various accidental perfections and what they consist in. This use is, I suggest, a metaphysical mistake. (b) But they can also be considered as the effects of actually existing items, which are their content-determining causes, and thus are revelatory of those very causes. Hence they can serve as a starting point for a direct inference, which terminates in one's assenting: "Yes, accidental perfections of both relational and nonrelational caliber do actually exist, and they have such-and-such natures." This utilization seems legitimate and is quite different from the former.

But what about the contrast between "predicamental" and "transcendental" relations? If predicaments are dropped from metaphysics, what of this contrast? The notion of "transcendental" relation became popular among Renaissance authors, where at least one of its functions appears to have been to unite components within a thing. When a philosopher conceives of components as themselves "things" (for example, of prime matter as having an act of its own), something is required to coalesce them into a single existent. One way of meeting that requirement is to call upon transcendental relations: "Of course, the components are united—they are *transcendentally related to one another.*" But if one accurately conceives of a component as "that *by which*" and not as a "thing," then unity is no problem, and the need for the doctrine of "transcendental" relation drops. (On transcendental relations, see Krempel, *op. cit.,* "Table Analytique"

Does that mean, then, that metaphysics has no predicaments? Yes, although at the end of his study a metaphysician separates accidents into various classes. But notice that this occurs at the end, not at the beginning of metaphysics, and second, that these classes are mere summaries of knowledge already gained about actually existing accidents and not initial steps toward acquiring that cognition. The metaphysician observes change/stability on the accidental level—the loss and acquirement of various individual perfections (operations, operative habits, color, and so on) in an existent remaining generically and specifically what it is. Thereupon he realizes both *that* the existent is composed of two components conveniently named "substance" and "accident" and *what* they are (each is a component, a "that by which," and so forth). His knowledge of various accidents grows through reflection upon individual perfections lost and acquired (for example, relations), coupled with consideration of quantity as operative in individuation. It culminates in a gradual, multilevel awareness: that there are accidents; what their general characteristics are (for example, all are components, all are known through intellection based upon data gained through perception, and so on); what the special characteristics of some are (for example, quantity as entering into individuation, relations as accidents but not accidental forms); finally, that accidental perfections show themselves to be either (1) quantity, (2) various qualities, (3) operations, or (4) relations. These last are the four classes which accidents themselves thrust upon the metaphysician toward the conclusion of his science. They are not predicaments.

5. Summary and Conclusions

Despite their independence and autonomy, material existents are immersed in multiple and deep-seated relationships because of an almost total vulnerability and openness with respect to their fellow existents in space and time. What is the nature of those relations?

(a) A relation involving an *S, F,* and *T* which are within the mind

---

[p. 709] for multiple references; especially see "Appendice: L'intrusion de la relation transcendentale dans l'école thomiste," pp. 645-70; also see Adriaan Pattin, O.M.I., "Contribution à l'histoire de la relation transcendantale," *Revue de l'Univ. d'Ottawa,* 28 [Juillet-Septembre, 1958], pp. 137*-55*).

Accordingly, elsewhere all the relations touched on in the present chapter would be called "predicamental." I prefer to speak of them simply as "relations."

is itself merely mental. In contrast, a relation which has an actually existing S, F, and T is real.[73]

(b) It genuinely depends upon those three factors. The S is that in which it inheres and exists. The F (which can be quantity, non-quantitative perfections, and causality of various kinds and complexity) is that which helps cause it. The T is that to which the S is referred and also that which at times helps cause the R by its very presence.

(c) Nonetheless, the R is really distinct from those three factors. Why so? The distinction is in certain cases experienced by us, as well as inferred from our direct statements about relations.

(d) In itself, then, the relation

1. is a component—for example, fatherhood is *that by which* a man is so ordered to another as to have such-and-such rights and duties;

2. is, accordingly, known by intellection working upon actual relational situations directly perceived;

3. is real because it actually exists;

4. is an accident because it is an individual perfection of the S in which it inheres;

5. yet is not an accidental form, because although it is that by which a subject is perfected within its essence in a static way, it does not perfect it in a *totally* intrinsic fashion: its unique nature is to orientate, refer, and open up the subject to what is without.

(e) Whenever a single real relation has many terms (as happens when a man is the father of several children, is bigger than all the people in Missouri), it has many "respects": the multiple "lookings-toward" which the single R actually has to its multiple terms and which the mind progressively recognizes.

Suggested Readings

Aristotle, *Basic Works,* ed. Richard McKeon, pp. 7-37. New York: Random House, Inc., 1941. On the categories.

Berry, K. K., "The Relation of the Aristotelian Categories to the Logic and the Metaphysics," *New Scholasticism,* 14 (1940), 406-11.

---

[73] Real relations are either bilateral or unilateral (mutual or nonmutual, double or single), depending upon whether or not the relation in the S to T is matched by a relation in the T to S (which T, of course, is the S of the second relation). An example of bilateral relations: filiation and fatherhood; of a unilateral relation: that of creature to God, of knowledge to what is known.

Blackwell, Richard J., "The Methodological Function of the Categories in Aristotle," *New Scholasticism*, 31 (1957), 526-37.

Kane, William J., *Philosophy of Relation in the Metaphysics of St. Thomas.* Washington, D. C., Catholic University Press, 1958.

Kossel, S.J., Clifford, "Principles of St. Thomas' Distinction between the *Esse* and *Ratio* of Relation," *Modern Schoolman*, 24 (1947), 19-36 and 93-107.

———, "The Problem of Relation in Some Nonscholastic Philosophies," *Modern Schoolman*, 23 (1946), 61-81.

———, "St. Thomas' Theory of the Causes of Relation," *Modern Schoolman*, 25 (1948), 151-72.

Owens, Joseph, *An Elementary Christian Metaphysics*, pp. 178-90. Milwaukee: Bruce Publishing Co., 1963. On real relations. Also pp. 191-209 on the relative categories other than relation.

———, "Aristotle on Categories," *Review of Metaphysics*, 14 (1960), 73-90.

Scheu, Sr. M. Marina, *The Categories of Being According to Aristotle and St. Thomas.* Washington, D. C.: Catholic University Press, 1944.

Wild, John, *Introduction to Realistic Philosophy*, pp. 330-55. New York: Harper & Row, Publishers, 1948. On relation and other categories.

———, "A Realistic Defense of Causal Efficacy," *Review of Metaphysics*, 2 (1949), 1-14. On real relations.

PART **III**

Causality

Efficient Causality   Whenever something unknown confronts us,[1] several questions spontane-
ously come to mind. The first is,
"What?" What is it? What is inside?
Of what is it made? This question we
already have technically answered concerning material existents. They are
composites of various components—
substance/accidents, prime matter/sub-
stantial form, essence/act of existing.
This last is the direct source of each
existent's reality and being, as well as
of its unity, individuality, truth, goodness, and beauty.[2] All these components
are its intrinsic causes. They *cause* it
because they help produce it: they make
it *be* and be what it is. They are its
intrinsic causes[3] because they are its

---

[1] For example, we return to our room and find an object concealed under a
sheet on the floor (see p. 151), or we unexpectedly receive a package in the
mail.

[2] On actual existence, see Chapters IV and V; also Chapter VI, Sections 3 and
5; on the other components, see Chapter III.

[3] "Intrinsic" with reference to the effect: they *are* the effect, they are the parts
which go to make it up. They are contrasted with efficient and final causes,
which are really other than the effect, and hence are "extrinsic" to it.

constitutive parts—they are not really other than the whole they constitute, which is the sum of its parts.[4] More precisely, in what does their
causality consist? It consists in the fact that they actually are present
within the existent, that they are what they are so that each can perform is own function (for example, the substantial form specifies, prime
matter individuates, the act of existing actualizes and realifies), that
thereby they join forces actually to constitute the existent. In the light
of their functions, intrinsic causes are of two sorts: they either are *actuating* causes (actual existence, substantial form, accidents—these are
acts and obviously cause the existent by their actuations) or *limiting*
causes (essence, prime matter, substance—these are potencies and manifestly cause the existent by receiving and limiting the acts).[5]

Although all these points are clear at this stage of our metaphysics,
nevertheless the fact that actual existence and the other components are
intrinsic causes is important. It emphasizes that they are not negations
or mere intramental constructs, but that they are real constitutive parts
of the existent, each with a unique contribution to make.

But an unknown object triggers another question in our minds—
namely, "Who?" After we know what it is, we instinctively wonder who
is responsible. Who did it? Who made it? What agent constructed it?
This is the consideration of *efficient cause,* to which we now turn.
However well we may understand material existents in their internal,
componential make-up, we still have not accounted for them completely
until we study the efficient causality which brings them into being and
by which they in turn produce other existents.

Many find this sort of causality baffling.

> The obscurity of the idea of causality is notorious. No idea has so
> persistently challenged analysis and criticism. To dispel its nebulous-

---

[4] At best there is between them and the whole a real distinction which is "inadequate" or "potential." See p. 170, n. 75.

[5] With the advent of the act of existence into metaphysics, Aristotle's description of intrinsic causes as "formal" and "material" is no longer adequate. "Prime
matter" and "substance" can be suitably designated as "material" causes, and
"substantial form" and "accident" as "formal causes" (although even here it
breaks down, for not all accidents [for example, relations] are forms); however,
the act of existing is not a form, and hence can hardly be called a "formal"
cause. One way of handling the problem is to deny that the act of existing is an
intrinsic cause (as was recently done by Joseph Bobik, "Some Disputable Points
Apropos of St. Thomas and Metaphysics," *New Scholasticism,* 37 [October,
1963], 428-30). But this is unfortunate, for what other component is so influential in producing an existent? Another way is to enlarge the description of intrinsic causes to include actual existence. Then they are either *actuating* or *limiting* causes.

ness by tracing its origin and defining its features has been the am-
bition of many subtle thinkers. Yet its genealogy and its nature are
still matters of great uncertainty. The ancestry of causality has been
imputed to various sources. What is its actual genesis? Shall we look
for it in the logical relation between ground and consequent, or in
the psychological connection between our wills and our acts, or in the
given conjunction between individual facts and events? The question
presupposes different conceptions of the nature of causality. Concerning its importance, too, how diverse the assertions! Causality has been
eulogized as the highest principle of explanation; it has been accepted
only as a descriptive law of limited applicability; it has been dispar-
aged altogether as being either otiose or self-contradictory. While all
agree that there is something opaque about the idea of causality, its
darkness has been accounted for in different ways, some ascribing it
to profundity, some to confusion, and others to mystery. No wonder,
then, that in some quarters causality has assumed the character of a
bête noire.[6]

Such a philosopher as Harold Chapman Brown even finds it dangerous:
"The concept of causation is the most treacherous concept that man
has fabricated to interpret his experiences in the physical world."[7]
Hume overcomes both obscurity and danger by reducing it entirely
to something merely intramental.

Necessity [and, a pari, power and efficacy] is . . . nothing but an
internal impression of the mind, or a determination to carry our
thoughts from one object to another. . . . The efficacy or energy of
causes is neither placed in the causes themselves nor in the deity nor
in the concurrence of these two principles; but belongs entirely to
the soul, which considers the union of two or more objects of all
past instances. 'Tis here that the real power of causes is placed, along
with their connection and necessity.[8]

---

[6] J. Loewenberg, "The Elasticity of the Idea of Causality," in *Causality*, ed.
George P. Adams *et al.* (Berkeley, Calif.: University of California Press, 1932),
p. 3.
[7] "Causality and the Cosmos," *ibid.*, p. 41.
[8] *A Treatise of Human Nature*, I, Part 3, Section 14 (Open Court Ed., pp.
214 and 215). Hume performs a similar reduction on beauty ("Beauty is no
quality in things themselves; it exists merely in the mind which contemplates
them") and on substance ("The idea of a *substance* . . . is nothing but a collection of simple ideas that are united by the imagination and have a particular
name assigned them by which we are able to recall, either to ourselves or others,
that collection"—*ibid.*, I, Part 1, Section 6, p. 16).
For an explanation and critique of Hume's position, see D. J. B. Hawkins,
Causality and Implication (New York: Sheed & Ward, 1937), pp. 65-88; also

Is there any alternative to Hume's reduction? How, in fact, does one achieve a valid knowledge of efficient cause? The answer is simple: by following the same inductive methodology used with the components—namely, turn to the actual universe, where the efficient-cause situation repeats itself constantly before our very eyes. Phosphorus bursts into flame on combining with oxygen; radioactive particles affect photographic plates, as well as living tissue; cosmic and light waves bombard us from outer space.[9] Plants grow, flower, and produce

---

idem, Being and Becoming (New York: Sheed & Ward, 1954), Chap. X: "Causality in Aristotle and Hume," pp. 137-49 (also see pp. 150-62); James Collins *A History of Modern European Philosophy* (Milwaukee: Bruce Publishing Co., 1954), pp. 423-33.

Hume's position on efficient causality (as on substance and other topics) is largely predetermined by his twofold attitude on human knowledge; human reason operates (as Collins observes, *ibid.*, p. 429) "in a purely abstract and a priori way, entirely apart from the guidance of sense observation" and, secondly, human cognition terminates immediately at the human knower himself, since "the immediate object of experience is the mental percept" (*ibid.*, p. 431). The first causes him to conclude that reason cannot formulate a theory of efficient causality which would be valid for the actual universe, because it does not and cannot discover it within that universe. The second forces him to picture efficiency on the horizon of his own mind. He restricts it to an intramental association: the conjunction of the *ideas* of cause-effect, of prior-posterior, and so forth.

Because Hume's metaphysics or causality rests upon his epistemology and psychology, it collapses when one realizes from his own actual cognitive operations that the human intellect is constantly nourished by the senses and spontaneously moves in an inductive direction and that nonconstructural human knowledge terminates directly at actual existents themselves.

[9] To many scientists causality tends to be identified with predictability. For example, Max Born, *The Restless Universe* (New York: Dover Publications, Inc., 1951), pp. 163-64: "We now have a *new form* of the law of causality, which has the advantage of explaining the objective validity of statistical laws. It is as follows: if in a certain process the initial conditions are determined as accurately as the uncertainty principle permits, then the probabilities of all possible subsequent states are governed by exact laws. If the experiment is repeated a great many times with the same initial conditions, the frequency of occurrence of the expected effects (and its fluctuations) can be predicted."

Such a conception of causality is in keeping with modern empiriological sciences and is valuable within that context. It is not, however, in conflict with a philosophical conception of causality, which has to do with the here-and-now situation of an agent's actually producing something new and with the ensuing real relationship between the new product and him.

On the extremely complicated question of the meaning of "cause" in empiriological sciences, see Ernest Nagel, *Structure of Science: Problems in the Logic of Scientific Explanation* (New York: Harcourt, Brace & World, Inc., 1961), pp. 73-78 and 277-335, especially pp. 316-24; Philipp Frank, *Philosophy of Science: The Link Between Science and Philosophy* (Englewood Cliffs, N. J.: Prentice-

the seeds which will reproduce the species. Birds build nests, lay eggs, hatch their young. Men erect houses, beget children, write poetry, carve statues, build rockets, pilot spaceships.

> Causal efficacy is a *relational* concept. What it means is the diffusion of something from one being (the cause) to another which is able to receive it (the effect). To the atomic analyst [Hume and his modern counterparts] such relational potencies and powers are sheer nonsense. Reality is made up of perfectly actual atomic capsules which are entirely insular and self-enclosed. Nature however is constantly confronting us with evidence of causal efficacy. The colourless gases O and H act on one another in certain ways to bring into existence a new fused substance quite distinct from any mere juxtaposition of O and H. Stones break windows, and murderers slit their victims' throats. No one who really disbelieved in causal efficacy would ever read a detective story.[10]

It is, then, from nature itself that we derive knowledge of causes. The doctrine we formulate is, in fact, nothing more than the intelligible representation of actual existents as they are produced by the activity of others and as they in turn produce still others by their activity.[11] Let us, then, concentrate upon actual cases of productivity.

1. Six Causal Factors

Let us begin with the simple case of a sculptor carving a statue from a piece of walnut. First of all, it is an instance of *causality*, because

---

Hall, Inc., 1957), Chap. 11: "Causal Laws" (pp. 260-77) and Chap. 12: "The Principle of Causality" (pp. 278-96); John G. Kemeny, *A Philosopher Looks at Science* (Princeton, N. J.: D. Van Nostrand Company, Inc., 1959), pp. 48-53; Andrew G. Van Melsen, *The Philosophy of Nature* (Pittsburgh, Pa.: Duquesne University Press, 1953), pp. 206-42; Victor F. Lenzen, *Causality in Natural Science* (Springfield, Ill.: Charles C. Thomas, 1954); L. de Raeymaeker, *Philosophy of Being* (St. Louis: B. Herder Book Co., 1954), pp. 262-70.

[10] John Wild, "Realistic Defense of Causal Efficacy," *Review of Metaphysics*, 2 (June, 1949), 6-7. Also see Paul Weiss, *Modes of Being* (Carbondale, Ill.: Southern Illinois University Press, 1958), p. 40: "To deny causation is thus to deny current evidence, to ignore an omnipresent category, to be faced with an inexplicable world, and to have an inexplicable belief that it is a mistake to say there is causation in fact."

[11] Our knowledge of other causes, too, is derived from the actual universe, where aluminum causes a canoe to be durable yet lightweight (intrinsic causes), money causes us to work (final cause), the fact that Boris Pasternak lived in Communist Russia makes *Doctor Zhivago* the novel it is (exemplary cause).

the sculptor does bring it about that there is a statue. With him present and working, the slab of wood turns into the figure of Stan Musial. Without him it remains a slab of wood. It is, moreover, *efficient* causality, for he produces the artifact through his activity.[12] An *efficient cause,* then, is *"that which produces another through activity."*

But the statue has at least two efficient causes, for the knife used by the sculptor also helps produce it. No matter how talented the sculptor may be, no matter how thrilling and compelling a vision of beauty he may be experiencing, no matter how plentiful the supply of wood, there would still be no statue without a knife, or at least some sharp instrument. And the very condition the instrument is in (sharp or dull, nicked or smooth) affects the final product. No less true is the fact that the artist's use of it affects its efficacy: he communicates to it his own exemplarity and finality (for instance, today the knife is carving Stan Musial's features, yesterday it carved John Glenn's), as well as actual motion.[13] In view of those facts, let us designate the knife as *"instrumental* cause," the artist as *"principal* cause." With reference to the single activity issuing from them, the former "acts when and as acted upon" (*movens motum*), the latter simple "acts" (*movens*). The efficacy of the former is colored both by its own nature (for example, it is a knife and is this particular knife) and by the exemplary and telic direction it receives by being moved.[14]

---

[12] Carving is such an activity as to perfect something which is other than the agent itself, and hence is called "transient" activity. But other activities (for example, assimilation of food, thinking) perfect the agent himself and are called "immanent." Efficient causality involves both sorts, since even the latter produce something new (for example, increase of size, concepts and propositions), although this is within the agent. In subsequent paragraphs we shall more frequently use transient activities as examples because their causal nature is more apparent and easier to work with.

[13] Actual motion is not communicated to such instruments as are active of their own nature (living things, acids, and so forth), but exemplarity and finality are communicated to all.

[14] See James S. Albertson, S.J., "Instrumental Causality in St. Thomas," *New Scholasticism,* 28 (1954), 409-35.

With respect to the human soul, which is not educed from matter but is directly created by God, human parents are manifestly not principal causes, nor are they even instrumental causes. Why not? An agent is an instrument by educing a new perfection from the potency of matter, but the sperm and ovum do not potentially contain the human soul, and, accordingly, the parents are not its instrumental cause. What sort of cause are they, then? The answer lies in what they *do* with regard to the soul: they furnish the matter within which the human soul is created and individuated. Let us call them, then, efficient "furnishing" causes. (If one calls them "dispositive" causes, [see Albertson, *ibid.,* p. 415,

But there being a statue also demands the artist has at hand wood or some other sort of material from which to make it. Of course this is not an efficient cause,[15] but still the material chosen makes a unique contribution to the final product (for example, a statue made from wood has different characteristics than one of bronze, marble, or aluminum). Also, it determines to a large measure what an efficient cause can do— for example, a cook can make clam chowder only if the pantry is stocked with clams, a male and female collie can beget collies from their sperms and ova but not French Toy Poodles, someone shooting an elephant in his parlor is responsible for different kinds and a greater quantity of chemicals than if he steps on a mouse. What this boils down to is that the material upon which efficient causes work is also a factor in the efficient cause complex.

Still another factor is the activity itself, in which efficient causality consists. It is the actual carving, begetting, writing, cooking, and similar operations by which agents (both principal and instrumental) bring forth the product. Looked at from one point of view, such an operation is in the agent itself in act insofar as it originates in the agent and is aligned with a state of actuation and perfection in him. But viewed from the other side, it is in the very thing which is being produced and precisely as being produced, precisely as changing from a state of potentiality to one of actuation. In this sense, obviously, the change, perfection, actuation resides in the product—in fact, the product *is* the operation, change, actuation as realized, externalized, concretized.[16]

A further factor is the real relation between the product and its agents, and it is one of origin, of belonging to, of dependence, of similarity. It is an unilateral relation (see p. 218, n. 73), since, as we

---

n. 18], then one must make sure that the adjective is given the force of the verb "deposit"—that which puts or lays down, provides, furnishes—and not the force of "dispose," which would be misleading.)

Accordingly, efficient causes are at least threefold: principal, instrumental, and "furnishing."

On the causality of human parents, see William Reany, *Creation of the Human Soul* (New York: Benziger Brothers, 1932); Henry J. Koren, C.S.Sp., *Introduction to the Philosophy of Animate Nature* (St. Louis: Herder, 1960). On other sorts of efficient causes, see above, Chap. VII, note 9.

[15] Because it is a constitutive part of the effect, the material is an intrinsic limiting and receiving cause. See n. 5.

[16] This property of an operation by which it is in both agent and patient is the background for the Aristotelian position that one and the same motion can be described as both action and passion. See J. Owens, *An Elementary Christian Metaphysics*, pp. 192-204. This description works most easily, of course, with transient operations—see n. 12.

have just seen, the change, actuation, and production is in the thing being changed, actuated, and produced. Thus, the agent *as agent* is not changed or produced, and hence has no real relation to the product.[17] But efficient causality consists essentially in that change, actuation, and production. Accordingly, such causality also consists in that relation of effect to agent. It is present in every efficient situation, whereas a real relation exists between agent and his product only when and because the agent is himself changed and perfected in the very act of producing the effect. Such a real relation exists in an agent as finite or as material, but never in him *precisely as agent*. The real relation of an effect to its agent is, then, at the very heart of efficient causality.[18]

The influence of those factors terminates in the product, which at times is an artifact, an extrinsic unit (the statue), where a new accidental perfection (the shape) has been drawn from the potency of second matter, now inheres in it, and is existentialized by the acts of existence actualizing the individual intrinsic units which make up that matter. But on occasion it is an intrinsic unit (this collie pup), where a new substantial form has been educed from matter (the sperm/ovum), is received and individuated by it, and is actualized by the act of existence existentializing the entire composite. Or it is the various chemical compounds resulting from the death of a living thing, where new substantial forms have been brought from a state of virtual presence to one of formal presence, are now individuated by the quantified matter of those compounds, and are existentialized by the acts of existence which actualize them.[19] Whatever the effect produced, it is

---

[17] The agent as agent is without a real relation to the effect because he is without the foundation required—namely, being changed, modified, perfected. Between the agent as agent and his product there is a mental relation—that put there by the mind as balancing the real relation between the product and agent. The real relation entailed in the effect-cause situation is, then, unilateral (see p. 218, n. 73).

Of course, the real relation between effect and agent is interpreted differently by the negative and affirmative views on relations. According to the former it consists in the S, F, and T, plus the mental activity of the one considering those three factors (see Chap. VII, Sec. 3); according to the latter it is an accidental perfection besides the S, F, and T (Chap. VII, Sec. 2).

[18] Efficient cause would, then, be more completely defined if a reference to the relation is included—for example, an efficient cause is "that through whose activity something new is produced and to which it is really related."

[19] With regard to human parents, the product is a new human existent, but many distinctions must be made. Because they furnish the matter within which the human soul is created and individuated, they are efficient "furnishing" causes of the soul (see n. 14). Because man consists of soul/body and because the parents furnish the matter, these parents are the principal causes of the body, while

the culmination of various causes, some of which are intrinsic (that is, the components which make it up, whether their function is to *actuate* [accidents, substantial form, actual existence] or to receive and *limit* [substance, prime matter, essence]). Others are extrinsic in the sense they are really *other than* the product, and these are the efficient causes (both principal and instrumental), together with the exemplarity and finality which efficiency involves.[20]

Here, then, are at least six factors which always are operative when material existents efficiently cause something:

> Principal agent: "that which acts without qualification."
> Instrumental agent: "that which acts while simultaneoulsy being acted upon."
> Pre-existing matter: that from which a new perfection is educed and in which it inheres and exists.
> Activity, whether transient or immanent.
> Real relation of origin, dependence, and similarity between the product and its agents.
> The product itself—the new accidental perfection or substantial form, existing in and individuated by its recipient.[21]

2. Some Corollaries

There are several points of information which additional reflection upon actual cases of efficient causality uncovers. These can be stated as corollaries to the basic causal factors already listed. In fact, the first has already been mentioned in connection with that list.

(a) *An agent precisely as agent is not changed by his activity.*[22] He may undergo changes inasmuch as he is material—for example, he expends energy while working. He may change insofar as he is finite: his operative powers pass from a state of potentiality to one of actuation in order that he be actually acting, and his activity can perfect his

---

their generative powers, together with sperm/ovum, are its instrumental causes. These last also become one of the new human existent's intrinsic causes (limiting, individuating) at the instant of conception and of the creation of the human soul.

[20] On final and exemplary causes, see Chapter IX.

[21] This list has to be carefully interpreted when applied to human parents. See n. 14 and n. 19.

[22] This corollary is concerned primarily with principal and not instrumental agents, and with transient and not immanent operations. See n. 12.

art and other operative habits so that the artifact he produces next time
will be even better. But granting all that, an agent precisely as agent
does not himself change. Why so? Because the very nature of his
activity (carving, writing, and so forth) is to be out-going, perfecting-
another. Secondly, the activity is *in* the thing which is being produced.
It *is*, actually, the thing's very change from the potential to the actual,
its being actuated and perfected under the influence of the agent.[23]
Because of what such activity is, then, an agent as agent undergoes
no change by acting, an efficient cause precisely as efficient cause is
not itself perfected in causing.

(b) *Whatever an agent produces is similar to himself*. At first sight
this point is extremely simple and what one would expect, as this
argument shows.

> In order to be an agent, something must actually *be* (obviously, since
> how could that which does not exist possibly act?) and must be
> *in a definite way* (since no one can simply *produce* but must pro-
> duce *something*—crab apples or collies or statues).
>
> But one is in a definite way either by nature (by its very nature, a
> crab-apple tree is a definite sort of tree and has its own type of
> natural operative powers) or through cognition (because of the
> singular vision of beauty and creative inspiration he is currently
> experiencing, this painter is the unique artist he is and is capable
> of producing a unique canvas).
>
> Accordingly, an existent's status as an agent originates in, flows from,
> is colored and influenced by what he is by nature or by cognition.
>
> Hence, an existent's very activity is in line with its nature or with its
> current state of knowledge. The activity is, in fact, nothing more
> than the agent projecting itself, externalizing what it itself is here
> and now.
>
> But the product is the result of that activity—it is, actually, the ac-
> tivity itself in a concretized and realized state.
>
> Therefore, the product also is basically nothing more than the agent-
> as-projected-and-externalized.
>
> Therefore, the product is similar to the agent, or, to say the same,
> whatever an agent produces is similar to himself.

But the point is not as simple as it looks when one inspects the
products of various agents. A collie pup is similar to its collie parents,
John-John Kennedy resembles his esteemed parents in myriad ways—

---

[23] As Aristotle remarked accurately, motion or change is the very actuation of
a potency as it continues to be in potency. See *Physics*, III, 1, 201a10-11.

but how is the statue of Stan Musial like its sculptor, and, also, like the knife he used? How is the patient's good health like the medicine which helped him recover it? How is my chill similar to the wind, or the growth this geranium has undergone similar to the sun? [24]

Such instances indicate that there are varying degrees of likeness between effect and cause. [1] At times the perfection found in the effect is intrinsically also in the agent, and this in the same manner and to the same degree (for example, the collie dogs). This class of causes let us call "univocal" (for obvious reasons). [2] At other times, the perfection of the effect is intrinsically found also in the cause, but in a different manner (for example, the statue and its sculptor). This class of causes let us call "analogous." [25] [3] On occasion the perfection of the effect is not as such in the cause, although something equivalent is there (for example, the patient's health and medicine, the knife and the statue, plant growth and the sun). This class of causes let us call "equivocal." [26]

What is responsible for those varying degrees of similarity? It is the fact that the agents themselves are so different. Some work through

---

[24] Other instances could be listed: an animal nourishing itself, someone seeing a red object or thinking on a philosophical problem, someone producing in his intellect the operative habit of geometry through working quantitative problems, and so on. What sort of similarity do these effects have to their causes? These instances indicate that perhaps the second corollary has reference only to transient operations. Since an agent perfects *himself* by immanent operations, what he produces by them is clearly like the agent.

[25] In general all artists are analogous causes. The perfection in question is found both in the artist and in the artifact—in the former, though, as contemplated and experienced; in the latter as concretized and incarnated. For example, *Oedipus Rex* is nothing but the dramatist's experience of grief as externalized in written and spoken symbols. *Death of a Salesman* is Arthur Miller's feeling of frustration and anger similarly expressed. *Heart of the Matter* is Graham Greene's vision of the complexity of the human situation projected into external expression. (We might add that each creature is likewise nothing but the divine Artist's vision of His own infinite perfection externalized in finite existents.)

At least one reason why the similarity between artifacts and artists is not as great as that between offspring and parents is that the latter produce the very matter of the offspring: the sperm and ovum not only are instrumental causes of the offspring but also become constitutive parts and thus intrinsic causes of him, and hence enter into his very make-up. See n. 19.

[26] Causes of this type would more consistently be entitled "extrinsically *analogous* causes," because their effects are not totally dissimilar to them. Actually, the perfection of the effect is predicated of the cause through extrinsic denomination because the cause has some equivalent perfection. For example, the chemical make-up of the medicine corresponds to health. See G. Klubertanz, *Philosophy of Being*, p. 161, n. 16.

knowledge and art (#2), others through natural powers (#1 and #3). Even among these last, though, there is a difference. Some are principal and proximate causes (#1), while others are principal but remote (the sun with regard to plant growth) or proximate but instrumental (medicine in relation to health, the knife in relation to the statue).

Despite these diversified levels of similarity, though, it remains true that every effect resembles its efficient cause to some extent, or in other words, that whatever an agent produces is somehow similar to itself.[27] And why so? Because the activity involved is the agent projecting and externalizing itself, and the product is that same activity in a concretized and realized condition.

(c) *Whenever a single effect is produced by two or more different agents* (for example, by principal and instrumental causes), *each agent makes a unique contribution to that effect* because each acts according to what it is if it is to act at all, and what each is makes it unique and diverse from everything else. *The unique contribution which an agent makes by acting according to what it is is called its "proper effect."* No matter what other effects it may have, then, *every agent has a proper effect, since an agent always acts according to what it is.*

By way of example, consider a teacher using a piece of red chalk to write "dog" upon the blackboard. The effect produced is composite and yet one. It is composite inasmuch as it is a symbol which is both meaningful and colored. It is one insofar as it is a single symbol where the color expresses the meaning, which in turn determines the precise position of chalk particles on the board. That effect is wholly caused by both the principal and instrumental agents, since each causes both meaning and color, but differently. The teacher causes the color through the chalk, but the meaning directly and of himself; the chalk causes the meaning only as moved by the teacher, and the color directly in virtue of its own nature. By directly causing the meaning, then, the teacher also causes the color; by directly causing the color, the

---

[27] This point may also be stated thus: "A cause contains in some way all the perfections of its effects." (Plotinus disagrees with respect to The One, Who is God and First Cause. If He is to cause the perfections of His effects, He must contain none of them. This position is necessary where to be real is to be one: that which is supremely real must also be supremely one, and thereby is unable to contain in any way the multiple perfections of the effects. It also suggests that the causality exercised by the One is not efficiency. See L. Sweeney, S.J., "Some Basic Principles of Plotinus' Philosophy," p. 506; *idem*, "Metaphysics and God: Plotinus and Aquinas," *Die Metaphysik im Mittelalter*, Vol. II of *Miscellanea Mediaevalia* [Berlin: Walter de Gruyter, 1962], pp. 232-39.)

instrument also causes the meaning. What is the *proper effect* of each
cause? For the teacher it is the meaning, because by nature he is an
intelligent being and agent. For the chalk it is the color, because by
nature it is a piece of red chalk.[28]

Whatever an agent causes in virtue of what it itself is, then, is its
proper effect. But the act of existing is really other than what any
material existent is. Therefore, the act of existing is not the proper
effect of any material existent. No such existent (or, for that matter,
no creature) can properly cause anything to exist. But more of this in
the next section.

3. Co-operation with God

When we realize that creatures cannot properly cause existence, an
entirely new dimension is added to our understanding of efficiency.
That realization is the basis for proving that God exists and for knowing to an extent the sort of existent He is. No material existent can
properly cause existence, because the act of existing is really distinct
from what each is and thus belongs to the nature of none of them.
Nevertheless, they do exist, they do have that supreme perfection. Therefore, there must be an Existent Whose very nature is to exist, Who
Himself needs no cause but Who can and does properly cause all other
existents to exist.[29]

The sequel to this proof is that every material existent is caused
both by God and by other material things. God properly causes them
to *exist*, creatures properly cause them to exist as *thus and so*. Accordingly, God and creatures *co-operate* (work together), and the question
is how this co-operation takes place. There are difficulties. In some instances agents are said to work together because they work side by
side—for example, two students writing two exams, three horses pulling three carts. Such is not the case here, which is more like two
students writing one and the same exam paper or three horses pulling
the same cart. But the current case differs even from these instances,
obviously, in that these agents are all creatures and thus are on the
same level of reality, whereas here one agent is infinite and the other

---

[28] This reflection on proper effect furnishes another definition of principal and
instrumental causes: a principal cause is one which properly causes the higher
perfection in an effect; an instrumental cause is one which causes the lower perfection.

[29] On God, see Chapter V, Section 6 and p. 127, n. 45.

finite, one the Creator and the other a creature. The danger in such co-operation is that either the higher cancels out the lower or the lower impedes the higher. What is to be said?

Manifestly, the parallel most relevant to God working with a creature is that of a principal agent working through an instrument to produce one and the same effect. This relevance is, actually, confirmed by these facts. As has already been indicated, God properly causes this dog to *exist,* while its parents properly cause it to exist *as this dog.* But the act of existing is itself a greater perfection than what determines and limits it. Therefore, God properly causes what is more perfect in the effect, whereas material things properly cause what is less perfect.[30] But that which causes what is more perfect is the principal agent, whereas the instrumental agent causes what is less perfect.[31] Consequently, God is to the creature with which He works as principal to instrumental cause.

The result of this parallel is that the characteristics of the principal-instrumental cause relationship are attributable, when rightly understood, to God and creatures. Consider a sculptor carving wood with a knife. A mutual dependence exists between them. If a sculptor is to carve, he needs a knife, which in turn can carve only if moved and directed by the artist. Far from hampering him, the tool complements him. On the other hand, the artist does not annihilate the influence of the instrument because he uses it according to its own nature as a sharp instrument (otherwise, why choose it?). Simultaneously he is enabling it to bring about an effect (a statue) which is well above its

---

[30] One's decision of what God properly causes is determined by his position on what it means to be real. If to be real is to be actual, then God's proper effect is that the thing actually exists. But if one holds that to be real is equivalent to being immutable and intelligible, then God properly causes creatures to be immutable and intelligible, whereas created agents properly cause them to actually exist.

One may note that this latter equivalence apparently generates difficulties in explaining creation, the process by which possibles become actuals. If possibles, by reason of their intelligibility and immutability, are already real, then creation is a passage from the real to the unreal, from the perfect to the imperfect (see p. 81, n. 35). But how can one then credit God with creation, Who would thereby be downgrading rather than ameliorating things? Or how can God's proper effect be, as the essentialists say, to confer immutability and intelligibility upon things? Or what would creation be? In the essentialist's interpretation, is it not going from being to nonbeing rather than from nonbeing to being?

[31] See n. 28. One should remember that God works *with* creatures because He works *in* and *through* them.

own mere sensible and immobile nature. The tie-up, then, between a principal agent and his instrument is mutually beneficial, as well as one of mutual dependence.

How are those properties verified with regard to God and creature? Of course, God could directly create all existents (as He did the initial stuff from which the present universe has evolved, and as He still does with reference to human souls). Absolutely speaking, then, He does not need creatures as co-workers. But in the present economy of things He has chosen to work through and with creatures and has given them requisite operative powers. Within the context of that free decision, then, He relies upon sculptors that there might be statues, upon plants that there might be seeds and eventually new plants, upon subhuman parents that there might be animal offspring, and even upon human parents that there might be matter within which He can create human souls (and thus that there might be new human existents).

From the side of creatures the dependence is, of course, absolute, since they cannot *be,* let alone act, without Him. The benefits likewise are extreme, for as instruments in the hands of God, they help bring about what is well above their nature—that countless things *actually exist.* This is a perfection which only God can properly cause, but which He achieves through them, who simultaneously are properly causing things to exist in a determinate, limited fashion.

Let us illustrate this co-operation briefly. Consider a newly existing statue. By properly causing the wood to be *this statue,* the sculptor also (instrumentally) causes this statue to exist. By properly causing the statue to *exist* (as well as the wood, the sculptor, and the carving to exist), God also (through the sculptor) makes the wood be a statue. Or take this existing collie pup. Its parents properly cause it to be this collie pup, and thereby instrumentally cause it to exist. God, though, properly causes it to exist, and thereby causes it to be this pup through its parents. Other illustrations could be given, but enough has been said to indicate that such co-operation benefits both God and creature.

This, then, is the new dimension given to a doctrine of efficient causality when one realizes that no creature properly causes existence. Because they do cause other actually existing creatures, they must literally *co-operate* with God in their causality. This co-operation is like that between an instrument and the principal agent—the former properly producing the lower perfection and the latter the higher, and yet each producing the entire effect. Applied to God and creatures:

God properly causes the thing to be, and, through the created agent, to be this thing; the creature properly causes it to be this thing, and, through God, actually to *be*.[32]

"Harmony," then, is the word best suited to describe the *co-operation* between material agents and God. As with any principal and instrumental causes, each is, rightly understood, dependent upon the other: God upon the creature as that *through which* He works, the creature upon God as Him *by Whom* it is used. Each has its own proper function because each acts in accordance with what it itself is. Yet each helps the other. God assists creatures so that by their activity other creatures begin *to be*; creatures assist God so that *these* creatures it is which come into being.[33]

In all this efficacy, though, God has primacy—He sustains, initiates, moves, directs all else. The basic reason for this primacy is the same as for that He enjoys in being: He is subsistent Actuality. Priority in being, then, spells priority in activity. Creatures' posteriority in efficient causality flows from their posteriority in being. They *are*, and because they are, they are active, and thus efficiently cause others. But the act

---

[32] A further problem arises when one tries to determine the co-operation more closely. There are at least two kinds of instruments—those which need to be physically moved, as well as directed exemplarily and telically (for example, a knife); and those which need only the latter because they are physically active of themselves (acids, radioactive materials, living things). Which kind do creatures resemble in reference to God? Are they like knives or like those things which already are physically active of themselves? Discussing those questions must be reserved to natural theology.

Incidentally, when speaking throughout this section of creatures as instrumental causes of existence, we do not intend that such instrumentality applies also to creation. Creatures cannot co-operate with God in creation, even instrumentally, for an agent is an instrument only by educing a new perfection from the potency of pre-existing matter. But creation, strictly understood, is a production which precisely excludes anything pre-existent. Hence, a creature cannot be an instrumental cause in strict creation. (See *S.T.*, I, 45, 5 resp.; also above, second paragraph of n. 14.) Creatures instrumentally cause actual existence only within noncreative causal situations.

[33] There are thus two sets of principal and instrumental causes: the one between God and creatures, the other between two creatures (for instance, between a sculptor and his knife—see Sec. 1 of this chapter). For the sake of clarity, let us call the causes in the first set "primary" and "secondary"; those in the other set simply "principal" and "instrumental." God is, then, the primary efficient cause, creatures are secondary causes, among which some are principal but others are instrumental agents.

See Robert O. Johann, "A Comment on Secondary Causality," *Modern Schoolman*, 25 (1947), 10-25.

of existing by which they are and are active[34] is really other than what they are, and thus is constantly caused by Another. Their efficiency, no less than their being, is itself *caused.*

4. The Efficient Cause Proposition

So far in this chapter we have been considering material existents as *efficient causes*—what the six factors are in a causal situation (Sec. 1); that precisely as agents such existents do not change, that whatever they produce is somehow similar to themselves, that they always properly cause something in the effect—namely, what it is (Sec. 2); finally, that they are co-workers with God (Sec. 3). The question we now face concerns existents as *effects.* How widespread is efficiency? How many existents are, actually, products of efficient causes? From one point of view, the answer is ready at hand: all of them, with one exception. Why so? Because all except God exist through an act of existence which is really other than what they themselves are. Actuality is not and never will be a part of their very nature. But they do exist, and therefore they must be efficiently caused by an Existent Who *is* actuality and Who properly causes them all to be actual. This convincing and obvious reply comes as a mere sequel to the real distinction between existence and essence.

*   (a) ANOTHER APPROACH

But another way of answering is frequently used, which substitutes deduction for induction and which elaborates a *"Principle* of Causality" rather than a corollary and a conclusion. This approach thrives best in a Cartesian atmosphere, where the human knower is not the body/soul composite but solely the soul; where data for human knowledge comes not from the senses but from ideas innate within the mind; where additional knowledge is achieved by deducing from those ideas the self-evident truths which they contain, which are formulated as analytic and a priori principles and to which one assents immediately.[35] This approach is that taken, for example, by John McCormick in his once

---

[34] The act of existing is, then, the root also of all efficient causality. See Sec. 5g of this chapter; also J. de Finance, *Etre et agir,* 2nd Ed. (Rome: Librarie Éditrice de l'Université Grégorienne, 1960), pp. 70-77, 241-53, 356 ff.

[35] For a history of the "Principle of Causality," see E. Gilson, "Les principes et les causes," *Revue Thomiste,* 52 (1952), 39-63; Joseph Owens, C.Ss.R., "The

widely used textbook, *Scholastic Metaphysics.*[36] First he turns to the Principles of Identity and Contradiction in a section entitled, "First Principles Derived from Notion of Being."

> Certain first principles of being are derived from the consideration of the notion of being. Comparing "being" with itself we find that it is identical with itself, and hence we derive the Principle of Identity: "Whatever is is," or, "If a being is, it is." Comparing "being" and "nothing" we find that they are directly opposed. What one affirms the other denies; one removes from a subject what the other predicates of it. They are therefore mutually exclusive and contradictory, and hence cannot be predicated of the same subject at the same time. From this comparison we derive the Principle of Contradiction as a self-evident principle. It may be formulated thus: "A thing cannot be and not be at the same time." [37]

In a later chapter he deals with the Principle of Sufficient Reason and the Principle of Causality.

Causal Proposition—Principle or Conclusion?" *Modern Schoolman,* 32 (January, 1955), 159-71. Also see John Gurr, S.J., "Genesis and Function of Principles in Philosophy," *Proceedings of American Catholic Philosophical Association,* 29 (1955), 121-33; *idem,* "Some Historical Origins of Rationalism in Catholic Philosophy Manuals," *ibid.,* 30 (1956), 170-80; *idem, The Principle of Sufficient Reason in Some Scholastic Systems, 1750-1900* (Milwaukee: Marquette University Press, 1959). These scholars show that Leibniz and Wolff, besides Descartes, play important roles in this history. According to Gurr ("Some Historical Origins," pp. 171-75), textbooks in the years 1750-1900 can be classified as follows in terms of the predominant influence at work upon their authors: 1750-1800— influence of Wolff; 1800-1850—influence of Descartes; 1850-1900—influence of Wolff again.

What I call a *"Cartesian* atmosphere" for reasons of convenience and simplification, Gurr in the studies cited above calls rationalism, primacy-of-essence position, geometry of being, and so forth. Despite that difference we are both describing the same thing. See Gurr, "Some Historical Origins," p. 178: "The ultimate source of first principles is within the realm of the rational, that is, the realm of the mind—more specifically, within the concept, which upon analysis yields a content whose necessity and universality is guaranteed because of the mind itself and the way it knows, that is, conceptually, that is, with a universality and a necessity which escapes the contingence and singularity of the sensible object by belonging to a realm distinct from it. Sometimes this process is explained in terms of an analysis made of the concept of being which yields the principle of contradiction, which, in turn, guarantees the principle of sufficient reason and thereby the mind can put itself in possession of the principle of causality, which by definition expresses a necessity and a universality the world of sense experience itself is incapable of yielding."

[36] Chicago: Loyola University Press, 1940.

[37] *Ibid.,* p. 21.

The Sufficient Reason

If reality is intelligible, there must be reason for things. It must be possible for intelligence to account for things, to find some intelligent answer to the question: Why is it? asked in regard to any being. The answer to this question will be the Sufficient Reason for the thing. On our assumption, then, that reality is intelligible, it will be possible to formulate a self-evident principle in regard to the reason for things, to the effect that: Everything that is has a sufficient reason for its being. Now reality . . . comprises the possible and the actual. Therefore, if a thing is possible, there must be reason for its possibility; if it is actual, there must be reason for its existence. . . .

The Principle of Causality

This sufficient reason [for the actual existence of things] may be looked for either in the being's own essence, or in something outside the being. . . . If we find the reason for existence completely within the being's own essence, we have a self-existent being, one which exists by reason of its own essence, by the necessity of its own essence. The answer to the question, Why does it exist? is, Because of the essence which it has. Its own essence is the completely sufficient reason for its existence. We know, however, that beyond the actually existing things, there are things which could exist and do not, beings, therefore, which have not the complete reason for existence in their own essence. If then such beings come to have existence, this cannot be entirely due to themselves, but, in part at least, to something else. They must also be extrinsically possible, that is, there must exist some other being that can give them existence, and the influence of this other being must have been exerted in their favor. Now the reason for existence of a being, which is found entirely or in part outside that being, is called a cause. A being, then, which begins to be must have part of its sufficient reason for existence in some being outside itself, or, in other words, must have a cause. In this way we can arrive at the Principle of Causality: Whatever begins to be must have a reason for its existence outside itself. But though this principle is thus shown to be a special application of the Principle of Sufficient Reason to a special class of beings, that is, beings that begin to be, it is really self-evident in its own right, for the two concepts, "to begin to be," and "to be without a cause," are evidently contradictory.[38]

---

[38] *Ibid.*, pp. 140-41. McCormick is not a Cartesian in other respects (for example, he holds that the human soul is the substantial form of the body—*ibid.*, pp. 235-37). Still his essentialism seems clear even from the paragraphs quoted. He there comes close to identifying reality with intelligibility ("If reality is intelligible, . . . On our assumption, then, that reality is intelligible. . . ."). Essence is

We have quoted McCormick at length because he illustrates sufficiently well the approach we have called "Cartesian." Its starting point is the notion of being, its procedure is comparison of various notions,[39] its cognitive movement is a descent from simple to complex awarenesses, its culmination is a series of self-evident and necessary principles, the last of which is called the "Principle of Causality: Whatever begins to be must have a reason for its existence outside itself." [40]

Suppose, though, that the human knower is not solely the soul but

---

for him the heart and center of a thing's existence (". . . a self-existing being, one which exists by reason of its own essence, by the necessity of its own essence. The answer to the question, Why does it exist? is, Because of the essence which it has").

On the importance of isolating a "pure position," but on the difficulty of finding it in any one philosopher, see Gurr, "Some Historical Origins," p. 175 and n. 13; *idem, The Principle of Sufficient Reason*, p. 160.

[39] He not only compares the notion of being with itself and with nonbeing ("Comparing 'being' with itself we find that it is identical with itself. . . . Comparing 'being' and 'nothing' we find that they are directly opposed"). In working out the Principle of Causality he also compares "beginning to be" with "causeless" and discovers that they violate the Principle of Contradiction ("[The Principle of Causality] is really self-evident in its own right, for the two concepts, 'to begin to be,' and 'to be without a cause,' are evidently contradictory").

[40] *Ibid.*, p. 141. Also see C. Frick, S.J., *Ontologia* (Friburgi Brisgoviae: Herder & Co., 1934), pp. 204-12. Not only does he derive the Principle of Causality by deduction from the Principle of Sufficient Reason, the Principle of Contradiction, and the intelligibility of "being" (in that order–pp. 204-5), but on p. 208 he makes the strong statement that one knows the Principle of Causality to be certain only from the ideas involved: *Ea certitudo autem nequit hauriri nisi ex ipsis ideis.*

Also see P. Coffey, S.J., *Ontology* (London: Longmans, Green & Company, Ltd., 1918), pp. 359-60 and 369-70. In the earlier reference two statements make clear the relationship between the Principle of Sufficient Reason and that of Causality: "To understand all the intrinsic principles which constitute the *essence* of anything is to know the *sufficient reason* of its *reality*. To understand all the extrinsic principles which account for its actual *existence* is to know the sufficient reason of its *existence;* and to understand this latter adequately is to realize that the thing depends ultimately for its actual existence on a Reality or Being which necessarily exists by virtue of its own essence." These statements also illumine his radical essentialism: reality is something apart from existence and is located in a thing's essence and ultimately in an Essence or Reality or Being. In the second reference he establishes the Principle of Causality to be "a self-evident, axiomatic, necessary principle" by stating that its opposite is "positively unthinkable and absolutely repugnant to our intelligence; all this our reason peremptorily declares to be intrinsically impossible." The result? "The Principle of Causality is therefore a necessary, *a priori*, self-evident principle." Also see H. Renard, *Philosophy of Being*, 2nd Ed. (Milwaukee: Bruce Publishing Co., 1946), p. 123.

also involves the body, that he has no innate ideas, and that his way
of knowing shows itself to be at best empirical—then this a priori
approach to causality collapses, and scepticism (or even disdain) sets
in. Such has been the attitude of many philosophers from Hume on
down to Bertrand Russell, who finds that "the law of causality, I
believe, like much that passes muster among philosophers, is a relic of
a bygone age, surviving, like the monarchy, only because it is erroneously
supposed to do no harm." [41]

The history of the doctrine of efficient causality consisted pretty much
of those two stages (the Cartesian approach and its rejection) until
recently, when some Thomists advised going back to what Aquinas had
affirmed long ago: the human knower is a composite of body/soul;
data for natural human knowledge (both spontaneous and philosophical) comes to him from the senses; knowledge largely entails induction.
Accordingly, knowledge of efficient causality is not a priori but a posteriori, is not analytic but (rightly understood) synthetic, is not a
principle but a conclusion.

> For St. Thomas, then, the basic metaphysical formulation of the
> causal proposition is that everything for which to be is other than
> its nature has its being (*esse*) from another. This is the conclusion
> of a strict demonstration. The first step in that demonstration is to
> show that a thing abstracts from its being without prescinding from
> it. . . . The second step is to show that the being of a thing is ac-
> cidental to it, not in the sense of a property or a predicamental acci-
> dent, which would be subsequent to the nature, but in the sense of
> an accident which is in its own way absolutely prior to that nature.
> The notion of accident in this sense is used as a middle term. The
> conclusion is that to be for such a nature is *ab alio* [from another].
> This is the causal proposition. . . . Where, in contrast [to the Car-
> tesian and Leibnizian background], sensible things are the origin of
> all human knowledge, and where those things are of a nature which
> is different from, but always open to, the act of being, they provide
> the basis for a rigorous demonstration in which the causal proposi-
> tion follows as a conclusion from the accidental character of their
> being.[42]

As far as it goes, this Thomistic advice is all to the good by re-

---

[41] Bertrand Russell, "On the Notion of Cause," in *Mysticism and Logic* (New
York: W. W. Norton & Company, Inc., 1929), p. 180.

[42] J. Owens, "The Causal Proposition—Principle or Conclusion?", *Modern
Schoolman,* 32 (May, 1955), pp. 335 and 339. E. Gilson initially advised returning to Aquinas in the article cited in n. 35.

emphasizing that man is a mind/matter complex, by reaffirming the inductive character of human knowledge,[43] and, most relevantly, by stressing that the causal proposition ("Everything for which to be is other than its nature has its being from another") is a *conclusion*.[44] It is that, as we have already indicated.[45] It is a sequel to the real otherness between existence and essence, as this inference shows.

> The act of existing in a material existent is really other than the essence of that existent, because the fact that this man *exists* is genuinely different than the fact that he is *this man*.
>
> But that which is really other than the essence of something must somehow be efficiently caused.
>
> Therefore, the act of existing in a material existent must somehow be efficiently caused.
>
> But it cannot be efficiently caused by that existent itself, because nothing can efficiently cause unless it actually exists.[46]
>
> Therefore, material existents are efficiently caused to exist by existents other than themselves (who eventually turn out to be God, since no existent whose existence is really distinct from its nature would suffice).

---

[43] Our approach in other areas of metaphysics has been inductive, and thus confirms this reaffirmation. On the components as inductively known, see Chap. III, Sec. 5, and Chap. IV, Sec. 5; on the transcendents, see Chap. VI, Sec. 3; on relations, see Chap. VII, Secs. 1 and 2.

[44] Owens' substitution of the phrase "causal proposition" for "principle of causality" is helpful. A proposition is any statement in which a predicate is affirmed or denied of a subject, whether that statement be a conclusion of a syllogism, one of its premises, or independent of any process. That substitution works well for Owens, to whom the Causal Proposition is a conclusion. It also works well for me, to whom the Efficient Cause Proposition (I prefer the more explicit expression) in one of its formulations is also a principle (see Sec. 4b of this chapter).

Owens interprets *De Ente et Essentia* accurately with respect to the Causal Proposition, but questionably with respect to the real distinction (see *art. cit.* [March, 1955], pp. 265-70). On the latter see L. Sweeney, S.J., "Existence/Essence in Aquinas' Early Writings," referred to on p. 68, n. 3.

[45] See p. 239.

[46] Actual existence is necessary not only for efficient causality, but also for intrinsic causality (for example, substantial form cannot specify and prime matter cannot individuate unless each actually exists), for emanative causality (quantity cannot flow from the composite of form/matter unless there actually is such a composite; intellect and will cannot come from the human soul unless the latter actually is), and so on.

Such, then, is the Efficient Cause Proposition—"Every material existent is efficiently caused by another," or, even more generally, "Every existent whose existence is really other than what it is is efficiently caused by another." In the light of the process it terminates, it is a conclusion and not a principle; it is mediately known through reasoning and is not self-evident. It is inductive and a posteriori, initiated as it is by our direct perception of two facts which material things disclose: *that* they exist and *what* they are.

✳ (b) IS THE CAUSAL PROPOSITION IMMEDIATELY KNOWN?

That approach to the Causal Proposition, then, is valid and important, as well as highly metaphysical, for it deals with existents precisely as existent, that is, precisely as existentially structured of existence and essence. Yet it is incomplete, since there is evidence that the Causal Proposition when differently formulated is also known immediately, and is, in fact, a self-evident principle of further cognition.

What is that evidence? The fact which we saw early in this chapter: when confronted with something new (for example, a raincoat pocket filled with syrup, a freshly baked cake in the cupboard, a smashed vase in the front hallway), everyone spontaneously and immediately asks, "Who?" Who is responsible? Who did it? Who made it? This question appears to follow from a syllogism, the major premise of which is the Causal Proposition:

> Every new item comes about because of some agent;
> But here is a new item;
> Therefore, some agent is responsible, and my question is: *Who?*

True enough, that proposition is operative on the purely practical level: it directs us with respect to the events we encounter in our day-by-day life. Also, it ordinarily is only implicit (we do not go about our daily tasks, repeating, "Every new item comes about because of some agent") —it becomes explicit solely under the force of such reflection as we are now making. Nonetheless, it *is* operative in our practical lives, and it must *be* there implicitly so as to be able to become explicated. Moreover, it must be *known* immediately, spontaneously, and by all, because everyone immediately and spontaneously does ask "Who?"

What would be the origin of that knowledge? In line with the nature of the human knower as a body/soul composite, and in keeping with the fact that human knowledge grows out of data obtained through perception, it would be a concrete case we observe of some agent constructing (or demolishing) something.[47] There we notice first the ingredients upon which he will work—the shortening, sugar, milk, flour, and so on which now and of themselves are nothing but shortening, sugar, and so forth, but which (unlike putty, lead, steel) can become a cake. We then see that the agent's activity of measuring, sifting, stirring, and so on transforms them from mere separate, sometimes distasteful ingredients into a delicious, edible combination. While observing such a concrete case, we become aware not only that *this* new item has resulted from *this* agent, but that in general every new item comes about through some agent, and this because of the very nature of ingredients and of an agent's function.[48] This awareness is the Causal Proposition, which becomes operative from then on in our everyday lives, so that whenever any new event touches us personally, we automatically know that some agent or other is responsible, and we instinctively inquire who it is.

As so formulated and known, that Proposition is inductive, for we know it from and within a concrete case (or cases). It is immediately known because it is known without reasoning. It is self-evident, not through mere analysis either of the terms used in its formulation or of the concepts they express, but because it is cognized immediately through the light of intelligibilities present within a concrete case of an agent making something. It is a principle because it serves as the major premise of the practical syllogism already discussed.[49]

[47] An instance of either construction or destruction would serve. In the first the many become one; in the second what is one becomes many.

[48] In this interpretation of the evidence, a child has accomplished a good deal in coming to know the Causal Proposition, in grasping the reasons why it must be true (the nature of ingredients as such and the function of an agent). Of course, all this he has done inarticulately and darkly, but he *has* done it, and this when a case (or cases) of an agent actually making something confronts him when he is psychologically and neurally ready for it.

For a child's knowledge of causality as interpreted by experimental psychologists, see J. Piaget, *The Child's Conception of Causality* (London: Routledge & Kegan Paul, Ltd., 1930); *idem*, "The Child and Modern Physics," *Scientific American*, 196 (March, 1957), 46-51; *idem*, *Le langage et la pensée chez l'enfant* (Paris: Delachaux et Niestle, 1948); *idem*, *Le répresentation du monde chez l'enfant* (Paris: Presses Univers. de France, 1947); E. Michaud, *Essai sur l'organisation de la connaissance entre 10 et 14 ans* (Paris: J. Vrin, 1949).

[49] Thus it is the initial step of a deductive process. Note that deduction has a place in human knowledge, but it is a subordinate one and generally begins from and deals with truths furnished by induction. On induction and deduction, see Chap. X, Sec. 3. From this later chapter it will be clear that I do not intend

It retains those properties even when philosophical reflection makes it explicit, speculative, and formally certain. While in the presence of a cook making a cake, a philosopher can concentrate technically upon the efficient causality taking place, upon the change being effected in the ingredients by the agent. That technical reflection would uncover at least these four facts: (1) that change is a process by which what is potential becomes actual; (2) that what is potential is not simultaneously and of itself also actual; (3) still that it has become actual when the change is terminated; (4) that, accordingly, the potential becomes actual not of itself but from something else—an agent.[50] Manifestly, the last fact is the Efficient Cause Proposition and can be formulated in various but synonymous ways—"Whatever goes from potency to act does so because of some agent," [51] or "Whatever changes, changes because of the influence of an agent," or "Whatever is moved is moved by another," or "Every new item comes about because of some agent," and so on. However formulated, it is explicit, technical, speculatively operative,[52] and formally certain (one not only assents to it without fear of erring, but one can also give a technical account for that absence of fear). Nevertheless, it remains inductive because it is initiated by concrete instances of efficiency. It still is immediate and self-evident, for it arises not from reasoning but from mere reflection upon evidence directly presented within those concrete cases.[53] It is a principle because it can and does serve as a premise within reasoning processes.[54]

"induction" to have the meaning it has in the writings of scholastic rationalists: "They make it a kind of appendage to the syllogistic process. Induction involves the deduction of universality and necessity from a principle possessed prior to and independently of the experience supposed to yield this intelligibility" (Gurr, *The Principle of Sufficient Reason*, p. 173).

[50] See G. Klubertanz, *Philosophy of Being*, p. 158. Also see n. 54 of this chapter.

[51] In the light of this formulation, cannot one also express it as, "Whatever is *composed of potency/act* demands an agent"? If so, the Efficient Cause Proposition known through reflection here meets that known through reasoning ("Every existent whose existence is really other than what it is is efficiently caused by another").

[52] That is, it is used in speculative philosophical processes. See n. 54 for an example.

[53] On the difference between reflection and reasoning, see Chap. X, Sec. 3.

[54] For example, Aquinas uses it as a premise in his First Way for proving the existence of God (*S.T.*, I, 2, 3 resp.): "It is certain and evident to our senses, that in the world some things are in motion. *Now whatever is moved is moved by another.*" Immediately thereafter he spells out the reflection by which one arrives at that proposition: "For nothing can be moved except it is in potentiality

The topic discussed in this fourth section has been existents as effects of efficient causality. How widespread is efficient causality? How many existents result from the activity of others? From one point of view, the answer is direct and easy: they all do, with the exception of God, because in all save Him actuality is really other than essence, and because all except Him change, going from potency to act on one or many levels.

On the other hand, the reply is more complicated if one takes into account the Cartesian tradition and discusses the knowledge involved. Then one must reject a cognition which would be immediate and self-evident in a deductive, analytic, a priori sense. Rather one finds it to be inductive and a posteriori because it entirely issues from our observing agents which actually are producing things by their activities. This inductive cognition is at least twofold. Either it is a conclusion to the reasoning process by which one realizes the impact which the real distinction between existence and essence in existents has upon their origin, in which case it is formulated as "Every existent whose existence is really other than what it is is efficiently caused by another." Or it is a self-evident principle known inductively through immediate insight into or technical reflection upon what change itself entails, as manifested in concrete cases of various changes effected by agents, and it is then formulated in some such fashion as "Every new item comes about

---

to that towards which it is moved; whereas a thing moves inasmuch as it is in act. For motion is nothing else than the reduction of something from potentiality to actuality. But nothing can be reduced from potentiality to actuality, except by something in a state of actuality. . . . Now it is not possible that the same thing should be at once in actuality and potentiality in the same respect, but only in different respects. . . . It is therefore impossible that in the same respect and in the same way a thing should be both moved and mover."

It also furnishes the basis for psychoanalysis. See Charles Brenner, *Elementary Textbook of Psychoanalysis* (New York: International Universities Press, 1957), p. 2: "Let us start with the principle of psychic determinism. The sense of this principle . . . is that each psychic event is determined by the ones which preceded it. . . . Mental phenomena are no more capable of such a lack of causal connection with what preceded them than are physical ones. . . . If we do understand and apply [this principle] correctly, we shall never dismiss any psychic phenomenon as meaningless or accidental. We shall always ask ourselves, in relation to any such phenomenon in which we are interested: 'What caused it? Why did it happen?' We ask ourselves these questions because we are confident that an answer to them exists. Whether we can discover the answer quickly and easily is another matter, of course, but we know that the answer is there."

because of an agent," or "Whatever goes from potency to act does so under the influence of an agent."

5. Summary and Conclusions

(a) However thoroughly a philosopher may have studied existents in the light of their intrinsic causes (the act of existing and the other components), he must still investigate their efficient causes if he is to understand them completely. The question "Who?" comes as automatically to mind as does "What?"

(b) The investigation of efficient causality made in this chapter centers around two problems—existents as efficient causes (Sections 1-3) and also as effects of efficiency (Section 4). Let us review the discussion of the second problem first.

1. How many existents result from efficient causality? With the exception of God, all of them, and this for two reasons. First, all except Him entail change—the transition from potency to act. Second, all besides Him actually *are* in such a way that the act by which each *is* differs really from that by which each is what it is.

2. Through what sort of knowledge is that answer achieved? Through induction, which is either immediate insight or reflection—then the knowledge is an immediate, self-evident principle, and can be formulated as "Every new item comes about because of an agent," or "Whatever passes from potency to act does so under the influence of an agent"; or through reasoning—then the knowledge is a conclusion, and can be formulated as "Every existent whose existence is really distinct from what it is is efficiently caused by another."

(c) Granted, then, that all material existents are effects of efficient causes, but in what exactly does that causality consist? How does it come about? In what way do material agents produce their fellow existents? There are several preliminary points of information to be considered. First of all, when material existents efficiently cause other existents, at least six factors are involved:

> Principal agent: "that which acts without qualification" or "that which causes the higher perfection in an effect."
>
> Instrumental agent: "that which acts while simultaneously being acted upon" or "that which causes the lower perfection in an effect."

Pre-existing matter: that from which a new perfection is educed and in which it inheres and exists.

Activity, whether transient or immanent.

Real relation of origin, dependence, and similarity between the product and its agents.

The product itself: that which is produced through activity and which is really dependent upon and similar to the agents (with respect to material agents, it is a new accidental perfection or substantial form, existing in and individuated by its recipient).

(d) Still additional preliminary information can be stated in these corollaries:

1. *An agent precisely as agent is not changed by his activity,* because the activity is in the thing being produced—it is, actually, the thing's very change from the potential to the actual.

2. *Whatever an agent produces is similar to itself.* Why so? Because the activity involved in the production is the agent projecting and externalizing itself, and the product is that same activity in a concretized and realized condition. According to the degrees of similarity, agents are called univocal, analogous, and equivocal.

3. *Every agent, whether principal or instrumental, has a proper effect in the product*—that which it produces by acting precisely according to what it is.

(e) The last corollary has important and relevant consequences. Because the act of existing is really other than what any material existent (or, for that matter, any creature) is, it is not the proper effect of any material existent. No such existent can properly cause anything to exist. It is the proper effect only of that Existent Whose very nature is to exist—namely, God, Who is subsistent actuality. But we know from direct perception that material existents help produce other material existents; hence they must literally *work together* with God as His instruments.

(f) In that co-operation between God and other existents lies the reply to how material existents are efficient causes. Instrumentally they account for the fact *that* other existents do exist, and properly they account for *what* they are. God properly accounts for the fact *that* they exist, and through His created and material co-workers He accounts for *what* they are.

(g) Obviously, actual existence is at the heart of all efficiency, created and divine. Creatures are active, ultimately, because they *are*. But

since they *are* through an act which is really other than *what* they are
and which must continuously be efficiently caused by God, their very
efficiency is efficiently caused, and they only instrumentally cause others to exist. God's activity too is rooted in His actuality, which, being
perfect (because subsistent), issues into efficiency which is perfect and
totally uncaused. He properly causes existence in others. Accordingly,
although creatures are secondary efficient causes, He alone is the primary Cause.

SUGGESTED READINGS

Albertson, S.J., James S., "Instrumental Causality in St. Thomas," *New
Scholasticism*, 28 (1954), 409-35.

Anderson, James F., *The Cause of Being*, pp. 1-31. St. Louis: B. Herder
Book Co., 1952. On God as primary efficient cause; on the co-operation of creatures with God.

De Raeymaeker, Louis, "The Metaphysical Problem of Causality," trans.
A. J. Heiman, *Philosophy Today*, 1 (1957), 219-29.

Gilson, Etienne, *The Spirit of Mediaeval Philosophy*, trans. A. H. C.
Downes, pp. 128-47. New York: Charles Scribner's Sons, 1940. On
creatures as efficient causes in relationship to God.

Gurr, S.J., John Edwin, *The Principle of Sufficient Reason in Some Scholastic Systems, 1750-1900*. Milwaukee: Marquette University Press,
1959. On "sufficient reason" in reference to the Efficient Cause Proposition as a Cartesian "principle."

———, "Genesis and Function of Principles in Philosophy," *Proceedings
of the American Catholic Philosophical Association*, 29 (1955), 121-
33.

Hart, Charles A., *Thomistic Metaphysics*, pp. 241-70. Englewood Cliffs,
N.J.: Prentice-Hall, Inc., 1959. On efficient causality.

Hawkins, D. J. B., "Causality in Aristotle and Hume" (Chap. X), "Simultaneous and Successive Causation" (Chap. XI), "Principles of Causality and Intelligibility" (Chap. XII), in *Being and Becoming*, pp.
137-49, 150-62, 163-76. New York: Sheed & Ward, 1954.

Johann, S.J., Robert O., "A Comment on Secondary Causality," *Modern
Schoolman*, 25 (1947), 19-25.

Meehan, F. X., *Efficient Causality in Aristotle and St. Thomas*. Washington, D. C.: The Catholic University of America Press, 1940.

Owens, Joseph, "The Causal Proposition—Principle or Conclusion?" *Modern Schoolman*, 32 (1955), 159-71, 257-70, 323-39.

Smith, S.J., Gerard, *Natural Theology*, pp. 77-100 and 116-56. New
    York: The Macmillan Company, 1951. Concerning efficient causes.
Wild, John, *Introduction to Realistic Philosophy*, pp. 297-318. New York:
    Harper & Row, Publishers, 1948. On efficient causality.
————, "A Realistic Defense of Causal Efficacy," *Review of Metaphysics*,
    2 (1949), 1-14.

CHAPTER **IX**

Final Causality

"What?" and "Who?" are not the only questions which arise when we are confronted with an unknown object.[1] We also ask "Why?" Why did the agent do it? For what reason? What is his goal and motive in acting as he does? This third question concerns final causality, which we shall now consider.

* 1. Several Opinions

Finality is totally rejected by many contemporary philosophers and scientists. No one has stated and explained this rejection better than the prominent American philosopher, W. T. Stace, professor at Princeton University. "Why is religion disappearing?" he asks.[2] Why, consequently, must the universe be purposeless, man's ideals be his own creation, man himself be alone and friendless in the world? Because of modern

[1] See pp. 223-24.
[2] W. T. Stace, "Man Against Darkness," *Atlantic* 182 (September, 1948), 53.

science, he answered, and this not because of any "particular discoveries or theories, such as the Darwinian theory of evolution, or the views of geologists about the age of the earth," but rather because of the "general spirit of science and certain basic assumptions upon which modern science, from the seventeenth century onwards, has proceeded." Who, in particular, was responsible for that general spirit of science and thus destroyed "the old comfortable picture of a friendly universe governed by spiritual values?" Galileo and Newton, by the "general picture of the world which these men and others of their time made the basis of the science, not only of their own day, but of all succeeding generations down to the present."

> Neither the Copernican hypothesis nor any of Newton's or Galileo's particular discoveries were the real causes. Religious faith might well have accommodated itself to the new astronomy. The real turning point between the medieval age of faith and the modern age of unfaith came when the scientists of the seventeenth century turned their backs upon what used to be called "final causes." The final cause of a thing or event meant the purpose which it was supposed to serve in the universe, its cosmic purposes. What lay back of this was the presupposition that there is a cosmic order or plan and that everything which exists could in the last analysis be explained in terms of its place in this cosmic plan, that is, in terms of its purpose.
>
> Plato and Aristotle believed this, and so did the whole medieval Christian world. For instance, if it were true that the sun and the moon were created and exist for the purpose of giving light to man, then this fact would explain why the sun and the moon exist. We might not be able to discover the purpose of everything, but everything must have a purpose. Belief in final causes thus amounted to a belief that the world is governed by purposes, presumably the purposes of some overruling mind. This belief was not the invention of Christianity. It was basic to the whole of Western civilization, whether in the ancient pagan world or in Christendom, from the time of Socrates to the rise of science in the seventeenth century.[3]

How did Galileo, Newton, and the other founders of modern science accomplish this revolution? Although they were mostly pious men who did not doubt God's purposes, nevertheless

> they took the revolutionary step of consciously and deliberately expelling the idea of purpose as controlling nature from their new sci-

---

[3] *Ibid.*, pp. 53-54.

ence of nature. They did this on the ground that inquiry into purposes is useless for what science aims at: namely, the prediction and
control of events. To predict an eclipse, what you have to know is
not its purpose but its causes. Hence, science from the seventeenth
century onwards became exclusively an inquiry into causes. The
conception of purpose in the world was ignored and frowned upon.
This, though silent and almost unnoticed, was the greatest revolution
in human history, far outweighing in importance any of the political
revolutions whose thunder has reverberated through the world.[4]

And the result?

For the past three hundred years there has been growing up in
men's minds, dominated as they are by science, a new imaginative
picture of the world. The world, according to this new picture, is
purposeless, senseless, meaningless. Nature is nothing but matter in
motion. The motions of matter are governed, not by any purpose, but
by blind forces and laws. Nature on this view, says Whitehead, . . .
is "merely the hurrying of material, endlessly, meaninglessly. . . ."
If the scheme of things is purposeless and meaningless, then the
life of man is purposeless and meaningless too. Everything is futile,
all effort is in the end worthless. A man may, of course, still pursue
disconnected ends, money, fame, art, science, and may gain pleasure
from them. But his life is hollow at the center. Hence, the dissatis-
fied, disillusioned, restless, spirit of modern man. . . . Along with
the ruin of the religious vision there went the ruin of moral principles and indeed of all values. . . . If our moral rules do not proceed
from something outside us in the nature of the universe—whether
we say it is God or simply the universe itself—then they must be
our own inventions. Thus it came to be believed that moral rules
must be merely an expression of our own likes and dislikes. But likes
and dislikes are notoriously variable. What pleases one man, people,
or culture, displeases another. Therefore, morals are wholly relative.[5]

---

[4] *Ibid.* See also Robert B. MacLeod, "Teleology and Theory of Human Behavior," *Science* 125 (March 15, 1957), 478, col. 1: "The revolution of the
New Science banished Aristotle's final cause, at least so far as physical nature
was concerned, and even Aristotle's formal causes were laid open to question.
The physical world that Newton envisaged was a world that could be described
in terms of material and efficient causes, in terms of particles of matter that
exist in space and time and are moved by force. Since Newton's day matter
has lost much of its materiality; space and time have ceased to be absolutes,
and force has been transmuted into a mathematical formula; but for all practical
purposes the Newtonian scheme still works, and deep down we still have the
conviction that Newton had his fingers on the fundamentals."

[5] Stace, *art. cit.*, pp. 54-55.

Stace goes on to suggest two remedies to help us in enduring those evils of our times (first, face the truth that such *is* the universe in which we live, and second, learn to live with that truth as best and as decently as we can),[6] but limits of space forbid following him. Even so, the points relevant for our purposes have been made amply clear: the root of our contemporary *malaise* is the rejection by modern science of final causes, of cosmic purposes; this was done because of the very aim of science—to predict and control events; the result is that modern sciences became an inquiry into causes other than final ones.

Since Stace's article, some have tried to insert finality into at least one of the modern sciences. Robert B. MacLeod, an experimental psychologist of Cornell University, tentatively suggested at the 1956 New York meeting of the American Association for the Advancement of Science that the concept of finality be introduced into the social sciences.

> In reviving the old question of teleology, I realize that I am venturing down a pathway that for some centuries has appeared forbidding even to the angels, and that in taking a hesitant step in this direction I am identifying myself with a nonangelic group. Teleology means the explanation of natural events in terms of purposive constructs. This is a currently unpopular approach. I submit, however, that we should from time to time look again at the phenomena that invite a teleological explanation and make sure that we have done full justice to them.[7]

The social sciences lack the significant upheavals and advances that mark the histories of astronomy, physics, and biology, and MacLeod locates that lack precisely in the fact that the social scientists, slavishly imitating the natural scientists, have apriorily excluded Aristotle and his theory of causality.

> We look for [the great revolution of the social sciences] in vain because it has not yet taken place. Why? I suggest that it is because the students of man have cravenly tried to pattern their fundamental concepts and methods after those of the natural sciences. I do not propose to canonize Aristotle, as the medieval theologians nearly did; but I do think that, just as the Renaissance was sparked by the rediscovery of the real Aristotle, so the social sciences of today can

---

[6] *Ibid.*, pp. 57-58. Also see *idem, Religion and the Modern Mind* (Philadelphia: J. B. Lippincott Co., 1952), where Stace covers much the same ground.

[7] *Art. cit.*, in n. 4, p. 477, col. 1.

profit from a fresh look at Aristotle's argument for the unity of man
and nature [which rests upon] a fourfold theory of causality.[8]

He then proposes that social scientists should at least consider whether
teleology would not help their very science.

> I am not arguing that science should suddenly have a change of
> heart and reinstate Aristotle's final causes. The physical sciences have
> done fairly well without them. The biological sciences seem to be
> admitting formal causes without yielding to final causes, although
> some biologists are striving manfully to reduce formal to material and
> efficient causes. What I do suggest is that the social sciences, dealing
> as they do with the very phenomena that invite a teleological expla-
> nation, should not scurry away from these phenomena but should
> look at them fearlessly and be prepared to think in more global terms.
> A quarter of a century ago a much maligned psychologist, William
> McDougall, analyzed what he called "the marks of behavior," the
> most important of which was purposive striving. I think he was right.
> Among the many things that are characteristic of organisms is that
> they strive toward goals. We may deduce goals from the observed
> behavior of simpler organisms or we may observe them directly in
> our own experience. The fact remains that goal directedness is some-
> thing we can observe. If science is to include the behavior of man,
> it must include the fact of purposive striving. Sticks and stones do
> not strive, but people do.[9]

Even this proposal he tempers with the suggestion that if the time is
not yet ripe for the direct introduction of final causes, let social scientists begin with formal causes and eventually move over to final causes.

> My present feeling is that, if we were to reintroduce final causes
> now, we would be moving too fast. Some day we may have a natural

---

[8] *Ibid.,* p. 477, col. 3. See *ibid.,* p. 479, col. 3: "The most influential of contemporary psychologists, the American behaviorists, are still trying to stuff the
science of man into a Newtonian bottle. They would like to see all of human
behavior plotted bidimensionally within a simple scheme of space-time coordinates.
I do not really deplore this. The scheme works well with rats, and with human
beings who have the fortitude to memorize endless chains of nonsense syllables.
It is a healthy and humbling experience to know that human, as well as animal,
organisms can be made to behave like well-oiled machines. In a world that cries
for a deeper understanding of man, however. . . , I think it is high time that
the students of man stop pretending to be scientists in the traditional sense and
settle down to the business of looking at man as he really behaves."
[9] *Ibid.,* p. 479, col. 3.

science that is broad enough, both in its concepts and in its methods, to include the facts of human purpose. For the time being, I think it is expedient to concentrate on Aristotle's formal causes, and I suspect that the solution of formal causality may automatically resolve the problem of final causality.

One's thinking is always culture-bound. My own bias is against any sort of teleology. I do not want to admit transcendent, or even immanent, purposes into the universe. This may be a relic of my Newtonian upbringing. Nevertheless, the facts of human behavior and experience reveal purposiveness. Shall we consider these facts of nature, or shall we deny them? If we accept them, shall we reduce them to "purposeless" terms, or shall we try to discover a unified science that is broad enough to encompass the full richness of experience? [10]

MacLeod's suggestion has not been universally welcomed by his fellow scientists. In an address at the 1959 convention of the same American Association for the Advancement of Science and later published also in its organ, *Science,* George Gaylord Simpson, Professor of Vertebrate Paleontology at Harvard, showed himself to be uninfluenced by MacLeod—in fact, he made statements directly opposing the latter's thesis that "What is most challenging about Darwin . . . is his reintroduction of purpose into the natural world. He may not have intended to do this . . . but this was clearly one of the consequences." [11] Simpson rejoins:

The sort of testable evidence that would suggest vitalism or finalism would be the steady progression of life, and of each of its evolving lineages, toward a final and transcendentally worthy goal. That is not, in fact, what the known record of life's history shows. There is no clear over-all progression. . . . [The sort of evidence Simpson offers in rebuttal] convinces me, at least, that the hypotheses of vitalism and finalism are not necessary. Everything proceeds as if they were nonexistent. . . . [Vitalism and finalism] are sometimes advanced with the avowed hope of retaining something from the world of superstition. Vitalism then pretends to find a place in nature for the supernatural. Finalism tries to bring in by the back door *the teleology that Darwin swept out the front door.*[12]

---

[10] *Ibid.,* p. 480, col. 2.
[11] *Ibid.,* p. 478, col. 3.
[12] George Gaylord Simpson, "The World Into Which Darwin Led Us," *Science,* 131 (April 1, 1960), 973, col. 2. On the link between vitalism and finalism, see *ibid.,* p. 973, col. 1: "There is no absolute logical necessity that vitalism and

In the following year and in the same journal Ernst Mayr, professor of zoology at Harvard, shows a direct acquaintance with MacLeod and reduces "teleology" to "teleonomy" in an important and interesting paper on "Cause and Effect in Biology." First he indicates the evidence generally adduced for final causes.

> No discussion of causality is complete which does not come to grips with the problem of teleology. This problem had its beginning with Aristotle's classification of causes, one of the categories being the "final" causes. This category is based on the observation of the orderly and purposive development of the individual from the egg to the "final" stage of the adult, and of the development of the whole world from its beginnings (chaos?) to its present order. Final cause has been defined as "the cause responsible for the orderly reaching of a preconceived ultimate goal." . . . Thinkers from Aristotle to the present have been challenged by the apparent contradiction between a mechanistic interpretation of natural processes and the seemingly purposive sequence of events in organic growth, in reproduction, and in animal behavior.[13]

But "what is the *x*, this seemingly purposive agent, this 'vital force,' in organic phenomena?" It is not *élan vital* or *entelechia*, whereby "the finalistic and vitalistic philosophies of the past merely replaced the unknown *x* by a different unknown, *y* or *z*. . . . The supernaturalistic conclusions drawn from these observations are altogether misleading." [14] What, then, is it?

> Where, then, is it legitimate to speak of purpose and purposiveness in nature, and where is it not? To this question we can now give a firm and unambiguous answer. An individual who—to use the language of the computer—has been "programmed" can act purposefully. Historical processes, however, can *not* act purposefully. A bird that starts its migration, an insect that selects its host plant, an animal that avoids a predator, a male that displays to a female—they all act purposefully because they have been programmed to do so.[15]

---

finalism should go together, but the ideas are related if only because both are to some degree nonnaturalistic, and in that sense nonmaterialistic. More often than not, vitalists are finalists and finalists are vitalists." On this point, see the entire section, p. 972, col. 3 to p. 973, col. 2.

[13] Ernst Mayr, "Cause and Effect in Biology," *Science* 134 (November 10, 1961), 1503, cols. 2 and 3.

[14] *Ibid.*, col. 3.

[15] *Ibid.*, col. 3-p. 1504, col. 1.

In what does this "programming" consist?

> The completely individualistic and yet also species-specific DNA code
> of every zygote (fertilized egg cell), which controls the development
> of the central and peripheral nervous systems, of the sense organs, of
> the hormones, of physiology and morphology, is the *program* for the
> behavior computer of this individual.[16]

It is completely mechanistic.

> The purposive action of an individual, insofar as it is based on the
> properties of its genetic code, therefore is no more nor less purposive
> than the actions of a computer that has been programmed to respond
> appropriately to various inputs. It is, if I may say so, a purely mechan-
> istic purposiveness.[17]

It is in fact better not to call such a mechanistic purposiveness "teleological" but "teleonomic."

> It would seem useful to [substitute *teleonomy* for *teleology* and then
> to] restrict the term *teleonomic* rigidly to systems operating on the
> basis of a program, a code of information. Teleonomy in biology
> designates "the apparent purposefulness of organisms and their
> characteristics," as Julian Huxley expressed it.
>   Such a clear-cut separation of teleonomy, which has an analyzable
> physico-chemical basis, from teleology, which deals more broadly
> with the over-all harmony of the organic world, is most useful because
> these two entirely different phenomena have so often been confused
> with each other.[18]

He then turns to MacLeod's position on Darwin.

> The development or behavior of an individual is purposive, natural
> selection is definitely not. When MacLeod stated, "What is most
> challenging about Darwin, however, is his reintroduction of purpose
> into the natural world," he chose the wrong word. The word *purpose*
> is singularly inapplicable to evolutionary change, which is, after all,
> what Darwin was considering. If an organism is well adapted, if it
> shows superior fitness, this is not due to any purpose of its ancestors
> or of an outside agency, such as "Nature" or "God," Who created a

---

[16] *Ibid.*
[17] *Ibid.*
[18] *Ibid.*, p. 1504, col. 2.

superior design or plan. Darwin "has swept out such finalistic teleology by the front door," as Simpson has rightly said.

We can summarize this discussion by stating that there is no conflict between causality and teleonomy, but that scientific biology has not found any evidence that would support teleology in the sense of various vitalistic or finalistic theories.[19]

In the light of those articles by MacLeod, Simpson, and Mayr, there are within the realm of modern science two opposing camps. One of these, numerically smaller and almost apologetic, timidly suggests reinstating finality. The other vigorously opposes that move, or at least wants it reduced to merely a mechanistic, psycho-chemical, immanent condition of material things.[20]

Another attitude towards finality is that of those Scholastics whose way of proceeding fits best into a Cartesian atmosphere[21] and for whom finality is a genuine and obvious factor in all reality. That every agent acts necessarily for the sake of an end is a self-evident and a priori principle. Consider what R. Garrigou-Lagrange, O.P., says in his well-known book, *God: His Existence and His Nature.*[22]

As soon as we understand what is meant by the word *end,* this principle ["Every agent acts for an end"] is self-evident. End is not only the terminus or result of an action, but the *reason why* the action has taken place. . . . It is a *definite perfection,* which directly *refers* to the agent as its own good, and for the sake of which the agent acts. . . . Now every agent . . . produces a *definite* effect according to its own natural law. . . . It cannot produce this definite and appropriate effect rather than any other, except on condition that it has a *tendency* to produce this particular effect rather than any other. It is not necessary for the agent to know the cause of this tendency, but at least that it is by its nature *ordained* towards this object. Thus the sense of sight produces an act which is not indifferent, but determined. . . . The reason why the sense of

[19] *Ibid.*

[20] For other representatives of those two camps, see Edmund W. Sinnott, *The Biology of the Spirit* (New York: The Viking Press, Inc., 1955) and Lecomte DuNoüy, *The Road to Reason* (New York: David McKay Co., Inc., 1949), who energetically champion telism. On the other side is Leo Francis Koch, "Vitalistic-Mechanistic Controversy," *Scientific Monthly,* 85 (November, 1957), 245-55.

[21] On this attitude with reference to the Efficient Cause Proposition, see Chap. VIII, Sec. 4a.

[22] St. Louis: B. Herder, 1934. All the references are to volume I of this work.

sight perceives colors instead of hearing sounds is because it is naturally *ordained* to seeing and not to hearing, because seeing is its very *raison d'être*. This is a self-evident truth, which certainly transcends the range of sense perception, but is perceived at once by the intellect, a faculty of being, when it considers such an organ as the eye or ear. . . . The mind has intuitive knowledge of this fact.[23]

The Principle of Finality is for him immediately evident also because of its direct connection with the Principles of Sufficient Reason and of Contradiction.

This principle of finality . . . is not only self-evident as soon as the terms of the proposition are understood, but it can also be proved indirectly by showing that to deny it leads to the absurdity of denying the principle of sufficient reason, which latter cannot be rejected without necessarily rejecting the principle of contradiction.

If every agent produces, not an indifferent effect whatsoever, but a determined effect which belongs to it by right, *though it does not tend towards this effect,* and is not *ordained* for it; . . . it follows that there is no way of explaining by the *principle of sufficient reason* how it is that the effect is definitely established and essentially refers to a definite cause. . . . If the agent did not *tend* towards its effect, if it did not have at least a natural *intention* for it, if it were not naturally ordained to produce it, it would no more produce this particular effect than any other, except by accident or chance. . . . In other words, action is essentially *intentional,* that is, ordained towards some end. Without this tendency not only the effect, but the activity itself, would be without a sufficient cause, that is, without determination or congruity, or, to put it differently, it could no more be said to be an attraction than a repulsion, vision than audition, digestion than respiration. . . .[24]

Our author draws his final conclusion.

Therefore, every agent acts *for* an end. The word *for* has a meaning, not only when applied to human activity, in which the end is known and intended, but also when applied to any other kind of activity. Whereas the efficient cause is the sufficient reason as a realizing principle (or that by which a thing is accomplished), the final cause is the sufficient reason for the thing which is accomplished. The eyes are made for seeing, and not for hearing. Therefore, the principle

---

[23] *Ibid.*, pp. 200-201.
[24] *Ibid.*, pp. 201-2.

of finality, like that of causality, is an analytical one in the Aristotelian sense.[25]

This third group could be illustrated by more recent authors,[26] but the paragraphs from the prominent Dominican writer disclose with sufficient clarity its diversity from the previous groups. They are hesitant or even hostile with regard to finality; their approach tends to be a posteriori; they fear any tie-in teleology might have with God, with the supernatural, the transcendent. But the last group welcomes finality wholeheartedly; they approach it in an a priori, analytic way so that it is formulated as a self-evident principle; they use it as a way of knowing God, Who is the intelligent Designer of the finalized universe.

Such, then, are various opinions on finality, which can serve as an introduction to our study of it. The excerpts from Stace indicate how important that study is if religioin and morality hinge upon it, as well as how its rejection by modern scientists came about. The selections from the other authors set up some of the questions we must discuss. What is finality or teleology? Is it synonymous with teleonomy, or does it involve more? Is finality found only on the cognitive level, or is it found also among living existents and even among inanimates? What is its relation with God? Does it lead to God, or does knowing Him lead us to it? Are the charges of superstition and supernaturalism valid?

Contact with these authors also confirms that the methodology to be followed is not an a priori descent from innate ideas to a so-called self-evident, analytic but largely gratuitous Principle of Finality. Rather, it should be that of a hardheaded but open-minded student of nature:

---

[25] *Ibid.*, p. 203.

[26] For example, see Kevin J. O'Brien, C.Ss.R., *The Proximate End of Education* (Milwaukee: Bruce Publishing Co., 1958), p. 48: "The Principle of Finality is traditionally and best formulated: *Omne agens agit propter finem.* . . . Its validity, though impugned in diverse ways by some writers—materialists, pantheists, positivists, evolutionists—is in practice an accepted part of daily life. It is of itself evident according to the second mode of perseity; its denial leads to absurdity and to a violation of the principle of sufficient reason." Also see *ibid.*, pp. 32-33. See J. Maritain, *Preface to Metaphysics* (New York: Sheed & Ward, 1945), "Fifth Lecture: The Principles of Identity, Sufficient Reason, and Finality," pp. 90-109, and "Sixth Lecture: The Principle of Finality (Second Aspect)," pp. 110-131; R. Arnou, S.J., *Metaphysica Generalis* (Romae: Typis Pontificiae Universitatis Gregorianae, 1941), pp. 231-34. Interestingly enough, P. Coffey, *Ontology* (London: Longmans, Green & Company, Ltd., 1918), p. 370 holds that the Principle of Efficient Causality is self-evident but not so with finality: "We shall see that as a matter of fact nothing happens without a *final* cause; that intelligent purpose pervades reality through and through. This, however, is a conclusion, not a principle."

an a posteriori and inductive observation of actual cases. As MacLeod advised,

> [We] should not scurry away from these phenomena [which invite a teleological explanation] but should look at them fearlessly and be prepared to think in more global terms. . . . Among the many things that are characteristic of organisms is that they strive toward goals. We may deduce goals from the observed behavior of simpler organisms, or we may observe them directly in our own experience. *The fact remains that goal directedness is something we can observe.* If science is to include the behavior of man, it must include the fact of purposive striving.[27]

2. Finality on the Cognitive Level

Let us begin by considering what happens when an industrious student in serious financial straits learns that a wealthy alumnus of the school is now on campus ready to give deserving students a gift of three thousand dollars with no strings attached. The student of course begins to *want* that money, but the coming about of that desire involves several stages which need explicitation. First of all, there is the student before he learns of the possible gift. Suppose that he is asleep in his room. In that condition he is not consciously desiring anything, and

---

[27] *Art. cit.,* p. 479, col. 3. In the third sentence of the quotation, he does not mean "deduce" in the sense of an a priori deduction from innate ideas, such as a Cartesian would advise, but in the sense of an inductive inference.

As to methodology, also see John L. Russell, S.J., "The Principle of Finality in the Philosophy of Aristotle and Teilhard de Chardin," *Heythrop Journal,* 3 (October, 1962), p. 351: "The difference in approach to philosophy between Descartes and Aristotle can be summarized without too much oversimplification by saying that for Descartes the philosopher is a [mere] spectator of the physical world; for Aristotle he is a participant. The Cartesian philosopher seeks to detach himself from the world; he withdraws to his study and contemplates the mundane scene with a qausi-angelic intellectual regard which has been purged, as far as possible, from the distractions of sensible experience. The Aristotelian, on the other hand, goes out into the world; he picks things up and handles them; he pushes and pulls them about. He recognizes that he has, in varying degrees, a common nature with animals, plants, and even lifeless things. . . . The philosopher must go to school with the physicist, the biologist, and the artist if he is to acquire the 'feel' of the world which it is his business to elucidate. It is no accident that Aristotle the philosopher was also a first-class biologist and one of the world's great writers on aesthetics and political theory. His philosophy is essentially that of a man who knows the world from the inside, not simply as a spectator."

yet, unlike the bed upon which he is lying, he is of such a nature as to be capable (when awake) of desiring, and of desiring many different objects (for example, he might desire to study, to swim, to dance, to earn money, and so on). The telephone rings, and someone informs him of the alumnus' generosity and tells him the alumnus is now present on the campus. The result is that the student's appetitive powers become active, he now *actually wants that money,* and he hurries for an interview.

That is the sort of situation which "finality" is used to describe on the cognitive level—an agent who can know and love, his awareness of a good, his actual love of the good known.[28] The "final" or telic *cause* is the good-as-known.[29] The causality it exercises is the attraction

---

[28] "Love," "desire," and similar terms can refer to different operations (see H. Renard, S.J., and Martin Vaske, S.J., *Philosophy of Man,* 2nd Ed. (Milwaukee: Bruce Publishing Co., 1956), pp. 212-13; G. Klubertanz, *Philosophy of Human Nature* (New York: Appleton-Century-Crofts, 1953), pp. 211-224). But it is more convenient for us to use them in the meaning which they have in common: they are all actuations of a cognitive agent's appetitive powers. For our purposes, then, they can be taken as synonymous. The distinction between will and sense appetites also is not crucial for our purposes, and we shall generally use these terms also without reference to that distinction. We shall also speak of love (or desire and so on) as an "operation" or "activity" or "act" without intending any difference in meaning.

Both men and animals are cognitive agents because both have appetitive powers, the former having both will and sense appetites (concupiscible and irascible), the latter only sense appetites. (See H. Renard, *op. cit.,* Chaps. VII and VIII; G. Klubertanz, *op. cit.,* Chaps. X and XI.) Although we shall speak only of men throughout these pages, what is said of them is also applicable, *mutatis mutandis,* to animals. But not all the operations of a man (or animal) are relevant to cognitive finality—only his appetition and those operations which it directly instigates. For example, in his vegetative functions (for example, assimilation of food, growth, respiration, and the like), in his unconscious relieving of tension by yawning or scratching his head, even in his cognitive activity when actuated by stimuli from without and not by a will-act, he is not acting as a cognitive agent.

A *cognitive agent,* then, is *an agent with reference to its appetitive operations, as well as to other operations directly caused by them.* A noncognitive agent is an agent with reference to all other operations except these.

[29] The adjective "final" is ambiguous. It can mean what is chronologically last ("The final task of the day") or what is definitive ("His book is the final word on the subject"), and so on. It can also be derived from *finis* as "goal." This last is the meaning in which we shall be using it: a good-as-known is the *final* cause because it is the goal which initiates a man's love and ensuing activity. Since *telos* in Greek means "goal," we shall use the adjective "telic" also as a synonym. This latter term has been brought into prominence by Donald C. Williams in his phrase, "telic tugs" (see "Form and Matter," *Philosophical Review,* 67 [1958], 312).

it exerts upon the agent. The final or telic *effect* is the agent's love for the good. The efficient cause of that act of love is the agent's appetitive powers—his will and/or sense appetites. Let us briefly touch upon each of these factors.

(a) FOUR CAUSAL FACTORS

1. The final cause is, then, the *good-as-known,* in which phrase each word is important. As seen previously, a good is "an actually existing item *as perfect,* and hence in relation to love." [30] The goodness of an existent (money, a building, a person, and so forth) resides precisely in its perfections—those possessions which are due to it in view of what it is.[31]

But the final cause with respect to cognitive agents is not simply a good, but, more exactly, a good *qua known.* The addition of the last two words has several important consequences. First of all, they explain how we can love what is in itself evil—we *look upon* it as good, and thus it seems a good because of our erroneous knowledge. Second, some of the goods which are final causes by triggering love in us do actually exist—the money desired by the student in the previous example, the person living next door, the sports car in the show window, and so on. But in order actually to be final causes, they must be known: only then can they attract us and set up desire within us. Some goods which are final causes, though, do not yet exist—the house to be built, the statue to be carved, the fame to be achieved, and so on. In fact, bringing them into existence is exactly what we want, and thus enters into their final causality. This they can exert, even though they are not yet actual, because a final cause is not simply a good, but a good precisely *as known.*[32]

To sum up: a final cause is a good-as-known, because this is what causes love in a cognitive agent. This can be something which is objectively evil, provided it is viewed as good. It can also be something which is objectively good, and this in two ways: either it is something which does not yet actually exist and we want to make it, or it is something which already is in existence and we want to obtain it.

---

[30] See Chap. VI, Sec. 3c.

[31] On perfections, see Chap. V, Sec. 2.

[32] The house to be built, the statue to be carved, and other final causes which do not yet exist are, strictly speaking, good only through extrinsic denomination: they are the awarenesses of what *will be* actual and thus good. See p. 154 and p. 160, and n. 54. Also see R. Kreyche, "How the End Functions as a Cause," *First Philosophy* (New York: Holt, Rinehart & Winston, Inc., 1959), pp. 248-50.

The very last point opens up a further complexity which cognitive finality entails, because one can have many reasons for obtaining something already actually existing. For example, I may want the hundred dollar bill you have in order to spend it or deposit it or cut it up. I may want to own that house on the corner lot so as to burn it, remodel it, rent it, or live in it. But the complexity does not stop there, for the person for whom I want it can vary. I may desire that I myself own the house, but I also may wish that you or your mother-in-law or the Young Democrats Club may own it.

The precise use to be made of a thing, as well as the person for whom it is intended, then, enters into why a cognitive agent desires something. Accordingly, a final cause in its concrete circumstances (for example, I want you to deposit the money) involves not only the thing itself (the money), but also the person for whom (you) and the precise use to be made of it (its deposit).[33] In saying that a final cause is a good-as-known, one must intend the last phrase to embrace those three elements: the thing itself (*finis cuius* or *qui*), its use (*finis quo*) and the person for whom it is done (*finis cui*). They are not, though, three final causes: they constitute a single, concrete goal, for they constitute a single object of the agent's appetitive power.

An actual final cause involves a further intricacy, because one good is frequently desired because of another. For example, you can desire that you own this mansion so that your son may be socially accepted at an Ivy League school so that he may eventually find a place in the United States Foreign Service. Or an artist may want to carve a statue so that he may obtain money so that he can feed his family. Obviously, then, a single goal may be made up of a series of subordinated goods (each of which involves the three elements mentioned in the previous paragraph). However multiple that series may be, though, it constitutes a single object for the appetitive power, and thus is a single final cause.[34]

---

[33] Traditionally, the first is called the *finis qui*, or at times *finis cuius*; the second, *finis cui*; the third, *finis quo*. These three conceptions and terms can also be applied analogously to a good which is to be made. For example, if I wish to carve a statue out of oak, the *finis qui* is the statue, the *finis cui* is the slab of oak, the *finis quo* is the carving.

[34] For semantic reasons the main goal has traditionally been called *finis operantis* (literally, the "end of the agent," the end in which the agent himself is primarily interested, whereas the others he considers as means); the subordinate goal (or goals, since they can be multiple) has been called *finis operis* (the "end of the work," the end which *is* the work). The original force of the latter phrase is clear in such an instance as this: a man wishes to fashion

Despite the complexities which can mark a final-cause situation, though, this must be clearly understood: the final *cause* therein is the good-as-known which is attracting the cognitive agent and thus causing him to love and tend towards it.

2. In what does the final causality of that good-as-known consist? What does it do? It does not strictly *do* anything, for it is not an efficient cause. It is a cause, though, because it brings about an effect—immediately, the agent's love; mediately (that is, through him), his obtaining or making something or other. The question is, then, *how* does it produce that act of love? By the attraction it exerts upon the agent. Because of its perfections it attracts or draws him, although not in any physical way, because it is not an efficient cause.[35] The thing known and loved is not itself changed by being known and loved—for example, the bottle of beer which attracts the thirsty laborer undergoes no change in that attraction: the change occurs in him—upon seeing the beer, he begins now to want it.

On two points the situation here is somewhat parallel to what one finds with respect to the transient activity of an efficient cause. Although an agent is truly an efficient cause, still precisely as agent he undergoes no change; the change is entirely in the patient, in the thing worked upon. So too here: the good-as-known is truly a final cause, and yet it itself does not change—only the one loving changes. Also, on the level of efficient causality a single physical activity is both action and passion: it is the former insofar as it comes from the agent, it is the latter inasmuch as it is in and perfects the patient.[36] Likewise, the act of love which arises within a final-cause situation is both the attraction which the good exerts upon the lover and simultaneously the response of the lover to the good. It is the former insofar as that act is telicly caused by the good-as-known; it is the latter insofar as that same act is efficiently caused by the agent through his operative powers. It is a single operation which is open to and the result of both causes.

The good-as-known is, then, a genuine cause because it helps produce the activity of love within a cognitive agent. Its causality is the non-physical attraction which the agent experiences within himself and

---

a mobile sculpture from metal rods and delicate wire in order to earn money. The *finis operis* refers to fashioning the sculpture—that is, a goal (hence, *finis*) which *is* the very object to be produced (hence, *opus*). The *finis operantis* is, of course, the sculptor's earning of the money.

[35] A final cause does not, then, attract or draw the agent as a magnet draws iron filings or horses a buggy.

[36] On action/passion, see p. 229, n. 16.

which is, actually, also his very act of love as produced not efficiently but telicly by that good. The attraction is his act of love in reference not to himself but to the good.

3. That operation of love is, then, the final *effect*: that which the good-as-known produces precisely as a final cause. It has two important characteristics—it is a determination and it is a tendency. It is a determination because, along the lines of what precisely is to be loved, a cognitive agent is indeterminate: *as far as he himself is concerned*, he is not now loving A or B. Yet he is determinable: he is by nature such as to be able to love A or B, or, for that matter, almost anything else (the student in our previous instance is capable of wanting to study, to swim, to go to the cafeteria, to dance, and so on). What determines him? The good which he comes to know, which attracts him and causes him to love it rather than something else. Hence, that act of love is an actual determination within him, a state of definiteness which directs him to *this* rather than *that* object and which issues into a determinate way of acting in order to implement that love and to achieve that object. In a telic situation, then, the cognitive agent of himself is determinable, the good as known is the determinant, and the act of love it telicly causes is the resultant determination.

But that operation of love is also a tendency, an inclination. Because of it an agent tends toward, is directed and orientated and pointed toward, some definite goal. It energizes his whole being, so that he undertakes labor and undergoes hardships in order to acquire or construct (as the case may be) the thing in question.[37]

The act of love is, accordingly, both a determination and a tendency. But that act is the telic effect in a final-cause situation; hence, determination and tendency are effects of finality. So truly are they thus linked with finality that they become a criterion of deciding whether or not finality is present in a situation.[38] If an agent acts in a determinate way

---

[37] As an example of the energy that love for a goal can release, consider Konrad Adenauer. This elderly man had already been Chancellor of West Germany for several years when a reporter asked him how he managed to keep going under hard work and pressure. He replied: "First, one must be of good stock. Second, one must have great patience. There is also a third necessity: one must do everything within one's power for an *ideal* that one believes in. In my case, it is the *ideal* of *saving Christian civilization*" (*Time*, August 31, 1953). "Ideal" I take to be synonymous with "goal."

[38] This criterion is useful not only for cognitive agents but for noncognitive ones as well. No matter where found, determination essentially entails that what is multiple is reduced to unity and what is potential becomes actual, with the result that the agent thus affected is pointed and directed to a definite

and if he spontaneously tends to that activity, then he is finalized towards that activity. What we are then observing are the *effects* of finality. Finality is present in its results.

4. The efficient cause of that act of love is, as has already been mentioned, the agent through his appetitive powers (will and sense appetites). He is a *cause* because he helps produce it. He is an *efficient* cause because he produces it by his activity: in fact, it is the very activity and actuation of his appetitive powers.[39]

Such are, then, the causal factors in a teleological situation involving cognitive agents.

The telic cause:	a good-as-known.
Its causality:	the attraction it exerts on the agent (which is rooted in its perfections but which *is* the ensuing act of love as telicly caused).
The telic effect:	the act of love (which is determinate and tendential).
The efficient cause:	the agent through his appetitive powers.

Manifestly, the act of love is midway between final and efficient causes:

[good as known] ⟶ [love] ⟵ [appetitive powers]
    final   *effect*   *efficient*
    cause   *cause*

(b) THE FINAL CAUSE PROPOSITION ON THE COGNITIVE LEVEL

Another question now emerges. How widespread is such finality? Is a known good absolutely necessary for bringing about love in a cognitive agent? Is this true: if no known good, then no love, then no ensuing activity?

---

goal. In a cognitive agent, that multiplicity or potentiality resides in his appetitive powers with their ability to love all sorts of goods, whereas the unity or state of actuation is his loving one of them. In a noncognitive agent the multiplicity and potentiality are the materials, the basic stuff which constitute it, but which as far as they themselves are concerned could have formed various other sorts of things, which virtually they are even now and which they will formally become through eventual substantial change. The unity or actuation is the very entity of the agent itself, organized, structured, programmed to produce definite activities. See Sec. 3a of this chapter.

[39] As we shall see later, his appetitive powers (as well as all his other operative powers) are also final effects. They tend to operations and to determinate operations. See Sec. 2b2 of this chapter.

One can easily answer that inquiry in the light of those four causal factors. A known good is absolutely necessary in order for a cognitive agent to love: such is the very nature of his appetitive powers and of a good as known. The former make him determinable with respect to what precisely is to be loved: they give him a capacity to love and yet they do not determine what exactly he is to love. This determination comes from something other than himself—from the good-as-known, which because of its perfections can attract him and settle what is to be the precise object of his love. The act of love is, then, a joint product of both his appetitive powers and the good. Without the former, there is no ability to love; without the latter there is nothing to love. If either were absent, there would be no love. Hence, the good-as-known is absolutely necessary that there be love (and the consequent activities it initiates) in a cognitive agent. To say the same: every cognitive agent acts because of a goal which is a good-as-known.

    *   1. IS THE FINAL CAUSE PROPOSITION IMMEDIATELY KNOWN? Such an answer is simple and clear, based as it is upon what appetitive powers and a good-as-known show themselves to be in our experience. They are to one another as the determinable to the determinant, the perfectible to the perfective, the actuable to the actuating. Another way of replying is to set the question within the framework of the Cartesian tradition and to investigate the sort of knowledge involved. Although this approach is more intricate, it is profitable because of the additional information it affords.

In our discussion of the Efficient Cause Proposition (see Chap. VIII, Sec. 4a), we have seen the fundamentals of this Cartesian approach. In a Cartesianism which is a "pure position," the human knower is not the body/soul composite but solely the soul. Data for human knowledge come not from the senses but from ideas innate within the mind. Additional knowledge is achieved by deducing from those ideas the self-evident truths they contain, which are formulated as analytic and a priori principles and to which one assents directly. In this chapter on finality (see pp. 261-63), it became clear that Garrigou-Lagrange and other scholastic authors take this approach to finality. According to them, every agent necessarily acts for the sake of an end, and this is a self-evident and a priori principle. It is immediately known to be true by analysis of its terms[40] and by consideration of its intimate con-

---

[40] See R. Garrigou-Lagrange, *op. cit.*, p. 200: "This principle . . . is self-evident to all who correctly understand the terms. . . . As soon as we understand what is meant by the word *end*, this principle is self-evident."

nection with the prior Principles of Sufficient Reason and of Contradiction.[41]

Against that Cartesian background, the question we now face is how the Final Cause Proposition is in fact known. What sort of knowledge is our awareness of it? Is it immediately known in any of its formulations? [42] Within the inductive movement which characterizes all basic human knowledge (spontaneous and philosophic), is it a self-evident principle?

My answer is yes, because of this evidence. When confronted with something new (for example, a raincoat pocket filled with syrup, a freshly baked cake in the pantry), everyone spontaneously asks not only "Who?" but also "Why?" Why did the agent do it? For what reason? What is his goal and motive in acting as he does? This inquiry seemingly is a sequel to a syllogism, the major premise of which is the Final Cause Proposition:

> Every new item comes about through an agent acting because of a goal;
>
> But here is a new item;
>
> Therefore, the agent responsible for it had some goal in mind and my question is: "*Why* did he do it? What is his goal?"

What we said previously concerning the Efficient Cause Proposition can also be applied here.[43] The Final Cause Proposition which is the major in that inference ("Every new item comes about through an agent acting because of some goal," or, more simply, "Every cognitive agent acts because of a goal") is operative on the purely practical level: it guides us in the events we encounter in our daily lives. Also it normally is implicit, becoming explicit only under the force of such considerations as we are now making. Nevertheless, it *is* operative in our practical lives, and it *is* in our minds implicitly if we are able to make it explicit. What is more, it necessarily is *known* immediately, spontaneously, and by all, because everyone immediately and spontaneously asks "Why?"

What would be the genesis of that knowledge? In harmony with the basic inductive character of human knowledge, it would be a concrete case a child observes in which an agent makes (or breaks) some-

---

[41] See Garrigou-Lagrange, *ibid.,* pp. 201-2. Also see the references to other authors in n. 26.

[42] We have already seen one formulation—see p. 271.

[43] See pp. 245-47.

thing under the influence of the end he has in mind. Consider a child witnessing Mother reacting favorably to Father's telephoned message that his employer would dine with them that evening. Everything else being equal, Mother begins to *desire* to prepare a special dinner to please the boss, thereby gaining a raise for her husband, a winter vacation in Florida for herself, and so forth. The child would notice several stages in the coming about of that desire. To begin with, there is Mother before she learns of the employer's visit. She is sleeping on the sofa. In that state she is not consciously desiring anything, and yet, unlike the sofa upon which she is lying, she is capable (when awake) of desiring and of desiring many different things (for instance, she might want to view TV or to sew or to clean house or to rake leaves, and so on). The telephone rings and her husband delivers the news of the visit. The knowledge of this good actuates her appetitive powers. She *now actually desires* to fix a special meal, and she heads for the kitchen.[44]

While observing such a concrete case, the child becomes aware not only that *his Mother's* desire (plus the efficiency into which it issues) is the result of *this* known good but, more generally, that desire in any cognitive agent results from a good-as-known, and this because of the very nature of a cognitive agent (indeterminate with reference to what precisely to desire and yet determinable) and of the very nature of a good-as-known.[45] This awareness is the Final Cause Proposition, which becomes operative from then on in his everyday life; thus whenever cognitive agents act in virtue of their cognitive natures, he automatically knows that they are acting under the influence of goals which are goods-as-known. And he instinctively inquires what they are, *why* they are acting.

As so known and as so formulated ("Desire in any cognitive agent results from a good-as-known" or, less complexly, "Every cognitive agent acts because of a goal"), the Final Cause Proposition is inductive, since we know it from and within a concrete case (or cases). It is immediately known because it is known without reasoning. It is self-evident not through analysis of the terms and concepts involved, not

---

[44] The coming about of the meal itself would, of course, provide data for someone's coming to know the Efficient Cause Proposition in case he has not already achieved that knowledge.

[45] What we remarked previously with reference to the Efficient Cause Proposition also holds here: the child has achieved a lot in knowing the Final Cause Proposition. In an inarticulate but genuine way he has grasped from a concrete case what a cognitive agent is and what a good-as-known is, as well as their mutual *rapport*.

through deduction from the Principles of Sufficient Reason and Contradiction, but because cognized immediately under the light of intelligibilities present within a concrete case in which a cognitive agent begins to love when influenced by a good-as-known. It is a principle inasmuch as it serves as the major premise of the practical syllogism already indicated.[46]

It keeps those properties even when philosophical reflection makes it explicit, speculative, and formally certain. While in the presence of that Mother as she begins to *desire* to prepare the special meal for her husband's boss, a philosopher can concentrate technically upon the final causality taking place, upon the change occurring in her because of a known good.[47] Such technical reflection would disclose at least these four facts:

1. Change within such an agent is a process by which what is potential becomes actual (she who can desire A or B or C now actually desires C).

2. What is potential is not simultaneously and of itself also actual.

3. Still, it has become actual when the change is terminated.

4. Accordingly, the potential becomes actual not of itself but from something else, which is, in this case, the goal, the good-as-known.[48]

Obviously, the last fact is the Final Cause Proposition; it can be formulated in various ways, all of which come down to the same thing: "A cognitive agent goes from potency to act under the influence of a good-as-known," or "Every cognitive agent acts because of a goal." However formulated, it is now explicit, technical, speculatively operative, and formally certain (one not only assents to it with no fear of erring, but one can also give a technical account for that absence of fear). Nevertheless, it remains inductive because it issues from concrete instances of finality. It still is immediate and self-evident because it arises not from reasoning but from mere reflection upon evidence

---

[46] See p. 272. As we noted with reference to the Efficient Cause Proposition (p. 246, n. 49), the Final Cause Proposition is also an initial step in a deductive process.

[47] This is no longer reflection on the "fieri *operis*" (the coming about of the thing), as is the case with the Efficient Cause Proposition, but on the "fieri *operantis*" (a coming about within the agent himself), or, more exactly, "fieri *amoris* in operante" (the coming about of the operation of love within the agent).

[48] See pp. 272-73.

directly presented within those concrete cases. It is a principle because it can serve as a premise within reasoning processes.[49]

*   2. IS THE FINAL CAUSE PROPOSITION KNOWN THROUGH REASONING? Can this Proposition also be known through reasoning? Is it ever a conclusion to a reasoning process?[50] I would say yes, and substantiating that affirmative answer can add a deeper dimension to our understanding of finality.

Its substantiation rests on the inductively known fact that whenever an agent produces an object, that product is the goal he had in mind as concretized and realized, and, consequently, it acts according to finality simply by acting according to what it itself is, merely by "doing what comes naturally." Suppose a man is shipwrecked on an island. What he desires is safe, dry, and convenient transportation across the water separating him from the mainland. With that in mind, he builds a wooden boat and a gasoline motor. His goal dictates his every move—his choice of materials and the construction of the boat and motor, all the parts of which are made to have and tend towards a determinate function. Because of its determinate, tendential and (to use Mayr's word)[51] teleonomic nature, that product is the telic *effect* in the final-cause situation just outlined. It is nothing but the man's goal as externalized and realized in various materials. Hence, by acting precisely as a motor boat, it acts for a goal (that of its maker) and according to finality.[52]

---

[49] For example, Aquinas could have used it in a version of his "Fifth Way" for proving the existence of God, although what he actually used was finality in noncognitive agents (see *S.T.*, I, 2, 3 resp., last par.).

[50] Such as is the Efficient Cause Proposition—see pp. 239, 243-45.

Two points should be remembered as we move into this section on knowledge of the Final Proposition through reasoning: (1) Such knowledge and our immediate knowledge of that Proposition (see Sec. 2b1 of this chapter) are each self-contained: each has its own basis for assent; each is, at bottom, independent of the other (although each complements the other); each is valid by and of itself. (2) We may legitimately introduce God into the consideration of finality in view of the fact that without relying on finality we previously have proved Him to exist and have some awareness of the sort of Existent He is (see Chap. V, Sec. 6).

[51] Ernst Mayr, *art. cit.*, p. 1504, col. 2. On determination and tendency, see pp. 269-70 and n. 38.

[52] Another example in which a thing's tendency to act is even more noticeable would be as follows. A man wishing to hurl an object across a narrow but deep crevice bends back a supple tree on the edge of the crevice and ties the object to it. When released, the tree will swing back into place and thus catapult the object across the space. Before its release, though, it strains to snap

But why is this relevant to the problem at hand? Because cognitive agents (as well, of course, as all other agents) are products of God, Who makes them with definite goals in mind. Thus by acting precisely according to their natures as cognitive agents, they automatically act for a goal (God's) and according to teleology. Let us try to understand these points a bit.

What is the end God intends in making a particular human existent? It is not to receive anything, but to give. As subsistent Actuality and thus infinite Perfection, God is completely self-sufficient. He does not need any creature, for creatures add nothing to Him. Consequently, the divine will to create is entirely free; it bases itself solely upon love—the love God has for Himself and for His creatures as finite re-presentations of the divine perfections. Hence, God's attitude towards creatures is a loving generosity: He wishes to give, to share with them His perfections until they become as like Himself as their created natures and capacities allow.

Coming back now to cognitive agents, and more specifically to this human existent, what is the goal God has in mind in making him? It is to uniquely communicate Himself in a manner apropos to an existent who is cognitive and humanly so. That is to say, He is to be possessed through a contemplation and love achieved by the human existent in question going through sensible existents, which are to nourish the human existent in question, to furnish data for his knowledge, and so on. In view of those various operations, God has constructed this man accordingly. So that he nourish himself, God gave him operative powers by which he could assimilate food; so that he could propagate the human race, God gave him remarkable generative powers; so that he could see colors, hear sounds, and so on, God gave him various powers of sense cognition; so that he could know truth (and, eventually, Truth), God gave him an intellect; so that he could love goods (and, eventually, the Good), God gave him appetitive powers (sense appetites and will). Those operations are the goals God directly had in mind. The operative powers themselves, as well as the human existent himself from which they stem, are the telic effects. They are nothing more than those goals as concretized and realized. They are determinate tendencies to those operations. In simply acting according to what they are, in letting them do what comes naturally, in allow-

---

back into its former position (so much so that the man must use force to hold it back): it is a *tendency* to that motion. The point of the example is that all products are such tendencies to activity.

ing them each to seek its own formal object, a human existent is
acting for the goals God intended, that is, according to finality.[53]

But the appetitive powers are those by which a man acts precisely
as a cognitive agent (and this is the point under discussion), and they
differ from all his other operative powers in this—that their very
object is the *good-as-known*. Accordingly, simply by letting them act
according to their natures as *appetitive powers,* a man is not only acting
for the goal God intended,[54] but he simultaneously is also acting
because of a good-as-known.

What this comes down to is that the operation of love is unlike
the operations of all other operative powers in that it is involved in
two telic situations. [1] It is the telic *cause* of the appetitive powers
insofar as it is the goal God intended in making those powers; they
are that goal as achieved, they are its telic effects, they are tendencies
to it. [2] It is also the telic *effect* here and now of a good-as-known:
when some good or other is presented to a cognitive agent, he begins
to desire and love it, and that act of desire and love is a determinate
tendency to it. [3] It also is, we may add, the efficient effect of the

---

[53] We might add that this picture of God making man with definite operations in mind and fitting him out with operative powers orientated to those
operations is paralleled in the supernatural order. Divine revelation tells us that
man's possession of God is not merely to be through natural contemplation
and love (that is, the kind achieved by going through material existents), but
through a participation in the divine life itself and ultimately through direct
union with God. He intends us to know and love Him somewhat as He knows
and loves Himself. How is this plan to be carried out? He would personally
come and dwell in each human soul, and His very coming and indwelling
would necessarily and simultaneously result in the elevation and quasi-deification
of the human person through sanctifying grace. (See M. de la Taille, *Hypostatic
Union* [cited on p. 172, n. 80].) Such a man would, in a sense, truly live as
God lives, and thereby would personally know and love God in Himself; through
that love and knowledge he would thus be intimately united to God, Who
would dwell within Him.

Such are the supernatural operations God intends for man. What are the
operative powers given him to achieve these operations? The theological virtues
(faith, hope, charity), the infused moral virtues (prudence, fortitude, and so
forth), and the gifts of the Holy Spirit. All of these flow from and complement
sanctifying grace, the entitative change effected in man by God. All of these
are determinate tendencies to these operations.

"Supernatural" aptly fits all such factors, since they genuinely transcend that
to which human nature itself entitles man. For an erroneous use of the term,
see Sec. 5b of this chapter, 2nd prgr.

[54] This property they have in common with all other operative powers, each
of which is by nature a divine goal as concretized and realized.

appetitive powers, which however can efficiently cause it only because
in God's plan they are its telic effect.[55]

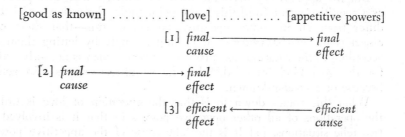

[good as known] . . . . [love] . . . . [appetitive powers]

[1] *final* ———————————→ *final*
      cause   *effect*

[2] *final* ———————————→ *final*
      cause   *effect*

[3] *efficient* ←——————————— *efficient*
      effect   *cause*

Manifestly, then, when someone is involved in a final-cause situation, there are two tendencies operative—that of his appetitive powers
themselves to love and that of the act of love itself to the good-as-known.
In this, appetitive powers are unlike other operative powers, which are
a tendency to their operations, but these operations themselves are
not strictly further tendencies.

Let us now marshal the points just made into an orderly sequence.

> A product, in what it is, is the end its maker had in mind as con-
> cretized and externalized;
> But activity flows from, is determined and influenced by, what some-
> thing is;
> Therefore, a product acts for an end (that of its maker) and ac-
> cording to finality by acting according to what it is;
> But every cognitive existent is a product of God and thus is the end
> He had in view as realized and concretized;
> Therefore, every cognitive existent, in acting according to its cogni-
> tive nature, acts for an end (God's) and in accordance with
> finality;
> But in virtue of his cognitive nature every cognitive existent has
> among its operative powers appetitive ones, which are tendencies
> to known goods and whose function is to love those goods;
> Therefore, every cognitive existent, when acting according to its
> cognitive nature, tends to and loves goods-as-known;
> Therefore, a cognitive agent, when acting in accordance with what
> he is as a cognitive existent, acts for a goal which is a good-as-
> known and which simultaneously is also the goal intended by God;

---

[55] See Sec. 2a of this chapter.

That is to say, if a cognitive existent is to act at all, he must act in accordance with what he is; but for a cognitive existent to act in accordance with what he is is equivalent to his acting for the goal set up for him by his Maker, which in turn is equivalent to his acting for goods-as-known.

Obviously, then, every cognitive agent acts because of a goal.

Obviously, too, the last statement is the Final Cause Proposition, which terminates a long and complex reasoning process and, thus, is a conclusion and not a principle.[56] It is mediately known, and thereby is not self-evident. It is inductive and a posteriori inasmuch as that process is directly initiated by information on the tie-in between products and goals (see the first two propositions of the process) which is gathered within concrete cases and which governs our subsequent viewing of cognitive existents in relationship to God.

(c) RÉSUMÉ

Let us bring the preceding sections into better focus by a survey.

1. There actually are situations in which cognitive agents begin to love because they become aware of some good or other. The result is a determinate tendency to that good through the act of love they efficiently cause. How can we describe that sort of situation? Let us say it is one of "finality" or "teleology." The good-as-known is the telic cause. The operation of love is the telic effect and is also the efficient effect of the agent working through his appetitive powers.

No one can validly challenge the existence of such situations because everyone frequently experiences them in himself and observes them in others. No one should, then, challenge finality in this its initial meaning, because it is nothing but a direct description of those situations.

2. Those same situations entail another finality when they are viewed in relationship to God. Cognitive existents are the handiwork of God, and thus in what they are (especially in their operative, and, above all, appetitive powers) they are His goals as concretized and incarnated. Hence, in acting in accordance with what they are as cognitive existents, they necessarily act for a goal (God's).

---

[56] This process allows us to know not only *that* cognitive agents act because of a goal but also *why*. That is to say, it affords not only *quia* but also *propter quid* knowledge.

On reasoning in contrast to mere reflection, see Chap. X, Sec. 3. We may note that the fifth proposition in the process is also a formulation of the Final Cause Proposition.

Let us emphasize that those existents, together with their operative powers, are telic effects. They are *determinate tendencies* to the operations He intended. Hence, when someone begins to love upon becoming aware of a good and through love begins to tend to it (#1), that tendency rests upon the deeper, prior tendency which is his appetitive powers themselves.

This second sort of finality is based upon the fact that God exists and makes us with goals in mind. Anyone who doubts that fact will also be skeptical of this finality. But this skepticism has to contend with the fact that we all experience our operative powers and their tendential character. Who has not felt the internal unrest caused by an unsolved problem (practical or speculative)? Until the mind finds an answer, it is uneasy, it probes and seeks, all of which reveals that it is a tendency to knowledge, to solutions. Or who has not experienced the disquiet brought on when there is no one or no thing to love? The will is a tendency to the good and is restless unless some good terminates that search.

But if one realizes through experience that his operative powers are determinate tendencies and if determination and tendency are marks of telic effects,[57] he should realize also that his operative powers are telic effects. In such an event his skepticism should be somewhat shaken.

3. But however that may be, we can clearly affirm finality with regard to cognitive agents. They act because of goals, which are goods-as-known. This acting because of goals is absolutely necessary, since the very nature of the appetitive powers demands them: those powers are to a good-as-known as the determinable to the determinant, the perfectible to the perfective, the actuable to the actuant. This we know inductively and immediately (either through immediate insight or through reflection), and we formulate it in a self-evident principle: "A cognitive agent goes from potency to act under the influence of a good-as-known" or "In a cognitive agent love comes about because of a known good" or, simply, "Every cognitive agent acts because of a goal."

4. Secondly, cognitive agents act because of goals which are goods-as-known since they are products of God, and thus are His goals as concretized and realized. Hence, in acting as cognitive existents, by acting in accordance with their appetitive powers, they automatically act for goals (God's), which are, in fact, goods-as-known, for such is the formal object of those powers. This we know inductively but medi-

---

[57] On determination and tendency, see Sec. 2a3 of this chapter and p. 269, n. 38.

ately as the conclusion of a reasoning process, and it is expressed simply as "Every cognitive agent acts because of a goal."

3. Finality on the Noncognitive Level

Cognitive agents' acting for a goal centers around the fact that they have appetitive powers, whose very formal object is the good-as-known. But what about existents which do not have such powers? Do they act because of a goal? In a word, is finality found on the noncognitive level? Such is the next question we face.[58]

An affirmative answer is obvious if we view noncognitive agents in reference to God. They are His products no less than cognitive existents (see section #2b2), and thus He has made them with definite goals in mind—the various operations and activities He intends for them.[59] Consequently, by acting according to their natures as noncognitive agents, by acting in accordance with the operative powers or active qualities[60] which God has given them to perform those operations, they automatically act for a goal (those activities) and according to finality. They are tendencies to determinate operations. They are effects in a telic situation. The universe is shot through with finality.

(a) CAUSAL FACTORS

But if we remove God from the picture and look at noncognitive agents merely in themselves, do they show any evidence of finality? If

---

[58] On what a noncognitive agent is, see n. 28. Chemicals and plants are not the only noncognitive agents. Men and animals are too with reference to all operations save their appetitions and those under their direct influence.

[59] We cannot tell what these operations are in an a priori way, but instead we know them from observation, from experience, and from the progress of science as it discloses more and more what material things are, the uses to which they can be put, and thus, gradually, what God intends through them. Also see R. Kreyche, *First Philosophy*, p. 256: "Neither must it be supposed that man must in every instance be able to 'read' final causes in nature, as though there were some peculiar significance *for man* in the formation of clouds or as though mosquitoes were made in order to try men's patience. True enough, there is abundant evidence of extrinsic finality in nature, by which things of a lower nature are ordered to the good of things of a higher nature, especially man. However, one must not be arbitrary in assigning specific ends to specific events." Because of the limits of human cognition we shall never be able to know the specific ends of all or even many subhuman agents and existents.

[60] For purposes of clarity, that by which living things effect an activity is called an "operative power"; that by which an inanimate thing effects an activity is an "active quality."

determination and tendency are signs of finality,[61] that question is the same as asking whether their activity entails those two factors.

Nothing is more evident than that noncognitive existents act, within limits, in a determinate and constant way.[62] Cherry trees grow in a definite way and produce cherries. A Concord grapevine grows in its own fashion and produces grapes. A mixture of hydrogen and oxygen, when an electric spark is passed through it, turns into water, not into petroleum. And so on through countless other examples which could be given: plants and chemicals act in a determinate, constant manner so as to produce definite results.

In such things tendency is less easily observed, perhaps, but it does manifest itself adequately enough. For example, sodium and phosphorus are so active (*tend* so strongly to activity) that they must be kept under kerosene to remain in a pure state. If exposed to air, phosphorus is so active that it bursts into flames. Sodium oxidizes slowly if exposed to air, but bursts into flames when placed near water. Bromine must be kept in a dark bottle at ordinary room temperature or else it will oxidize. Fluorine is so active that chemists do not attempt to produce it in a pure state. Acids can burn spontaneously without any outside

---

[61] On tendency and determination, see pp. 269-70 and n. 38.

[62] The phrase, "within limits," is added mainly in view of outside interference. When this occurs (for example, by application of X-rays or radioactive materials or through grafting) the activity of those existents will change (although the change in activity arises only from a prior change in the agents themselves).

On the "Principle of Indeterminacy" spoken of by empiriological scientists today, see M. Vaske, *Introduction to Metaphysics* (New York: McGraw-Hill Book Company, 1963), p. 136, n. 4: "The Heisenberg principle of 'uncertainty,' or 'indeterminacy,' does not seem to be a denial of determinacy of action, but a denial of certainty of observation, prediction, and manipulation of microcosmic events. Morever, the principle (primarily at least) seems to be concerned with the measurable *phenomena* of action, not with the proper *causes* of the phenomena." On indeterminacy in biology, see E. Mayr, *art. cit.*, p. 1505. He lists four reasons why a biologist meets indeterminacy in the objects of his study: randomness of an event with respect to the significance of the event; uniqueness of all entities at the higher levels of biological integration; extreme complexity; emergence of new qualities at higher levels of integration. But he adds: "Let us remember that indeterminacy does not mean lack of cause, but merely unpredictability."

Also see G. Klubertanz, *Philosophy of Being* (New York: Appleton-Century-Crofts, 1963), p. 173: "The results of nonvital activities are consistent results. Of course, there is not an absolute invariability of action and result. But there is a definite *constancy*, within limits, so much so that physicists and chemists can construct mathematical formulas for these activities, and so much so that in the past two generations entire industries have been built on the exact, universal knowledge acquired by scientists."

prodding. Plants also grow spontaneously, sending their roots down to water, pushing their stalks up through the soil to the sun. We may say, then, that noncognitive agents not only act determinately but also *tend* to their activities.[63]

This tendency or spontaneity, as well as the fact of determination, discloses that noncognitive agents are finalized. Their operations (together with the products to which these at times give rise) are the final causes.[64] Those very agents, in themselves, in their structure, in their operative powers and active qualities, are the final effects: they are determinate tendencies to the operations they also efficiently cause.

[operations] . . . . [noncognitive agent itself]

$$
\begin{array}{ll}
\text{final} \longrightarrow & \text{final} \\
\text{cause} & \text{effect} \\
\\
\text{efficient} \longleftarrow & \text{efficient} \\
\text{effect} & \text{cause}
\end{array}
$$

[63] What would tendency be on the noncognitive level? Do we have a parallel which might help us understand it better? Yes, since all our operative powers are the same sort of determinate tendencies to operations (see Sec. 2c2 of this chapter, 3rd prgr.) and we directly experience them as such. In our awareness of our own determinate tendencies, then, we gain an insight into what such tendencies are in plants and chemicals. On this level we are like plants and chemicals, save that we experience our tendencies, whereas they do not experience theirs.

J. Russell, "Principle of Finality," p. 350, gives these examples of tendency on the nonliving level: "Gravitational attraction between two bodies is not the only instance of inorganic seeking or striving. This is a far more universal property than Aristotle or the medievals could have suspected. It is present wherever there are forces of attraction or repulsion. Among the ultimate particles of matter, protons and neutrons seek each other, and this accounts for the great stability of most types of atomic nucleus. Electrons and protons are drawn to each other; hence arise all the chemical properties of matter. Magnetized bodies seek to orientate themselves in each other's field. The mutual repulsion of two electrons, or of two protons, is again a type of striving: in this case a striving to separate rather than to approach. Attraction and repulsion are both necessary for the manifold chemical and physical activities of matter. Seeking and striving are therefore to be found throughout all nature." In offering gravity as an example, Russell stresses (as well he should) that gravity as currently conceived has nothing to do with Aristotle's outmoded theory of natural place.

[64] Here lies the reason why so many refuse to see finality on the noncognitive level: it would inevitably lead them to God. If noncognitive existents are the telic effects of operations which do not yet exist, and if they are already structured today to produce tomorrow's operations, someone must have made them with those operations in mind. Consequently, finality on the noncognitive level demands God ultimately as its complement.

Those, then, are three causal factors in the teleological situation on the noncognitive level: final cause, final effect, efficient cause. If the final cause in a situation involving cognitive agents is "a good-as-known to which the agent tends through love," here a final cause is "a good to which an agent tends under the impulse of its very being." The good of a cognitive agent is its operations, as well as the products which ensue from those operations.

(b) THE FINAL CAUSE PROPOSITION ON THE NONCOGNITIVE LEVEL

We are now confronted with the problem of how widespread such finality is. Do all noncognitive agents act according to finality? Is this necessarily so?

If we take into account the causal factors just discussed, the answer is yes. Because noncognitive agents act in a determinate and tendential way by acting according to what they are, they all act in accordance with teleology. They all act for a goal (the operations which they efficiently cause and to which they direct themselves).

*   1. IS THE FINAL CAUSE PROPOSITION IMMEDIATELY KNOWN? Perhaps if we again place the question in a Cartesian perspective and consider the kind of knowledge at issue, we shall gain further information.[65] How, then, is the proposition, "Every noncognitive agent acts for an end," known? Do we have immediate cognition of it, so that it is a self-evident (although inductive) principle?

One can reply affirmatively as a result of the following evidence, which is complex and rather difficult to handle. When confronted with a change in the activity of a noncognitive agent, everyone spontaneously asks, "Why?" and looks to the structure of the noncognitive agent as the immediate explanation and to the cognitive agent responsible for the changed structure as the ultimate explanation.[66] For example, if I throw a cork into a basin of water, I notice that it floats. But suppose someone secretly fills the cork with lead and then throws it into the water. Seeing it sink, I inevitably ask, "Why did it happen?" and seek the reason by investigating the cork and eventually seeking the motive my friend had in mind when he made the change. This question

---

[65] See Sec. 2b of this chapter.

[66] Not all changes in activity are caused directly by cognitive agents; some are caused by deterioration of the thing itself (see n. 67), some by other noncognitive agents (which seemingly would be ultimately dependent upon cognitive agents, however). Then, too, the proposition can be known not only through a *change* in activity but also through *activity* (see n. 68).

and subsequent investigation appear as the sequel of a syllogism, the first premise of which is a version of the Final Cause Proposition:

> On the noncognitive level a change in activity comes about through a change in the thing acting, which in turn comes about because of the goal the cognitive agent making the change had in mind;
> But here is a change in activity;
> Therefore, there is a change in the thing acting, coming about because of a cognitive agent's goal, and my inquiry is, "Why did it happen? What in the noncognitive agent accounts for it? Why did the cognitive agent change the thing?"

Several comments can be made concerning that major premise. Why is the first portion of it true? Why does a change in activity result from the thing's being changed? First, because an agent acts according to what it is, and this for the reason that it could hardly act according to what it is not; second, because its structure is a determination to that activity. Hence, the first part of the major is equivalent to stating that "Noncognitive agents act for an end (their activities) because they are determinate tendencies to it." [67] But why does a change occur in the thing? In some cases at least, because a cognitive agent engineers that change with an aim in mind. Because a product (here, the thing as changed) is the goal of its maker (here, the cognitive agent changing the thing) as concretized and realized, it acts for a goal by acting according to what it is, since what it is has been determined to that goal by the one changing it. Consequently, the major in its entirety is equivalent to affirming that "Noncognitive agents act for an end because they are determinate tendencies to it by reason of the fact that they are the end their maker intended as realized and concretized."

That major premise is, then, the Final Cause Proposition as formulated with regard to activity issuing from noncognitive agents. It is operative on the purely practical level: it guides our re-actions to events we meet in our daily lives. Normally we do not go around repeating, "On the noncognitive level a change in activity comes about because of a change in the thing acting." Hence, it ordinarily is implicit, becoming explicit only when subjected to the sort of consideration we are currently making. However, it *is* influential in our daily lives, and it *is* implicit in our minds, for it can be explicitated. Moreover, it must be

---

[67] This consideration would take care of cases in which change occurs through the thing itself (see n. 66). One should remember that the thing itself is not the final cause, but rather the *effect*.

known immediately, spontaneously, and by all if everyone immediately and spontaneously asks, "Why?"

What would be the origin of that knowledge? In line with the fundamental inductive orientation of human knowledge, it would be some concrete case in which a child observes that a cognitive agent changes the structure of a noncognitive agent so as also to change its activity. It could, in fact, be an actual incident as simple as the one involving the cork made to sink by the insertion of lead. There the child not only would become aware that the activity of *this* object is now different because the object itself is different due to the influence of this cognitive agent changing it. But he would also realize more generally that the activity of any noncognitive agent becomes different if that agent is itself modified by a cognitive agent acting for some good-as-known. And this realization stems from the necessary tie-in between a noncognitive agent and its activity and between that agent and the cognitive agent changing it. This realization is the Final Cause Proposition expressed in terms relevant to activity on the noncognitive level; from then on it becomes applicable in events which touch his personal life, enabling him spontaneously to ask, "Why did it happen? What in the noncognitive agent accounts for it?" and, eventually, even, "Why did the cognitive agent change the structure of the non-cognitive agent?"

As so known and expressed, the Final Cause Proposition is inductive, since we know it from and within a concrete case (or cases). It is immediately known because known without reasoning. It is self-evident —not through analysis of terms and concepts, not through deduction, but because known directly under the light of intelligibilities present within a concrete case in which a cognitive agent modifies what a noncognitive agent is so as also to change its activity. It is a principle because it serves as the major premise of the practical syllogism already discussed.

It retains those marks even when philosophical reflection renders it explicit, speculative, and formally certain. While in the presence of someone inserting lead into a cork so that it may sink when placed in water, a philosopher can concentrate technically upon these points:

1. The influence of the known good upon the cognitive agent involved (it determines, perfects, actuates him).
2. The fact that the product which results from his activity is nothing but his goal as realized and incarnated—it is a determinate tendency to definite operations.

3. The fact that, consequently, the product acts according to finality in acting in accordance with what it is—what it is is not only the efficient cause of its activities, but is their final effect as well: it tends to them as to what is to be produced.

4. That, consequently, any change in what it is results in a change in what it does.

Such reflection brings it about that the Final Cause Proposition is now explicit, technical, speculatively operative, and formally certain. It is, though, still inductive, because all those realizations are made within concrete instances of finality on the noncognitive level. It remains immediate and self-evident because it issues not from reasoning, but from reflection upon evidence directly offered by those concrete instances. It is a principle because it can serve as a premise within reasoning processes.[68]

* 2. IS THE FINAL CAUSE PROPOSITION KNOWN THROUGH REASONING? Can the Final Cause Proposition itself be known through reasoning? Is it ever a conclusion to a reasoning process? The affirmative answer is so clear from previous discussions that here we need only organize the points made earlier[69] into an orderly sequence.

---

[68] Aquinas uses it within his "Fifth Way" for establishing that God exists. See *S.T.*, I, 2, 3 resp., final par.

The Final Cause Proposition can also be known immediately not merely through a *change* in activity but through activity itself, although probably this knowledge would first occur when we encounter something new. For example, when confronted with the activity of a new machine, we spontaneously ask, "Why the activity? Why does this agent act this way?" Then we investigate the structure of the thing for the immediate explanation. This question and subsequent investigation appear as the sequel to a syllogism, the first premise of which is a version of the Final Cause Proposition.

Every noncognitive agent acts according to what it is;

But here is an activity;

Therefore, the explanation of its activity lies in what it is, and this I shall investigate so as to understand its activity.

Behind the major premise stands the fact that an agent is not only the efficient cause of its activities but is also structured and programmed for them, is a determinate tendency to them. The major, then, is equivalent to: "Every noncognitive agent acts for an end by acting according to what it is, because what it is is a determinate tendency to its activity."

This process is implied in that elaborated above concerning a change in activity.

[69] Concerning cognitives, see Sec. 2b2 of this chapter; concerning noncognitives, see the initial paragraphs of Sec. 3.

A product in what it is is the end its maker had in mind as concretized and externalized;

But activity flows from, is determined and influenced by, what something is;

Therefore, a product acts for an end (that of its maker) and according to finality by acting according to what it is;

But every noncognitive agent is a product of God and thus is the end He had in view as realized and concretized;

Therefore, every noncognitive existent, by acting according to its nature as a noncognitive existent, that is, by acting in accordance with the operative powers and active qualities which God has given him as properties of that nature, acts for an end (God's) and according to finality.

The last statement, obviously, is the Final Cause Proposition, a conclusion which terminates a reasoning process. It is mediately known, and thus is not self-evident. It is inductive and a posteriori insofar as that process is directly instigated by information on the link between products and goals which is gathered within concrete cases and which affects our understanding of noncognitive agents in relationship to God.

(c) RÉSUMÉ

In cognitive agents finality is detected by the fact that they begin to love upon becoming aware of a good: this actuates their appetitive powers, and the resultant actuation is the very operation of love, telicly caused by the good and efficiently caused by the appetitive powers (see pp. 266-70). Such detection is impossible in noncognitive agents, which do not have appetitive or cognitive powers and which therefore elicit no operations of love.[70]

What does finality consist in, then, with respect to these agents? It consists in the determinate tendencies to activities which they have and, in fact, are. Nothing is more obvious than that various noncogni-

---

[70] "Love," as well as such terms as "appetite," "striving," and "seeking," seems so intimately linked with cognition that preferably it is not predicated of noncognitive agents. Other authors do not share this preference—for example, M. Vaske, *Introduction to Metaphysics*, p. 141; R. Kreyche, *First Philosophy*, pp. 195 and 252; J. Russell, "The Principle of Finality in the Philosophy of Aristotle and Teilhard de Chardin," *Heythrop Journal*, 3 (October, 1962), *passim*. "Tendency" and "inclination," though, do not appear to have that intimate connection, and hence I apply them with reference to cognitives and noncognitives alike.

tive existents do act; that they act in a definite, programmed, and spontaneous way; that, everything else being equal, they produce definite results.[71] Finality in them is that spontaneous, tendential, intrinsic, teleonomic determination to activities which is their very nature, structure, entity. They act according to finality by acting according to what they are, and this because what they are is a determined tendency to activity.[72] Hence, a noncognitive agent through its operative powers or active qualities is not only the efficient cause of its activities: together with those powers and qualities, it is also the telic effect of those very operations (how else can we explain the fact that it tends to produce them by reason of its structured nature?). They are its final causes, which it is programmed to produce efficiently and to which it tends.

Obviously, this picture of finality is incomplete. If these noncognitive existents are the telic effects of operations which do not yet exist, if they are already structured today to produce tomorrow's operations, Someone must have made them with those operations in mind, and this Someone must have a mind so as to make them. Thus, finality on the noncognitive level also requires an intelligent Agent (who ultimately proves to be God) as its complement. These noncognitive agents act for an end (God's) by acting according to what they are, because what they are is God's goal as concretized and realized.[73]

But even without this complement, finality in its initial phase is genuinely found on the noncognitive level. Just as all cognitive agents are determinate tendencies to a goal (the good-as-known) by reason of love, so too all noncognitive agents are determinate tendencies to a goal (their operations) by reason of their very entities, which are programmed for those very operations. Even one who withholds God from the picture can and should admit this teleonomic teleology.[74]

---

[71] The phrase "everything else being equal" is added to take care of external interference. When this occurs everything is not equal, and their activity is changed if their entity has been changed. See n. 62.

[72] This is the Final Cause Proposition, known immediately (either through immediate insight or through reflection).

[73] This is the Final Cause Proposition as known through reasoning.

[74] The adjective in the expression utilizes Mayr's term (see n. 51). The tendential determination of a noncognitive agent to operations, which is its structure and entity, is teleonomic precisely because it *is* that very entitative structure. It is woven into the very fibers of its being. But that determination is teleological too inasmuch as it is the result of finality: it is the telic effect of those operations. On the noncognitive level there is no conflict between teleonomy and teleology.

4. Chance in the Universe

If all cognitive and noncognitive agents act for an end, then one would expect that no event escapes finality. But such is not the case, as any daily newspaper testifies. Because its steering wheel locked, a southbound car swerved over into the path of a northbound car, which in turn pulled over onto the sidewalk and hit two pedestrians. Their deaths were not intended by the driver of either car, yet the second driver did hit them and their fatal injuries did actually occur. A delivery man steps from the back door of an apartment building after making a delivery and finds himself catching a three-year-old boy who had fallen from a fourth-floor window ledge. When he came to the building, his purpose was not to save the boy, yet he did actually catch him—another actual occurrence which is over and beyond the finality of the agents involved. Such events which escape finality we shall call "chance." Now let us investigate them more thoroughly in order to know how widespread chance is.

Suppose that a man invites two of his former classmates to his home for dinner. These two men have not seen each other for years, and neither of them knows the other will be there. The meeting will be chance as far as the two guests are concerned because neither had intended to see the other, but it will not be chance on the part of the host because he planned the meeting. But suppose the moment they meet in the driveway, the host's wife hurriedly backs her car out of the garage and accidentally runs over them. Their injury is still another chance event, but this time involving not only the two guests and the wife, but even the host. He did not intend it, but he could not have prevented it because of a lack of either knowledge (he did not know it was going to happen) or power (he saw what was about to occur but was too far away to stop the car or to warn his guests).

This instance enables us to make several points.

1. A *chance event is the crossing-over of two or more lines of efficient causality, so that the crossing-over itself (as well as that which results from it) is not intended by any of the agents directly involved.*

2. Chance events are of at least two sorts:
   (a) only two lines of efficient causality are directly involved (one guest meets another unexpectedly)—let us call these *"relative chance"*;

(b) more than two lines are directly involved (the wife runs over the two guests against her own and her husband's intention)— let us call these *"absolute* chance."

3. Evidently, an event which is chance on one level may not be so on another (the meeting of the two guests is accidental with respect to them but not to the host; the injury of the two guests is a chance event to them and to their host, but not to his wife if she intended it).

4. A chance event occurs because the agents involved lack knowledge or power—otherwise they would stop it, since it is over and beyond or even against their wishes.

Now to the question of how widespread chance is. Relative chance events are, of course, frequent enough in our own lives as to need no additional comment. What about absolute chance events? If taken in a sufficiently restricted sense (involving three or four chains of efficiency), they too occur occasionally, as each one can testify from his own experience. Whenever finite cognitive agents with ability to make frequent and disparate decisions by reason of free will are close to one another in space and time, the various lines of efficiency they initiate are bound to intersect one another with unintended results.

But is absolute chance on what might be called a "global" scale possible? For example, might a nuclear world war be triggered accidentally? It would be against the wishes of every nation, yet none of them could prevent it—either because they are unaware of the chain of events leading up to the accidental launching of the first missile or because they are powerless to stop it. Obviously, it could happen, for each government has only limited knowledge and power. Despite the precautions currently taken (for example, no one man at a launching site or at SAC headquarters has full access to the crucial machines or information, a direct telephone line has been installed between Washington and Moscow, and so forth), still it is conceivable that a chain of events could get out of control of any and all men, and thus a nuclear war could be started accidentally. Just as obviously, though, no series of events can escape the control of God, Whose knowledge and power are both infinite. Therefore, what might be called "total" chance is impossible.[75] All the happenings in this universe (even those which

---

[75] "Total chance" aims at expressing an event which would escape the finality even of God. "Relative," "absolute," and "total," arbitrary terms though they be, are useful in view of the three possible combinations of agents: two creatures, more than two creatures, creatures and God.

are chance as far as we created agents are concerned) are framed, stabilized, guided by the infinite wisdom, love and power of divine providence.

Is chance found on the noncognitive level? In order to answer, we must first establish what chance there would be. It would be an event which escapes finality. But noncognitive agents act according to finality by acting according to what they are, and since they act according to what they are whenever they act, they act in accordance with finality every time they act. The only way in which a noncognitive agent could escape finality, then, would be not to act at all. But in that case there would be no event, either. Hence, every event brought about by noncognitive agents is necessarily according to finality, and chance on the noncognitive level seems impossible. For example, baking soda stirred into the batter will inevitably leaven the cake. The atmospheric conditions here today will necessarily bring about rain tomorrow. As far as the noncognitive agents within it are concerned, then, our universe is one of finality, of tendency to definite results, of determinism, of necessity.[76]

*   But there are examples which make us pause. Suppose rain falls immediately after an earthquake which somehow started a number of fires. Because the rain is falling now and here, it quenches fires—an effect it does not have always or elsewhere. Is not that effect a chance event? I would say no, but several points must be clarified. A noncognitive agent such as rain has what might be called an essential effect (providing moisture) and various side effects (here it is beneficial to growing crops, there it cleanses dusty buildings, here it quenches fires). The essential effect it procures directly of itself, and hence always; the others it procures in conjunction with other noncognitive agents, which vary, so that these effects vary also. But not even the

---

[76] Although predictability is not at the heart of finality, in some areas it is its sequel. Take, for example, weather forecasting. Because noncognitive agents act according to what they are, they act in a determined, necessary way. Hence, by studying what atmospheric conditions are today, meteorologists can tell with reasonable accuracy what the weather will be tomorrow, everything else being equal (see n. 71). In fact, Dr. Irving P. Krick, head of a commercial meteorological laboratory in Denver, makes forecasts months or even years in advance. How does he go about it? "His forecasts are based on past performances the weather has given throughout history. He believes that the whole solar system is orderly and can be relied on, given the same atmospheric causes, to produce the same atmospheric effects. Today the Krick laboratory knows what the weather was like for every day back to 1899" (*This Week Magazine*, April 8, 1962, p. 5).

second sort of effect is chance, because the space-time relations in which noncognitive agents find themselves also help constitute what they are. This rainstorm, by acting in compliance with what it is here and now, puts out fires, whereas that one soaks vineyards and acts in compliance with what it is there and then.

* Apparently, the only way chance can enter the arena of noncognitive agents is through the interference of cognitive agents. Rain can be produced "artificially" by airplanes seeding clouds with pellets of Dry Ice. In such a case rain could perhaps be called "chance," insofar as its falling in this place and at this time (with varying side effects) is not the result of natural atmospheric processes. Nevertheless, in their chemical reactions Dry Ice and clouds both act according to what they are, and thus according to finality. The element of "chance" (that the condensation should be here and now, with its own attendant side effects) is directly due to the cognitive agents.[77] Perhaps a clearer example would occur if someone by mistake filled the sugar containers in the obstetric section of a hospital with salt. Suppose a nurse adds this to milk and gives bottles filled with this mixture to the babies, so that several of them die from this "chance" event. It is chance, though, only as far as the nurse is concerned, for she does not intend their deaths. It is not chance as far as the salt is concerned, for it acted in compliance with finality in acting precisely according to its nature as sodium chloride when mixed with milk and taken internally by infants. This event is another illustration of the third point made earlier (see p. 291): that which is not chance with reference to noncognitive agents may be so with respect to cognitive ones.[78]

---

[77] Explosions of atomic and hydrogen bombs by various nations may have so disturbed the natural meteorological conditions that our weather will never again be entirely "natural."

[78] Because evils frequently occur through chance, a brief word can be appropriately added here on the causes of evils. Take the case of a man with poor eyesight. What are the efficient and final causes of the lack of 20/20 vision? Obviously, the efficient cause is the man himself through his visual organs and powers insofar as he efficiently causes an act of seeing which suffers from a lack of full vision. In efficiently causing the seeing, he also and inevitably causes the lack (to the extent that it can have a cause: it is, one must remember, a privation, an absence, a nothingness—see pp. 167-69).

But what about the final cause of that privation? The man directly desires to see, but inasmuch as his seeing is imperfect, he cannot help but desire (at least, permit) the imperfection along with the seeing: if he is going to see at all, he must see imperfectly. Evil, then, can be desired only insofar as it is connected somehow with good (see pp. 167, 266). Hence, evil as evil has no final cause; it is never directly desired.

Does an evil entail intrinsic causes (that is, receiving and actuating causes—

5. Summary and Conclusions

Because of the two previous summaries (see Secs. 2c and 3c of this chapter), this section can be brief. It will center around the question which finality entails above all: *"Why?"*

(a) *Why* do cognitive agents act? For the sake of goals which are goods-as-known. These actuate their appetitive powers and the resultant actuation is their operations of love, which are caused telicly by the goods and efficiently by those powers and which are determinate tendencies to make or obtain those goods.

(b) *Why* do noncognitive agents act? Because of what they are. By reason of their very entity, by reason of the operative powers and active qualities stemming naturally from them, they are determinate structures for and tendencies to activities. These latter are the telic causes, whereas the agents themselves in their entity and structure are the telic effects. By acting in compliance with what they are, then, they automatically act in accordance with finality and for a goal (those activities).[79]

Such finality is naturalistic in the sense that it *is* the natures of things; it is deterministic, programmed, teleonomic, since it is nothing more than their very entitative structure. But such is not the whole story, because finality here necessarily points to God. If noncognitive existents are the telic effects of operations which do not yet exist, if they are already structured now to produce future operations, Someone must have made them with those operations in mind. Thus, finality on the noncognitive level requires God as its ultimate complement. Does this requirement merit the charges of superstition and supernaturalism?[80] Hardly, since God is demanded by the agents' very natures, entities, and structures as their ultimate explanation.

---

see p. 224)? Obviously, it has an intrinsic receiving cause—the subject of which it is predicated and which it affects (in the case of poor vision, that subject is the man, and, more proximately, his visual powers and operations—see pp. 167-68 and n. 68). Just as obviously it has no intrinsic actuating cause, for evil is the very absence of a perfection.

See M. Vaske, *Introduction to Metaphysics*, pp. 195-96.

[79] With reference to a noncognitive agent, then, a final cause may be described as "a good to which an agent tends because of its very being"; with reference to cognitives, "a good to which an agent tends through love." In the light of those two definitions, the heart of both noncognitive and cognitive finality is that agents determinately tend to a good.

[80] As examples of those charges, see the texts of Simpson and Mayr cited in n. 12 and n. 14. For an accurate meaning of "supernatural," see n. 53.

(c) *Why* did this or that chance event happen? To the extent that they are chance, no answer is possible, for they are outside the realm of finality. The cognitive agents responsible for them did not intend them, although they did efficiently cause them. Of course, one can understand how they can happen—cognitive agents are limited in knowledge and in power, their freedom of choice makes them capable of multiple and disparate decisions, their proximity to one another in space and time makes them mutually vulnerable. But as far as the agents directly involved in an accident themselves are concerned, it has no reason, no motive, no telic explanation, because it was beyond or even against their intention. It escapes finality.

(d) In view of the finality to be found in cognitive and noncognitive agents alike, our universe is a dynamic one, shot through with tendencies and consequent activities. But in view of the factors which make chance events (both relative and absolute) possible and almost inevitable, it is a precarious and challenging one. On how delicate a point is our well-being balanced. How precious does actual existence become.

> To grasp what it means to exist, one needs to grasp the fact that he might not exist, that he treads at every moment on the sharp edge of possible annihilation and can never escape the fact that death will arrive at some unknown moment in the future. Existence, never automatic, not only can be sloughed off and forfeited but is indeed at every instant threatened by non-being. Without this awareness of non-being—that is, awareness of the threats to one's being in death . . . existence is vapid, unreal, and characterized by lack of concrete self-awareness. But with the confronting of non-being, existence takes on vitality and immediacy, and the individual experiences a heightened consciousness of himself, his world, and others around him.[81]

* 6. Exemplary Causality

Since exemplarity is closely linked with finality,[82] we shall add a brief consideration of exemplary causes. Let us begin by recounting

---

[81] Rollo May, *Existence: A New Dimension in Psychiatry and Psychology* (New York: Basic Books, Inc., 1958), pp. 47-48. Also see p. 42: "[Man] is that particular being who knows that at some future moment he will not be; he is the being who is always in a dialectical relation with non-being, death."; F. Wilhelmsen, *Metaphysics of Love* (New York: Sheed & Ward, 1962), pp. 97-145, especially 124-45.

[82] See M. Vaske, *Introduction to Metaphysics*, p. 150; R. Kreyche, *First Philosophy*, p. 262; H. Renard, *Philosophy of Being*, pp. 161-64.

how exemplarity worked in one concrete case. As told in the *New Yorker*, Richard Lippold was asked to construct two mobile sculptures for the foyer in the Lincoln Center, New York, according to these plans:

> "From the street level two escalators carry the public up to an area two hundred feet long, thirty feet wide, and fifty feet high. All the levels of auditorium and balcony open on to this promenade. It is suggested that two vertical Lippolds be suspended at some point above or just in front of the escalators, brilliantly lighted and visible from all eye levels from the balconies. Seen from the balconies, they will hang surrounded by glass and the city as a background. Does this perchance set your imagination to work?" [83]

Lippold realized that this commission presented special problems because

> ". . . the space was so long and narrow, and because there would be very strong competition from the balconies and the vertical columns of the building. The sculpture would have to be pretty strong to hold its own against that kind of architecture."

How did the final artifact come about? In retrospect, Lippold feels that two unrelated incidents of that summer went a long way toward shaping his final concept.

> The first was a warm, spontaneous friendship that had sprung up on board the *Queen Frederica* between the Lippolds [on their way to Europe for the summer] and two young Italians, a girl of seventeen and her nineteen-year-old brother. "It was a vitalizing experience to be with them, and the friendship did a lot for me," Lippold recalls. "There was something about it, the idea of strangers reaching out to one another across a generation, that touched me deeply, and I think now it may have influenced the form of my sculpture, with its two forms reaching out and its father-son connotation in my mind." The other incident occurred at the end of the summer, in Denmark. . . . By this time, Lippold had become anxious and depressed; it was nearly time to go home, and he had nothing to show to Abramovitz [who had given him the commission]. "I was waiting and waiting for something to happen," he says. One morning, walking in the formal garden of a neighboring castle, with its clipped

---

[83] Calvin Tomkins, "A Thing Among Things," *New Yorker*, March 30, 1963, p. 49, col. 2. The plans are a quotation from a letter to Lippold.

borders and elaborately shaped shrubs, he wandered off across the lawn toward a great tree, whose lower branches swept the ground. He made his way through the branches and stood there looking up into the inverted green bowl of the tree, and it struck him that there was something in that shape—that "open yet closed form," as he has called it—that should be his sculpture. All at once, "a roundness with forms reaching across it like the limbs of a tree" seemed to him the only concept that could hold its own against the strong vertical columns of Abramovitz's building without violating the space. "From then on the form of the sculpture determined itself in my mind," Lippold says. "Of course, it was transformed, like all my artistic ideas, into concepts of space and of form in space, and the inverted-bowl thing was reversed, so that it opened upward, but the essential idea stuck." [84]

Once he had his basic concept, idea, exemplar for the mobiles, what remained was to implement it, first in a series of sketches and finally in whatever material he would choose.

His first renderings [of sketches] consisted merely of a generalized impression of two masses stretching out toward one another. . . . [Later] he began in his drawings to fragment the forms, breaking them up into smaller elements that would hang every which way and would glitter and sparkle like the leaves of a tree in sunlight. This led him naturally to the idea of using milled metal sheets of various lengths, suspended from the ceiling by fine cables. . . . By deciding to use solid metal sheets, he virtually ruled out the kind of geometrical symmetry that had characterized many of his previous large constructions, and he also found himself moving in a direction that rather surprised him. "Although I did not intend these forms to be figurative . . . they seem to be acting like people. By their gestures . . . these two figures seem to me like friendly gods (atomically conceived like all of us), reflecting in their splendor the splendor of man." [85]

After the sketches came a scale model, and, finally, the artifact itself. We have quoted from this article at length because it gives an artist's own account of how he acquired his exemplar (which he calls "concept" or "idea"), as well as an indication of how it exercises its causality upon the artist and the artifact. It was acquired from actual existents (his friendship with the two Italian youths, the inverted

---

[84] *Ibid.*, p. 49, col. 3-p. 50, col. 1.
[85] *Ibid.*, p. 50, col. 2-p. 52, col. 2.

green bowl of the enormous tree). But one must note that it came from
them in a special way: insofar as the data they provided was worked
upon by the artist's imagination, was fused together into a whole, was
"transformed . . . into concepts of space and of form in space," which
in turn became figurative and symbolical. The result was a dynamic,
compelling, pregnant idea which directed his activity from drawing
preliminary sketches to suspending the final metal sheet. Through his
activity it also directed, specified, and determined what the artifact
itself is.[86]

This instance includes all the main elements of exemplarity. The
exemplary cause is the idea directing the artist in his making. The
causality it exercises is that very direction or specification of his activity
and, through it, of the artifact.[87] The exemplary-effect is that activity
as so directed and specified. The efficient cause of that activity is the
artist through his operative powers and habits (these last are various
arts, together with the artistic talents and technique they demand and
arise from). Let us very briefly comment on each of those factors.[88]

(a) The exemplary cause is, then, the concept or idea directing the
artist in his artistic activity. It is the "beautiful-as-known," in which
phrase each term is important. As seen earlier, the beautiful is "an
actually existing item as splendent, and thus in relationship to contemplation and joy."[89] Since the beautiful is an actually existing item,
the exemplar arises too from actual existents (and frequently not from
just one, but from many). The beauty of those existents consists
precisely in their objective splendor—the wealth of their perfections
(among which are surely to be counted brilliant colors, comely shapes,
and other sensible qualities), harmoniously ordered to one another and
flashing forth in attention-catching radiance.

Nonetheless, the exemplary cause is precisely what is beautiful *as*

---

[86] In Lippold's own words, "The idea of strangers reaching out to one another . . . influenced the form of my sculpture, with its two forms reaching
out." Again, his awareness of "A great tree, whose lower branches swept the
ground . . . the inverted green bowl of the tree" produced "a roundness with
forms reaching across it like the limbs of a tree . . . smaller elements that
would hang every which way and would glitter and sparkle like the leaves of
a tree in sunlight."

[87] Because of the close and necessary liaison between activity and artifact,
whenever in subsequent sentences of this section we say "activity," we should
be interpreted as saying, "activity and artifact."

[88] We can be brief because what we shall say will closely parallel the earlier
section on the causal factors in cognitive finality (see Sec. 2a of this chapter).

[89] On the beautiful, see pp. 161-62.

known. The addition explains why not one but several actual existents generally form the basis of an exemplar: the creative imagination of the artist automatically and instinctively welds them together, bringing into sharp relief some factors and downplaying others. It also explains how the exemplar can grow and develop, especially during the initial stages of the artistic process: the artist's fertile mind is always at work.

(b) In what does exemplary causality of the beautiful-as-known consist? What does it do? It does not strictly *do* anything, since it is not an efficient cause. It is a cause, though, because it produces an effect—the agent's activity by which he endeavors to project that exemplar into matter. But how does it produce that activity? By the direction it exerts upon the agent. This is not, however, to be understood in a physical sense (in which, for example, a jockey directs a race horse): it is not an efficient cause. The beautiful-as-known sets the artist into a state of absorbing and ecstatic[90] contemplation, so that the ensuing efficiency by which he tries to externalize the contents of that contemplation is itself colored, influenced, specified, and directed by that very contemplation. This state in which the artist finds himself is the exemplar.

One and the same set of activities is, then, simultaneously caused in a twofold way: exemplarily by the beautiful-as-contemplated, efficiently by the agent through his operative powers and art habits. Just as a single operation of love within a final-cause situation is both the attraction which the good exerts upon the lover and at the same time the response of the lover to the good, so too a single line of efficiency is both the direction which the beautiful-as-known exerts upon the artist and simultaneously the response of the artist to the beautiful.

The beautiful as contemplated is a genuine cause because it helps produce the efficiency of an artist. Its causality is the nonphysical direction which the artist experiences within himself and which is, in fact, also his very artistic activity as produced not efficiently, but exemplarily, by the beautiful. The direction or specification is that activity in reference not to himself, but to the beautiful.[91]

---

[90] "Ecstatic" in the sense that he transcends himself, his usual surroundings, and the petty routine and concerns of his day-by-day life. The term is not used in any religious or mystical sense.

[91] Is an exemplar a final cause as well? One and the same object can be both an exemplary cause and a final cause (in the sense of the initial *finis operis*— see n. 34), since it can be both beautiful and good. Even so, it exerts a different causality as an exemplar than it does as a goal. As the former it directs the artistic activity of the artist, and that direction *is* that efficiency as exemplarily caused (see Sec. 6b of this chapter). As the latter it attracts and actuates his

(c) Because the factors of exemplary-effect and efficient cause have been given rather full treatment in connection with exemplary-cause and its causality, we shall mention them without discussion. The artistic activity of the artist is the exemplary effect. Its efficient cause is the artist through his operative powers and art habits. One and the same activity is midway between two sets of causes, exemplary and efficient.

[beautiful as contemplated]	→ [activity of artist] ←	[artist's operative powers and art habits]
exemplary cause	*effect*	*efficient cause*

(d) Such, then, are the causal factors in exemplarity:

Exemplary cause:	beautiful-as-contemplated.
Its causality:	the direction it exerts on the agent (which is rooted in its objective splendor but which *is* the agent's artistic activity as exemplarily caused).
Exemplary effect:	the agent's artistic activity, together with the artifact it produces.
Efficient cause:	the agent himself, through his operative powers and art habits.

SUGGESTED READINGS

De Raeymaeker, Louis, *The Philosophy of Being*, trans. E. H. Ziegelmeyer, S.J., pp. 270-81. St. Louis: B. Herder Book Co., 1954. On final and exemplary causality.

Gerrity, Brother Benignus, *Nature, Knowledge, and God*, pp. 83-101. Milwaukee: Bruce Publishing Co., 1947. On finality.

Hart, Charles A., *Thomistic Metaphysics*, pp. 297-324. Englewood Cliffs, N. J.: Prentice-Hall, Inc., 1959. On finality.

Janet, Paul, *Final Causes*, trans. Robert Flint. New York: Charles Scribner's Sons, 1892. An interesting testimony to a nineteenth-century approach to finality.

---

appetitive powers, and that attraction *is* that operation of love as telicly caused by the good (see Sec. 2a2). On exemplarity, see C. Hart, *Thomistic Metaphysics* (Englewood Cliffs, N. J.: Prentice-Hall, Inc., 1959), pp. 386-403.

Klubertanz, S.J., G. P., "St. Thomas' Treatment of the Axiom, '*Omne Agens Agit Propter Finem*'," in *An Etienne Gilson Tribute,* ed. Charles O'Neil, pp. 101-17. Milwaukee: Marquette University Press, 1959. Contains a collection of Thomas' texts on the Final Cause Proposition.

Smith, S.J., Gerard and Lottie H. Kendzierski, *The Philosophy of Being,* pp. 96-148. New York: The Macmillan Company, 1961. On exemplary cause; on finality.

Van Melsen, Andrew Gerard, *The Philosophy of Nature,* pp. 217-34. Pittsburgh: Duquesne University Press, 1953. On determinism, scientific causality, predictability, probability, random events.

Ward, Leo R., *God and the World Order.* St. Louis: B. Herder Book Co., 1961.

Wild, John, "Tendency: The Ontological Ground of Ethics," *Journal of Philosophy,* 49 (1952), 468-72. On tendency in relationship to finality.

PART IV

Metaphysics
as a Science

CHAPTER **X**

Separation
and Knowledge
of the Real

"The science of pure being cannot be called a science," we heard R. G. Collingwood exclaim at the beginning of this book, "in the sense in which an ordinary science is so called. . . . This is only a roundabout way of saying that there can be no such science. There is not even a quasi-science of pure being."[1] Why does he, as well as other contemporary authors, take this attitude towards metaphysics? Fundamentally because for them a genuine science can be based only on the measurable, the quantitative. Metaphysics, however, is not built upon such evidence, and consequently cannot be a valid science. In their opinion only mathematics, physics, chemistry, experimental psychology, and other empiriological knowledges are genuine and valid sciences.

Against this view we contended that

[1] R. G. Collingwood, *An Essay on Metaphysics* (Oxford: The Clarendon Press, 1940), pp. 15-16, quoted on p. 5, n. 9. For other pessimistic statements on metaphysics, see those collected by Robert Miller, C.S.B., "The Empiricist's Dilemma: Either Metaphysics or Nonsense," *Proceedings of American Catholic Philosophical Association*, 29 (1955), p. 151 sq.

perhaps material existents give out evidence not only as they are viewed under laboratory conditions, but also as they are directly perceived in their actual, day-by-day conditions, and that, consequently, a genuine science of metaphysics is possible. Our contention has proved true. Material existents in their very status of actuality have provided evidence for a science which is valid, because that evidence cannot be gainsaid. Since sensible things not only involve change/stability but also actually exist, we came to conclude that they consist not only of substance/accidents and prime matter/substantial form[2] but also of another component, the act of existing.[3] Because the fact that they actually exist is what contributes perfection and objective worth to them, we realized that to be real is to be actual, with the result that the act of existing is the source of an existent's reality[4] (and, we might add, of its unity, truth, goodness, beauty, and individuality as well).[5] Since nothing acts unless it actually is, the act of existing is also the root of efficient causality in an existent. In fact, the *rapport* between an existent and its actuality determines what it can do in efficiently causing existence. Only subsistent actuality can properly cause things to exist, and, accordingly, material existents cause existents solely by co-operating with God as instruments with a principal cause.[6] Finality too rests on actuality, insofar as a final cause is a good to which an agent tends (either through love or under the impetus of its very entity) and insofar as goodness or perfection stems ultimately from existence.[7] Even the very peril to which chance makes us heirs sharpens our appreciation of existence. "With the confronting of non-being [through death], existence takes on vitality and immediacy, and the individual experiences a heightened consciousness of himself, his world, and others around him." [8]

These conclusions coalesce into a body of organized knowledge, and thus are the science we call "metaphysics." Because they are grounded in objective data gained through direct perception of existents and are carefully worked out through reflection and reasoning, metaphysics is a valid science. Because they have to do with existents precisely as existent (the formal object of no other science), metaphysics is a dis-

---

[2] See Chap. III.
[3] See Chap. IV.
[4] See Chap. V.
[5] Chap. VI, Secs. 3-5.
[6] Chap. VIII, especially Sec. 3.
[7] Chap. IX.
[8] R. May, *Existence: A New Dimension,* p. 48. On chance, see Chap. IX, Sec. 4.

tinct science.[9] It is not a radical essentialism, since there essence (with attendant immutability, intelligibility, and other such properties) is the heart of reality, but here actuality has primacy.[10] It is, then, an existentialism, but not of the radical sort, where to be actual is to be sheer change and fluency (with concomitant unintelligibility and forlornness), or, in some interpretations, to be human, to be a self, to be a subject.[11] But here to be actual is to be actually existing, whether the existent be changing or stable, subject or object, human or subhuman, subsistent or participant, infinite or finite. Actuality is the common denominator of them all, the heart of every reality. The science which recognizes that primacy of actuality is a metaphysics of authentic existentialism.[12]

* 1. Metaphysics and Separation

But is it possible to understand more exactly the nature of metaphysics as a science? Can we more keenly appreciate the unique sort of knowledge it is?

Contemporary Thomists reply by pointing to the fact that metaphysics alone involves *separation* and therein differs from all other sciences. But what is separation? On this they hold rather widely differing views. For some, separation is not to be classified as an abstraction, and this for several reasons.[13] The former is a negative judgment,

[9] See Chap. I, especially Sec. 5 and n. 17.

[10] On essentialism, see Chap. II, Sec. 3. On the primacy of actual existence, see Chaps. V and VI.

[11] See Chap. II, Sec. 2; also p. 176, n. 86.

[12] See Chap. V, especially Sec. 1. For a different interpretation of authentic existentialism, see John Wild, "Christian Rationalism (Aquinas, Gilson, Maritain)," in *Christianity and Existentialism* (Chicago: Northwestern University Press, 1963), pp. 40-65.

[13] For example, Louis Geiger, O.P., *La participation dans la philosophie de s. Thomas d'Aquin.*" (Paris: J. Vrin, 1942), p. 315 sq.; *idem,* "Abstraction et séparation d'après S. Thomas," *Revue des sciences philosophique et theologique,* 31 (1947), 3-40; Louis Marie Régis, O.P., "Quelques apories," *Études et recherches,* 1 (1936), 127-156; *idem,* "Analyse et synthèse dans l'oeuvre de S. Thomas," *Studia Mediaevalia* (Bruges: de Tempel, 1948), pp. 301-30; Philip Merlan, "Abstraction and Metaphysics in St. Thomas' *Summa,*" *Journal of History of Ideas,* 14 (1953), 284-91; Jean Dominique Robert, O.P., "La métaphysique, science distincte de toute autre discipline philosophique selon s. Thomas d'Aquin," *Divus Thomas* (Piacenza), 50 (1947), 206-22; G. P. Klubertanz, S.J., *Introduction to Philosophy of Being,* (New York: Appleton-Century-Crofts, 1963), pp. 45-52; Robert W. Schmidt, S.J., "The Use of

whereas the latter is a simple apprehension. The former concerns existence, the latter involves only essences. The former deals with items which actually are not the same and merely expresses that ontological nonidentity; the latter deals with items which are associated in the real order and simply does not consider the one while concentrating on the other.[14] According to others, though, abstraction may occur either through simple apprehension or through judgment. That abstraction which one makes through judgment is called separation, and, accordingly, separation is one sort of abstraction.[15]

A third and original position has recently been outlined by Henri J. Renard, S.J.[16] All abstraction involves judgments. Total abstraction terminates in a judgment of *unity*—namely, "that the subject of the philosophy of nature is concerned with things which must exist in matter."-[17] Formal abstraction concludes also with a judgment of *unity* —that quantitative forms can exist only in matter.[18] But the sort of

---

Separation in Metaphysics," *Proceedings of the Twentieth Annual Convention of the Jesuit Philosophical Association* (Woodstock, Md.: Woodstock College Press, 1958), pp. 10-33. For a competent survey of the authors listed here and in notes 14-16, see Sr. Mary Roberta McMahon, O.P., "Separation: Its Development in Recent Thomism" (Doctoral Dissertation, St. Louis University, St. Louis, Missouri, 1963).

[14] Members of this same group rather commonly maintain that the doctrine on abstraction and separation of Aquinas (whom they claim to be following) is not identical with that of Cajetan, an important Renaissance Thomist commentator. They maintain that Cajetan's three degrees of abstraction distort Aquinas' position. See Jean Dominique Robert, *art. cit.*; G. P. Klubertanz, *op. cit.*

[15] Matthias Thiel, "De abstractione," *Studia Anselmiana*, 7 (1938), 99-119; F. A. Blanche, O.P., "La théorie de l'abstraction chez S. Thomas Aquin," *Mélanges thomistes* (Paris: Vrin, 1934), pp. 237-51; J.-M. Ramirez, O.P., "De Ipsa Philosophia in Universum secundum Doctrinam Aristotelico-thomisticam," *Ciencia tomista*, 27 (1922), 325-64 and 29 (1924), 48-52; Jacques Maritain, *Existence and the Existent* (New York: Pantheon Books, Inc., 1948), pp. 26-32 and notes 13 and 14; Marie Vincent Leroy, O.P., "Le savoir speculatif," *Revue thomiste*, 48 (1948), 328-39.

These same scholars tend to view Cajetan's degrees of abstraction as basically harmonizing with those of Aquinas. (For example, see M. V. Leroy, *ibid.*; J. Maritain, *op. cit.*, p. 30, n. 14.) Separation is the third degree of abstraction, or, in Maritain's language, eidetic visualization (see *ibid.*, p. 30: "The abstraction proper to metaphysics . . . proceeds from the eidetic visualization of a transcendental which permeates everything").

[16] "What is St. Thomas' Approach to Metaphysics?" *New Scholasticism*, 30 (1956), 64-83.

[17] *Ibid.*, p. 71.

[18] *Ibid.*: "From a consideration of the *rationes abstractae* studied in mathematics such as quantities and geometric figures, we are able to judge likewise

abstraction proper to metaphysics ends in a judgment of *separation*—that the concept of substance (and, in general, of being) shows it need *not* exist in matter, "that matter does not enter into the definition of substance, that it does not belong to its *ratio* to exist in matter." [19]

Such, then, are at least three divergent interpretations of the nature of separation in metaphysical knowledge—it is judgmental but not an abstraction, it is judgmental and an abstraction, it is judgmental but so too are the other two abstractions. However different these interpretations may be, though, they all agree in this—separation is a mental operation, it is an intellectual activity, it is fundamentally a negative judgment.

The position which I think accurate differs from all three. If described strictly and directly, separation (and, more generally, abstraction) is itself not an intellectual operation at all. Rather it is a property, condition, status (call it what you will) of our intellectual awarenesses. Truth is one such property or condition—namely, the conformity existing between an intellection and the thing known. Certitude, together with probability and doubt, is another such. Abstraction is a third, although a negative one and concerned with the *content* of our awarenesses. It is the absence of matter within the very content of an intelligibility. As one sort of abstraction, separation is the absence of matter within the content of intelligibilities proper to metaphysics. The unique factor in separation is that the absence within our metaphysical awarenesses arises because the things known somehow are themselves actually nonmaterial.

Let us now endeavor to explain and defend this position, thereby coming also to understand the unusual nature of metaphysics better.

2. Twofold Description of Knowledge

First of all, we must note that human knowledge arises from at least two causes, one of which is the intellect itself (together with the senses, of course), which efficiently produces the knowledge. The other is the

---

in a judgment of unity, that quantitative forms cannot exist without matter, because quantity . . . cannot be understood without its relation to intelligible matter."

[19] *Ibid.*, p. 72. Why the emphasis on substance? Because "substance is the principal, the most important of the *rationes* which are connected with the subject of metaphysics" (p. 73).

However, one should note that all three abstractions or judgments arise from an analysis of *rationes,* concepts, definitions (*ibid.*, p. 71).

thing known, which determines the content of the knowledge, and thus is its (for want of a better word) content-determining cause.[20] That the *cognitum* is a genuine cause of cognition can be easily seen in one's spontaneous knowledge of "dog." The reason why I am aware of "dog" and not "giraffe" is that a dog and not a giraffe is present before me and determining what I am thinking about.

Since, then, human knowledge has two sources, it can and must be described in a twofold way—from the point of view of the mind itself and from that of the *cognitum*. When a philosopher undertakes the first sort of description, he speaks in terms of the intellectual operations involved. He asks whether the process consists of simple or complex apprehensions, of perceptual or intellectual judgments, of affirmative or negative judgments, of reasoning or mere reflection. He investigates whether the process as a whole is inductive or deductive.[21]

But in the second description his concern is quite different. He considers whether the conclusion to which the process in question leads is actually in conformity with reality, and this consideration involves the truth of the proposition and of the process. He also inquires whether the firmness of his assent to the proposition is justified by objective evidence; this inquiry concerns certitude. He can also reflect upon the content of the awarenesses in which the process culminates, thereby realizing that by his intellection he has to some degree transcended the singular, the restrictive, the limiting—in a word, matter. By this reflection abstraction lies disclosed. It is a property of those awarenesses: the absence of matter within the very content of the intelligibilities in which our mental operations terminate.

Let us now endeavor to describe various philosophic processes from the point of view of those two causes, first with reference to their efficient cause (the intellect). Such descriptions will disclose where one is to locate the difference between metaphysics and other sciences.

---

[20] This is one more example of the enlargement which the notion and nomenclature of cause must undergo (see p. 194, n. 9, p. 209, n. 53, and p. 224, n. 5). The *cognitum* is like an exemplary cause (see Chap. IX, Sec. 6) in that it specifies what the content of the concept will be. But it also differs from the exemplar. The latter is an idea influencing the thing made; the former is a thing influencing an idea. For the time being at least, the best description of the *cognitum* seems "content-determining cause."

[21] On these operations, see Sec. 3 of this chapter where intellectual operations are first viewed generally and in themselves (pp. 311-13) and then seen in relationship to the various philosophical processes by which we established substance/accidents, matter/form and essence/existence (pp. 314-18).

* 3. First Description: Intellectual Operations Involved

When we undertake the first description, we speak in terms of the intellectual operations which knowledge involves. What are those operations? Through knowledge the knower becomes the known.[22] This becoming or be-ing another does not occur physically, as happens when the food we eat is assimilated and becomes part of us, since what is known is not changed or destroyed in being known. It must, then, occur in a nonphysical way: "intentional" is the word commonly used to describe it. By stimulating the sense cognitive powers of the knower, a dog or any other sensible thing helps cause its re-presentation, image, likeness in those powers. This re-presentation sets off a chain-reaction of *operations* in the cognitive powers of the knower, with the result that the knower comes to know the thing by intentionally becoming it and the thing is (literally) re-presented anew within the knower in a nonphysical manner.[23]

Those are the operations in which we are currently interested with reference to the various philosophical processes. But before attending to them there, we must view them more generally and in themselves: how many there are, what the nature of each is, how they differ from one another. Prior to this, however, two points should be mentioned. First, we know the sort of operations an intellect has not in an a priori way, but rather by reflecting upon the multiple and varied cognitive activities we actually experience in ourselves and observe in others. Second, only the results of this reflection can be given here because of the limits space and time impose.[24]

A human intellect shows itself, then, to have at least three main operations, each of which has its own subdivisions, as the following table shows:

---

[22] This aspect of knowledge will be more readily understood if we recall what we experience in reading a novel or seeing a movie: we enter into its characters, suffer and rejoice with them. In short, we somehow *become* what we read and see.

[23] On "intentional being," see Chap. VI, Sec. 1.

[24] On the cognitive operations of the human knower, see the books on the philosophy of man listed on p. 13, n. 17. Also see the following: L. M. Régis, O.P., *Epistemology* (The Macmillan Company, 1959), pp. 151-74, 253-306; Frederick D. Wilhelmsen, *Man's Knowledge of Reality* (Englewood Cliffs, N.J.: Prentice-Hall, Inc., 1956), pp. 75-133; Donald Williams, *The Ground of Induction* (New York: Russell and Russell, Inc., 1963).

1. Awareness of what an item is   1. *apprehension*
   (a) which arises spontaneously, nontech-   (a) simple
       nically
   (b) which arises technically and which   (b) complex
       summarizes some such previous opera-
       tion as reflection, reasoning, judgment
2. Assent that an item is such or is not such,   2. *judgment*
   is or is not
   (a) directly based upon sense percep-   (a) perceptual
       tion
   (b) directly based upon intellection   (b) intellectual
       (which may itself, however, be work-
       ing upon data furnished by perception)
3. Activities by which we prepare ourselves   3. *thinking*
   for #2—for example, inference, anal-
   ysis, synthesis, and so on.
Inference which
   (a) moves from general to particular: Deduction
   (b) moves from particular to general
       or from sensibles to nonsensible: Induction
                                             through immediate in-
                                               sight
                                             through reflection
                                             through reasoning

The last type of operation (#3) is so complex that we should pause briefly to describe it in more detail. When sufficient evidence is not at hand to enable the mind to make a judgment, it must first analyze, synthesize, compare, consider, infer—in fact, use any sort of intellectual activity which helps. All of these activities constitute another sort of operation, which traditionally has been described as *cogitatio* and in English can be called "thinking." Of those various activities, inference seems most important and frequent.

Inference is a process by which our mind proceeds from one item to another which is somehow seen to be implied in the former. This process reveals itself to be of two general kinds inasmuch as the human mind arrives at truths in two rather obviously different ways. Either it proceeds from the singular to the universal, from the perceptible to the nonperceptible, or it proceeds from the universal to the singular, from the more general to the less general. The first process let us call "induction"; the second, "deduction." Note that a process is inductive or deductive because of its starting point and general direction. If it starts with sensibles and moves upward, it is induction. If it starts with general knowledge and moves downward, it is deduction. Induction and deduction, then, are used to describe mental processes in which the mind is actually proceeding in a unified, organically developing manner.[25]

The human knower moves inductively in three ways, the first of which is immediate insight: a spontaneous and immediate realization of a truth from data presented within a concrete case, as occurs when he realizes that (for example) every nonmathematical whole is greater than its parts or that every new event comes about because of an agent acting for a goal.[26] The second and third ways are reflection and reasoning, which differ inasmuch as the latter involves the use of a middle term, while the former does not. Often it is difficult to determine whether or not a process does entail a middle term. This much, though, can be said. If the concrete cases upon which the process centers furnish all the intelligibilities needed, it does not entail a middle term, and thus is reflection rather than reasoning. For example, we know through reflection that every cognitive agent acts because of a goal which is a good-as-known if we achieve that knowledge by realizing within a concrete case that a cognitive agent and a known good are to one another as the determinable to the determinant. For that realization we need no middle term because the intelligibilities furnished by the concrete instance are sufficient.[27] But if we achieve that knowledge by bringing God into the scene (God has produced such agents with a goal in mind; but a product is its maker's goal as concretized; therefore . . .), the intelligibilities embedded in a concrete case of a cognitive agent acting because of a known good are supplemented by the additional one of the agent's relationship to his Creator. Then the process is not reflection, but reasoning.[28]

---

[25] The difference between induction and deduction is not the absence or presence of reasoning (which can be present in either), but rather the starting point and consequent direction in which the mind moves. The starting point of the former is material existents; that of the latter is general knowledge. For clear examples of deduction, see the practical syllogisms in which the major premises are the Efficient Cause Proposition (Chap. VIII, Sec. 4b) and the Final Cause Proposition (Chap. IX, Secs. 2b1 and 3b1).

[26] See the references to Efficient and Final Propositions given in the previous note.

[27] See pp. 274-75.

[28] See Chap. IX, Sec. 2b2. Immediate insight, reflection, and reasoning are all instances of *intellective* induction: an inductive process which culminates in our seeing the intrinsic necessity underlying our assent. For example, my knowledge that a nonmathematical whole is greater than any of its parts is an intellective induction because it issues from my awareness within a concrete case of what a

Such, then, are the three main intellectual operations of a human knower: apprehension, judgment, and thinking, the last of which can be inductive or deductive inference. Let us now investigate various philosophic processes to see which operations each entails.

Let us begin with the process by which we came to assent to substance and accidents as actual components of a material existent.[29]

1. [Directly perceived fact:] In accidental changes one and the same thing
    (a) remains specifically and generically what it is [stability]
    (b) and yet acquires new individual perfections (change);
2. But evidence #a is other than evidence #b;
3. But diverse evidences indicate the actual presence within of diverse constitutive parts;
4. Therefore, such evidences indicate that the thing is actually made up of diverse constitutive parts:
    (a) that by which the thing specifically and generically remains what it is and yet receives various individual perfections—"substance";
    (b) that by which the thing, while remaining specifically and generically what it is, is actually modified through a new individual perfection—"an accident."

Through this process, then, we come to realize that a material thing is composed of at least two different components, substance and accidents. The question now is how to describe the mental operations which underlie that process. Obviously it involves judgments, since it

---

whole is and what a part is. Intellective induction is contrasted with *rational* induction: an inductive process which does not culminate in my seeing the intrinsic reasons why I assent. Since rational induction is found only in the physical sciences, little attention is paid to it here. For additional information, see G. Klubertanz, *Philosophy of Human Nature*, pp. 385-401.

Intellective induction is also contrasted with what can be called "induction by enumeration"—the process by which I assent that "All the birds in this thicket except two are sparrows." Such an assent can be certain, but it fits only a definite situation and that at a particular time. And I make such an assent solely by sensibly observing and cataloguing relevant factors in the situation. It does not rest upon any intrinsic necessity: there is no necessary, universally operative reason why sparrows should be here rather than blackbirds. Obviously, such an assent is nonscientific, and if "induction by enumeration" were the only inductive process of which man is capable, metaphysics or any other science would be impossible.

[29] We first saw this process in Chap. III, Sec. 3. It is repeated here for easy reference.

consists of four propositions which have arisen because the mind has assented (for example) that in accidental changes one and the same thing does remain specifically what it is while acquiring new individual perfections, and so forth. Some of those judgments are perceptual (for example, Proposition #1), others are intellectual (for example, #3 and #4). Some are negative (#2 and the judgment implied in #4 that substance is really other than the accidents it receives), others are affirmative (#3 and the affirmation in #4 that substance and accidents actually are constitutive parts of a sensible existent). That process also involves apprehensions, since in and through it we become aware of what various items are. Some of these apprehensions are simple— for example, in Proposition #1 the spontaneous awarenesses of various existents which are accidentally changing (this man, this dog, this flower). Others are complex: our technical cumulative awareness of what substance is and what accidents are (#4). Also, the process is an induction, because the intellect starts with sensible existents, together with the twofold evidence of change/stability they furnish, and terminates by assenting to the imperceptible components which compose them. It is an intellective induction, since we see why we assent: change/stability are nothing more than accidents/substance manifesting themselves.[30] It is an intellective induction which involves reflection rather than reasoning because, however complex the process may be, we can find within concrete cases of change/stability all the intelligible data needed for the process, and hence do not use a middle term.[31]

Next let us diagnose the process by which we came to realize that a material existent involves an additional composition—that of prime matter and substantial form. The structure of the process is similar to the preceding one.

1. [Directly perceived fact:] A substantial change in a thing involves
   (a) the loss and acquirement of specific perfection [change]
   (b) together with corporeal continuity [stability];
2. But evidence #a is other than evidence #b;
3. But diverse evidences indicate the actual presence within of diverse components;
4. Therefore, such evidences indicate that on the substantial level a material thing is actually made up of two real and diverse components:

---

[30] On intellective induction, see n. 28.
[31] See p. 313.

(a) that by which a thing is of such-and-such a specific nature, and hence has its own distinctive characteristics—"substantial form";

(b) that by which a material thing receives a substantial form and yet which is capable, through subsequent substantial change, of receiving other substantial forms—"prime matter."

As the process itself is similarly structured to that by which we know substance and accidents, so too the intellectual operations it entails are similar to those of the earlier operations. Accordingly, it will suffice if we list them with little or no explanation. It involves judgments (#1-#4), some of which are perceptual (#1), others intellectual (#3, #4). Some are negative (#2 and the assent implicated in #4 that prime matter is not the same as the substantial form it receives and limits), some are affirmative (#3 and the affirmation in #4 that prime matter and substantial form actually are components of the substance within a sensible existent). Also the process involves apprehensions, some of which are simple (in #1 our spontaneous awareness of various material things capable of substantial change or actually undergoing such a change), others are complex (our technical and dynamic awareness of what matter and form are in #4). Finally, because it moves from sensible existents to a new set of imperceptible components, the process is an induction. It is an intellective induction because we see why we assent: corporeal continuity and the newly acquired specific perfection are nothing else than prime matter and substantial form manifesting themselves. It involves reflection rather than reasoning because we do not use a middle term, but rather find within concrete cases of such change all the intelligible data needed.

Now, how did we as metaphysicians acquire our knowledge that, over and above the components so far discovered, a material existent also involves an act of existing? The process can be outlined as follows:

1. [Directly perceived fact:] An actual material existent
   (a) not only is what it is (Paul is this man)
   (b) but also actually exists (Paul *is*);
2. But evidence #a is other than evidence #b;
3. But diverse evidences indicate the actual presence within of diverse components;
4. Therefore, such evidences indicate that an existent is actually made up of two real and distinct components:
   (a) that by which it is what it is—"essence" (that is, the com-

posite of substance [prime matter/substantial form] and accidents);

(b) that by which it actually exists—the "act of existing."

Obviously, the structure here is again similar to that found in the
two previous processes, but it contains great diversity in content. Here,
the directly perceived facts are no longer merely change and stability
within one or other order. They involve the contrast between *what* a
material existent is and the fact *that* it does actually exist. In the last
analysis, this contrast is rooted in the fact that to be real is to be actual.
Actual existence perfects and literally realifies that which does exist. A
consequence is that the act of existing, the component which actualizes the thing and manifests itself through this evidence, is perfection
par excellence, is the ultimate source of all other perfections within the
existent, has primacy over essence, and so on. Another consequence is
that "being" ("any actually existing item") expresses both *what* a thing
is and *that* it is, both essence and existence, and yet emphasizes existence. That which makes a being be *being* is its actual existence.[32]
Metaphysics, then, is a science other than the philosophy of nature because the metaphysician no longer studies beings-as-mobile but beings-
as-being, or existents *precisely as existing*.

Despite those important differences, though, the fact still remains that
this third process is similar in structure to its two predecessors. Consequently, the intellectual operations which underlie it are similar to
those found in the previous ones, and we shall catalogue them with
little or no comment.

This process, then, involves judgments (#1-#4) some of which are
perceptual (#1 includes both attributive ["Paul is this man"] and existential ones ["Paul actually is"]),[33] others intellectual (#3, #4).
Some are negative (#2 itself, the judgment implied in #4 that the
act of existing is not identical with the essence which it actualizes, the
realization permeating the entire procedure that "To be real is not to
be material or to be any other kind of being, is not to be this or that"),
others are affirmative (#3, the affirmation in #4 that the act of existing actually is a component within the existent, the realization operative throughout that "To be real is to be actual"). The process also
involves apprehensions, some of which are simple (in #1 our sponta-

---

[32] On "being," see Chap. VI, Sec. 1 and Appendix B.

[33] Existential judgments are of extreme importance in metaphysics, for they are
a cognitive means through which the human knower achieves contact with actual existence. For helpful studies, see p. 88, n. 45.

neous awareness of this or that existent), others complex (in #4, our technical and dynamic awareness of what the act of existence is, of its nature, and of its relationship to essence). Finally, the process is an induction because the intellect moves from sensible existents to the component which intrinsically accounts for their existential status. It is an intellective induction because we understand why we assent: the fact something actually exists is the perceived result of the act of existing functioning within. It involves reflection rather than reasoning because we do not use a middle term but rather find within actual existents all the intelligible data we need.

Such, then, are three basic philosophic processes, together with a description of them in reference to their efficient cause, the intellect. However complex and tedious, that description illustrates the fact that isolating the intellectual operations which underlie them can and should be done if one's account of his philosophic knowledge is to be adequate. But it performs a function even more relevant to our present discussion by revealing that negative judgments are not restricted to metaphysics. A philosopher of nature also uses them, as when he concludes that substance is not identical with accidents and that prime matter is not the same as substantial form.[34] Moreover, it discloses that the distinction between philosophic disciplines is not grounded in intellectual operations as such. All such disciplines are judgmental. They all terminate in awarenesses which arise within complex apprehensions, gathering together into a dynamic, psychological unity all the cognitive treasure amassed in immediately preceding reflection and judgments.

In what, then, is the distinction between the various philosophic sciences rooted? Not in the intellectual operations as such, but in the content of the insights gained through those operations.

Manifestly, our next step is to consider our philosophic cognition in the light of its content and, ultimately, of the *cognita* causing it. This consideration will illuminate what abstraction and separation are.

* 4. Second Description of Philosophic Knowledge: Abstraction

When a philosopher attempts an inventory of the various sorts of knowledge he possesses, certainly one sort he finds is his spontaneous, nontechnical, and therefore nonphilosophic awareness of other material

---

[34] In the first two processes we were working as philosophers of nature, since we were studying existents precisely as mobile.

existents—trees, animals, plants, other men, rocks, and so forth. Even that knowledge is twofold: he knows "this dog" both as "this" and as "dog." If we suppose that he could only know the dog as "this," then his knowledge of dogs would be confined merely to sensation of now this [dog], now that [dog]. But, actually, his cognitive powers are such that he also knows this dog as "dog." Thereby he cognitively transcends signate matter, which would restrict and limit his cognition to this or that individual. Within the very content of his awareness of "dog," then, there occurs an absence of signate matter. An absence of matter within the very content of an intelligibility is what we mean by abstraction, and, to some degree, is the property of every intelligibility.

Two additional facts must be noted. The absence of matter in such an intelligibility as "dog" does not arise because actual dogs are themselves without signate matter, but rather because the human knower, in concentrating on a dog as "dog," simply leaves the "thisness" out of consideration. Yet that absence is grounded in reality, in the *cognita*: if what makes a dog be *dog* would also make him be *this*, it would be impossible even intentionally to separate "this" and "dog." That is, this first sort of abstraction[35] ultimately rests upon the real composition within a dog of prime matter (that, ultimately, by which he is *this*) and of substantial form (that by which he is *dog*). In addition, although our awareness of "dog" does not contain signate matter, matter is not entirely absent from its content, since a dog even as *dog* does involve matter: it is his very nature to be a material, living, sentient, canine substance. Accordingly, abstraction here involves only a partial absence of matter, and this again because of the *cognitum,* whose very nature includes matter as a constitutive part.

Another kind of knowledge a philosopher discovers within himself is a spontaneous and nontechnical awareness of the external characteristics of various material things—the softness of human flesh, feathers,

---

[35] How shall we name this abstraction? The Latin term given it has been *abstractio totius*. The force of the second word is that the relation of a common nature to the individuals sharing it is like that of a *whole* to its parts.

What English expression seems best suited? Perhaps "abstraction of whatness" will do, the last word pointing to what the human knower is concentrating upon: he is aware of *what* sort of thing a dog is. The whole phrase, then, can be spelled out as follows: "The absence of matter within the content of an intelligibility through nonconsideration (abstraction) because of concentration upon what sort of thing the existent is (whatness)." On the meaning of "whatness," "quiddity," "essence," see pp. 90-92, and n. 52. We are here using "whatness" in its spontaneous, nontechnical, nonphilosophical meaning.

In expressions for subsequent kinds of abstraction, the last words in the phrase will have the similar function of indicating what the human knower is concentrating upon in his nonconsideration of matter.

sponges, foam rubber; the durability of oaken floorboards, mahogany panels, steel plates, granite slabs; the roundness of water tumblers, basketballs, wedding rings, automobile wheels; the whiteness of swans, newly fallen snow, cirrus clouds, bed linen, Caucasian men and women. This knowledge also is in its own way twofold, for a human knower not only knows the various kinds of things[36] which are, say, white but is also aware of "whiteness," the characteristic they have in common. Suppose that he could only know whiteness as inherent in swans. Then his knowledge of it would be restricted to that sort of existent. But, actually, he also is aware that fresh snow, cirrus clouds, and so on also are white, and he is cognizant of "whiteness" itself as a common attribute. Thus he cognitively transcends the various kinds of things which would confine and limit his cognition to this or that sort of existent. Within the very content of his awareness of "whiteness," then, there occurs an absence of the restrictive, confining, limiting—factors which we can call "matter." Here, then, is another absence of matter within the very content of an intelligibility, and, consequently, a second sort of abstraction.[37]

As with the first sort, so too here additional facts are to be mentioned. The absence of matter in such an intelligibility as "whiteness" does not arise because whiteness as actually found in white things has no connection with matter, but rather because the human knower, in concentrating on this or that sort of white thing precisely as *white,* simply does not consider what the sort of thing is which is white. Yet that absence is rooted in the actual *cognita:* if what makes a swan be *white* would also make him a *swan,* then it would be impossible even intentionally to distinguish validly between swan and whiteness. In other words, this kind of abstraction basically is grounded upon the fact that (for instance) a white swan is composed of really distinct components of substance (that by which he is a swan) and the accidental perfection by which he is white. And, although our awareness of "whiteness" does not contain "swan" or any other definite sort of thing which is white, matter is not entirely absent from its content, since whiteness itself does involve matter: by its very nature whiteness demands there be extended surfaces which reflect light of all wave lengths. Accordingly, abstraction here involves only a partial absence of matter, and

---

[36] This knowledge would, of course, be another example of "abstraction of whatness."

[37] Let us call it "abstraction of external characteristics," where the last words point to what the mind concentrates upon (see n. 35).

this, again, because the *cognitum* is such as actually to be intrinsically linked with extension and matter.

Still a third kind of knowledge a philosopher can possess is a technical grasp of logic, mathematics, physics, and other constructural sciences. For instance, he is aware of what genus, species, and other logical conceptions are. He may be conversant with Euclidean geometry, with current theories on the atomic and subatomic structure of matter or with biological classification of plants and animals. Such knowledge is twofold, although it differs from the two previous kinds because it is constructural. Perhaps we might preferably say that such knowledge involves two stages—the "stuff" as it exists (a) originally and then (b) as worked upon by the human knower.[38] Instances of those stages with reference to logic are: (a) "dog" as a direct universal and (b) as a reflex universal; or with reference to mathematics: (a) "roundness" as an external characteristic of various material things and (b) "circularity" as a strictly mathematical conception; with reference to physics: (a) hydrogen before and (b) after entering a cyclotron, with results expressed in mathematical formulae.

Suppose that the human knower could know only stage #a. Then the sciences of logic, mathematics, and physics would be non-existent, and, in fact, impossible. But his cognitional power and ingenuity are so great that he actually transcends stage #a, together with the restriction and confinement it connotes. Within the very content of his awareness of "dog" as a reflex universal, of "circle," and so forth, there occurs an absence of what would restrict, confine, and limit and which can be again designated as "matter." [39] Here, then, is another absence of matter within the very content of intelligibilities, and accordingly a third type of abstraction.[40]

Once again, two facts are to be stressed. The absence of matter, in the sense just indicated, within constructural intelligibilities does not occur because they have no connection with the first stage (#a), which has the important function of providing a basis for the subsequent process. Rather, that absence arises because the mind concentrates upon

---

[38] Although "stuff" is an inelegant term, it is useful as applicable to items which are both intramental (our awareness of "dog" and of "round") and extramental (hydrogen).

[39] By this time it should be clear that matter is an extremely analogous term. In general, it is that which, if present, would restrict, confine, and limit the content of an intelligibility.

[40] Let us designate it as "abstraction of addition," however paradoxical that may sound. The final word expresses what the mind fixes its attention upon while ignoring the original "stuff"—it attends to its own contribution.

the contribution it itself makes to those intelligibilities and upon the various changes it has effected in the original data (#a), so that the latter no longer holds its attention. Also, the absence of matter (again, in the sense explained) in our constructural intelligibilities is not complete. True, such intelligibilities are a significant advance over stage #a. Still they are not entirely independent of it, they are not divorced from it. In fashioning those awarenesses the intellect cannot proceed arbitrarily. The original data still exercises an influence.

A fourth knowledge which a philosopher can have acquired is a philosophy of nature—a study of material, mobile beings precisely as mobile. Reflecting upon the evidences of change/stability which such existents show in both the accidental and substantial orders, he concludes that they are composed of substance/accidents and prime matter/substantial form. This judgmental process culminates in his technical awareness, within complex apprehensions, of what those two sets of imperceptible but actual components are.[41] Obviously, such knowledge involves two levels, the first of which is occupied by mobile things as we directly perceive them undergoing various kinds of accidental changes (that is, quantitative, qualitative, local) and of substantial changes (generation, corruption). The second is occupied by those same things, but now undestood as constituted by transsensible but real components: substance/accidents and matter/form. We now know the intrinsic causes of such existents in their very mobility. On the first level change/stability are mere facts; on the second they are evidences pointing to components within, and the thing lies transparent before our intellectual gaze.

Suppose, though, that the human knower could not rise above the first level. He might achieve a phenomenological, day-by-day description of material things (a history, a biography), but any philosophic science of nature would escape him. His intellectual powers are such, though, that he actually can and does ascend to the second level, thereby transcending the first, as well as the cognitional restriction and limitation it implies. Within the very content of his awareness of mobile beings *precisely as mobile* and of the components which intrinsically cause them, then, there is to be found an absence of the restrictive, limiting, confining—that is to say, of matter. Here, accordingly, is another absence of matter within the content of intelligibilities, and thus another type of abstraction.[42]

---

[41] See pp. 314-16.

[42] This let us term "abstraction of natural components," where the final words indicate that to which the knower attends as a philosopher of nature: the components of substance, and so forth.

Again, several additional facts must be listed. First, the absence of matter in the sense indicated (that is, directly perceived data of this or that definite kind of accidental or substantial change) in such intelligibilities as "substance," "accident," "prime matter," and "substantial form" does not occur because the material thing they constitute is to be found without various and perceptible accidental or substantial modifications, or because the components exist independently of it, or because the sensible evidences of change and stability have no bearing upon them (in fact, change/stability are nothing more than the components, so to speak, externalizing themselves). Rather, that absence arises because the philosopher of nature, having been guided by various actual manifestations of change/stability to the components, now concentrates upon the latter with inattention to the former. This absence, though, is fundamentally grounded in the components themselves, none of which can itself be perceived but is known through intellectual judgments (albeit formulated by a mind working upon perceived data), and each of which has no extended parts outside of parts, and thus is itself somehow immaterial.[43] Second, although our awareness of such components is free in content from directly perceived data of this or that definite kind of accidental and substantial change, matter is not entirely absent from such awarenesses, because the components, however imperceptible and immaterial each may be in itself, do constitute a thing which is perceptible, material, and changing, and they are dependent upon it. A general reference to change/stability enters into the definition of them all.[44] Consequently, abstraction here involves

---

[43] Although the components studied by a philosopher of nature are intrinsically dependent upon matter, they can still be described as immaterial because none of them is itself extended or has parts outside of parts. To contrast them with the act of existing and the human soul, we have previously called them "barely immaterial" (see Chap. V, Sec. 4)—that is, components within a material essence which are immaterial in such a way as to be intrinsically dependent upon matter. The act of existing is *amaterial* because it is a component which can be within a material existent (although not within the material essence) and yet which is immaterial to such a degree as to be both extrinsically and intrinsically independent of matter. The human soul (together with its operative powers of intellect and will and their operations and operative habits) is *spiritual* because it is a component within a material essence and yet it is immaterial to such a degree that it is intrinsically independent of matter. One should note that the human soul lies within the range of a philosophy of nature when considered precisely as the substantial form of the body (as spiritual and subsistent, it belongs to metaphysics).

[44] For example, "Substance is that by which the thing specifically and generically remains what it is and yet receives various individual perfections"; "prime matter is that by which a material thing receives a substantial form and yet

only a partial absence of matter, and this because the *cognita* (the components) are such as actually to be linked with matter.

Another sort of knowledge which a philosopher must include in his inventory is metaphysics—the science of beings precisely as being, of existents precisely as existing. By reflecting upon the existential status of material things which confront him and which are known through existential judgments, by realizing that actual existence is an important factor in them—in fact, even more important than what they are— and by granting that actuality is the font of reality, he is led to ac- knowledge the actual presence of the act of existing in these material things. This is a component over and beyond those discovered through the evidences of change/stability, and its disclosure lifts the philosopher from the science of beings-as-mobile to the science of beings-as-being, since what makes a being *be* being is the fact that it does actually exist, that it is actualized by the act of existing.[45]

Obviously, such cognition occurs in two stages. The first is that of perceptual judgments, by which we spontaneously realize not only that this man, that woman, this horse, this mimosa tree, and so on are in- deed this man, woman, and so on, but also that they actually are. The second is the moment of intellection and insight when we realize that each actual existent involves a component which is other than those accounting for what it is and which ultimately accounts even for what *they* are—namely, the act of existing. Here we know actual existents in the light of the intrinsic cause of their very actuality, reality, and being. In the first stage actual existence is a mere fact; in the second it is an evidence indicating the act of existence within, and an actual existent in its reality and being lies unfolded before us.

But let us suppose that the human knower could not go beyond the first stage. He might achieve a census of actual existents, a catalogue, a chronicle. But metaphysics in the sense of a philosophy of beings qua being would be out of the question. However, the human knower can and does attain the second stage, and thus transcends the first with its limitation and confinement. Within the very content of his awareness of the act of existing and of his consequent understanding of "beings- as-being," then, an absence of the restrictive and limiting is to be found, and, accordingly, another instance of abstraction appears. This time, though, the abstraction is quite unique, for here the mind has come upon a component with no inherent link to any matter whatsoever.

which is capable, through subsequent substantial change, of receiving other sub- stantial forms."

[45] See above, pp. 316-18.

Even when actualizing a material existent, the act of existing is both intrinsically and extrinsically independent of matter: unlike the other components, the reason it is present is that the material existent is *existent* and not that it is material.[46] This ontic absence of matter simply transfers itself to the intentional order, and our awareness of "act of existing," of "being," and of the other transcendents contains no matter because there actually is no matter in the *cognita*.[47] Unlike all four previous abstractions, then, the abstraction proper to a metaphysician tends to be a complete and not merely a partial absence of matter within the content of his intelligibilities; it occurs because of the absolute freedom of matter in the *cognita* themselves and not because the mind simply does not consider the matter which nonetheless actually is there.

In view of its special status, then, a metaphysician's abstraction is given the special name of "separation," signifying an absence of matter within the very content of intelligibilities caused by *cognita* which themselves are actually independent of matter and, in that sense, separated from it.[48]

---

[46] See n. 43. Not only does the act of existing have no necessary or intrinsic link with physical matter, but also it is itself free from any sort of potency or limitation. As far as it itself is concerned, it is *pure* act because *nothing but* act, since its sole function is to actuate and the sole relationship it has to any other component is that of the perfective to the perfected.

Accordingly, the freedom from restriction and limitation which the act of existing as such enjoys is freedom both from physical matter and from any sort of potency.

[47] The intelligibilities of "being" and the other transcendents are somewhat different from that of the "act of existing." The former refer to more than actual existence: "being," for example, signifies "an actually existing item," where the last word points to essence, which in all existents save God is potency and in some even includes physical matter. Accordingly, the absence of matter characterizing the former intelligibilities also differs somewhat from that characterizing the latter. Nonetheless, it continues to be an ontic abstraction inasmuch as the transcendent intelligibilities signify essence not in itself but only in reference to existence, not as material or potential but only as actualized and realified. Thus they share in all the characteristics which "act of existing" itself has, one of which is ontic abstraction.

[48] Such seems to be the derivation of "separation." Aquinas seems to have been one of the first to apply it to knowledge. He used it to describe actual things free from matter and motion ("separated substances"—see *De Ente et Essentia*, Chap. 4 (Maurer translation, p. 43 [The translation referred to here and in subsequent quotes is that listed in the bibliography at the end of this chapter.]): "It remains for us to see in what way essence is in separated substances, namely, in the soul, in the intelligences, and in the First Cause" (Latin text in Roland-Gosselin Ed., p .29, ll. 1-3; *De Potentia*, 5, 8, resp.; *S.T.*, I, 7,

Such, then, are several kinds of knowledge which a philosopher can find within himself. No attempt has been made to ask whether his appreciation of literature and other fine arts directly involves abstraction, or what sort a philosophy of art, ethics, epistemology, psychology, and sacred theology entail. But the other kinds of knowledge investigated provide enough information, I hope, to clarify what abstraction is, why it is manifold, and what separation (the abstraction peculiar to metaphysics) entails. In separation the unique nature of metaphysics lies exposed: a knowledge whose content is caused by *cognita* which themselves are unique—items genuinely independent of matter, actuals qua actual, beings precisely in their be-ing.

* 5. Summary and Conclusions

(a) Intellectual knowledge can be adequately described only if both its causes are taken into account—its efficient cause, which is the intellect itself, and its content-determining cause, which is the *cognitum*. A description made with respect to the former will investigate the various sorts of mental operations involved. In the case of the basic processes by which a philosopher learns of the act of existing and of the other components, these would include both simple and complex apprehensions, perceptual and intellectual judgments (both affirmative and negative), and intellective induction through reflection. Note that the presence of judgmental knowledge (even of a negative sort) is not what distinguishes one philosophic science from another: they all are judgmental.

(b) A description made with respect to the content-determining cause of knowledge (the *cognita*) will include a discussion of abstraction: the absence of matter within the very content of intelligibilities.[49]

---

2 ad 2; *In Meta.*, Proemium). But he also transferred it to the knowledge they cause in us (*In Boet. de Trin.*, 5, 3, resp. [Decker Ed., pp. 183, 186]).

In its remote origins the words as applied to *cognita* free from matter reaches back to Aristotle (for example, *Metaphysics*, XII, Chap. 7, 1073a2: "It is clear . . . that there is a substance which is eternal and unmovable and separate from sensible things"), and, even earlier, to Plato (see F. Astius, *Lexicon Platonicum* [Bonn: Rudolf Habelt Verlag, 1956], III, 564-66). Whether other medieval authors besides Aquinas applied it also to the knowledge proper to a metaphysician has not yet been investigated.

[49] Obviously, abstraction does not involve merely the actual exclusion of physical matter, an exclusion which even sense knowledge entails, because the sense faculty, as well as its operation and sensible species, is immaterial. It is rather an exclusion within the content of knowledge, within what-is-represented-and-

Manifestly, abstraction itself is not an intellectual operation. It is, rather, the negative property or condition of an intellectual awareness as omitting matter (in some sense and to some degree) from its ken. It can be predicated of mental operations only through extrinsic denomination—they are that which produce intelligibilities characterized by an absence of matter. But abstraction itself is directly and intrinsically predicable only of the content of intelligibilities. In line with this, negative judgments can be termed separation, but only in the sense that they are among the operations through which a metaphysician attains awarenesses which contain no matter whatsoever inasmuch as the act of existence and other *cognita* actually are genuinely immaterial. Separation as such is an immediate attribute only of the content of those awarenesses; it is predicable of negative judgments merely through extrinsic denomination.

(c) A partial inventory of various kinds of knowledge which a philosopher can possess discloses five instances of abstraction. These in turn fit into two general categories, inasmuch as matter is absent from the content of the intelligibilities involved for two reasons: either the mind simply does not consider the matter (in some sense or other) which the *cognita* actually involve or the *cognita* themselves are actually without matter. The following table locates these five abstractions with respect to that twofold category:

"ABSENCE OF MATTER WITHIN THE CONTENT OF AN INTELLIGIBILITY"	= ABSTRACTION
1. Because of the nonconsideration of matter, which nonconsideration arises because of one's concentration upon	through nonconsideration
(a) the sort of thing an existent is ("dog" vs. signate matter)	abstraction of whatness
(b) external characteristics ("white" vs. various definite kinds of white things [swans, snow, and so on])	abstraction of external characteristics
(c) contribution which mind itself imposes upon the original data in the elaboration of constructs ("dog" as reflex universal vs. "dog" as direct universal; "circle" vs. "roundness")	abstraction of addition

known. In this sense it is found only within intellection and not within sense cognition, which is an awareness of something as here-and-now-and-this, and, accordingly, within whose content matter is present.

(d) components within a mobile being studied as mobile ("substance," "accidents," "prime matter," "substantial form" vs. various definite kinds of directly perceived accidental and substantial changes)	abstraction of natural components
2. Because of the actual absence of matter in the *cognita*, which either are amaterial (act of existing) or spiritual (God, the human soul as subsistent, and so forth)	through actual absence = SEPARATION

(d) This table makes several points clear. First, "matter" has an extremely analogous meaning. In general, it is any factor which would restrict, confine, or limit the content of an awareness. That factor can be signate sensible matter (see #1a), various kinds of existents with reference to an external characteristic shared in common (#1b), the original "stuff" (whether intramental or extramental) in contrast to its intelligible status after the human knower has worked upon it (#1c), definite kinds of directly perceived accidental and substantial changes (#1d), and, finally, any matter whatsoever (whether sensible or intelligible, whether signate or common), and, in some cases, any potency whatsoever (#2).

Second, separation is one sort of abstraction because it is an absence of matter within the content of metaphysical intelligibilities. In fact, it is abstraction *par excellence* inasmuch as it involves a complete absence of matter within intelligibilities and what they contain.

Third, "abstraction" itself is obviously an extremely analogous concept. A genuine similarity exists between abstraction through actual absence (#2: separation) and that through nonconsideration (#1): each is an absence of matter within intelligibilities. But they also differ greatly, and for reasons now too evident to need comment. The various abstractions listed as arising through nonconsideration (#1) also differ widely from one another. They are not, for instance, mere degrees of one and the same univocal sort, but rather differ greatly in nature and kind from each other. Nor is the list of abstractions necessarily complete, because no account has been taken of such knowledges as philosophy of art, moral philosophy and moral theology, sacred theology, or epistemology.[50]

---

[50] This much seems clear with regard to moral philosophy or ethics, which is the science of what man ought to do. A philosopher knows what man *is*, and, thereafter, comes to know what he *ought to do*. But suppose that he could not

(e) Finally, why is metaphysics distinct from all other sciences? Why is it an unusual sort of knowledge? There are two answers: because it studies being precisely as being and because it is marked by separation. Those replies seem different, because the former is concerned with the formal object of metaphysics, the latter with its special mode of abstraction. The former expresses what is present in the content of its intelligibilities, whereas the latter signifies what is absent. Nevertheless, the two amount to the same. That by which a being is being is the act of existence. But this is amaterial: even within a material existent it is a component which is immaterial to such a degree as to be both extrinsically and intrinsically independent of matter.[51] But by reason of this independence the act of existing, when known, causes the content of a metaphysician's awareness of being to be free from matter. But this cognitive freedom from matter is separation. Therefore, affirming that the subject of metaphysics is actuals qua actual is equivalent to stating that metaphysics is characterized by separation. They are two sides of the same coin. Since no other science has identically the same inscriptions, metaphysics is indeed a rare coin, quite unlike any other. It is a coin of great price.[52]

---

rise above the first sort of knowledge. It would confine and restrict him. Actually, however, he does transcend it, together with its relative confinement and restriction, and comes to know what man ought to do. In the content of the intelligibilities on this second level of knowledge, there is an absence of the restrictive and limiting (= matter, which here is equivalent to a mere knowledge of what man is), and this is the abstraction proper to ethics.

So too with sacred theology, which can be described as the science derived from divine revelation. If someone is unaware of that revelation or refuses to accept it, he is restricted to purely natural knowledges achieved from data given by sensible existents through perception and elaborated by human reason alone. But by accepting and elaborating divine revelation, a sacred theologian transcends merely natural knowledges with the restriction and confinement they would embody in this context. In the content of intelligibilities within sacred theology, then, there is an absence of the restrictive and limiting (here, merely natural knowledge), and hence an abstraction peculiar to sacred theology.

[51] See n. 43.

[52] Because Thomas was among the first to transfer the term "separation" from existents to knowledge, it would be interesting to check our interpretation with his texts. For this check, see Appendix C.

SUGGESTED READINGS

Anderson, James F., "On Demonstration in Thomistic Metaphysics," *New Scholasticism*, 32 (1958), 476-94.

————, "Some Disputed Questions on Our Knowledge of Being," *Review of Metaphysics*, 11 (1958), 550-60. An important article on metaphysical knowledge.

Copleston, S.J., F. C., "Man and Metaphysics," *The Heythrop Journal*, 1 (1960), 3-17.

Eslick, Leonard, "What is the Starting Point of Metaphysics?" *Modern Schoolman*, 34 (May, 1957), 247-63. On metaphysics as grounded in sensible existents.

Gilson, Etienne, *The Spirit of Mediaeval Philosophy*, trans. A. H. C. Downes, pp. 1-41 and 403-26. New York: Charles Scribner's Sons, 1940. On Thomistic Metaphysics in relationship to divine revelation and sacred theology.

Griesbach, M. F., "Judgment and Existence," in *Proceedings of the American Catholic Philosophical Association*, 30 (1956), 205-11.

Henle, S.J., Robert J., "Existentialism and the Judgment," in *Proceedings of the American Catholic Philosophical Association*, 21 (1946), 40-53.

————, *Method in Metaphysics*, Aquinas Lecture, 1950. Milwaukee: Marquette University Press, 1951.

————, "A Phenomenological Approach to Realism," in *An Etienne Gilson Tribute*, ed. Charles J. O'Neil, pp. 68-85. Milwaukee: Marquette University Press, 1959. On the necessity of induction in metaphysics.

Kane, O. P., William H., "The Subject of Metaphysics," *Thomist*, 18 (1955), 503-21.

Maritain, Jacques, *The Degrees of Knowledge*, trans. G. B. Phelan, New York: Charles Scribner's Sons, 1959.

Maurer, Armand, *On the Division and Method of the Sciences*. Toronto: Pontifical Institute of Mediaeval Studies, 1953. A translation of Aquinas' *In Librum Boethii de Trinitate*, questions 5 and 6.

Owens, Joseph, *An Elementary Christian Metaphysics*, pp. 213-308. Milwaukee: Bruce Publishing Co., 1963. On knowledge (its operations of apprehension, judgment, demonstration, and so forth; intentional being; truth); on sciences (their division, nature).

————, *St. Thomas and the Future of Metaphysics*, Aquinas Lecture, 1957. Milwaukee: Marquette University Press, 1957.

Schmidt, Kenneth, "Toward a Metaphysical Restoration of Natural Things," in *An Etienne Gilson Tribute,* ed. Charles J. O'Neil, pp. 245-62. Milwaukee: Marquette University Press, 1959.

Schmidt, S.J., Robert W., "The Evidence Grounding Judgments of Existence," in *An Etienne Gilson Tribute,* ed. Charles J. O'Neil, pp. 228-44. Milwaukee: Marquette University Press, 1959.

Simmons, Edward D., "The Thomistic Doctrine of the Three Degrees of Formal Abstraction," *The Thomist,* 22 (1959), 37-67. [See references to other authors in notes 13-15].

Tyrrell, Francis M., "Concerning the Nature and Function of Judgment," *New Scholasticism,* 26 (1952), 393-423.

Appendices

Jacques Maritain on Existence / Essence

In view of the fact that Jacques Maritain is one of the most prominent present-day Thomists and has had widespread influence, it will be profitable to review what he says concerning the real distinction between existence and essence. He has explained his view in some detail in at least two treatises— *Preface to Metaphysics: Seven Lectures on Being,* the English translation of which first appeared in 1939, and *Existence and the Existent,* translated in 1948.

One's awareness of essence and existence arises, Maritain informs us in the *Preface to Metaphysics,* as a result of a metaphysical intuition of being.

> I will attempt to bring out more clearly the intelligible subsistence contained in . . . [being], the first object grasped by the metaphysician's intuition. We are immediately aware

of this characteristic of it, that when we consider different things there is in each alike a typical relationship between *what* is, that which philosophers term essence or nature, and its *esse,* or existence. That is to say this notion of being involves a species of polarity, essence-existence.[1]

Accordingly, we must briefly consider what our French author states concerning this intuition.

First of all, it is not the "primitive"[2] or "obscure"[3] intuition by which a man first apprehends *being* vaguely, blindly,[4] infra-scientifi-cally,[5] as the general class into which all diverse sensible things can be placed.[6] But what, positively, is it? In answering, let us first quote the two actual examples Maritain gives, which can be kept in mind when we then recount his own description of it. The first instance given is that of his wife Raïssa, who describes it thus:

> I have often experienced in a sudden intuition the reality of my being, the profound first principle which makes me exist outside nonentity. It is a powerful intuition whose violence has sometimes frightened me and which first revealed to me a metaphysical absolute.

The second instance he takes from the autobiography of Jean-Paul Richter:

> One morning when I was still a child, I was standing on the threshold of the house and looking to my left in the direction of the woodpile when suddenly there came to me from heaven like a lightening flash the thought: *I am a self,* a thought which has never since left me. I perceived my self for the first time and for good.[7]

Now, how does Maritain describe this intuition?

> We are confronted here with a genuine intuition, a perception direct and immediate, an intuition not in the technical sense which the

---

[1] Jacques Maritain, *Preface to Metaphysics* (New York: Sheed & Ward, 1948), p. 64.

[2] *Ibid.,* p. 63. Maritain also calls this a concrete (*vs.* abstract) intuition, "like that of an external sense or of introspection, of an intuition centered upon a reality grasped concretely in its singular existence" (p. 58).

[3] *Ibid.,* p. 60.

[4] *Ibid.,* p. 29.

[5] *Ibid.*

[6] *Ibid.,* p. 31 sq.

[7] *Ibid.,* p. 47.

ancients attached to the term, but in the sense we may accept from modern philosophy. It is a very simple sight, superior to any discursive reasoning or demonstration, because it is the source of demonstration. It is a sight whose content and implications no words of human speech can exhaust or adequately express and in which in a moment of decisive emotion, as it were, of spiritual conflagration, the soul is in contact, a living, penetrating, and illuminating contact, with a reality which it touches and which takes hold of it. Now what I want to emphasize is that it is being more than anything else which produces such an intuition. . . . Thus we are confronted with objects and as we confront them, the diverse realities made known by our senses or by the several sciences, we receive at a given moment, as it were, the revelation of an intelligible mystery concealed in them.[8]

One final quotation, which occurs immediately after Maritain had given the two examples already referred to:

There are, therefore, metaphysical intuitions which are a natural revelation to the soul, invested with the decisive, imperious, and dominant character of a "Substantial word" uttered by reality. They reveal the intelligible treasure, the unforgettable transobjective fact, which is either her own subsistence, the "Self" that she is, or being either her own or the being apprehended in objects. . . . [This intuition] is always, so to speak, a gift bestowed upon the intellect, and beyond question it is in one form or another indispensable to every metaphysician. . . . Moreover, it is as true to say that this intuition produces itself through the medium of the vital action of our intellect, I mean as vitally receptive and contemplative, as to say that we produce it. It is difficult . . . inasmuch as it is difficult to arrive at the degree of intellectual purification at which this act is produced in us, at which we become sufficiently disengaged, sufficiently empty to *hear* what all things whisper and to *listen* instead of composing answers.[9]

In the light of the preceding quotations, then, what is this metaphysical intuition of being? Replying to that question is difficult, among other reasons, because of Maritain's somewhat lyrical language, but this attempt seems accurate. The intuition he describes is a perception which has these characteristics: (1) It is relatively spectacular and sudden. (2) It is direct and immediate, "a very simple sight," superior

---

[8] *Ibid.*, p. 45 sq.
[9] *Ibid.*, p. 48.

and prior to reasoning and demonstration. (3) It is intellectual and abstractive.[10] (4) It is absolutely necessary for every metaphysician.[11] (5) It is passive rather than active insofar as it can occur only when the mind is sufficiently purified and empty so as to listen to reality rather than to dictate to it; then actual existents can reveal their intelligible mystery—namely, that being is "that which exists or can exist." [12] (6) Its object is being precisely as the subject matter of metaphysics,[13] being-as-being, being "beheld in itself and in its essential properties, . . . in its essentially analogous value." [14] In short, the intuition of a metaphysician is the immediate, unique, sudden awareness by which he knows being precisely as being.

What is to be said of Maritain's contention? Some have rejected it because such an intuition can find no place in Thomistic psychology.[15] Such rejection seems a bit hasty. If actual cases of such intuition have occurred (they seemingly have—see p. 83 f.), then one's psychological theory must be enlarged to include them. Still others may hesitate to accept his stand because an intuition is commonly regarded as an intensely individual, personal, private affair. How then can it ground a science, which has connotations of universality and certitude? Granted that an intuition is personal and individual with reference to its efficient cause (as is any act of knowledge)—it is *I* or *you* who is knowing. Still, if what is known is universal and common, if I intuit the nature of being and of existence themselves, if I realize what "to exist" means not just for myself but for any existent, then the hesitation is needless.

A much more serious reservation can be lodged against Maritain's position, and this directly concerns existence/essence. As we have already seen, he talks as though the notions of essence and existence are handed over in one's intuition simultaneously with the notion of being. This latter contains, involves, implies, includes them:

---

[10] *Ibid.*, pp. 58-61.

[11] Also see *Degrees of Knowledge* (London: Geoffrey Bles, 1959), p. 215: "[This intellectual perception of being] constitutes our primordial philosophical intuition without which we can no more acquire the science of metaphysical realities than a man born blind acquires the science of colors."

[12] *Preface to Metaphysics,* p. 63.

[13] *Ibid.*, p. 62.

[14] *Ibid.*, p. 63.

[15] See Etienne Gilson, *Elements of Christian Philosophy* (Garden City, N. Y.: Doubleday & Company, Inc., 1960), p. 130: "[The recognition of the notion of the act-of-being] cannot possibly be an intellectual intuition, because there is no such thing in Thomism."

In virtue of its essential structure the concept of being also includes in itself indissolubly . . . these two linked and associated members of the pair essence-existence, which the mind cannot *isolate* in separate concepts. Whatever being I may think of, its concept implies this double aspect.

According to such statements, one's knowledge of essence/existence is as immediate as that of being itself. But he continues:

Metaphysics teaches us that in God the distinction between essence and existence is a *distinctio rationis*, a purely ideal distinction, but that in all created objects there is a real distinction between them.[16]

What are we to conclude from that sentence? Although we know from intuition that being somehow involves essence/existence, yet we can decide whether their relationship is one of identity (as in God) or of real diversity (as in creatures) only from other sources—"metaphysics teaches. . . ." But the difficult question which every metaphysician must face is precisely how he can conclusively establish that real distinction. On this point Maritain is not very informative.

In *Existence and the Existent* he does furnish a bit more information. On the topic of intuition this second book differs somewhat from the *Preface*, although mainly by explicitating what remains implicit in the earlier treatise. For instance, he devotes more attention to how judgment functions in the intuition[17] and to the fact that the senses play a primordial and indispensable part in attaining such intuition.[18] He more frequently stresses the role of existence—for example, the intuition terminates above all in an awareness of the act of existing.[19] What he

---

[16] *Preface to Metaphysics,* p. 65.

[17] *Existence and the Existent* (New York: Pantheon Books, Inc., 1948), p. 15 sq.

[18] *Ibid.,* p. 20.

[19] *Ibid.,* p. 19: "At the root of metaphysical knowledge, St. Thomas placed the intellectual inutition of that mysterious reality disguised under the most commonplace and commonly used word in the language, the word *to be;* a reality revealed to us . . . when we release . . . the act of existing. . . ." *Ibid.,* p. 20: "[This intuition of being] owes its purity and power of illumination only to the fact that the intellect, one day, was stirred to its depths and trans-illuminated by the impact of the act of existing apprehended in things, and because it was quickened to the point of receiving this act. . . ." *Ibid.,* p. 26: "When . . . the intellect . . . conceptualises the metaphysical intuition of being . . . what the intellect releases into that same light is, here again, first and foremost, the act of existing."

says on the distinction between essence/existence is another case in point, since his comments can be looked upon as developing what he left largely unstated in the *Preface*.

After sections devoted to "The Intuition of Being" [20] and to "The Concepts of Existence . . . and That of Being," [21] he discusses "The Implications of the Intuition of Being," [22] where he shows how all the major Thomist theses are rooted in the act of existing, the insight into which is gained through intuition. The real distinction is the first of those theses: [23]

> The most fundamental and most characteristic metaphysical thesis of Aristotelianism as re-thought by Thomas Aquinas, the thesis of the real distinction between essence and existence in all that is not God—in other words, the extension of the doctrine of potency and act to the relation between essence and existence, is directly connected with this intuition. This is, in truth, a thesis of extreme boldness, for in it potency (essence) . . . is completed or actuated by an act *of another order* which adds absolutely nothing to essence as essence, intelligible structure, or quiddity, yet adds everything to it in as much as it posits it *extra causas* or *extra nihil*. . . . Made real by the act of existing—that is to say, placed outside the state of simple possibility—they [essences] are really distinct from it as potency is really distinct from the act that actuates it; for if they were their own existence they would be Existence and Intelligibility in pure act, and would no longer be created essences. [24]

The doctrine of the real distinction is, then, an application of act/potency to existence/essence. Because act is really distinct from potency and because existence is act and essence is potency, existence is really distinct from essence. Moreover, if an essence were not really other than existence, it would be pure, subsistent act, and thus it would be God rather than a creature.

But doubts can be raised against each of Maritain's arguments. How do I know that existence *is* act, that essence *is* potency? Does not this knowledge presuppose I already am aware that existence is actually

---

[20] *Ibid.*, pp. 19-22.
[21] *Ibid.*, pp. 22-34.
[22] *Ibid.*, pp. 35-46.
[23] The other theses pertain to universals and virtual distinction, potency and prime matter, the human composite, evil, immanent acts of knowing and loving, liberty and the *rapport* divine motion has to liberty, efficient and final causality, and the superabundance of being.
[24] *Existence and the Existent*, pp. 35-36.

present in an existent as a component? Is not my knowledge of existence/essence as act/potency a sequel to that prior awareness? Also, if existence means simply (as an essentialist asserts) that an essence has been efficiently caused by God, then the identity of essence and existence does not destroy creaturehood but rather establishes it by setting up the relationship of effect-to-cause between that essence and God.

As a final comment: actual intuitional experiences (see p. 83 f.) seem each to be an awareness not of the act of existing itself (as Maritain would have them) but of actual existence as a fact. In such an intuition one realizes vividly and enduringly that he actually exists and that this fact is of prime importance, affecting him profoundly.

How the Meaning of "Being" Is Worked Out

The deliberate elaboration of the metaphysical meaning given "being" entails reflection upon at least the following steps.

(a) If this man, that plant, and other such intrinsic unities were the only subjects of which the term is predicated, then its meaning could be formulated as "an actually existing thing," with "thing" referring to essence and "actually existing" to act of existence, which is really distinct from the former.

(b) But once components are known to exist, and thus to be real, the formulation becomes "an actually existing item." "Item" is general enough to express what a component is, as well as what an intrinsic unity is (#a). The other words in the formula point to actual existence, which is really other than what each component is, with the exception of the act of existing itself, which exists by being what it is (although only within some existent).

(c) When one is confronted with the

peculiar nature of such extrinsic unities as a family, a machine, or a painting (they are, and hence are real, but what they are is a mere complex of real relations [see Chap. VI, Sec. 1, *ad finem*, and Chap. VII]), then one realizes that "item" signifies this relational complex, whereas "actually existing" points to the acts of existing actualizing the various subjects in which the relations inhere and through which they exist.

(d) Once God is known to exist, then "item" is made to refer to an essence which is identical with the actuality expressed by "actually existing," because it is God's very nature to exist (Chap. V, Sec. 6).

(e) As predicable of such extremely divergent actual items, then, "being" is shown to be a very general awareness. It expresses both *what* an actual is (whether God, this man, a component, a family) and *that* it is. Despite its generalness, though, "being" is also most rich in content—in fact, it is as rich in content as is possible for a concept with maximal extension. Why so? Because it also expresses everything in each actual of which it is predicated: "item" has to do with what each is, the other words to the fact that it is. Insofar as it signifies each *as actual*, it points to each in its very uniqueness and determinateness, for everything is actual in a determinate, unique, individual way. (See pp. 149-50.)

(f) There is this difference between "being" (as well as the concepts of other transcendents and of any pure perfection) and such a concept as "man" or "animal." The common perfection which the latter signifies is never found actually existing precisely as such, of and in itself. There is no Man or Animal: there is this or that man, this or that dog, none of which exhausts the intelligibility. But Being (as well as Truth, Goodness, Wisdom, and so forth) does exist as such, of and in itself. This *is* God, in Whom all other existents participate and thereby are beings. In summary, "man" or "animal" is, as such, only an intelligibility and never extramental. "Being" is both an intelligibility and an extramental subsistent.

(g) There is this similarity, however, between "being" and "man." One who understand truly and deeply what to be human means thereby also knows all men, whoever and wherever they may be, precisely as human. So too, one who finally understands what to be actual means also grasps all beings (whether they be God, creatures, components, or accidental unities) precisely as being, all existents qua existent, whatever is real precisely as real. And this is a much greater victory, for this has extended the mind to a much greater degree than in the previous example or in almost any other kind of knowledge. In attaining this understanding, then, the human knower has performed a tremendous intellectual feat and has achieved what is certainly one of the aims of metaphysics as a science.

(h) See L. Sweeney, S.J., "Analogy and Being," *Modern Schoolman,* 39 (March, 1962), 261-62; *idem,* "Existence/Essence in Early Writings of Aquinas," *Proceedings of the American Catholic Philosophical Association,* 37 (1963), 124, n. 43; James F. Anderson, "Some Disputed Questions on Our Knowledge of Being," *Review of Metaphysics,* 11 (June, 1958), p. 553 sq. and p. 566 sq.; J. Owens, *Elementary Christian Metaphysics* (Milwaukee: Bruce Publishing Co., 1963), pp. 115-17.

APPENDIX C

Aquinas on
Separation

How does our interpretation of separation and abstraction (see Chap. X, Secs. 4 and 5) square with Thomas' texts? Considerably better than might appear at first sight, although our aim has not been textual exegesis but rather presentation of our own position. True, in both key passages (*In Boethii de Trinitate*, 5, 3, resp. and *S.T.*, I, 85, 1 ad 1 and ad 2) Thomas speaks of abstraction in terms of the intellectual operations involved, and thus seems to combine the description of knowledge in reference to its efficient cause with that in reference to the *cognita* or even seems to be oblivious of the latter as cause. But according to him knowledge does flow from those two causes,[1] and his apparent identification of abstraction with simple apprehension and judgment[2] perhaps might

---

[1] For example, see *De Veritate*, 10, 6, resp.

[2] *S.T.*, I, 85, 1 ad 1: "Abstraction comes about in two ways. First, through composition and division [Thomas' language for "judgment"]. . . . Second, through simple and absolute consideration." Also see *In Boet. de Trin.*, 5, 3, resp., especially *ad finem* (Decker Ed., p. 186, l. 13 sq.; Maurer translation, pp. 31-32).

345

more accurately be understood as predication through intrinsic denomination: apprehension and judgment are the operations by which we produce knowledges marked by various abstractions. Moreover, the various abstractions involved in diverse kinds of knowledge are determined by the objective status of the *cognita*. When one item actually is not the other,[3] we have that abstraction called separation.[4] When one is linked with the other but is somehow independent, we have a nonseparative abstraction.[5] When the one is dependent upon the other, even such nonseparative abstraction is impossible.[6] Thus, the *cognita* themselves decide whether or not abstraction is possible, and, if so, which kind it will be and whether matter is to be partially or totally absent from the awareness.

Accordingly, Thomas would seem to agree with our theory of abstraction as a description of knowledge in the light of the *cognita*. It is a negative property of our intelligibilities: the absence of matter within their very content. Separation too is a abstraction, and thus is the negative property of the intelligibilities arising within the study of beings-as-being: the absence of matter within the content of awarenesses caused by *cognita* which are intrinsically independent of matter.

---

[3] *Ibid.* (Maurer's translation, p. 31): "In the case of things which can exist separately, separation rather than abstraction obtains" (Latin text in Decker Ed., p. 185, l. 31). S.T., I, 85, 1 ad 1: "[The first way in which abstraction occurs is] through composition and division, as happens when we realize that something is not in another but is separated from it."

[4] In the S.T. passage (I, 85, 1 ad 1), separation is an abstraction: "*Abstraction* comes about in two ways. First, through composition and division, as happens when we realize that something . . . is *separated* from another" (Italics mine). Also *ibid.*, ad 2 *ad finem*.

In the *In Boet. de Trin.* passage (p. 184, l. 2; p. 186, l. 1; Maurer's translation, pp. 28 and 31), separation is contrasted with abstraction in its strict sense.

[5] *Ibid.* (Maurer's translation, p. 28): "If one thing does not depend on another with regard to what constitutes the intelligibility of the nature, then the intellect can abstract it from that other thing so as to know it without that other" (Latin text in Decker Ed., p. 183, ll. 14-16). Among the examples Thomas gives of items having that independence are animal re feet, hands, and so on; letter of alphabet re syllables of words; quantity re quality; nose re pug-shaped; man re whiteness; whiteness re man; elements re mixtures; circle re semicircle.

[6] *Ibid.* (Maurer's translation, pp. 27-28): "When that through which the intelligibility of a nature is constituted and through which the nature itself is understood, has a relation to, and a dependence on, something else, clearly we cannot know the nature without that other thing" (Latin text in Decker Ed., p. 183, ll. 3-6). Among the instances Aquinas gives of items which are thus dependent: feet, hands, and so on re animal; syllables re letters of the alphabet; pug-shape re nose; father re son; quantity re intelligible matter; accidents re substance; mixtures re elements; triangle re lines; man re soul/body; this soul/body re Socrates.

Index of Names

Italicized numbers indicate footnote or "Suggested Readings"; non-italicized numbers accompanied by letter "n" indicate text itself and footnote.

Index

of

Topics

Italicized numbers indicate footnote; non-italicized numbers accompanied by letter "n" indicate text itself and footnote.

of knowledge:
content-determining: *cognitum*,
309-10n, 326-27
efficient: cognitive powers, 309,
310, 326
presential, re relations, 209
primary/secondary, 238, 251
proper: re God/creatures, 127, 234-
38
Certain (probable, doubtful) conclusions, 158
Certitude, formal (*vs.* material) 247,
274, 286
Chance, 290-93, 295
on noncognitive level, 292-93
relative/absolute, 290-92
total, 291n-92
Change:
center of unreality for Platonists, 27
(*see also* Radical essentialism)
claimed impossible, 48
factor in reality, 26-27, 33-34
heart of reality (Heraclitus; Sartre),
20-21, 25
material/immaterial, 11
shown possible through act/potency,
48-49
Changes in activity:
variously caused, 284
Change/stability, 11 (*see also* Stability)
on accidental level, 37-38, 40, 44-50
as evidences, 45
as facts, evidences, 322-23
make-up of individuals, 36
on substantial level, 37-38, 50-58
Chemicals, 42
"pure," 53n
virtual, 43, 53n
Christ, 171-73, 176 (*see also* Supposit;
Nature)
Circularity, 321
Cognitive agent:
final situation, 264-81 (*see especially*
265n)
Cognitum:
content-determining cause, 309-10,
318-28, 345-46 (*see also* Knowledge)
Complex apprehension, 312, 315, 316,
318, 322, 326 (*see also* Apprehension)

Component:
re abstraction of natural components,
322-24
Aristotle: only four, 61
defined, 48, 59-60
on inanimate level, 61
Concrete case, 38
re inductive knowledge, 246-47, 272-
75, 279, 286-87
Constancy, 282n
Constitutive part (*see* Part)
Construct:
re evil, 168
re predicaments, 215n
re relation, 201n
in teleology, 256
Constructural sciences, 6, 137
involve "abstraction of addition,"
321-22 (*see also* Construct;
Knowledge)
Contemplation:
re beautiful, 161-62
means of possessing God, 276-77n
"Corporeal" continuity, 52-53, 106
Corporeity, 179
Cosmic influences, 191
Creation, 238
Creature:
defined, 127
not instrumental cause in creation,
238
not proper cause of existence, 127
proper cause of existence as determined, 235-38, 250
posterior in being and efficiency, 238,
250-51

D

Death, 295n
as evidence, 50-53
not annihilation, 52, 106
Deduction, 312-13n (*see also* Inference)
place of in human knowledge, 246
re "Principle of Causality," 239-42
Definition:
metaphysical *vs.* cosmological, 133-34
(*see also* Metaphysical knowledge)

Good-as-known, 266, 268, 270, 279
(_see also_ Finality re cognitive agents)
causes without changing, 268
object of appetitive powers, 277-79
Grammatical predications, 213-16 (_see also_ Predicaments)
Gravity, 283

H

Habit, operative, 13
Habitus (_see_ State)
Harmony:
re co-operation between creatures/ God, 238
History of philosophy:
aid to philosophizing, 19, 34
as methodology in metaphysics, 12, 16-17
Humanity, a construct, 215
Human parents:
causes of body, 230
efficient "furnishing" causes re soul, 228, 230
Human soul:
efficient causes of, 228
individuation of, 178
mutable for Platonist, 29
Plotinus, 31-32
spiritual, 123, 126, 323, 328
Hylomorphism, 37

I

Ideal, 269 (_see also_ Goal)
Imagination of artist, 299
Immanent activity (_see_ Activity; Operation)
Immaterial, 123-24, 126-27 (_see also_ Amateriality; Material; Spiritual)
amaterial, 124, 127, 323, 329
"barely" _vs._ "spiritual," 56, 123-24, 323
blanket description, 123
re natural components, 323n (_see also_ Abstraction of natural components)
re sense cognition, 326
spiritual, 56, 123, 323

Immediate insight, 312
Immutability (_see_ Stability)
Indeterminacy in biology, 282
Indeterminate/determinate:
re awarenesses (restrictive, transcendent), 151-153n
re essence-argument, 70-71
Individual, 170-82, 185-86 (_see also_ Supposit; Nature)
analogous, 177
contemporary thinkers, 175n
re extramentals, 170
re intramentals, 170
meaning prior to divine revelation, 174
modern education, 175
re nature, "individuation," 176-82, 185
supposit, 170-76, 185
Cajetan/Maritain, 172-73
divinely revealed, 170-72, 174n
primacy of existence, 175-76
Scotus, 172
Suarez, 172-73
De la Taille, 173
Individual existents:
combinations of change/stability, 34, 36
devaluated:
by radical essentialists, 31-32 (_see also_ Radical essentialism)
by radical existentialists, 36
show themselves knowable, 33, 34
show themselves real, 33
starting-point of metaphysics, 34
Individuality:
two sorts (supposit/nature), 175, 176-77n, 185-86
Individuation:
in artifacts, 177-78
_vs._ individuality, 115
none for Plato/Ockham, 181n
principle of, 176-82, 185
from quantified (signate) matter, 178n-79
radically from prime matter, 114-15, 176-82
four questions/answers, 178-81
of soul, 178
from substantial form, 179-81

L

Literature, 136
Logic, *195*
  involves "abstraction of addition," 321 (*see also* Abstraction)
Logical accident (*see* Accident)
Logical property (*see* Property)
Logician re predicaments, 215, 216 (*see also 92*)
Love:
  attraction/response, 268-69
  cause of human openness, 191
  determination of cognitive agent, 269
  efficiently caused by agent, 268, 270 (*table*), 278
  re good, *154, 160*
  means of possessing God, 276, 277
  not applied to noncognitive agents, *288*
  "outside of numbers," 10, 44-45, 50
  synonymous with desire, etc., *265*
  telic cause and effect (*table*), 278
  telicly caused by good-as-known, 268-69
  tendency to goal, 269
  unlike other operations, 277

M

Material (*vs.* formal), 56-58
Material (*vs.* immaterial):
  defined, 56, 121-22
  how predicated, 121-22
    of act of existing, 122n
    of essence, 122n
    of essential components, 122n
    of quantity, 122
    of "that which," "that by which," 56n, 122
Material universe:
  aggregation of appearances (Sartre), 22-24
  mirrors Forms, 28
  Plato, 27
Materialistic monism, 19
Mathematics, *195*
  involves "abstraction of addition," 321 (*see also* Abstraction)
Matter:

re abstraction: a restricting factor in content of intelligibility, 328
factor in efficient-cause situation, 229
prime, 53-58, 60-61
  cause of individuation, 114-15
  defined, 53, 60
  for essentialist, 206
  how called "material," 122n
  known through intellection, 54-55, 60-61
  metaphysical definition, 134
  more direct cause of quantity, 114n
  not form, 207n
  a perfection, 108n (*see also* Perfection)
  Pesch, 206
  principle of individuation, 164n, 177-81, 185
  pure potency, 55n, 61, 97, 206, 207n
  as "that by which," 54
  transcends perception, 54-55, 60-61
  why so named, 55-58
  second, 58n, 230
  signate, 328 (*see also* Quantified matter)
  re "abstraction of whatness," 319
  "signed by quantity," *178*
Matter/form:
  basis for "abstraction of whatness," 319
  knowledge-process described, 315-16
  knowledge of, marked by "abstraction of natural components," 322-24 (*see also* Abstraction)
  not synonymous with potency/act, 57
Matter *vs.* form, 57
Mental distinction, 76n (*see also* Real distinction)
  between essential perfections, *114,* 179-80
  major, *114, 180*
  between predicaments, 214n
  between restrictive awarenesses, *152*
  between transcendents, *153*
Mental relation, 195n, 217-18
  of cause to effect, 230

in supernatural order, 277
telic effects because determinate tendencies, 276-77n
Otherness, 170-82, 185-86 (*see also* Individual)
"Other than" (*see* Individual):
  transcendent:
    known metaphysically, 157-58
    known spontaneously, 152-53

P

Parts:
  constitutive, 40-41, 45-46, 53, 59
    of accidental unity, 40, 47
    called "principles," 47-48
    indicated by diverse evidences, 38-39, 59
    integral (physical), 41-42, 47, 170
    intrinsic causes, 39, 46, 54, 87, 112, 223-24
Passion (*see* Action)
Perception:
  analogous, *143*
  re existence/essence, 88, 94, 317 (*see also* Judgment, perceptual)
  re matter/form, 54-55, 60-61, 316
  re substance/accidents, 46-47, 60, 315
"Perfect," linked with good, *154*, 160
Perfection, 107-10
  re act of existing (source of all perfections), 109-10, 125-26
  defined, 107-8
  essential, 178-80
    how distinct, 114n, 180n
  not identical with act, 108-9
  mixed/pure, 108
  re prime matter, 108n
  specific:
    from substantial form, 113, 180-81
    specific/generic, 114n
    three sorts (*see* Value)
Person: one kind of supposit, *176* (*see* Supposit)
Personalism, 176
Philosopher (*see* Thomistic philosopher)
Philosophy:
  Christian, *174*

of morality:
  abstraction in, 328 (*see also* Abstraction)
of nature, 27, 62, 92n, *318*, 322n-23
  Aristotle's: inadequate, inaccurate, 37
  Frick, 32
  re predicaments, 216 (*see also* Predicaments)
  uses "abstraction of natural components," 322n-23 (*see also* Abstraction)
of subjectivity, 176
Physical evil, *167*
Physics:
  involves "abstraction of addition," 321n-22 (*see also* Abstraction)
Place, *213*, 214
Possibles:
  in authentic existentialism:
    are nonbeing, 138n
    [essence/existence]-as-known, 139-40
    real through extrinsic denomination, *81*
  in natural theology, *138*
  in radical essentialism, real because of immutability, *81*, 138n, 139n
Possible/actual, 80-81n
  in radical essentialism, *81*
Posture (*situs*), 213
Potency (*see* Act/potency):
  pure, 55n, 61, *97*, 206, 207n
Predicaments, 211-17
  Aristotle, 213
  in authentic existentialism, 213-17
    based on grammatical predications, 213-16
    defined, 213
    grammatical "forms," 215-16
    grammatical, not metaphysical accidents, 215
    have no function, 216n-17
    not constructs, 215n
  re relations:
    Coffey, 211
    Klubertanz, 211-13
Predictability: 226
  sequel of finality, 292
Presence, virtual/formal, 42, 53n, 230
Primacy (*see* Existing, act of)